Beyond Paradise

Beyond Paradise

Technology and the Kingdom of God

A Prophetic Primer for Church Leaders

JACK CLAYTON SWEARENGEN

Wipf & Stock
PUBLISHERS
Eugene, Oregon

BEYOND PARADISE
Technology and the Kingdom of God

ISBN 10: 1-59752-842-0
ISBN 13: 978-1-59752-842-9

Manufactured in the U.S.A.

To my family—

who tolerated me during four years of writing.
And, come to think of it,
forty years of preparation.

And to the reviewers—of chapters and more:

Bev Beckendorf, Peter Bosscher, Andy Dryden, Denis Haack, Ginny Hearn, Walt Hearn, Adrienne Kuehl, Joel Lipkin, Dan Melligan, Ron Miller, Terry Morrison, Al Segall, Tim Stafford, Pete Swearengen, Ken Touryan, Diana Van Konynenberg, Rich Van Konynenberg, Bob Wauzzinski, John Wood, Ned Woodhouse.

Many, many thanks.

Contents

Prologue

ONE DAY, while I was working on this book, my wife, Nancy, went to see our family physician about upper back pain. The visit took longer than we expected, so on the way home she called me on the cell phone to say she would arrive shortly. Such is the convenience of the cell phone. But an all-too-common hazard of the technology intervened: she took her eyes off the road while dialing, ran over the curb, and into a fire hydrant.

Another technology then came into play: air bags. Because she is barely 5'2", the driver's side air bag hit her with full force, breaking her right arm in four places and removing much skin from her lips—and also knocking the cell phone to the floor. When the telephone rang at home, I could hear traffic noise and eventually a policeman speaking to Nancy. I realized I was listening in on the aftermath of her accident. Because the cell phone had alerted me, I drove the route I knew she would travel, and found her unconscious in the driver's seat but with an ambulance already on the scene. Thanks to wireless communications technology she was able to get rapid medical attention; and thanks to advanced medical technology she has recovered. The industry has now learned that explosive deployment of "first-generation" air bags could injure children and small adults. Hence "second-generation" bags were designed to inflate less violently, and "third-generation" systems now include a seat sensor that prevents deployment if the occupant weighs less than eighty-five pounds. So, cell phone technology "caused" Nancy's accident, but also allowed emergency personnel (and me) to reach the scene quickly. Air bag technology was developed to prevent injuries, but in this case it was the source of injury.

Cell phones offer the great convenience of mobile communication. Gone are the days of searching for a phone booth, a parking place, and coins only to discover the phone book missing. But multitasking drivers—using cell phones, fiddling with their radios or applying makeup—are involved in nearly eight out of ten collisions or near-crashes.[1] Headsets or "hands-free" cell phones do not solve the problem, because it seems that using mobile phones while driving is just as dangerous whether drivers are

---

[1] Klauer et al., "The Impact of Driver Inattention."

chatting through a headset or holding on to the hand set.[2] It's not just keying in phone numbers or calling up messages but the conversation itself that is distracting.[3] A similar outcome applies to air bags. They protect us from one kind of hazard but introduce a new one.

If we study technology and technological society we will discover these are just small examples of a recurring pattern. It turns out that *all* technologies have consequences that were not part of the original intent and are usually not anticipated. When we implement technological solutions to these introduced problems we discover new surprises which then need to be solved and so on. And as we get locked into this pattern we may be distracting ourselves from seeking more durable social solutions to the problems we are trying to solve. Moreover, technology is a distraction by itself—demanding our time and attention for selecting, acquiring, learning, operating, maintaining, and disposing. Ellen Goodman wryly noted that with the countless hours she spent learning how to operate and maintain high-tech devices she could have learned Mandarin. But, she lamented, the language skill would have been of lasting value whereas the procedures she had to master for the devices became obsolete and utterly useless.[4] Clearly along with technological progress our lives have become much more complicated. Ultimately technology may be a *profound* distraction, diverting us individually and collectively from our highest calling—the kingdom of God.

All this serves to introduce the first purpose of this book, which is to convince Christians that technology assessment is worthy of inclusion in discipleship. Actually it is more than worthy—it is an indispensable part of faithfully obeying the Scriptural directives to fill, subdue, rule, cultivate, and keep. These directives comprise the foundations of the *culture mandate;* and if our response is measured by population growth, industrialization, wealth, consumption, and the human "footprint" on the planet we have done superbly. Technology has been the key. It has enabled Earth to support many more human numbers, protected us against the forces of nature, relieved suffering and drudgery, provided great advances in communication, mobility, biology, information and other fields, and produced great wealth for many people, at least in Western nations. All this success has convinced some that progress based upon technology is unlimited.

[2] McEvoy et al., "Role of mobile phones in motor vehicle crashes."

[3] Quoted in Granelli, "Headsets don't reduce accident rate," A1, A13.

[4] Goodman, "Have your toothbrush call my laptop," G1, G8.

But along the way we have fashioned a society that is technological before anything else.

Most Christian leaders avoid discussion of science and technology because they don't know the languages of either discipline and don't understand the issues that science and technology are hurling at us. What, for example, might be the biblical position on globalization? On energy use and global warming? On eugenics, transgenics, nanotechnology, and GMOs? On privacy and surveillance? Some may question whether these are biblical issues at all. As a result of this lack of understanding, both leaders and their congregations are at a loss when the opportunity arises to provide biblical insights into contemporary issues. And they become vulnerable to unnecessary polemics between science and faith.

Hence the Church needs a crash course in technology and culture. In my structured engineer-type way of thinking I would describe the need this way: To grow as disciples of Jesus Christ we must discern how much our lifestyle, values, and worldviews are shaped by non-biblical influences. This in turn means that we understand whether or to what degree the scientific-technical worldview is biblical. Next, believers must be equipped to serve as God's agents. To carry out the *Shema* and the Great Commission we must understand the spiritual forces that stand in opposition to the gospel. What are the gods and idols of our time? What things are replacing God in people's lives? Serving as God's agents for the advance of His kingdom means that we work for His purposes of reconciliation, healing, and transformation. Because technology dominates our lives and our culture, authentic discipleship must include steering the technological enterprise toward biblical norms.

The second purpose of *Beyond Paradise* is to explain how the Church can use biblical values to confront the scientific-technical worldview and influence contemporary technological culture. Practical means are presented for assessing the "arrows" of technology and progress and redirecting—i.e. steering—them toward spiritual, social-cultural, aesthetic, and environmental sustainability. A theology of technology begins to emerge from the process. Such a theology has yet to be discussed—let alone adopted—by the Church. Nor to my knowledge has any previous author set forth a path for the Church to serve as transformational agent for technology. Unfortunately, becoming a Christian does not automatically transform our worldviews or even give us new discernment.

Beyond Paradise is intended as a *primer* for readers who aren't ready yet to grapple with the existing philosophical treatments of the subject. It is intended for Christians who are seeking to be faithful to the whole of

God's revelation and to church leaders who desire to help their congregations apply biblical principles to the contemporary issues of Western society. I presume that all of my readers are users of technology, and that no Luddites will be attracted to the book. Principles for developing and using technology and steering the technological enterprise are developed from Scripture, including the means for influencing our culture. The book is also for Christians who develop technology. Some technology students may not be sure why they are in engineering or other applied sciences, or have some doubts about being there. The book will help in choosing a first job, which should entail more than selling oneself to the highest bidder. If you are already employed in technology, you may find ideas to help you exert an influence in your workplace, perhaps through innovative approaches that achieve organizational objectives but come closer to biblical ideals. That is good preparation for a time in your career when you may become a decision-maker for your organization.

Chapters 1–3 present a time-scale portrayal of technological civilization. Technology's origins and development are reviewed, and its effects on human civilization, other species, and the planet itself are examined. The development affirms that "technological" probably characterizes contemporary Western civilization better than any other word. Chapters 4–9 comprise a discussion of the consequences. Working with the engineering concept of limits, likely techno-futures are described and examined in terms of environmental, social, and aesthetic sustainability. The scientific-technological worldview confuses progress with growth, exalts personal mobility as the greatest freedom, and discounts any notion of limits to human endeavor. As a result the social and spiritual elements of our culture are threatened as much as the physical environment is— perhaps more. Chapters 10 and 11 present a biblical foundation for technology as the platform from which technological civilization may be redirected toward four-fold sustainability. Acting individually—and collectively through the Church—God's people can provide the missing vision and lead the way toward healing of society.

I have endeavored to use contemporary illustrations that should be familiar to both laity and clergy. Many of the illustrations are from my personal experiences, and to a significant degree the book integrates the separate pieces that comprised the topics of my journal papers in the field of technology and society. In summary, my objectives are to:

1. convince Christians that technology is shaping our culture and dominating our lives for better or worse;

2. persuade us to be proactive; to manage the impact of technology in our lives individually and to demonstrate that alternative to the general culture;

3. "unpack" the scriptural mandate for doing these things;

4. develop a biblical foundation for technology; and

5. provide practical means for assessing and steering technology toward biblical norms.

Objectives 1 and 2 are developed by means of examples from past, present, and future technologies. Items 3 and 4 are derived from Scripture—together with insights from theological and sociological treatises. The means for pursuing objective number 5 are adapted from an analysis of industrial ecology (IE). We discover that the foundations of the young discipline can be derived from Scripture; so the methodology can be extended from environmental sustainability to the social, aesthetic, and spiritual realms. The concept of "Hippocratic engineering" is introduced for biblically-based technology development.

JCS
October 2006

Chapter 1

Technology Changed the World

Announcements proclaiming that particular technologies will change the world are familiar—and some technologies have changed things in big ways. The social and cultural changes brought about by the printing press, gunpowder, personal computers, automobiles, railroads, steamships, airplanes, antibiotics, and many of other technologies were profound. But *revolutions* are easier to identify using hindsight rather than foresight. In 1883 Lord Kelvin predicted "X rays will prove to be a hoax." In 1932 Albert Einstein remarked "there is not the slightest indication that nuclear energy will ever be obtainable." Thomas Edison thought alternating current would be a waste of time. "Everything that can be invented, has been invented," announced Charles H. Duell, commissioner of the U.S. Patent Office in 1889.[1] Franklin Delano Roosevelt, when he was Secretary of the Navy, predicted that airplanes would never be useful in battle against a fleet of ships. In 1960 the *New York Times* predicted "a flourishing civilization on the moon twenty or thirty years hence."[2]

In terms of technology, people living at the time of the Civil War had more in common with the patriarch Abraham (ca. 2000 BC) than with people living in America in the latter half of the twentieth century.[3] If a person were transplanted from 1865 to our modern society, he/she would struggle to comprehend the leaps that had occurred in military technology, transportation, communications, medicine, and many other areas. Commercial jet aircraft service was inaugurated in 1952; Sputnik—the first man-made satellite—orbited Earth in 1957; and in 1962 the first U.S. nuclear power plant began generating electricity. In July 1969 Neil Armstrong walked on the moon; and in 1972 the American Board of Nuclear Medicine administered its first certification exam. The entire

[1] Grossman, "Forward Thinking," 136.

[2] Winters, "What's Always Next?" 62.

[3] Moreland, *Christianity and the Nature of Science.* Quoted in Samples, "Just Another Animal?" 102.

semiconductor revolution, with microchips leading to a new world of communications, information management, automation, labor-saving devices, and entertainment occurred during the second half of the century. In 1990 when the Cold War ended, the atomic Scientists turned their "doomsday clock" back an additional few minutes before midnight.

Perhaps of all technological "breakthroughs," those in medicine affect our lives in the most personal ways. When I was two years old I came down with a severe case of pneumonia. I faintly recall being in the Good Samaritan Hospital in Zanesville, Ohio, in an oxygen tent. Years later my mother told me that our family physician doubted that I would survive unless he could obtain some penicillin, which was being hailed as a new "wonder drug." That was the year after Pearl Harbor, and all of the limited supplies were reserved for the military. Somehow our doctor must have succeeded in finding enough penicillin, because I recovered. My early childhood memories also include seeing houses posted with quarantine notices because some child inside had scarlet fever or some other contagious disease.

After the Second World War we moved to Pasadena, California. My mother enrolled her three children in swimming classes at the nearby public pool just as an epidemic of poliomyelitis began sweeping the nation, paralyzing and killing children. Everyone knew of someone who had gotten polio; three of my cousins in Chicago—all in the same family—contracted it. Summers became seasons of fear for parents. All they knew to do was to keep their children away from public places and have them avoid excess exertion. So, as the days warmed into summer we had to drop out of swimming and stay at home. But the Salk vaccine ended the siege; and since my childhood pneumonia bout, vaccines have been developed for many of the other diseases that had previously gripped people in a climate of fear—tuberculosis, measles, mumps, smallpox, chickenpox, plague, and influenza.

When I was in high school, my pal Greg's brother died of kidney disease, followed soon after by his father. Doctors informed Greg that he was genetically destined for the same fate. His kidneys did fail, but by then the dialysis machine was available, so Greg went into the hospital three times a week for dialysis. He had headaches afterward, but the treatment kept him alive for several years until finally he was able to have a kidney transplant. Without that dialysis machine, my friend could not have lived to see his two children grow up. Today, even when dialysis is still required, the treatment for kidney failure has greatly improved. Medical science has learned to transplant internal organs, provide artificial life support when vital organs fail, perform fantastic skin treatments for burn patients, and even cure some types of cancer. The human genome has been mapped, biological science is beginning to develop means to treat and cure some hereditary diseases, and bioengineers are developing mechanical or electromechanical replacements for damaged body parts.

Not long ago the National Academy of Engineering and a consortium of engineering societies sought to identify the most significant engineering triumphs of the twentieth century. The top twenty vote-getters were compiled in "A Century of Innovation,"[4] along with a description of the benefits delivered. The "winners" are listed in Table 1.1. Abundant,

Table 1.1.

1. Electrification	8. Computers and Peripherals	15. Household Appliances
2. Automobile	9. Telephony	16. Health Technologies
3. Water Supply and Distribution	10. Air Conditioning and Refrigeration	17. Petroleum and Petrochemicals
4. Electronics	11. Highways	18. Lasers and Fiber Optics
5. Airplane	12. Spacecraft	19. Nuclear Technologies
6. Agricultural Mechanization	13. Internet	20. High Performance Materials
7. Radio and Television	14. Imaging	

available electric power was voted the top innovation, because it helped spur America's economic development, and the benefits were distributed from cities to farms. Health technologies indisputably belong on the list, but would not have progressed without electrification, refrigeration, electronics, imaging, and quite probably clean water supply. Air conditioning and refrigeration were included because "often we take the likes of refrigeration and air conditioning for granted even though they have significantly improved our sense of comfort and contributed to our physical health, giving us the ability to transport and extend the shelf life of food." Radio and TV were included because they are "much more than mere entertainment devices. They have changed the way we view the world and our place in it." And the telephone "has made the whole planet a smaller but much more connected place for all of us."

---

[4] Constable and Somerville, "A Century of Innovation."

3

Computers are in the list, as we would expect. Today's young people can hardly imagine living without computers. Yet at the end of the 1950s only 2,000 computers were functioning in the whole world. The best of them, such as the UNIVAC, the IBM 702, and the DEC PDP-11, could execute maybe 10,000 machine instructions in one second. By the year 2000 there were 300 *million* active computers capable of executing several hundred million instructions per second. That represents a four-billion-fold increase in computing power in 40 years, or an annual growth rate of 56%! This phenomenal increase in computing power is manifest in the growth and increased sophistication of both embedded systems (such as microprocessors) and outside systems (such as the Internet). In addition, manufacturing and distribution processes have been enhanced by increased use of computing power and technology, so that our automobiles are assembled and painted by robots, and laser scanners provide retail check-out and re-order inventory at the same time.[5]

Many of us have been directly affected by recent advances in medical science. For about a decade, our adult son—and father of three school-age children—had suffered from epileptic seizures. In recent years they became more frequent and more debilitating. Anti-seizure drugs, although initially effective, were no longer able to control the episodes, and eventually Peter had to give up driving. Perhaps in bygone days when extended families lived under one roof, the family could have distributed the care-giving and shared the chores, but in contemporary American culture young families are on their own. Although facing a difficult existence, Peter had the advantage of living in a big U.S. city (San Francisco, California) where modern medicine was available, specifically in a neuroscience unit specializing in epilepsy. A week spent in the hospital for advanced diagnostic testing enabled the doctors to pinpoint the source of the seizures to a small region in his brain. Joyously, we learned that the seizures originated in his temporal lobe, in a place accessible to surgery. Additional tests permitted the doctors to understand his brain's neural patterns and predict the impact of surgery. Each brain hemisphere was sedated in turn while he responded to a variety of questions and stimuli. It became clear that Peter had a congenital vascular abnormality that was causing blood to leak. Could the leakage have been exacerbated by years of playing soccer, one of his favorite sports? At any rate, certain decay products of the leaked blood had been toxic to his brain tissue.

[5] DeLong, "Productivity Growth in the 2000s,"9–10.

A few weeks later, a neurosurgeon removed the abnormal vessels and the damaged tissue. His surgery was guided by the battery of diagnostic data previously acquired on Peter's condition. Peter was even awakened during the surgery to answer questions! I might be less inclined to tell this story if the outcome weren't positive; but it was. Peter is healed. A few months after surgery, he had one seizure while playing squash, but the neurosurgeon dismissed its significance as due to overstressing his still-not-fully-healed brain. Now he takes minimal medication and has been free of seizures for more than two years. But even if he hadn't been cured, the medical diagnostic and surgical procedures make quite a story, and Peter is telling it. With his doctors' encouragement, he made a video record of his tests and surgery. With support from the Epilepsy Foundation, that record is being edited into an instructional video.

Innovation in health technologies shows no signs of slowing. Consider some developments from the year 2003 alone. Surgeons in Napa, California, used robotic extensions of their arms and hands to perform "minimally invasive surgeries" (MIS) through tiny incisions, while still having the three-dimensional view of open operations. In a classic heart operation, a foot-long incision might be made and rib bones broken to open the chest cavity. With the robot, the surgeon cuts only two or three small holes, 5 to 8 millimeters in diameter, for the robotic arms to enter. The patient's heart does not have to be stopped for the procedure, nor must the patient be put on a heart-lung machine to survive.[6] A company in Sunnyvale, California, has gone into business as the world's first producer of surgical robotic arms. Scientists in North Carolina built a brain implant that permits monkeys to control a mechanical arm with their thoughts. The remote arm was connected to the monkey's brain, possibly the first time that mental intentions have been harnessed to move a mechanical object.[7] In England a neurosurgeon implanted an electrode into the medial nerve of his arm to link his nervous system to a computer. Then, from a laboratory in New York, he was able to move a mechanical hand in England by thinking about it and moving his own fingers.[8] At Walter Reed Army Medical Center an amputee learned to control his prosthetic arms and hands by electrical impulses from muscles in his forearms—the same muscles he once used to move his real hands and wrists. The impulses went to microprocessors powering motors in his new electromechanical wrists

---

[6] Gamel, "St. Joseph Health System," 28–33.

[7] Weiss, "Monkey Brains Run Robot."

[8] Kusnetz, "Cyborgs No Longer Science Fiction," D1.

and arms.[9] A U.S. research consortium announced progress on a retinal prosthesis, a "seeing eye" chip with as many as 1,000 tiny electrodes, to be implanted in the eye. It has the potential to allow people who have lost their sight to regain enough vision to function independently.[10]

Changes in communication have been almost as dramatic as those in medicine. The Gutenberg printing press first made it easy to communicate the exact same message to a large number of people beyond voice contact and for the readers to absorb the message at their own pace. Today many modes of telecommunication supplement the printed page. The Internet and other media are interconnected by satellite, fiber optic cable, or atmospheric radio waves. Some futurists have predicted that within a generation, up to half of all human interactions will be via "tele-living." Photos, movies, and videos provide experiences that are both "virtual" and "repeatable," even for those who cannot travel.[11]

For those who *are* mobile, transportation has expanded to all the "firmaments," from land and water to the sky and finally space. Think of how the power to propel us on our journeys has changed: from human to animal to wind power, then steam and electric power, the internal combustion engine, jet aircraft, rocketry, and nuclear power for ships. Much of today's transportation is guided by inertial navigation, radar, or a global positioning system (GPS). According to the National Highway Transportation Safety Administration, in 2003 there were 230.2 million registered vehicles in the United States, up from 225.7 million in 2002 and more than the number of licensed drivers.[12] A vast infrastructure has grown up to support the use of automobiles. Following the same course, an industrial complex called "general aviation" now supports a growing number of private pilots and aircraft, and another supports recreational boating.

What Do We Mean by "Technology" and "Culture"?

So far, I have been using the word *technology* and describing *culture* without defining the terms, so it is time to develop some working definitions before delving more deeply into the relationship between them. If we were to give theologians the first opportunity to define the terms, they would probably point to the first two chapters of Genesis, which describe God's

[9] Loeb, "You Still Feel Like You Have a Hand," 35.
[10] Ehrenman, "New Retinas for Old," 42–46.
[11] Boorstin, "Technology and Democracy," 152–66.
[12] Tyson, "DOT Releases Preliminary Estimates."

work of creation and present His first instructions. The Creator gave human beings freedom not just to enjoy the creation, but to use it, within limits, to develop *culture*. In that context, culture refers to the total result of human activity; *civilization* would have a similar meaning. So defined, culture encompasses all human achievement: the work of human minds and hands. It is the "artificial, secondary environment" that humans superimpose on the natural. It includes language, habits, ideas, beliefs, customs, social organization, inherited artifacts, technical processes, and values. As theologian Richard Niebuhr pointed out, "gifts of nature" are received as they are communicated, without human intent or conscious effort; but "gifts of culture" cannot be possessed without effort on the part of the recipient.[13]

What definitions would an anthropologist contribute? In anthropology books from the 1880s, it is the making and use of tools that distinguishes humans from animals. Benjamin Franklin allegedly coined the term *homo faber*—man the tool maker—and Karl Marx used it in his writings.[14] Today it seems clear, however, that some animals, birds, and even insects use objects such as sticks and rocks as rudimentary tools. One might argue that a spider web and a cocoon are manufactured tools. Looking back on the Industrial Revolution and its consequences, I am compelled to add *potens* (power, powerful) to Franklin's definition, because the distinguishing characteristic of industrialization is the harnessing of natural energy to accomplish human purposes. So my definition of human becomes *Homo potens faber*—Man the *power* tool maker/user. I concede that an eagle flying on updrafts and turtles using the high tide to lay their eggs also are harnessing natural energy. But they are merely using it, not consciously transforming it to accomplish new ends. A psychologist would probably add self-awareness to the definition of what it means to be human, although self-awareness is arguably present in certain animals. If the psychologist added "seeking of purpose and meaning in existence to their definition then the theologians might agree.

In both common and academic usage, the word *technology* is variously used to refer to tools, instruments, machines, organizations, media, methods, techniques, and systems. French sociologist Jacques Ellul adopted an even broader umbrella of "technique," which he defined as the "totality of methods rationally arrived at and having absolute efficiency

---

[13] Niebuhr, *Christ and Culture.*

[14] Chandler, "Technological or Media Determinism."

. . . in every field of human activity."[15] For now, the following set of definitions for technology will suffice, along with the association of an academic discipline for each definition.

- The process of extending or modifying the natural world: bigger, smaller, faster (engineering)
- Bodies of skills, knowledge, and procedures for making and doing useful things (social science)
- The defining mark of human beings (anthropology)
- A special form of knowledge that is compatible with science and controllable by the scientific method, and produces some practical end (philosophers of science)
- The definitive characteristic of modern society (sociology)

What Purpose Does Technology Serve?

Western societies have moved far beyond the simple identification of technology with tools and machines. According to social critic Lewis Mumford, today technology includes the whole of our material culture.[16] Engineering students have been taught for years that technological developments arise to "fill needs," as reflected in the saying that "necessity is the mother of invention." But as social philosopher Carroll Purcell puts it, "many modern 'needs' are themselves inventions, the product of an economy that stimulates consumption so that it can make and market things for a profit."[17]

The broader *definitions* of technology have given rise to correspondingly broader visions of the *purposes* of technology. The first and probably most familiar purpose is to make human life safer. Before the Industrial Revolution, that objective was more or less limited to subduing or managing the hostile forces of nature, including wild beasts and "acts of God" such as extreme weather, flood, fire, or famine. Today, although we would add subduing pathogens and developing artificial organs and new treatments for disease, congenital defects, even the effects of aging, we still refer to acts of God, and look for technological solutions to harness nature or make it more predictable.

---

[15] Ellul, *Technological Society*, v.

[16] Mumford, *The Pentagon of Power*. Quoted in Purcell, *White Heat*, 26.

[17] Purcell, *loc. cit.*, 40.

A second purpose is more recent in origin than the first; certainly it emerged subsequent to the Industrial Revolution and perhaps since the age of automation. This purpose is to relieve drudgery and suffering, especially as related to repetitive, dangerous, or arduous tasks. 'Labor-saving devices' for the household and robots to replace assembly-line workers are examples. From a theological perspective, the first two purposes could be understood as mitigating some of the effects of humanity's fall from the state of innocence that humans enjoyed in the Garden of Eden.

A third purpose of technology is to provide material prosperity, by increasing the rates of resource extraction, goods production, and global commerce. This is arguably the most notable aspect of technology's contribution to human welfare, because three major advances—the initial development of tool use, the agricultural revolution, and the Industrial Revolution—each revolutionized human culture and enabled quantum jumps in the population of the planet. Each revolution allowed people to be better fed, clothed, housed, protected, and healed.

The Industrial Revolution actually included a second agricultural revolution, which went beyond the initial use of tools to cultivate and irrigate the soil.[18] This second revolution was characterized by mechanization of agriculture, and it was enabled by inventions such as:

- Jethro Tull's seed drill (1701)
- James Small's cast iron plow (1765)
- Andrew Meicle's threshing machine (1780)
- Cyrus McCormick's mechanical reaper and binder (1834)
- Anna Baldwin's suction machine to milk cows (1878)
- The Haber-Bosch process for "fixing" atmospheric nitrogen (early twentieth century)

Today the entire food system has been industrialized and automated—by refrigeration for crop transportation and storage; fossil-fuel based fertilizers, pesticides, and herbicides; irrigation, ever larger mechanical systems for cultivating, planting, and harvesting; global positioning systems, and computer analysis to optimize fertilizing & harvesting. Crop hybridization produced the first green revolution; but today innovators hope that agricultural biotechnology (genetically modified organisms, or GMOs) will lead to a new green revolution.

---

[18] Purcell, *loc. cit*, 2–3.

It could be argued that the U.S. is undergoing a contemporary *knowledge revolution* as it morphs from a manufacturing to an information society. An optimistic assessment has globalization of information technology (IT) producing a new wave of job growth in the U.S.,[19] and a case may be made that the knowledge revolution is revolutionizing culture. However, IT has not yet enabled a jump in the Earth's carrying capacity—its ability to support life. If it can affect such global issues, the most likely avenue will be indirect—through genomics, biotechnology, high-tech agriculture, and *miniaturization*.

Each technological revolution established what appeared at the time to be unlimited resources for population growth. Since the Industrial Revolution, however, the third purpose of technology has taken on additional significance, because concerns are growing about the long-term impacts of human activity on Earth's life-support systems. Population levels, economies, and cultures are inextricably linked to how we use, produce, process, dispose of, and recover or recycle natural and synthetic materials and energy, and the innumerable products made from them.[20] For those reasons, the future trajectory of Earth's human population is uncertain. Will we experience continued growth, or are we approaching decline, even crash?

A fourth purpose of technology is to achieve security and hopefully even world peace. During the hunter-gatherer period weapons were used to fend off enemies; but in the twentieth century the development of armaments accelerated dramatically, along with their applications in battle. When we apply satellite imaging technology to watch our adversaries we are even using technology to manage uncertainty. Beyond national security, people increasingly look to technology to provide domestic, social, and personal safety and security. Examples include detection, tracking, and access denial systems; intelligence technologies (such as eavesdropping, wiretapping, and); cyber security through "spam" blockers, antiviral software and anti-spyware.

A fifth purpose follows closely from the fourth, although it is more closely related to economic security than to military security. In this case, technololgy is used to export democracy and capitalism in the process of globalization. Globalization is technology-enabled, through the Internet, jet transport, and containerized freight. Advocates of globalization believe that trading partners don't make war on each other; democracies don't start wars, and that global commerce is the best way to increase the mate-

---

[19] Mann, "Globalization of IT Services and White Collar Jobs," 6.

[20] Graedel and Allenby, *Industrial Ecology*.

rial well-being of the less-developed nations who are often our adversaries. The fourth and fifth purposes for technology were combined to justify the U.S. invasion of Iraq in 2003. The pre-emptive attack was rationalized on the basis of a threat to U.S. domestic security, and the political objective was to install Western-style democracy. For better or worse, however, globalization includes the export of Western (especially U.S.) culture.

A sixth purpose is more futuristic and actually cross-cuts all the others: use of technology to shape our destiny as a species. Today science news, and to some degree popular news, is replete with announcements of scientific advances and speculations about where they are leading. Engineers collaborate with geneticists, biologists, biochemists, and materials scientists in efforts to redesign living organisms. Cross-disciplinary research programs combine molecular-level computing, nanotechnology (with characteristic dimensions on the order of molecular dimensions), and genetic manipulation to develop human-machine hybrids—or cyborgs. What was once science fiction is being touted as the next step in human evolution.

Big Technology—Big Impacts

Western civilization was revolutionized by industry and commerce, but not without cost. Samples of hair from historical figures like Newton and Napoleon show the presence of toxic elements such as antimony and mercury. By the 1800s, certain trades were associated with characteristic occupational diseases: chimney sweeps contracted cancer of the scrotum from hydrocarbons in chimney soot; hatters became 'mad' from nerve-destroying mercury salts used to treat felt fabric; and bootblacks suffered liver damage from boot polish solvents.

Industrial economies were built of iron and steel. Early craftsmen found that wood, burned in contact with certain minerals, changed them into metallic substances of great usefulness. But wherever the iron industry took hold, the production of charcoal consumed the forests of the land. That early material shortage became a crisis that led to the next great advance in metallurgical engineering. The smelting of iron using coal instead of charcoal determined the subsequent history of Britain and, indeed, of the rest of the world.[21]

As the end of Britain's forests drew nearer, admirals and statesmen became alarmed for the future of British supremacy at sea if their oak timber were depleted. Thus one of the purposes of the colony to be es-

---

[21] Kirby et al., *Engineering in History*.

tablished in America for Queen Elizabeth by Raleigh's expedition of 1585 was the production of iron from the ores and immense forests of the new continent. After Virginia was at last founded in 1607, one furnace and two small forges were erected at Falling Creek, 66 miles above Jamestown. According to historian Richard Kirby, it was their lighting that provoked the massacre of March 22, 1622. In order to preserve their forests, the Indians wrecked the furnaces and slaughtered the workmen.[22]

Pursuit of prosperity through technology made the first industrial cities nearly uninhabitable. The London of the novels of Charles Dickens and Arthur Conan Doyle was enveloped in darkness from coal smoke and soot; slag heaps accumulated in neighborhoods; the Thames River was an open sewer; and the stench of industrial, human, and animal waste filled the air. Child labor was the norm; many children and adults died from typhus, cholera, and pneumonia. Pittsburgh and Chicago in the U.S. were not much different, although child labor was less common. In the twentieth century *Automation* caught on as a means to reduce human exposure to hazardous industrial activities as well as to increase productivity.

Individual technologies intended for social good can be misused. Some analysts argued that the mere possibility of the Strategic Defense Initiative was sufficient to force the Soviets to capitulate in the arms race. In the moment of triumph at the end of the Cold War, a U.S. State Department employee suggested that we might have arrived at "the end of history."[23] He meant that Western capitalism and liberal democracy had trumped all other human achievements in self-government and human welfare. Then on September 11, 2001, I was teaching an engineering class on systems design when the news came that four American commercial jets had been hijacked and turned into "weapons of mass destruction," a phrase that until now had only been assigned to devices—nuclear, chemical, and biological—whose design purpose was large-scale destruction in wartime.

Military conflicts are notoriously damaging to the environment as well as to people. In the 1991 conflict in the Persian Gulf, the Iraqi military intentionally released over 330 million gallons of crude oil into the Gulf and set fire to over 700 oil wells, sending thick, black smoke into the

---

[22] Ibid.

[23] Fukuyama, "Are We at the End of History?" 75–78.

atmosphere.[24] But even that environmental insult was miniscule compared to the legacy of the nuclear arms race.[25]

Historical Example:
the Chicago Hog Packing Industry

The later stages of the nineteenth century in the U.S. were associated with a synergy of mass production, large corporations, continent-wide markets, and electric power. All of these enabled industry in general, and the Chicago meat packing industry in particular, to flourish. From the late nineteenth century through the mid-twentieth, Western societies pursued material prosperity and military security through mass production of goods on assembly lines. A fascinating documentary film aired on public television in 2003 showed the rise of Chicago as an industrial city. It gave viewers a perspective on the enormous increase in productivity that technology provided—and the technological optimism that accompanied it. As depicted in that documentary, the U.S. led the world in developing automation.[26]

A device called the Hereford wheel was perfected by the Chicago meat packers. Shackled to it by a hind leg, hogs were lifted into the air so a "sticker" could slit their throats. Many writers of the time, including English poet Rudyard Kipling, described the bloody, noisy scene of the hog kill using the Hereford wheel.[27] From the kill to the cutlets, pork packing developed into a labor-intensive, lightning-fast disassembly line. In about 15 minutes, a hog went through the whole process, passing perhaps 150 workers, depending on the packinghouse. By the turn of the century, some Chicago meat packing houses were killing five or six thousand hogs a day. A record run at the Union Stockyards was about 190,000 hogs in one day.

Largest of the pork packers was Philip Armour's company. Armour could keep in communication with his global pork-packing empire through the trans-Atlantic cable laid in 1860, the telegraph line, and the telephone. Today we are familiar with great global industries such as oil and steel, but the first of them was pork packing, established nearly 150 years ago. Son of a farmer from Stockbridge, New York and unsuccessful in school, Armour went west and made enough money in the California gold rush to

24 "Pollution."

25 See for example Hoffman, "Radioactivity Threatens a Mighty River," A1.

26 "Chicago."

27 Rudyard Kipling. Quoted in "Chicago," *loc. cit.*

enter the grain and pork business. He poured his profits into an efficient packing plant alongside the Union Stock Yards of Chicago, undermining other packers who could not compete. He was a disciplined, ruthless businessman who had his finger in every aspect of the business that made Chicago "hog butcher of the world." In Armour's Chicago, industrialists "did it straight," as Norman Mailer would write. "Chicagoans were greedy, direct, too impatient for hypocrisy, in love with honest plunder."[28]

The Chicago packinghouses became the city's foremost tourist attraction. Visitors could see that their familiar world of pasture and butcher was gone, replaced by the mechanization of slaughter. What was it that made the slaughterhouses attractive to tourists? They were witnessing what was new, what was "modern." It was the Industrial Revolution at its most starkly dramatic. Observers were horrified and repelled by it on the one hand, but they also marveled at what their age had accomplished, and what was happening to the world as a result. Novelist Upton Sinclair wrote that while watching that disassembly line, one could begin to "hear the hog-squeal of the universe."[29] His novel caused a sensation and led to changes in the packinghouses and the nation's approach to meat sanitation. Two years after Sinclair's novel was published the federal government established the first standards for food sanitation—the beginnings of the USDA and FDA.

In those same animal disassembly lines, Henry Ford found the inspiration for his Model T automobile assembly line. And today's commodity futures markets grew out of the trading activities around the Union Stock Yards. In addition to hogs, grain was also bought and sold. Through a new Board of Trade, traders bought and sold receipts for grain deposited in elevators by the Chicago River. A telegraph in the trading room sent instant market reports to New York buyers, who bought grain in the elevators for future delivery. Speculators then developed a futures market, enabling buyers in New York to buy for future delivery Chicago hogs or grain that did not yet exist—a market not in hogs or grain as such, but in their future prices.

When a growing Chicago needed a new water system, a sanitary engineer from Boston named Ellis Chesbrough was hired to bring clean water from Lake Michigan. His grandiose project featured a tunnel going two miles out to an intake point. It opened in 1867 but never worked. Spring rains washed sewage two miles out into the lake, right into the

---

[28] Norman Mailer. Quoted in "Chicago," *loc. cit.*

[29] Upton Sinclair. Quoted in "Chicago," *loc. cit.*

water intakes. Chesbrough was given another chance, however, and his bold plan to reverse the flow of the Chicago River succeeded in sending its waters through a canal westward into the Illinois River and eventually into the Mississippi. The river no longer flowed east into Lake Michigan. Businessmen honored Chesbrough for "purifying the river" without "interfering" with the city's business or its "unparalleled growth."[30]

To the city fathers, that was the beauty of a man like Chesbrough. He came with the attitude that technology could solve any problem—even problems created by technology. He was feted at banquets because he allowed Chicago to grow without changing anybody's behavior, without controlling any of the economic interests who were dumping waste into the river. Now they could continue to use that river as a sewer and send their garbage down-river toward complaining but less powerful canal towns. "The stench has been almost unendurable," wrote a downstream resident, "What right has Chicago to . . . reduce the value of property and bring sickness and death to the citizens?"[31]

Chicago has always been the beneficiary of the stored resources of the Great Plains. As Wes Jackson of the Land Institute in Salina, Kansas, notes, "we must count the cattlemen as miners of the soil nutrients with each animal shipped out of the region. Later, oil and natural gas were discovered and the fossil carbon miners became richer than the ranchers. Those who appropriate sun energy pooled over millions of years are certain to have economic advantage over those who harvest a scant supply of contemporary sunlight in the form of food crops or grass-fed livestock. The plowing of the prairies, most notably during World War I, turned the settlers and their descendants into soil miners. The Dust Bowl years of the 1930s were a major consequence of this Great Plowing. Next the water miners, with their Chevy and Ford engines burning fossil carbon, sucked down the Ogallala Aquifer, a reserve accumulated in geologic time. This fossil water irrigates corn in arid country for feedlot beef."[32] In addition to automation, other factors such as agriculture, technologies for transportation, communication, and sanitation were crucial for marshalling the resources of the Great Plains into the large industrial organizations and high-productivity, mass-production economy that flourished in Chicago.[33]

[30] Quoted in "Chicago," *loc. cit.*

[31] Ibid.

[32] Jackson, 3.

[33] An economist would no doubt insist that more than technology was needed to build the economy. In order for enough capital to be assembled, developments like limited liability,

Where Are We Now?

It is important to try to assess where we are now and to try to determine where our present course is taking us. Is the optimism of the technologists justified? Can technological acceleration continue forever? Some believe that the past achievements of science indicate that all limits can be overcome with suitable applications of science. Whatever we determine in response to these questions, is it wise to attempt to steer technology? Or would such efforts backfire because any attempt to steer the enterprise will kill the goose that is laying the golden eggs?

The Chicago meat packing industry and the other examples illustrate the optimism that characterized the technological enterprise in the U.S. during the nineteenth and twentieth centuries. The optimism included belief in inexhaustible resources, continuous progress, and limitless horizons. An optimistic outlook asserts that appropriate technological and other changes can produce replacements for scarce natural resources, control pollution, and allow production and consumption to continue to rise. That view is dominant in most discussions of sustainability by government officials and business executives, whose emphasis is rarely on limiting consumption. Some observers are convinced that the rising consumption of raw materials enabled by—and required for—technology is neither equitable nor sustainable. Others believe that mal-distribution is the only problem, with many people in the world having too little while others have over-abundance. Despite the insistence of environmental advocates that achieving sustainability requires reduction of per-capita consumption and stabilizing population, most engineers limit their focus to increasing technological efficiency and decreasing pollution per unit produced.[34]

More than a century after Sinclair's exposé of the Chicago slaughterhouses, social impacts still accompany technological benefits. The rise in labor productivity (the amount of goods and services produced per labor hour) enabled by technology means that fewer workers are needed. In 1980, when manufacturing employment in the U.S. peaked at about twenty million, General Motors employed 454,000 workers to produce 56 million cars and trucks a year. In 2004 GM made roughly the same number of vehicles, but needed only 118,000 people to do so.[35] According

the stock market, investment banking, a continent-wide market, and an anti-trust policy were also required. Cf. DeLong, *loc. cit.*, 42.

[34] *Green Products by Design;* Reijnders, "The Factor X Debate," 13–22.

[35] Berry, "Doing More With Fewer Workers," 19. Unfortunately for GM, those productivity gains were not enough. In June 2005 GM announced a reduction of 25,000 workers, or roughly 22% of its North American work force. The company blamed the cost of work-

to Bloomberg News columnist John Berry, the amount of labor required to assemble a vehicle has been reduced, on average, to 24 person-hours.[36] GM's experience reflects what has been happening throughout the U.S. manufacturing industry for the past two decades. New technologies have delivered huge gains in productivity so that the cost of manufactured goods has come down. According to material measures such as gross domestic product (GDP) per capita or labor-saving devices per household, the average standard of living has risen as well. The corresponding concern about continuing loss of manufacturing jobs due to rising productivity is that the real gains seem to accrue only to the already well off, while a growing number of displaced workers can find only minimum-wage jobs or none at all.

Automobiles, drive-up windows, and fast food contribute to a U.S. epidemic of obesity, with an increased cost of health care shared by everyone. Telecommunications, air conditioning, and home entertainment centers permit people to work, shop, and be entertained at home instead of gathering with others. Remote garage door openers may provide protection, but reduce the number of encounters with one's neighbors. Many Americans have withdrawn into private, gated enclaves. Even without the gates and guards, increasing numbers seem to be withdrawing from their neighbors and sometimes from members of their own families.[37]

The Acceleration of Just About Everything

Any description of a particular culture will have to be tied to a particular period of history, because culture does not remain fixed. Everywhere we look, new technologies spawn new industries, and the pace seems only to quicken. "In the twenty-first century," wrote historian Steven Ambrose, "everything seems to be in a constant flux, and change is so ubiquitous as to be taken for granted. This leads to a popular question: which generation lived through the greatest change? The ones who lived through the coming of the automobile and the airplane and the beginning of modern medicine? Or those who were around for the invention and first use of the atomic bomb and the jet airplane? Or the computer? Or the Internet and email?"[38] Ambrose chose not only a period of time but a specific people:

---

ers' health care, but the fact remained that the largest sport utility vehicles—sales of which GM (and Ford) had been counting on to continue their profitable run—were declining.

[36] Ibid.

[37] Baumgartner, *The Moral Order of a Suburb*; Lynch, *A Cry Unheard*.

[38] Ambrose, *Nothing Like It in the World*, 358.

Americans who lived through the second half of the nineteenth century. He cited the locomotive as the first great triumph over space and time and America as the one place where it was utilized fully, in a transcontinental railroad. That railroad (and the telegraph) made it possible to have a nationwide stock market, a continent-wide economy, and a continent-wide culture.

But today even the word *change* no longer suffices to characterize what is happening. New technologies are arriving with ever-increasing frequency. Social historian Theodore Zeldin notes: "Technology has a rapid heartbeat, compressing housework, travel, entertainment, squeezing more and more into the allotted space."[39] In his book *Faster: The Acceleration of Just About Everything,* technology writer James Gleick labels the phenomenon "time compression." He says: "We have learned to grasp quickly. We can read signs, change lanes and avoid other vehicles at 70 mph while also listening to a song and planning our weekend. Things come at us at a rate our ancestors could not have imagined, and we handle them."[40]

Most futurists say that technology is growing exponentially.[41] One doesn't have to be an engineer to understand these things. Compare the lives your grandparents and parents lived with your own childhood and your current life. What did your grandparents do for entertainment in place of watching TV? How did your parents stay in touch with friends? What did they do for recreation? A little reflection should convince you that during the span of just two generations essentially all major socioeconomic sectors have been transformed. Think about the changes in the following economic sectors:[42]

- Communication
- Agriculture
- Transportation
- Medicine

- Recreation
- Government
- Warfare
- Research

- Manufacturing
- Finance
- Education
- Entertainment

---

[39] Quoted in Gleick, *Faster,* 11.

[40] Gleick, *loc. cit.,* 201.

[41] Kurzweil, "Technology in the 21st Century." For a contrasting view see Adler, "Entering a Dark Age of Innovation."

[42] Include the arts in entertainment. Spirituality also has been changed by technology, but as we shall see, in ways that are not readily discerned.

Odds are that most of the changes you identified resulted from introduction of new technologies. But if the technological driving force for change is still not evident, consider these facts from the last few years:

- Globalization, which is basically technology-driven, is changing the face of American manufacturing and consumption. Manufacturing jobs are moving overseas and the goods we purchase are likely to have been made in Asia or Indonesia.

- Toyota became the second largest worldwide automobile manufacturer, and the third largest in North America.

- Daimler Chrysler shortened the development concept-to-showroom cycle of a vehicle from 60 to 30 months.

- Dell Computer Corp claimed that parts spent only 8 hours in its factories before leaving in a finished PC.

- Intel Corp Chairman Craig Barrett said that 90% of the products his company delivered on the final day of each year did not exist on the first day of the same year.

- Kodak Corporation ceased to make film cameras, concentrating instead on digital versions.

- Software product cycles, already short at 18 to 24 mos., are evaporating. Instead of a distinct, tested, shrink-wrapped version, manufacturers distribute upgrades and patches on a monthly or even daily basis.

- New manufacturing technology produces fully functioning micro electromechanical systems (MEMS) just days after they are designed using 3-D computer-aided design (CAD) software.

- Product life cycles are getting shorter
    - The average life of a consumer product is 3 years until scrapped.
    - The average life of a computer is 4.7 months until obsolete.
    - The average life of a company is 7 years until out of business.

According to one futurist, "Eighty percent of what engineers need to know to be successful in the twenty first century is outside their field or industry today."[43] As a result, since 2001 the U. S. Accreditation Board for Engineering and Technology (ABET) has required that students be taught the imperative of *lifelong learning* for graduates who intend to remain in technology development.[44] For two decades—just as Moore's law predicted—computing power per microchip has doubled every eighteen months. Anything that doubles in a certain amount of time and continues to do so is growing exponentially, following the "J" curve in Figure 1.1. Most of us, however, are not trend-perceptive. That is, "we see around ourselves only the little bits and pieces that reach back to last week and

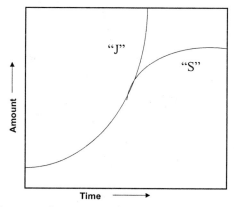

Figure 1.1. "J" curve of exponential growth and "S" curve of limited growth.

forward to tomorrow."[45] Technically trained persons refer to this kind of cognitive process as linear thinking. I recall commenting to my aging grandmother that traffic in her adopted city—a fast-growing suburb of San Francisco—certainly must be different than when she was young. I didn't expect that we could miss-communicate here, because she had lived in a small town in rural Ohio. "Why, no, not at all," she said, "we had traffic just like this." Because little in our everyday lives happens exponentially, our natural tendency is to underestimate what this means and to under-calculate how extraordinary this type of change occurs.[46] "Exponentials start slowly and remain disarmingly out of sight" says James Gleick. "Yet

[43] Barlow, *Creating the Future.*

[44] *Criteria for Accrediting Programs in Engineering.*

[45] Swenson, *Margin,* 41.

[46] Swenson, *Hurtling Toward Oblivion,* 53.

they build strength relentlessly until they've grown too large to ignore. By then, whole industries have changed and whole cultures have fallen."[47]

The history of thinking about exponential growth ranges from doomsday scenarios to technological optimism.[48] Scientific realism dictates that in a finite world, limits of one kind or another eventually must constrain such processes—forcing the trajectory from the J to the S curve in the figure. In biology, the population of a bio-organism in a Petri dish may grow exponentially until the walls of the dish stop the growth. In semiconductor technology the limits may be imposed by the ability of manufacturing equipment to accurately photo-etch the circuits, or by the way in which silicon atoms organize during solidification. By overcoming some of the apparent limits, however, manufacturing technologists have so far postponed the onset of the S curve.

Christian physician and futurist Richard Swenson has argued that exponential growth is bringing us into encounter with psychological and spiritual limits in addition to the physical ones.[49] Although the infamous Scopes trial in 1925 earned religious fundamentalists a reputation as antimodern, few Christian groups have tried to limit their use of technology. Evangelicals embrace the mass-communication technologies of radio, television, and the Internet to spread the gospel.[50] Many churches regularly make their services available via the Internet and use multimedia presentations to promote missionary activities. In contrast, the Amish subordinate technology to the good of God, family, and community—subordination that became a symbol of their separation from the evil world.[51]

The changes that technology imposes on cultures are not always for the better, and the impacts of technology on the spiritual domain are not readily discerned. By surrounding us with images that reflect ourselves and not God, for example, technology may damage our sense of the sacred. By supplanting natural things with artificial ones technology may deprive traditional religious symbols of their suggestive meanings.[52] The transcontinental railroad, which Ambrose credited with enabling a continental culture, transformed—some would say vanquished—Native American cultures. At first, passengers shot buffalo "for sport" from the windows

---

[47] Gleick, *loc. cit.*, 277.

[48] Swenson, *Hurtling Toward Oblivion*, 57–61.

[49] Swenson, *Hurtling Toward Oblivion*.

[50] Hendershot, *Shaking the World for Jesus*.

[51] Funk, "Technology and Christian Values."

[52] Kuhns, *Environmental Man*, 19.

of passenger trains; later freight trains made it profitable to ship the hides and meat to eastern markets where the hides could be made into robes or tanned and used for leather drive belts for machinery. Within a few years the number of buffalo had been reduced from twenty million to a few thousand, sealing the fate of the Plains Indians' culture, including their religious practices. "White" culture was also changed. The Mormon practice of polygamy required isolation from the persecution that had forced the church west. The coming of the railroad—right through the 'promised land' of northern Utah—brought commerce, prosperity, but also unbelievers. The necessary isolation disappeared, and polygamy eventually had to be dropped from church doctrine.[53]

Collectively, the argument about limits is compelling. One way or another, encounters with limits must force a shift from exponential growth to a sustainable rate. The shift could be painful, as in population limitation by starvation; or it could be catastrophic, as a result of sudden collapse of one or more of Earth's life-support systems. It is not too late to manage the shift deliberately, but time may be growing short. Science and technology have enabled exponential growth, but they also will be a key to achieving sustainability. Notice that I said "a" key: in addition to science and technology, I believe that other forces must be brought into the process. These other forces are social and spiritual, and we will explore them in subsequent chapters. Ultimately, technology may be a *profound* distraction, demanding our preoccupation with mundane things instead of the kingdom of God.[54]

---

[53] Burns and Ives, "The West: Fight no More Forever."
[54] Funk, *loc. cit.*

Chapter 2

In Technology We Trust

CULTURAL CHANGE *per se* was not among the six purposes of technology listed in chapter 1. But change to culture is certainly one of the outcomes. Prior to the Industrial Revolution, civilizations changed little unless they were overrun by a very different people and forced to adopt the ways of their conquerors.[1] Cultural *revolutions* from inside were rare. The early history of the United States portrays a rapidly evolving civilization as the colonies threw off their colonial master and the nation expanded westward. But prior to the Industrial Revolution the economy remained basically agrarian, supplemented by cottage industries that produced the tools for agriculture, exploration, and war-fighting.

When the Industrial Revolution spread to the U.S. in the nineteenth century it merged with the new spirit of exploration, conquest, and expansion to produce a uniquely American brand of technological optimism, remnants of which still permeate U.S. culture. The image of the rugged individualist, the lone inventor, the capitalist entrepreneur, the pioneer and the wandering cowboy—these caricatures still shape the American *psyche* and weave through our advertising campaigns. But the reality of the matter is that technological progress has changed the picture into a myth. Consider the situation of farmers, who must increase productivity just in

---

[1] From an anthropological perspective, warfare represents one means by which a society forces its will upon another, with the loser's culture inevitably changing as a consequence. Technology has always been the enabler of warfare, and thus warfare is one more example of technology forcing cultural change. Consider the impact of one simple development: rifled artillery. At the outset of the American Civil War, state-of-the-art military forts were protected by substantial brick walls. Fort Pulaski—which guarded the harbor at Savannah, GA—contained 25 million bricks and required 18 years to build. But on April 11, 1862, Pulaski fell after only 30 hours of bombardment from the Union's newly developed rifled cannons. The old ten-inch round shot fired from smooth bore cannons weighed 128 lbs. and had an effective range of 800 yards. In contrast, the new rifled and bullet-shaped James Bolt projectile weighed only 80 lbs. but had a devastating and accurate impact from more than two miles away. The result marked the end of masonry fortification and changed defense strategy worldwide. See Hinds and Fitzgerald, *Bulwark and Bastion*, 45–54.

order to survive in this era of rising costs and stagnant prices. Computer and GPS technologies are making them more efficient—by automatically dispensing the optimum amount of fertilizer or pesticide as determined from overhead images obtained during the growing season and yield measurements during harvest. But along with this increased efficiency, the days when a farmer could repair his own equipment are gone, just as they have passed for the owners of modern automobiles. The benefits of technology are many, but *simplification* is not one of them. Life has become much more complex. Today we all depend upon a complex system of production, distribution, maintenance, and consumption. Full development of the issue would require more space than is available, so I will focus on three examples that collectively portray how dependent on technology we have become.

Interdependency

Prosperity and Consumption

Pursuit of material well-being is a key characteristic of U.S. culture. One might say the same thing about any culture; certainly many societies have produced opulence—at least for their royalty. But a problem emerges when the objective, races past *sufficiency* and becomes focused on abundance. The U.S. economy achieved a level of production sufficient to feed, shelter, and clothe all its citizens by the early twentieth century. But then we turned our efforts to *creating and filling new needs*; yesterday's luxuries have become today's necessities.[2] As evidence of the creation of new "needs," one need only browse through a copy of *Sky Mall* on an airline flight—or check it out at www.skymall.com. The last time I looked, every single item in the 250-page catalog seem to me to fit in the category of excess. Contemporary U.S. grocery stores are roughly double the average size of a generation ago, which is also about double the size of a generation previously. A Barnes and Noble bookstore may now devote as much shelf space to recently published books as the British Museum had for the entire corpus of humanity's written history and literature when Karl Marx used its library a century and a half ago.[3]

The real estate section of our local newspaper recently included an article describing the features that "high-end" buyers demand in new homes. Granite counter tops are considered to be the norm, as are stainless steel appliances, built-in vegetable sinks, espresso-cappuccino makers, a butler's

[2] Sine, 83; Amato, *Stuff*; Friedel, "Scarcity and Promise."

[3] Swearengen and Woodhouse, "Overconsumption as an Ethics Challenge for Engineering Education," 15–31.

pantry, a separate wine refrigerator, and two dishwashers (which are "a big plus when entertaining"). Many of the new homes have outdoor kitchens, complete with built-in cabinets, gas BBQ, and outdoor fireplaces. Jetted tubs are still popular in the master suite, but walk-in rain showers (two to four massaging shower heads) with a roomy seating area while sitting in a steam bath are usually featured now. There are also his-and-her water closets with heated tiles, a personal valet for steaming clothes and a whirl-pool sink—a jetted laundry sink for hand-washing one's finer clothes. The homes generally have four- or five-car garages and wiring for many com-puters, multiple power lines, plasma televisions and an intercom system installed throughout the house. Smart features can be programmed via computers—the security system as well as the thermostat can actually be modified in cyberspace.[4] But before you conclude that only "high-end" homeowners are caught up in this phenomenon, you should count the number of electrical, electronic, and other power-driven devices in your home. Include battery-powered devices such as flashlights and remote controls, and outdoor tools such as edgers and mowers. Chances are your list will quickly exceed fifty, and most will approach eighty.

In 2005 the average house built in the United States was a record 2412 square feet—up 63 feet since 2004 and 60% since the 1970s.[5] But our houses still aren't big enough to hold all the stuff that we accumulate. The self-storage business has become a $15 billion industry, nearly 39,000 facilities containing 11.6 million units and 1.5 billion square feet of stor-age space. And that doesn't include companies that deal in portable storage units or those that store only vehicles and boats.[6] About 9% of America's 112 million households currently use self storage and about 25% have used it in the past. A survey by the Self Storage Association found that more than half of the renters had attics or garages in their homes—it's just that they were too full.

Admittedly, some consumer items that may seem frivolous on first encounter may meet some "unspoken" needs. Consider Mocha the cat, who has agreed to live with my sister in the Sierra Foothills. Sally loves Mocha, but Mocha whines to be let in or out, leaves rodents entrails on the doorstep, requires visits to the vet, is picky about his food, and sometimes doesn't come home at night. Enter NeCoRo.[7] As shown in figure 2.1with

[4] Howe, "Must Haves," 34–39.

[5] Brown, "Homes growing as families shrink," E5.

[6] Rose, Bleys W., "Stashing the Goods," D2, D8.

[7] Weeks, Linton, "no muss, no fuss with robo-pets," D1, D2.

siblings and friend, NeCoRo is a nearly-realistic cat-bot that weighs 3.5

Figure 2.1. NeCoRo and siblings   Figure 2.2. Scooba

pounds and is packed with visual, auditory, and movement sensors.[8] Some "robo-therapists" believe that robotic pets like NeCoRo will be easier for many people—the elderly, the allergy-stricken, the autistic and disabled children and adults—to deal with than a real cat. They don't have any of Mocha's shortcomings. NeCoRo meows obnoxiously and occasionally hisses unless you touch it in a certain way, tripping special sensors, and then it closes its eyes and purrs or mews contentedly. Robo-therapists believe there is a huge future for robotic pets. Sherry Turkle, Massachusetts Institute of Technology professor and author of *The Second Self: Computers and the Human Spirit*, has been studying the effects of robotic pets on people.[9] She is convinced that people respond to robo pets because people are basically lonely and vulnerable. They don't want to feed and clean up after their animals, but they do want more and more expressions of affection from them. "Of course, this puts us back into willing servitude," says writer Linton Weeks. Ironically, as we build more-needy machines that act more like animals, we are also trying to develop less-needy animals that act more like machines.[10] Brooks was alluding to the practice of breeding animals and treating them with steroids and antibiotics for increased productivity.

The company that gave us the cute robotic floor vacuum "Roomba" in 1999 further shortened the list of domestic chores in 2005 with the introduction of Scooba (see Figure 2.2). Scooba is a smart robotic mop that can pick up loose dirt, lay down a cleaning solution, scrub the floor

[8] Anon, "Robo-cat is out of the bag."

[9] Turkle, *The Second Self*.

[10] Weeks, *loc. cit.* We will return to this subject in the following chapter.

and then squeegee it dry. [11] A remote "brain" shoots a small beam of light to create a virtual wall to keep Scooba away from carpets, and sensors on the robot keeps it from tumbling down a flight of stairs. Roomba and Scooba illustrate one of the purposes for technology discussed in chapter 1—relieving drudgery. NeCoRo, on the other hand, is a techno-toy, but one that seems to be filling a social need. In this role, NeCoRo seems to be an example of technology making human life better. But is it a technology to solve a problem created by technology? Many analysts have argued that negative social consequences of industrialization include separating families and isolating individuals. We will return to this theme in chapter 6.

Technology Dependency

NeCoRo and Scooba would be useless without batteries, so we expect to be able to purchase them at retail outlets and recharge them at home. If the proper batteries are unavailable, not just NeCoRo comes to a halt. Our watches, cameras, TV remote controls, flashlights, power tools, thermostats and smoke alarms, toys, laptops, iPods, MP3s, cell phones and cordless hand sets, garage door openers and sprinkler controls all become useless. Yet batteries for electronic consumer items are the tip of an infrastructure iceberg. We just couldn't function without clean running water, refrigerators and ranges, supermarkets, automobiles and gasoline stations, and electronic communication. These things in turn depend upon a complex, inter-woven, and institutionalized network of production, distribution, operation, and maintenance. Retail stores depend upon reliable manufacturing and distribution systems, and the producers require raw materials, energy, labor, and waste management. Directly or indirectly, most of us are completely dependent upon an essentially invisible system that supplies the goods, services, and energy we need for our daily lives. Interruptions would have impacts ranging from frustrating to agonizing and potentially catastrophic. The "Y2K" computer software problem—which was predicted to create havoc in the nation's financial sector—did not materialize. But the OPEC oil embargo in 1973 caused a national gasoline shortage in the U.S. and near panic. The rolling blackouts in California during the summer of 2001 were attributed to human manipulation of energy markets; and in summer 2003 a switching problem in Ohio initiated a blackout that spread across the Northeastern U.S. and Southeastern Canada. In each case many elderly people died when their air conditioning stopped.

---

[11] Harris, "Floor-scrubbing robot sticks to its turf," F3.

Clearly the infrastructure must be reliable not just during normal operation, but during abnormal and even highly unusual situations.

But as technological systems grow more complex, the opportunities for technical failure grow too.[12] And as systems become more powerful and/or more toxic and the surrounding population increases, the consequences of failure become more severe.[13] In 1973 systems theorist Ervin Laszlo warned "In the remaining decades of this century, mankind's problems will be increasingly complex in detail and global in scope . . . Never before have so many people faced so many problems of such great complexity. Any attempt to isolate issues and apply short-range remedies will continue to fail by reason of the growing interdependency of all vital processes on this planet."[14] Although the general public seldom thinks about this issue in technical terms, individually and collectively we attempt to manage the risks of system breakdowns, from simple things like installing an emergency generator in our home to large-scale efforts like homeland security.

In fact, the effort may have seeped into our subconscious. "Today's America is all about avoiding risk," says senior writer Andre Seu of *World* magazine.[15] "We manage risk with Social Security, 401Ks, gated communities, burglar alarms, car alarms, life and malpractice insurance, insurance for vacations (against trip cancellation, interruption, or delay, medical emergencies, lost or stolen baggage, missed connections), and prenuptial pacts." Seu neglected to mention the far larger effort that we devote to managing the risks of the critical infrastructure, national security, and natural disasters. Yet when we think of ways to reduce risks, where do we turn first? Technology is our key source of protection against most of the "big" failures, and increasingly for the smaller ones. And wherever technology is not the key provider, *technique* is.

Surety

Technologies that can inflict great damage if they fail are called high-consequence systems. The public water supply, hydroelectric dams, jumbo jets, supertankers, the electric power grid, and petrochemical plants certainly qualify—but so do nuclear weapons and power plants, ammuni-

---

[12] Perrow, *Normal Accidents*.

[13] The consequences of failure are independent of the probability of failure; risk is the product of probability of failure and its consequences.

[14] Laszlo, *The World System*, 82. Quoted in Swenson, *Margin*, 59.

[15] Seu, "Risky Business," 35.

tion factories and the air traffic control system. The Internet is a high-consequence system because it has become indispensable to modern commerce. For this reason, terrorists are targeting the Internet and at the same time using it as a tool for their own pursuits. But because it is distributed over many sites rather than concentrated at one location it may be less vulnerable than some more centralized technical systems.

Formalized procedures for assuring the safety of high-consequence systems date back at least to the first ASME Boiler and Pressure Vessel Code in 1914–15. But as boilers increased in size and pressure and nuclear weapons and power plants entered the picture, approaches to safety had to become more sophisticated as well. Nuclear weapons, for example, must be immune to lightning strikes, fires, airplane crashes, and even old age—plus they must rebuff unauthorized use. The methodology for designing safety and reliability into high consequence systems is called *surety science and engineering*, "a generalized approach to designing complex systems that assures reliability under normal circumstances, safety under abnormal circumstances, and security and use control under hostile circumstances."[16] In other words, surety means not only obtaining safety, but having it guaranteed by technology and technique. The science and engineering approach to surety entails determining in advance the maximum consequences we can tolerate, and then taking well-defined steps to ensure that any possible failure will be less than that. Any desired level of surety is achieved through a layered approach, or redundancy. "Business as usual" would be level zero, but by adding certain technologies and making changes to the design, surety can be increased in steps. Each additional level reduces the probability of failure up to level four, at which point the failure of concern becomes physically impossible. But of course costs—and most likely complexity—rise as well.

Consider fire protection. At one time fire was a major threat to cities and even burned a number of them down. Now we have fire engines, water hydrants, and insurance. We also have smoke detectors, fire alarms, fire extinguishers, fire-resistant materials and building designs, all enforced by public codes. Although the problem wasn't approached from the beginning with surety methods, the collective result reveals the value of a layered approach. Driving while intoxicated (DWI) could be reduced via surety science and engineering, as shown in Table 2.1.

---

[16] "Surety White Paper."

Table 2.1. Surety engineering applied to DUI

Level	Description	Example of Prevention	Results
0	Do nothing	No prevention	High probability of DWI accidents
1	Inform	Publicize laws and societal expectations	Minor reduction of accident rates
2	Plan ahead and enforce with trained people	Police patrols on New Year's Eve and other "party-type" holidays	More accident prevention, depending on ratio of police to drunken drivers
3	Utilize automatic technological controls	Breathalyzers connected to all cars' ignition switches	Drunken drivers prevented from driving unless breathalyzer disengaged

Currently we use procedures—or techniques—that deliver surety at level 2. The procedures and technologies that can deliver surety at level 4 are readily available, so why don't we implement them? A likely answer is: because each additional layer increases the cost of prevention and interferes with individual liberties.

In 1999, engineers at Sandia National Laboratories and the National Academy of Science identified twelve major surety challenges that they forecast would be important for the U.S. in the twenty first century. The challenges are listed in Table 2.2.[17] Most of these challenges are unique to

Table 2.2. Surety challenges of the 21st century

- Manage increasing complexity of interdependent systems
- Counter cyber and physical terrorism
- Assure no nuclear yield by accident or hostile intent
- Counter the potential for nuclear proliferation
- Assure a reliable infrastructure so America is "the place where things work"
- Provide solutions for aging nuclear weapons stockpile
- Assure a safe, secure, and reliable energy supply
- Provide for a clean and sustainable environment

[17] *Surety White Paper, loc. cit.*

Table 2.2. Surety challenges of the 21ˢᵗ century (*continued*)

- Counter crime
- Provide safe and secure schools
- Advance solutions for aviation reliability, safety, and security
- Provide solutions for aging infrastructure

advanced technological societies—certainly the list for Sudan would look very different. It is interesting to consider how accurate the forecasts were. Most, if not all, of the objectives are in today's headlines. That technological solutions are being pursued for the twelve surety challenges is not surprising, because after all, the list was compiled by scientists and engineers in a national security laboratory. However, ever-increasing dependence upon technology brings its own kind of risks. One of these may include risks introduced in some inherent but often unanticipated way. Environmental impacts provide a case in point. Harm from misuse, or use by an adversary, of devices that we developed for our own protection are additional possibilities. But at some point pursuit of technological remedies may displace the search for social and even spiritual solutions.

Technology and Natural Disasters

All the surety challenges in the table result—directly or indirectly—from human activity. "Acts of God" were not included, but the disastrous tsunami in the Indian Ocean in December 2004, and Hurricane Katrina in August 2005 emphasize that protection from destructive natural events remains one of the key purposes of technology.[18] The tsunami alone killed more than 150,000 persons directly and many more died in the following weeks due to shortages of food and medical care and destruction of infrastructures. In each disaster families lost everything they owned, entire towns and villages were destroyed, roads, bridges, and railways damaged.

Technology provided a significant assist to the response efforts. Web sites and blogs became the announcement boards and lost and founds for missing persons, and cell phones around the world aided in searchs. Images and news of the destruction were transmitted over the Internet, including first-hand accounts from bloggers who lived through the waves and quickly posted pictures and descriptions. Government and global aid organizations used satellite images of affected areas before and after the

---

[18] Ironically, with respect to global warming, technology impacts are intensifying rather than taming nature.

tsunami to help in their relief efforts. The International Red Cross set up web sites to help people track down survivors, and America Online started a site for its members to make donations to relief agencies.[19] DNA testing helped identify bodies of the victims.[20]

Could technology have done more, especially if deployed in a surety context? If detection devices, communication channels, and warning systems were in place they might be able to provide additional time for evacuations of populations prior to a natural disasters such as tsunamis, cyclones or volcanic eruptions. The U.S. has six sensors on the floor of the Pacific Ocean to detect deep-water tsunamis and send a signal to surface buoys that—in turn—transmit the signal via satellite to the tsunami warning centers in Alaska and Hawaii. Although only three were working on December 26, 2004, even so sufficient data were received to cause the Center in Hawaii to issue a warning of the possibility of a tsunami near the epicenter of the quake. In the absence of information from the Indian Ocean, however, officials could not confirm that a tsunami had been generated. "This was a momentous event in both human and scientific terms," said Costas Synolakis, a civil engineer and tsunami researcher at the University of Southern California. "It was a failure of the entire hazards-mitigation community." [21] Synokalis was not only implying that technology is the solution, but also that people have a right to be free of risk. Within three weeks of the 2004 tsunami the governments of India, Indonesia and Thailand announced plans to set up a warning system in the Indian Ocean similar to the one in the Pacific. India alone plans to spend $30 million toward the effort.[22] The U.S. announced plans to spend $37.5 million to upgrade our Pacific system and to install new systems in the Atlantic, the Caribbean, and the Gulf of Mexico.

"The world's attention has been focused on the vulnerability of people who live on the edge of oceans, said President Bush's science advisor, "and we have a responsibility to respond to their need."[23] But social contributions to the problem, e.g. development in low-lying coastal regions; and technological contributions, e.g. large-scale civil engineering works that remove natural barriers to tidal surges, were not mentioned. Because natural disasters often ignore national boundaries, perhaps the burden of

[19] Moore, "Tech to the rescue," E1, E6.

[20] Ladika, "South Asian Tsunami," 504.

[21] Bhattacharjee, "In Wake of Disaster, Scientists Seek Out Clues to Prevention," 22–23.

[22] India may have had an additional motive—detection of underground nuclear tests by her neighbors.

[23] Eilperin, "U.S. to expand tsunami alarm net," A10.

installing and operating safety systems should involve international coop-eration. But more than that, why do we continue to build on our vulner-able coastlines and flood plains?

Technology and National Security

In writing about the Cold War, former nuclear weapons scientist Thomas Reed concluded that "technology counts. Turning your back on technolo-gy is a very foolish thing to do."[24] Just like the risks, benefits of technology may occur in unanticipated ways. The economy of the Soviet Union had always been so hard pressed that Western pundits sometimes called the USSR "a third world country with nukes."[25] But the nuclear arms race—especially the "Star Wars" missile defense program—finally destroyed the Soviet economy. Thus the Cold War was "won" not only by technology, but also by the adversary with the stronger economic system. The scientific and technological achievements of the Soviet Union show that planned economies can produce technological advances, but a market economy seems necessary for technology to disseminate into the general culture. The economic boom that has ensued since the government of the Peoples Republic of China began freeing the economy provides further confirma-tion. Nevertheless the concept of deterrence has always been hard to resist. It is based on peace through strength, that is, making the adversary more vulnerable than we are.

In recognition of the risks of failure, means to reduce the risks are sometimes pursued in tandem. Arms control—which has actually been pursued for thousands of years—is one of these means. Sometimes the agreements are bilateral; other times they are imposed. Instances of volun-tary disarmament are exceedingly rare. As shown in Table 2.3, one of the earliest recorded is described in I Sam, where the Philistines banned the practice of blacksmithing in Israel. Their objective was to ensure that the Israelites did not have access to agricultural instruments made from iron, because these could be fashioned into weapons that would outperform their bronze counterparts.

[24] Reed, Thomas, *At the Abyss.*
[25] Whether or not the missile defense system would have worked is beside the point. The Soviets respected U.S. technology to the degree that they feared it would work.

Table 2.3. Arms control before the nuclear age [26]

1269 BC	Earliest known peace treaty (Egypt and the Hittites) cemented by the marriage of Ramses II to a Hittite princess.
1100 BC	Philistines restrict the use of iron by the Israelites (I Sam 13:19–20)
800–700 BC	". . . and they shall beat their swords into plowshares . . . neither shall they make war anymore" (Isa 2:2–4; a prophesy)
546 BC	A "cessation of armaments" ends 72 years of hostilities in the Yangtze River Valley in Honan Province, China.
500–400 BC	Athens and Sparta agree to dismantle fortifications although during the negotiations the Athenians hedged by continuing to build their ramparts "high enough to be defended." (*Peloponnesian War*, Thucydides)
450 BC	Socrates to Glaucon—no use of poisoned weapons or poisoned water. (*The Republic*, Plato)
400–300 BC	No weapons concealed in wood, no barbed or poisoned points, no points "blazing with fire." *Book of Man*—India
202 BC	After the battle of Zama, Carthage is required to surrender all war elephants to Rome and is forbidden to train others. (*Book XXX*, Livy)
950–1027 AD	The European nations define noncombatants and other "rules of war" in the *Peace and Truce of God*.
1139 AD	The Second Lateran Council prohibits the use of crossbows against Christians. (Their use was encouraged against "infidels!")
1609	The use of poison or pollution of drinking water is banned. (*On the Law of War and Peace*, Grotius)
1817	The *Rush-Bagot Agreement* between the U.S. and the UK demilitarizes the Great Lakes.
1868	The *St. Petersburg Declaration* bans "400-gram projectiles with fulminating or flammable substances."
1899–1907	*The Hague Peace Conference* bans dum-dums and poison gas.
1907	*Hague Declaration XIV* prohibits discharge of projectiles and explosives from balloons or by other "new methods of similar nature."
1922	The *Washington Treaty* bans "noxious gasses."
1925	The *Geneva Protocol* bans first use of chemical weapons.
1920–1926	Stringent inspection provisions, including anytime, anywhere suspect-site inspections fail to prevent post World War I German rearmament.

[26] Information compiled by John M. Taylor of Sandia National Laboratories, private communication.

Modern weaponry has increased the urgency of arms control agreements. As weapons become more powerful the potential for casualties to innocent civilians and collateral damage to structures rises in concert. High-explosive and incendiary weapons can destroy extensive areas, and defoliating agents sprayed from the air can damage large vegetated areas. In contrast to spear, sword, bow-and-arrow, and rifles, "dumb" weapons—those that are fired, dropped, or launched in the general direction of the target—cannot discriminate between soldiers and noncombatants. [27] Land mines are of special concern with respect to civilian casualties long after hostilities have ceased; weapons of mass destruction (WMD) are of special concern with respect to both civilian casualties and collateral damage. Thus, in addition to the historical treaties and agreements in Table 2.3, more than twenty arms control agreements have been enacted since 1960 pertaining to WMD, especially nuclear ones. The U.S. has declined to join the global ban on incendiary weapons and land mines.

Because nations can hide clandestine weapons programs, arms limitation agreements must be monitored for compliance, a process sometimes called treaty verification. The U.S. relies upon technology to provide assurance that our adversaries are not cheating on agreements—or even apart from agreements are not pursuing WMD. The International Atomic Energy Agency (IAEA) is devoted solely to prohibiting the spread of nuclear arms. Recent concerns over WMD programs in Iran and North Korea reinforce the need. Many of the monitoring technologies are quite sophisticated, especially those that were intended for overhead use (spy airplanes, satellites, and now unmanned aerial drones). Monitoring also takes place on the ground remotely, at the perimeter of a facility, or on-site by cooperative agreement or from human intelligence agents. As with overhead monitoring, technology provides the key to effective ground-based monitoring. In the event that arms limitation fails, the second Bush Administration began constructing a "missile shield" to destroy ballistic missiles from "rogue states" before they can reach targets in the U.S. mainland. The effort is intended to increase our surety by the addition of another layer of technology. Funding continues for this anti-missile system, which in April 2004 the General Accounting Office labeled "largely unproven." [28] Up to 2006, this program has absorbed more R&D dollars than any other military program.

---

[27] Long-range weapon delivery systems such as ballistic missiles and guided "cruise" missiles have accuracies measured in hundreds of feet or better, thereby permitting—in principle—the use of smaller warheads and consequently less collateral damage.

[28] "Missile Defense."

Homeland Security

Two of the risks inherent in ever-increasing dependence upon technology include harm from misuse, and use by an adversary of devices that we developed for our own protection. The 9-11-2001 attacks on the World Trade Center and the Pentagon, using commercial airplanes commandeered by terrorists, include some features of each. Shortly afterward the Postal Service provided the unintended delivery method for a biological weapon. The attacks were different from anything in U.S. history. Suddenly we felt *vulnerable*. The attacks shook our belief that two oceans and technological supremacy could shield us from a troubled world, and replaced it with a realization that our technological society offers a very "target-rich" environment for terrorists. Transportation networks, gas and oil storage facilities, water supplies, telecommunications, energy supplies, banking/financial systems, government operations, and emergency services—all are possible targets.

Nevertheless, technology is a key part of our hope for protection in the future. "Terrorism isn't going to stop technology," said Northwestern University Professor Joel Mokyr, "It's only going to tweak its direction." Mohyr is a technological optimist. He predicted that the threat would stimulate R&D for technology to combat bio-terrorism, hasten the deployment of high-speed telecommunications networks, and promote development of low-cost, sophisticated video-conferencing to partly obviate the need for air travel.[29] Mokyr doesn't deny that reliance on technology has made us easier to target. But he predicts that not only will more technology eventually make us safe, but that the very effort will contribute to progress.

The federal government created the Department of Homeland Security (DHS) with the goal of reducing our vulnerability to terrorism. The Department's mission statement collects the functions of the several agencies that were rolled into DHS:[30]

- lead the unified national effort to secure America
- prevent and deter terrorist attacks
- protect against and respond to threats and hazards to the nation

---

[29] Quoted in Lohr, "A Time Out for Technophilia."
[30] U.S. Department of Homeland Security Home Page.

- ensure safe and secure borders, welcome lawful immigrants and visitors
- promote the free flow of commerce

The DHS mission requires identifying potential targets, assessing the probability of attack, forecasting the methods terrorists might use, estimating the likelihood they could be successful in attacking those targets, and calculating the possible consequences. DHS experts try to avoid a "failure of imagination," which is another way of saying they try to anticipate and counter anything a terrorist might try. This sounds like the problem that surety methodology was developed for, and indeed DHS is using surety science and engineering.[31] DHS is also using probabilistic risk assessment (PRA) methods to prioritize among the many competing demands for funding.[32] Such an application of PRA illustrates *technique*—Jacques Ellul's term for the process of applying scientific-technological methods to societal problems.[33] But DHS experts must still make subjective judgments about the likelihood of a particular scenario, including the value of the target.

For homeland security, threat, target vulnerability, and possible consequences of successful attack all must be assessed. The problem is complicated by the fact that threats with the greatest consequences may not be the most likely. Detonation of a nuclear explosive by terrorists would have devastating consequences, including casualties, economic loss, psychological and political damage—or all of them. But terrorists' capability to procure or build a fission or fusion weapon is probably very low. A "dirty bomb," where a chemical explosive is used to disperse highly radioactive debris—thereby rendering a region uninhabitable like Chernobyl—is much more likely. In order to counter this threat, international efforts to protect nuclear materials and weapons are more likely to be important than a homeland protection program. Unfortunately, neither the probability that terrorists will attempt a particular attack, nor the probability that they will succeed can be determined. Instead, "intent" is indicated by previous attempts or similar attacks or sometimes by intercepted messages. Only the vulnerability of targets and possible counter measures are under our control.

[31] DeGaspari, "Layered Security," 35.
[32] Hutchinson, "Calculating Risks," 40–41.
[33] Ellul, *The Technological Society*.

Because illegal immigration increases the threat of terrorism, identifying and intercepting illegal aliens is part of the DHS mission. Would-be terrorists can and have crossed into the U.S. from Mexico and Canada by land and sea, and have entered by air from overseas. Thus a database was developed to aid in the screening of air travelers. The first personal identifier is the tried-and-true (fingerprints), but more sophisticated biometric technologies are in the works. If the database "flags" the traveler, he/she will be subjected to extra inspection. A "no-fly" flag means that the traveler is turned away at the gate. No provision for challenge is included at present, and that alarms individual rights activists. Enhanced screening portals filled with sensors to detect explosives and bio-agents have replaced metal detectors in some airports. Sensitive multi-spectral sensors can detect even small, concealed objects.[34] Keeping track of sociopaths through electronic eavesdropping has been the stuff of spy movies. But this "signal intelligence" has become indispensable. Intercepted "chatter" can move federal officials to elevate the terrorism alert level from green to yellow to orange to red.

Another technology makes it harder for terrorists or domestic criminals—and law-abiding citizens as well—to disappear into society. Beginning with the 2001 Super Bowl at Tampa Bay, remote cameras connected to computers with image-recognition software scan the entering crowds.[35] People presently identify themselves with something they know, such as a password or social security number, or with something they carry, such as a driver's license or passport. But these items are easy to forge or steal, and digital photos are problematic for security purposes because the images can be altered on a PC. Thus experts are focusing on advanced biometrics—the measurement of unique biological characteristics—for positive identification. In early 2004 DHS began developing a program that will utilize biometrics to identify foreign visitors with non-immigrant visas. In addition to preventing suspected terrorists from entering the U.S., dangerous cargo must also be denied. This is a daunting task because of the scale of international commerce. Inspecting the 6 million shipping containers that enter the U.S. each year without greatly slowing the flow is a task that begs for technological help. Of course, all of this security will come at a cost to privacy and convenience. Freight and passengers alike must slow or stop for inspection, and invariably some innocent persons or benign cargo will be singled out for interrogation or denied passage.

---

[34] Hutchinson, "Technology vs. Terrorism," 48–52; Falcioni, "Terrorism on Alert," 4.

[35] Moran, "A Face in the Crowd," D1.

What if terrorists or weaponized cargo slip past all the detection and prevention barriers? Can we reduce the damage or casualties from an attack? The equivalent of a smoke detector for biological weapons is probably years away. If we could design such a device, it could transform some threats such as anthrax from weapons of mass destruction to scary nuisances. Without stealth, anthrax makes a feeble weapon, because if treatment begins promptly after exposure, almost everyone exposed to anthrax survives, even those who have inhaled spores.[36] In 2001, when aides to (then) Senate Majority Leader Tom Daschele (D-SD) received a letter containing suspicious powder, it took the rest of that day to determine that the substance contained anthrax spores. Lawrence Livermore National Laboratory, Livermore, California, is developing a hand held mini-DNA lab that can identify diseases such as anthrax or plague within 30 minutes. A private company is working on a plasma gun to kill pathogens with an electric current. Officials hope it can be used to decontaminate airplane cockpits, night-vision goggles, and other items that can't be sprayed with bleach.

In 1984, the followers of Bagwan Rajneesh contaminated the salad bar at a Sizzler Steak House in The Dalles, Oregon with *S. typhi*. The attack caused 751 cases of illness, many requiring hospitalization. That event, coupled with periodic outbreaks of *E. coli* 0157:H7 and salmonella and "mad cow" cases in Canada, Washington State, and Texas forced food safety on to the list of homeland security issues. Prospective technologies for safety of our food supply—from agriculture to supermarkets and restaurants—include sensors that can detect contamination of food coming across international borders or monitor agricultural pesticides to make sure they are not over-applied. Other sensors could monitor the quality of water and reduce the vulnerabilities of the supply system. A decontaminating foam known to kill anthrax is being evaluated for its ability to eradicate *E. coli*, salmonella, and spoilage organisms on food processing equipment. The formulation may also have potential for sanitizing meat cutter's equipment and livestock trucks and poultry houses.[37]

A rapid and automatic syndrome-reporting system also might provide enhanced damage control. This is a real-time computerized surveillance system program that would alert public health authorities to unusual patterns, such as clusters of people coming down with unusual symptoms.[38]

[36] Chang and Pollack, "Sniffing Out Pathogens," A14.

[37] Burroughs, "Sandia team investigates use of Labs' technology to ensure 'farm-to-fork' safety of the nation's food supply," 9.

[38] Chang and Pollack,; Burroughs, *loc. cit.*

In theory, such a system could track not only bio-terror attacks—such as the one in Oregon—but also the ebb and flow of more mundane conditions such as influenza. Had a mandatory trace-back system been in place at the time of the first mad-cow disease (Bovine Spongiform Encephalitis, BSE) incident in the U.S., it would have taken hours, not days, to figure out when and where the cow in question was born, what it had eaten, and which other animals had the same history. With such a system, every cow and bull would be tagged at birth with a radio frequency identification (RFID), or hand-written, ear tag and recorded in a national database. Every movement of the animal to and from farms, feedlots, and slaughterhouse would have been noted. But the beef industry continues to resist the technology because of its cost.[39] On the other hand, the very existence of BSE can be attributed to technique, in this case supplementing animal feed with processed remains in hopes of increased productivity.

Technological advances in surveillance, screening, and decontamination are encouraging, but technology alone cannot deliver surety. The technologies will have to be deployed within carefully configured *procedures*. In fact, the major portion of DHS FY2005 budget was for operations. If we've learned anything from 9-11-2001, it's that we are facing an enemy that compensates for its relative lack of power by identifying and targeting our vulnerabilities. Well-prepared terrorists will take the measure of our most sophisticated technologies and try to route their attacks around them. "Yes, we've sent a man to the moon," says Edward Tenner, author of *Why Things Bite Back: Technology and Unintended Consequences*, "but the moon did not take evasive action."[40] Experts acknowledge that vigilance by ordinary citizens is a key to reducing terror threats.[41] Out of necessity, we are becoming more suspicious of other people and things.

Personal Safety and Security

Because the threat of terrorism is new, it is difficult to compare the cost of protection with pre-9-11-2001 expenditures. President Bush's FY 2007 budget request for DHS of $42.7 billion seemed large, yet already in 1999 the business of public safety and private security in the U.S. was $38 billion per annum, not including law enforcement.[42] Private security guards are important, but technology is the major source of surety. Devices like

[39] Pressler, "Building a Better Burger," 10–11.
[40] Tenner, *Why Things Bite Back*. Quoted in Levy, "A High-Tech Home Front."
[41] Hutchinson, *loc. cit.*; Falcioni, *loc. cit.*
[42] Knox, "Sales to schools a major market for security firms."

traffic signals, "krypton" bicycle locks, auto alarms, and airport metal detectors have become ubiquitous. Audible and silent alarms for businesses and homes offer deterrence, but to increase surety special valuables can be marked with unique and tamper-resistant identifiers. Video surveillance, metal detection, interior and exterior intrusion detection sensors, anti-theft property marking, glass-break sensors, and duress alarms are deployed widely. Other technologies include portable explosives detectors, alcohol and drug residue detectors, anti-graffiti sealers, and miniaturized bio-recognition sensors. Some of the many technologies for safety and security are listed in Table 2.3.

In a general sense, all of the technologies in the table present attempts to prevent or mitigate malevolent behavior of others. Along with these intended purposes, however, comes the likelihood that the technologies and associated techniques may produce results that were not intended. Consider the emerging use of RFID tags in library books. This application promises to reduce the occurrence of repetitive-motion injuries in librarians, greatly speed up the check-out process, and assist librarians in locating and re-shelving books. RFID has been used for some time in card-key

Table 2.3. Technologies for safety and security[43]

Monitoring	Access Control	Deterrence
• wiretapping	• Video systems	• deadbolt locks
• signal intelligence	• Encryption	• timed switches
• satellite monitoring	• "V-chip"	• motion detectors
• portal monitoring	• passwords	• "firewall" software
• closed circuit TV	• firewall software	• anti-theft lug-nuts
• thermal imaging	• cipher locks	• portal detectors
• Night vision systems	• tamper resistant seals	• portal X-rays
• Ankle bracelet monitors	• coded keys	• watermarks
• Ultra wide band radar	• perimeter wheel locks	• pepper spray
• Recorders in rental cars	for shopping carts	• speed bumps
• RF tags for cattle	• gun trigger locks	• call blocking
• Smoke and CO detectors	• graffiti-resistant coatings	• "the club"

---

[43] Classification under the various headings is imprecise because some of the technologies may be used in more than one capacity.

Table 2.3. (*continued*)

Identification	Assurance	Enforcement
• fingerprinting • DNA testing and databases • biometrics • retinal imaging • forensics • unique identifiers • licenses • trace analysis • caller ID • RFID tags	• holographic images • security systems • breathalyzers • tamper-indicating seals • watermarks • fluorescent dyes • urinalysis • smoke detectors in lavatories • stun belts • voice stress analyzers • ankle bracelets • polygraph • antivirus software	• laser targeting • photo radar • radar guns • 'shoot-back' weapons • forensic science • handcuffs • truancy smart cards • rubber bullets • stun guns • GPS beepers in autos • governors on rental equipment • tear gas and mace • sticky foam

security systems and automated toll booths. The tags that the San Francisco Public Library is considering are only operative within three feet of an on-site reader. Thus they are unable to transmit messages that could be received by another system such as a cell phone broadcast antenna. There is no connection to a global positioning system and a library item cannot be tracked beyond the library doors.[44]

But opponents are not convinced. They envision a scenario where someone bent on identity theft could sneak up behind a person carrying RFID tags and "read" the tags with an interrogating electromagnetic radiation (EMR) beam. Opponents also fear for privacy rights and the erosion of protections against unreasonable search and seizures.[45] "It takes a determined act of self deception not to see how RFID tags could carry much more information over much greater distances in the near future," worries Cameron Sturdevant. "Using Moore's Law, it's easy to envision that in eighteen months, the tags and the readers that power and scan the

[44] Hildrith, "No reason to fear privacy invasion from library books," B9.

[45] Neither the Constitution nor the Bill of Rights explicitly mentions a general right to privacy.

tag's contents will dramatically increase in power." [46] The basic read-only chips used in these tags cost anywhere from 5 to 50 cents, and no doubt their prices will decline and their power will increase. Pressure to add the tags to everything that can be sold or rented will mean many more opportunities for anyone with an RFID scanner (similar to anti-theft scanners at store exits) to inventory the lives of individuals. If inventory thieves find it useful to harvest personal data, what is to prevent them?

Surety in Schools

The shooting by a student at Red Lake High School in Minnesota in March 2005 kept the issue of school violence on the front pages. The event recalled the rampage at Columbine High School in 1999 and earlier shootings at schools in Jonesboro, Arkansas; West Paducah and Fayetteville, Kentucky; Springfield, Oregon; Edinboro, Pennsylvania; and Pearl, Mississippi. In 1997, one in eight Oregon high school students, and 8% nationally, acknowledged that they had carried a gun, knife, or other weapon to school in the previous 30 days. [47] At least two hundred books on school violence were published in the past ten years, coupled with considerable media speculation on the subject. Violence at schools frequently occurs in small towns or suburbs—the very places of refuge where people have fled to escape urban disorder. [48] Garrett Metal Detectors once sold only to airports, courthouses, and prisons. [49] "We never dreamed there would be a market in schools," says the company's president, "[but] now it's the largest-selling segment of our business," with sales projected to keep growing. [50]

Some of the schools where shootings occurred already had surveillance cameras and armed guards. To date, however, most applications of surety technology in schools have been designed to enable response rather than prevention. But that may be changing. In a pilot program deemed very successful by school officials, engineers at Sandia National Laboratories, Albuquerque, New Mexico designed and installed a comprehensive security system at nearby Belen High School. [51] In 1999 U.S. Senator Jeff Bingaman of New Mexico introduced legislation to create

[46] Sturdevant, "When a transmitter becomes a blabbermouth," B9.

[47] Har, "Survey"; Hopkins, "Weapons and Oregon teens."

[48] Harrop, "Young and deadly"; Getlin, "Our Violent Nature"; "To Establish Truth, Insure Domestic Tranquility."

[49] www.garett.com.

[50] Parker and Kasindorf, "Schools taking security to heart," 1.

[51] Ibid.

a School Security Technology Center at Sandia. Under the auspices of the Center, Sandia began offering its security package to schools, tailored to meet their specific needs. They also placed a primer and guidebook for school administrators on the Internet.[52] In the guide one learns that "through technology, a school can introduce ways to collect information or enforce procedures and rules that it would not be able to afford or rely on security personnel to do," and "the peace of mind of both students and faculty can often be quickly enhanced by the installation of video cameras." Technologies offered include equipment to detect the presence of illegal drugs, prevent unauthorized individuals from entering the school building, curb vandalism, prevent fire alarms from being tripped falsely, and generally provide school officials more control over what takes place in the school buildings. However, such security is not cheap: it may cost $16,000 to apply the technology package at a single entrance of a single school.[53]

Technology is also available to combat the problem of students cutting classes. Each student must swipe a bar-coded card upon entering the school building, and teachers receive a computer-generated list of who is on campus. Each teacher then notifies the school office of any discrepancy between who was supposedly present that day and who was actually in class. The next morning, the security system lets out a loud "cock-a-doo-dle-do" rooster crow for any student who skipped a class the previous day. The Philadelphia school district spent over a million dollars on the system, which is operating in all high schools in the city. The principal of one school claimed that the system had reduced cutting by 75%. The firm that created the system, however, admits that the improvement rate is as low as 10% in some schools "where the rooster goes off and the child (ignores it and just) keeps walking."[54] A fringe benefit or drawback, depending on one's point of view, is that: "With a phone call, parents can get data on their child."[55] The system also plays a tune on a student's birthday, which no doubt is a big hit with a teenager who has gone to great lengths to fit in and not call attention to him or herself.

[52] Green, "The Appropriate and Effective Use of Security Technologies in U.S. Schools," 23.

[53] Getlin, *loc. cit.*

[54] Snyder, "High-tech student ID card sounds alarm if class is cut," A5.

[55] Ibid.

Discussion

After God created human beings in his image, He blessed them and said to them, "Be fruitful and increase in number; fill the Earth and subdue it" (Gen 1:28). Gen 2:15 adds "God put [them] in the Garden of Eden to work it and take care of it." These commands did not mean that Adam and Eve should be farmers and have lots of children. *Subdue* meant to transform untamed nature into a social environment. They were to bring order to the Garden, to introduce schemes for managing its affairs. They were to fill the Earth with the broader pattern of their interactions with nature and with each other. In these ways, human beings would add to that which God created.[56]

How well have we done with these directives, or mandates? Humans developed technology to assist them in the filling and subduing endeavors. But the picture that begins to emerge hints that technology may no longer be simply our servant. Our lives have become technologically determined, and along with it technology may have become our master. According to technology educator Ruth Conway "It is not enough to ensure that a technological activity or product is examined in its context, exposing the human and environmental implications and even asking questions about its purpose . . . Technology is itself shaping the value judgments we are making about it. This is the power that technology exercises over us. Living *in* and acting *on* the world cannot be separated. If by default or lack of more fundamental sources of inspiration and commitment we let the technological environment dominate our experience, then technology will itself become the guiding force for action."[57]

During the height of the Cold War, Dutch Parliamentarian and economist Bob Goudzwaard identified four dominant goals that he believed occupied peoples around the world—goals that *give meaning and purpose to those who pursue them*:[58]

1. Resisting all exploiting and oppressive powers in order to create a better society;

2. Survival of one's people or nation: the preservation of one's freedoms and/or cultural identity;

---

[56] Mouw, *When the Kings Come Marching In*, 16. Quoted in Monsma, *Responsible Technology*, 38–40. These concepts will be developed as we progress through the book, culminating in chapter 11.

[57] Conway, *Choices at the Heart of Technology*, 109.

[58] Goudzwaard, *Idols of Our Time*, 19–20.

3. Preservation of one's wealth or prosperity, and the opportunity for continued material progress; and

4. Guaranteed security: the protection of oneself, one's children, and one's fellow human beings against any attack from outside.

Although Goudzwaard considered these goals operative worldwide, it should be clear that in the U.S. we are looking to technology to assure every one of them. There is no reason to think that the authors of the surety challenges in Table 2.2 ever read Goudzwaard's book. But his four goals seem to explain—or justify—every item in the surety list. Not only do we pursue safety and security primarily by technical means, technology is also the source of our wealth and prosperity. Along the way, however, our culture has come to be *defined* by technology.

Reflect briefly on the use of technology for public and private safety and security. Americans don't feel as safe as they once did. Terrorism has arrived on our shores, violent crime has increased, and public civility has declined. There is little agreement, however, on why these things are happening, and even less on how the trends might be changed.[59] Technological remedies—if they can be found—are likely to be cheaper and quicker than social programs and the effectiveness of technical solutions are apparent more quickly. Is it surprising, therefore, that government, business, and individuals turn to technology for protection? But using technology to assure safety and security in effect moves a social problem into the scientific and technical arena,[60] and pursuit of safety and security by technological means can displace dependence upon God. Conway writes "Fear of the neighbor, rather than trust in God, becomes a governing factor in human relations. In this insecurity we do two things: we create our own 'substitute' gods [including technological ones], which belong exclusively to us and seem to offer the security we need. And we use our differences from others to give ourselves identity as individuals or a group. [61] This cycle . . . can be broken only by a readiness to abandon the *false security* that is bolstered by superior technological capability."[62]

---

[59] In the year 2000, travelers to war-torn Bosnia and Croatia reported feeling safer on the streets of Mostar and Sarajevo than they did in American cities (Glassner, *The Culture of Fear.*). The situation changed dramatically, however, on 9/11/2001.

[60] Sarewitz, *Frontiers of Illusion*, 164.

[61] Conway, *loc. cit.*, 66–67.

[62] Conway, *loc. cit.*, 68.

The Old Testament teaches that the vulnerable "other"—including the alien and stranger—shall be protected; and the Apostle Paul admonished us to "look to each other's interests and not merely our own."[63] These injunctions need to pervade the context within and for which technology should be developed.[64] With all of the foregoing in mind, educator David Layton added two new competencies that should be required in technological education: the ability to judge the worth of a technological development in the light of personal values, and the ability to step outside one's "mental set" to evaluate what that technology is doing to us and our culture. These competencies would also help all of society resist the tendency to view social problems in terms of a succession of "technological fixes" rather than addressing the root causes.[65]

[63] Phil 2:4.

[64] Conway, *loc. cit.*, 69.

[65] Layton, *Make the Future Work*. Quoted in Conway, *loc. cit.*, 109.

Chapter 3

Transcending All Limits

JESUS PREDICTED that we would outdo him. He said "Anyone who has faith in me will do . . . even greater things than these."[1] How can we possibly do greater things than Jesus? Consider that modern medicine has healed millions more people than Jesus did. Jet airplanes have carried missionaries far beyond the furthest extent of Paul's missionary journeys. Sonar and other technologies have increased the catch of fish a million-fold beyond the disciple's nets, and industrial agriculture has fed far more than the crowd that ate from the twelve baskets. Sound amplification enables evangelists to reach enormous audiences—and television carries their message around the globe. Granted, modern technology is thoroughly secularized. It typically offers no thanks to God. But that does not mean that God has taken Himself out of the process. "Everything good is part of God's kingdom," Tim Stafford insists, "and we must take joy in it."[2] When children of the kingdom use their abilities to alleviate poverty or extend healing, such wonders are signs of the kingdom. Jesus spoke in general terms; but perhaps he foresaw the social revolutions that future technologies would produce.

Futurology—peering into the future—is popular whether one is watching the weather report, investing in the stock market, or reading science fiction. Much more than an outlet for self-styled prophets and science fiction writers, however, futurology is serious business. Why, in this age of too little time and too many distractions, should we care so much about *next*? And for that matter, who has time to speculate? *Time* Magazine, for instance, publishes an annual "What's Next?" edition. Financial planners and investors search for emerging technologies and the companies that might profit from them. Writer James Poniewozik believes that our interest is intentionally cultivated. "Chasing the next big thing is as vital to the economy as the Fed's monetary policy," he says. "Tech companies need you

[1] John 14:12–13.
[2] Stafford, *Surprised by Jesus*, 134.

to realize how empty your life was in the primitive days before you could email your dishwasher. Celebrity magazines need you to care who the next Ashton Kutcher will be and not to think too much about why we needed the current one in the first place. And the self-help business needs you to despair occasionally of all of this trend-hopping so you can go out and buy the newest guide to simplifying your life and living in the moment."[3] Lev Grossman suggests a deeper cause: "Oracles, futurists, visionaries—some people make their living by trying to divine the shape of things to come before anybody else. And we all avidly await their predictions . . . [But] we desperately need prophets, even false ones, to help us narrow the infinity of plausible futures down to one or at least a manageable handful."[4] Manipulated by business interests desperately needing prophets, even false ones, to help us manage our options—is that characteristic of our culture? Some technological visionaries in the past seem to have pursued their craft with religious zeal; and some are doing so today. But the goals of the transformations that technology is expected to produce are not often spelled out.

Key Technologies for the Twenty-first Century

Scientific American devoted its 150th Anniversary Issue in 1995 to "Key Technologies for the 21st Century."[5] According to Editor John Rennie, "we decided to forsake the purely fabulous and concentrate on those that seemed most likely to have strong, steady, enduring effects on day-to-day life . . . As technologies pile upon technologies at an uneven pace, it becomes impossible to predict precisely what patterns will emerge. Can anyone truly foresee what the world will be like if for example genetic engineering matures rapidly to its full potential? If organisms can be tailored to serve any function, can anyone guess what a twenty first century factory will look like?"[6] "New technologies pose moral dilemmas, economic challenges, personal and social crises," Rinne added. "For example, after the Human Genome Project is completed, the genetic aspects of intelligence, violence, and other complex traits will be available for direct scrutiny, and conceivably, manipulation. How much will that transform the basis and practice of medicine, law, and government?"[7] How, indeed?

[3] Poniewozik, "Why we're So Obsessed with 'Next,'" 171.

[4] Grossman, *loc cit.,* 2004.

[5] *Scientific American* (September, 1995).

[6] Rennie, "The Uncertainties of Technological Revolution," 57–58.

[7] Ibid.

The Scientific American essay collection wasn't intended as an anthropological treatment. What the collection does provide is a comprehensive and fairly recent compilation of technologies that are important for Western civilization. With a little updating the collection provides a springboard for a current look at our technological future. The update follows, supplemented with thoughts on unintended consequences, emergent properties, and ethics.

Energy

The rate at which we are consuming our nonrenewable resources, especially fossil fuels, will lead to a global crisis by the middle of the twenty first century. The U.S. consumes 27% of the world's energy, yet constitutes only 5.5% of the world's population and owns but 4% of world oil reserves. The U.S. Geological Survey estimates that 75% of the world's conventional petroleum reserves and 66% of natural gas reserves have already been discovered, and more than half of the world's total oil supply will have been used by 2020.[8] As shown in Figure 3.1, at the present rate of use and with the rest of the developing countries striving to achieve increased technological sophistication, global power consumption will increase from 14 terawatts (TW) today to 30–60 TW by 2050.[9]

Where will this energy come from? The worldwide rate of new oil discoveries has been declining since the 1960s, and excess production

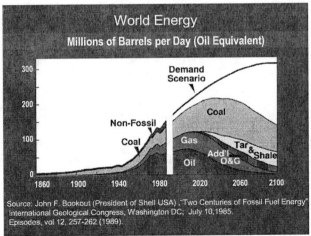

Figure 3.1. Global energy demand and supply through the year 2100

[8] "World Petroleum Assessment 2000."

[9] A terawatt is 10^{12} watts—equivalent to a thousand modern coal or nuclear power plants.

capacity is disappearing.[10] In March 2004, both Royal Dutch Shell Oil and El Paso Natural Gas revealed that they did not have the reserves that they had been claiming. A growing number of trend-watchers believe that humanity is about to reach a point of reckoning, when half of the oil that we will ever recover will have been extracted.[11] According to these "peak oil" theorists, global oil production will start falling at that point, never to rise again. Although oil will continue to provide a significant portion of world energy, prices will steadily rise. Developing nations aspire to live as we do, but that is simply not possible with a global economy based on oil. To maintain economic growth, the world will have to become radically more energy-efficient or shift quickly to renewable and nuclear energy. If the shift isn't fast enough, the global economy will undergo major convulsions.

Optimists insist that that peak oil theorists underestimate the power of technology to findmore oil, indeed, to broaden the concept of oil itself.[12] Michael Lynch, an industry consultant and a leading critic of peak-oil theory, believes peak oil forecasts are clouded by "Malthusian bias."[13] But if the peak oil model is correct, the U.S. hasn't gotten the message. U.S. oil production peaked in 1970 and domestic natural gas production is also in decline. We continue to live as if either the resource is limitless, or technology will provide a substitute when market forces dictate.

Considerable misinformation about energy supplies and alternatives—or perhaps just uninformed optimism—fills the popular media. Nuclear energy does not pollute the atmosphere or contribute to global warming. But unless public concern about radiation from accidents or sabotage can be resolved, a nuclear solution seems unlikely.[14] Hydropower supplies about 20% of the world's and 10% of U.S. energy, but is essentially "tapped out" in the continental U.S. Hydroelectricity is at risk from global warming and is not environmentally benign as commonly thought. Dams impair fish runs, warm the water, and obliterate scenic canyons. What about solar? In one year the earth receives as much energy from sunlight as is contained in all the known reserves of fossil fuels and

---

[10] Campbell et al., "Oil and Gas Liquids 2004 Scenario."

[11] Heinberg, *The Party's Over*; Campbell et al., *loc. cit.*

[12] Ball, "'Peak-oil' theorist sees global supply dwindling," E1-E2. One "optimistic" scenario holds that that oil and gas will run out before doomsday global warming scenarios can materialize (Coghlan, "Too little oil," 18).

[13] Ball, *loc. cit.*

[14] The pebble-bed reactor may be a safe alternative.

uranium combined.[15] In theory, solar energy could provide much of the energy required by humanity, but it is diffuse and impossible to store unless converted to some other form. Moreover, solar photocell fabrication demands lots of energy and is not any more environmentally benign that the rest of the microelectronics industry. Wind energy also represents a large resource—in theory. Roughly 0.25% of the sun's energy reaching the lower atmosphere is transformed into wind. This may seem small, but the source is so large that 80% of the electricity in the U.S. could potentially be supplied by wind farms in North and South Dakota alone.[16] But wind energy is intermittent and thus can only provide "peaking power" until new methods of energy storage are developed.

"Biomass"—a term that in practical usage refers to all living plant matter—contains energy that has been stored as organic material by photosynthesis; the energy can be recovered by various means. Agricultural wastes such as wood chips and wheat stubble can be burned to generate steam for turbines. Corn can be converted to ethanol or diesel fuel. But even if the nation's entire corn crop were used for ethanol it would replace only 15% of our petroleum use.[17] The next hope is ethanol from cellulose—the fibrous material in all plants. This additional source might enable the U.S. to displace up to 30% of its current petroleum consumption.[18] While some of the cellulose may come from agricultural residues, there will most likely be a need for crops designed and grown specifically for energy production. Each of these "biofuel" crops will entail diversion of agriculture from food to fuel production and will bring a new invasive species risk.[19] Modern agriculture also depends upon fossil fuel for pesticides, herbicides, fertilizer, cultivation, harvesting, and transportation; plus large supplies of fresh water. As a result, the Energy Return on Energy Invested (EROEI) for ethanol and other biofuels may be negative. One study concludes that the energy consumed in corn farming and ethanol production is *six times* greater than the amount the end product provides to automobile engines.[20]

Hydrogen is not an alternative source of energy, because it does not occur as such in nature. Like electricity, it is a "carrier" for energy trans-

[15] Hoagland, "Solar Energy," 170–73.

[16] Hoagland, *loc. cit.*; Cook, "Research Review."

[17] Featherstone, "B-2 in Odessa," 4–17.

[18] Baker and Zahniser, "Ethanol Reshapes Corn Market," 51–54.

[19] Raghu et al., "Adding Biofuels to the Invasive Species Fire?" 1472.

[20] Patcek, "Thermodynamics of the Corn-Ethanol Biofuel Cycle."

portation and storage. It is true that hydrogen burns "clean," producing only water vapor. But extracting elemental hydrogen from naturally-occurring compounds (such as water) may—like ethanol—also have a negative EROEI. Moreover, hydrogen is gaseous at standard conditions, so it must be compressed or liquefied before it can store energy efficiently. High-pressure gases are hazardous, hydrogen especially so because it embrittles metals. Thus hydrogen cannot be simply distributed via natural gas pipelines. The advantages of a "hydrogen economy," if indeed there are any, lie in shifting the pollution from vehicle tailpipes to remotely situated hydrogen plants.

All energy sources have severe technical limitations, not to mention the time required for developing the necessary production, storage, and distribution systems. The shifts from wood to coal, coal to oil, oil to natural gas, and the development of nuclear power each required thirty to fifty years—so did the shifts from canals to railways to roads.[21] However, the time remaining in which we must replace the fossil energy economy may be less than fifty years. If that estimate is correct,—and it seems increasingly likely—in order to avoid a crisis we may not be able to wait for market mechanisms. Government intervention in the market appears mandatory.

Transportation

In the transportation category, *Scientific American*'s key technologies included high-speed rail, non-polluting and "customized" automobiles, and intelligent transportation systems. "The future automobile will be clean and customized," wrote an industry executive. "While monitoring its surroundings, the car of the future will keep tabs on its driver as well. Fatigue and loss of concentration are leading causes of accidents, especially on long trips. But tired drivers give themselves away. Their reaction time increases and steering becomes erratic; eyelids begin to close; and the electrical resistance of the skin goes down. Once such signs are detected, an audible alarm can alert the driver it is time for a rest."[22] This scenario sounds like surety applied to DWI (Table 2.1).

In the foreseeable future every aircraft will have full knowledge of all other aircraft in its area and will be able to coordinate with them directly. Pilots will be able to look at the planned flight path at different scales: from a strategic view of the entire route to a tactical one showing the im-

---

[21] Ausubel, "Regularities in Technological Development," 70–91.

[22] Zetche, The Automobile: Clean and Customized," 102–6.

mediate surroundings. So said NASA's Office of Aerospace Technology, on the occasion of the 100th anniversary of the Wright Brother's flight at Kitty Hawk.[23] Advanced sensors, digital terrain databases, accurate geo-positioning, and digital imaging will provide pilots and air traffic controllers with 3-D pictures of terrain, obstacles, and other traffic. The information will be fed to intelligent systems that will re-compute flight trajectories in "real time."[24] The role of controllers will shift to space managers who oversee traffic flow and system demand.

No matter how much technology is brought to bear, however, automobile-based transportation systems are associated with gridlock, pollution, sprawl, personal injuries, and energy consumption. We now know that we will never be able to build enough lanes to eliminate congestion, since auto usage itself grows with every increment in highway construction. University of California, Berkeley Professor Robert Cevero suggested that people need to be "liberated from their automobiles" by designing communities that are not planned around the automobile, reducing the need to travel in the first place.[25] This concept is now embodied in new urbanism or "transit-oriented development." The issue of personal mobility holds such controlling influence on Western—especially U.S.—culture that it is worthy of separate treatment, which I provide in chapter 9.

High-speed rail offers much promise for relieving both urban gridlock and "winglock" at hub airports. Magnetic levitation ("maglev") appeals because it represents new technology; but steel-wheel-on steel-rail trains are operating at 300 kilometers per hour (KPH) today and have been tested at up to 520 KPH, faster than the maglev record.[26] Moreover, the steel wheel train retains significant energy advantage over the maglev concept. Either way, high-speed trains are the future for interurban travel corridors such as San Francisco–Los Angeles, Dallas–Houston, Portland–Seattle, and the Northeast Corridor. But the need for security applies to rail just as surely as it does to air transport. In March 2004, terrorists bombed commuter trains in Madrid, Spain, killing over 200 persons. Highway transport seems advantageous from a security standpoint, until we recognize that over 40,000 persons are killed in motor vehicle accidents each year in the U.S.

---

[23] Lebacqz and Pearce, "Future Air Traffic," 35.

[24] Ibid.

[25] Cevero, "Why Go Anywhere?" 118–20.

[26] Eastham, "High-Speed Rail?" 100–1.

NASA's successful missions to Mars in 2004 rejuvenated the U.S. enthusiasm for space exploration that had waned somewhat after the Columbia disaster. Breathtaking photographs of distant nebulae sent by the Hubble deep-space telescope abetted the enthusiasm. But the cost of materials and energy for unbridled space exploration is nearly prohibitive, unless—as Freeman Dyson proposed—we develop a fleet of miniaturized unmanned spacecraft.[27] Moreover, an astronaut traveling to Mars would absorb enough cosmic radiation to destroy every cell in his or her body. The craft that Dyson envisions will weigh only a few kilograms and be propelled through space by solar-electric systems. They will be able to wander freely about the solar system, altering their trajectories to follow the changing needs of science. "Nature has kindly arranged the solar system so that most of the potential destinations are smaller bodies whose gravity is weak," Dyson argues, [so that] landing spots will be easier to find than deep harbors were for nineteenth century steamships."[28] Robotic space travel is just one of the possible benefits of technology miniaturization.

Why, then, should we pursue a manned mission to Mars? According to science reporter Anne Applebaum the reasons are mostly political. "There is always the risk that yet another politician will seize on the idea of sending a person to Mars or building a manned station on the moon as a way of sounding far-sighted or futuristic or even patriotic. The search for 'life' on Mars is to find proof that we are not alone in the universe. It is not a search for sentient beings, but rather a search for evidence that billions of years ago there might possibly have been a few microbes. It's hard to see how that sort of information is going to heal our cosmic loneliness, let alone lead to the construction of condo units on Mars." Applebaum softens somewhat when it comes to *unmanned* missions. She notes "None of [this] is to say that it isn't interesting or important for NASA to send robotic probes to other planets. It's interesting in the way that the exploration of the bottom of the Pacific Ocean is interesting, or important in the way that the study of dead languages is important. Like space exploration, these are inspiring human pursuits. Like space exploration, they nevertheless have very few practical applications."[29] Technological optimists undoubtedly would counter by arguing that the endeavor will produce unpredicted serendipitous benefits.

[27] Dyson, "21st–Century Spacecraft," 114–16A.
[28] Ibid.
[29] Applebaum, "Mission to Nowhere," 27.

Technology for Sustainable Agriculture

For the past hundred years, technology has been a reliable force for pushing agriculture toward higher productivity. Much of the dramatic improvement has come through the use of more fertilizers, more pesticides, and more irrigation. Conventional plant breeding has boosted yields by roughly 1% annually—still not nearly enough to keep pace with population growth. I mentioned in chapter 1 how new technology is helping farmers increase productivity. But further increasing agricultural productivity by the methods of industrial agriculture is not a formula that can be followed much longer. Human demand on the biosphere from agriculture, forestry, and fisheries is not sustainable, just as it is not for fossil fuel use. We used 70% of the earth's regenerative capacity in 1961, 100% by the mid-1970s, and more than 125% since 1999.[30] The rate of species extinction now exceeds one per day.[31] The next green revolution needs to increase yields without damage to the biosphere. We must produce an agriculture that does not require subsidy from fossil fuels, does not deplete soil carbon, and does not build up salts and toxic residues in the soil. Making agriculture sustainable requires making plants more efficient in converting sunlight, nutrients, and water into food and fiber products. This is a tall order.

Agricultural biotechnology may be opening the door by crossbreeding plants that would never do so naturally. Desirable traits are being directly engineered into crop lines called "genetically modified organisms [GMOs]."[32] From a purely biological perspective, genetic manipulation is simply augmenting conventional breeding, bioengineering plants to withstand various diseases or pests as well as to resist stress from high-acidity or alkaline soils, drought, or toxic elements. These efforts may increase the yield of food crops and boost productivity on some of the world's marginal lands. But pessimists fear an irrecoverable release of "frankenfoods" into the biosphere—foods which may turn out to be unsafe for consumption. Although biologists and geneticists discount such fears, corruption of natural crops with biotech varieties is happening. It has not been possible to limit biotech or GMO crops to certain contract fields. Seed gets across fence lines and gets mixed with non-GMO seed at the elevator and mill.

---

[30] "Global Biodiversity Outlook 2002"; Thomas et al., "Extinction Risk from Climate Change," 145–48.

[31] "Global Species Assessment."

[32] Plucknett and Winkelmann, "Technology for Sustainable Agriculture," 182–86.

As GMO crops spread, native species will gradually disappear, and so will the genetic information that they contain.

The Land Institute in Salina, Kansas, is working to achieve sustainable agriculture through development of perennial food crops that can co-exist and even subsidize each other. Examples include alfalfa and wheat. Institute scientists hope to develop an agricultural system with the ecological stability of the prairie and with a yield comparable to annual crops. "We feel comfortable in saying that we have demonstrated the scientific feasibility of our proposal for a Natural Systems Agriculture," they report. If Natural Systems Agriculture were fully adopted, we could one day see the end of agricultural scientists from industrialized societies delivering agronomic methods and technologies from their fossil fuel-intensive infrastructures into developing countries and thereby saddling them with brittle economies."[33]

The Machine That Changed the World

On January 22, 1984, the huge TV audience watching Super Bowl XVIII also saw a memorable Apple Computer commercial that helped propel the Macintosh into the computer mainstream. The $1.5 million Orwellian-style spot showed an athletic woman running past rows of oppressed humans and smashing a giant telescreen image of "Big Brother," which was supposed to represent IBM. When Apple officially introduced the Macintosh two days later, employees who designed the new computer fervently believed that they had created something that would change the world. In many ways, they were right. That first $2,500 Macintosh, and the way Apple marketed it as "the computer for the rest of us," popularized the idea that you didn't have to work for a big company or be a computer scientist to benefit from owning a personal computer. Twenty years later inexpensive personal computers, controlled with the point and click of a mouse are as embedded into the fabric of everyday American life as the automobile and the airplane, even though most people now own computers built by companies other than Apple.[34]

"We all believed that the world could be a better place because of the personal computer," said Guy Kawasaki, the 50th employee hired for the Macintosh Division. Kawasaki's title of "software evangelist" told of his mission to spread the gospel according to Apple and get developers to write programs for the Mac. "I think that if you were to ask the Macintosh

---

[33] The Land Institute home page.

[34] Evangelistica, "The Machine that Changed the World," A1–A2.

Division employees today "are you disappointed in the results of the Macintosh?" we would say we really thought it would be the predominant operating system in the world today," Kawasaki said. "On the other hand, it has made millions of people happy and has lasted 20 years."[35]

Now jump forward twenty years from the debut of the Mac to the November 2004 issue of *Technology Review*. Rodney Brooks, director of MIT's Computer Science and Artificial Intelligence Laboratory, speculates about exponential growth of information storage, processing power, wireless connections, and DNA sequencing. If the annual doubling of information storage continues, he says, ten years from now an iPod will be able to hold 20 million books—more than Harvard University's entire collection. In 2017, we will be able to carry around the complete text for all the volumes in the Library of Congress. Twenty years from now a teenager will be able to "shuffle down the street with every movie ever made stored in a $400 iPod."[36] Tremendous business opportunities will be realized in digitizing old television and shows and films, and developing technologies that will let users browse and search them all. Finally, by sometime in the 2020s advances in computing power and storage will make DNA sequencing so cheap that determining a person's genetic fingerprint and disease susceptibility would cost only about one dollar. "One can find plenty more exponentials out there," says Brooks, "from the volume of scientific literature to the number of networked sensors that surround us, to the amount of spam we all receive. They, and others, are all going to have an impact on research and development opportunities and on our lives. Brooks opinion about these new technologies? *Bring them on!*"[37]

On February 9, 2004, while I was working on the section in chapter 2 about safety and security, the U.S. Department of Homeland Security changed its home page and I lost the reference for a quote. Volatility—disappearing sources—is a problem with the World Wide Web as a research tool. A growing number of scientists and scholars are nervous about increasing reliance on a medium that is proving more ephemeral than archival. In one recent study, one-fifth of the Internet addresses used in a Web-based high school science curriculum disappeared during a 12 month period. Another study found that 40 to 50% of the URLs referenced in articles in two computing journals became inaccessible within four years. The average lifespan of a Web page is currently about 100 days. Of the

[35] Ibid.
[36] Brooks, "The Other Exponentials," 33.
[37] Ibid.

2,483 British government Web sites, 25% change their URL each year. All this matters a lot because some documents exist only as Web pages, meaning that there are no definitive references where future historians might find them.[38] In hopes of countering this trend, several organizations, including the search engine Google and Kahles Internet Archive are taking snapshots of Web pages and archiving them as fast as they can so that they can be viewed even after they are pulled. [39] The Kahles Archive contained more than 200 terabytes of information in 2003, equivalent to about 200 million books. Every month 20 more terabytes are added, equivalent to the number of words in the Library of Congress. But with an estimated 7 million new pages added to the Web every day, archivists can do little more than play catch up.[40]

Use of the Internet by terrorists is another unintended outcome. Like volatility, this too has an analog in printed media, except that the Internet is much faster and more widely disseminated. Supplemented by mobile communications, the Internet enables the phenomenon defense experts call "netwar," a campaign of terror, crime, and propaganda waged by networks of small, ideologically-motivated groups attuned to the tools of the information age. Either network enables terrorist groups to share information, stay loosely connected across international boundaries, and operate semi-autonomously without the need for a traditional leader. As our society becomes increasingly dependent on knowledge-based technology in every sector, new vulnerabilities to such attacks will arise.[41] But high tech is not simply a set of tools for terrorists. It also provides essential services for countering terrorism. A Web site jointly operated by the FBI and the National White-Collar Crime Center has generated thousands of leads for criminal investigations. In addition, offsite computer backups enabled many companies to promptly restore data destroyed when the World Trade Center towers collapsed.[42] The problem is that it will be a never-ending race for the good guys to stay ahead of the bad guys.

Communication Technologies

Cell phones and seat-back phones helped provide investigators with a clearer picture of activities on the airliners hijacked on 9/11/2001, and ap-

[38] Weiss, "Missing Links," 34.

[39] www.archive.org.

[40] Weiss, *loc. cit.*

[41] Woodward, "Modern World Faces Specter of 'Netwar,'" B1.

[42] Ibid.

parently galvanized the passengers aboard United Airlines flight 93 to take action. Using a combination of signals from satellites, GPS receivers can pinpoint the location of a caller within about 100 feet. Equipping mini-cell sites to locate devices by triangulation may offer a cheaper and possibly even more accurate alternative. In emergencies, such techniques can help services reach callers who do not know where they are. More routinely, networks are beginning to provide interactive data services, such as a traveler in an unfamiliar town requesting the addresses of nearby restaurants.[43] All-optical communication networks provide so much capacity that on-line exchange of video and large computer files is becoming routine in technological societies. In the future, a video camcorder owner will be able to plug the camera into a cable wall outlet and invite relatives across the country to participate in a child's birthday party through video linkages. In fact, as bandwidth becomes as cheap as electricity, gas, or water, one can hardly imagine future varied uses for the network.[44]

Vast regions of the developing world are completely without either telephone or Internet. Wireless systems, whether they employ satellites, cellular transceivers, or some combination of the two, can provide a way to extend services to underserved areas at low cost. The same wireless technology that has turned coffeehouses into Internet portals is about to go global. Tiny wireless hubs, connected to the Internet, presently are open to any computer within fifty feet, but the range will soon be extended to tens of kilometers. Satellites can serve vast areas at a cost that is indifferent to location, because satellite terminals can be deployed much more quickly and flexibly than cables can be laid. As the distances between users increase, the satellites' wide area of coverage makes them more cost-effective than cellular systems.

Perhaps most important, satellite communications in the developing world might help stem the large-scale migration of people from the countryside to cities and from the developing world to developed nations. According to industry executive Russell Daggatt, wire-line technologies just extend the industrial-age paradigm in which the economics of infrastructure drives people into overcrowded, overburdened urban centers. He believes that satellites can help people choose where they live and work, based on such considerations as family, community and quality of life rather than access to infrastructure.[45] I present an analogous argument

---

[43] Zysman, "Wireless Networks," 68–71.

[44] Chan, "All-Optical Networks," 72–76.

[45] Daggatt, "Satellites for a Developing World," 94.

in chapter 9 where the role of the automobile in inducing sprawl is contrasted with the centralizing influence of rail. Like other defenders of an auto-based culture, Daggatt has not considered land and energy as finite resources.

The same RFID technology that protects against shoplifting also permits drivers to zip through toll booths without stopping. The FDA has approved "biochips" for pets and livestock; and in 2004 approved a human version that will monitor vital signs.[46] RFID wristbands at some prisons keep track of inmates and guards. "Of course there's a dark side to tracking humans," said technophile Jim Louderbeck; but "fortunately we can expect to see a commercial RFID blocker next year."[47] As we proceed toward this wireless world, it might also be wise to consider the cumulative effects of ever-increasing amounts of electromagnetic radiation on biological life.

Gadget Nirvana

"Future computer interfaces will be as pleasant and personal as a well-trained butler," *Scientific American* futurists predicted in 1995. "They will handle our affairs, assemble personalized newspapers and help free us from the constraints of time and place." The annual consumer electronics show in Las Vegas showcases progress toward that vision with home entertainment hubs, wireless displays, Internet appliances, and entertainment systems for autos that receive broadcasts of digital music and television. Also enormous flat panel TVs that are digital cable-ready, personal video players (PVPs) with flat-screen technology called organic LED (OLED) that produce crisp images on a screen the size and thickness of a credit card, smart computer displays that permit users to wander the house or office with a screen that links wirelessly with the computer, and personal data assistants (PDAs) with telephones and picture messaging. Converging home entertainment devices that permit multiple formats from MP3s to recorded TV shows to be controlled from a single device are just over the horizon.[48] Some analysts suggest the emerging "digital lifestyle" will steer people back into their own homes, away from terrorists and foreign vacations.

But the smarter a device becomes, the greater the risk that its complexity will baffle the user. Donald Norman, former VP of advanced technology at Apple, noted that the operation of modern machines and

[46] "Is that a Verichip Under Your Skin?" 67.

[47] Louderback, "2004: Welcome to the Wonderful World of Wireless," 6.

[48] Krane, "Its Gadget Time in Las Vegas," D10.

the concepts behind their design are invisible and abstract. There may be nothing to see, nothing to guide understanding. Consequently, workers know less and less about the inner workings of the systems under their control, and they are at an immediate disadvantage when trouble erupts.[49] Philosopher Albert Borgmann refers to this emergent property as *opacity*.[50] With people spending a growing proportion of their lives in front of computer screens, informing and entertaining one another, exchanging correspondence, working, shopping, and falling in love, some accommodation must be found between limited human attention spans and increasingly complex collections of software and data. As interactive television, palmtop diaries and smart credit cards proliferate, the gap between millions of untrained users and an equal number of sophisticated microprocessors will become even more apparent. According to experts, one way to simplify the operation of networked gadgets and make them more user-friendly is to embed some of the intelligence needed to accomplish useful tasks in the network.[51] Intelligent network services may make more sophisticated interactions possible, but will that increase opacity?

Artificial Intelligence and Intelligent Software

Future word processors will check content, not just spelling and grammar. If you promise your readers to discuss an issue later in a document and fail to do so, a warning may appear on your computer screen. Spreadsheets will highlight entries that are technically permissible but violate common sense. Document retrieval programs will understand enough of the content of what they are searching—and of your queries—to find the texts you are looking for regardless of whether or not they contain the words you specify. These kinds of programs will act in concert with computer hardware and networks to make computer-based services ever less expensive and more ubiquitous.[52]

Intelligent software will begin to function as a personal secretary—extended memories that remind people where they have put things, whom they have talked to, what tasks they have accomplished and which remain to be finished.[53] That computer on your desktop is just your helper today. But soon it may become a very close friend. Now it sends your

[49] Norman, "Designing the Future," 194–98.

[50] Borgmann, *Power Failure.*

[51] Zysman, *loc. cit.*

[52] Lenat, "Artificial Intelligence," 80–82.

[53] Maes, "Intelligent Software," 84–86.

emails, links you to the Internet, does your computations, and pays your bills. Soon it could warn you if you are talking too much at a meeting. Or it could alert others in your group to be attentive when you feel you have something important to say.[54] Aided by tiny sensors and transmitters called a PAL (Personal Assistance Link), your machine (with your permission) will become an "anthroscope," an investigator of your up-to-the-moment vital signs. It will monitor your perspiration and heartbeat, read your facial expressions and head motions, analyze your voice tones, and correlate all these to keep you informed with a running account of how you are feeling, something you may be ignoring. It will also transmit this information to others in your group so that everyone can work together more effectively. If someone is too excited to produce peak performance, the machine might tell him via a pop-up message to slow down. On the other hand, it might tell the team leader, "take Bill out of the loop, we don't want him monitoring the space shuttle today. He's had too much coffee and too little sleep."[55] This scenario brings to mind the smart car that will refuse to continue when its driver becomes drowsy.

Research centers at Stanford, MIT, And Toronto are developing "wearable" computers—devices that are part of our apparel yet allow 24/7 connection to the Internet and other computer databases. We're getting close to taking the ultimate step toward "seamless" interfacing with computer systems via direct brain implants.[56] Such interfacing will be attractive to people who need access to lots of information. The "anthroscopic computer project" at Sandia National Laboratories seeks to map characteristics that correlate with "personal best" performance. The tools for this project—accelerometers to measure motion, face-recognition software, EMGs to measure muscle activity, EKGs to measure heart beat, blood volume pulse oximetry to measure oxygen saturation, a Pneumotrace™ respiration monitor to measure breathing depth and rapidity—are all off-the-shelf items. According to the project director, "We give off so much information. But our only current way of interacting with a computer is very limited: through, essentially, a keyboard and mouse. So the limitation of my computer's ability to help me—this increasingly complex, wonderful machine with its ability to recognize intricate patterns—is its inability to recognize complex patterns in me." Asked whether this might be an overly mechanistic view of human nature, he replied "I would not say we have

54 Singer, "Desktop Computers to Counsel Users on Decisions," 6.
55 Ibid.
56 Hook, "The Techno Sapiens are Coming," 37–40.

a mechanistic view, unless one considers a precedent to be a mechanism." He said that it is no different from making decisions based on baseball statistics.[57] The potential for mischief, however, seems profound.

The limited intelligent software agents now available commercially rely on programming, one way or another. A possibly more promising approach is offered by "artificial life agents" that program themselves. Their software will be designed to change its characteristics based on experience and interactions with other agents. Obviously the widespread dissemination of such agents will have enormous social, economic, and political impact. Such agents will bring about a social revolution—almost anyone will have access to the kind of support staff that today is the mark of a few privileged people. As a result, more people will be able to ingest and digest large amounts of information and engage in several different activities at once. But who will be responsible for the actions of the agents?[58]

From AI to Intelligent Robots

Soon inanimate objects such as appliances will converse with the user, and converse and coordinate with one another, computer science professor Douglas Lenat predicted in 1995. Voice-activated technologies are familiar today. From here it is just a small jump to personal-service robots, just as science-fiction writer Isaac Asimov envisioned.[59] The robots that serve us personally in the near future will be even more anthropomorphic than NeCoRo the cat described in chapter 2. To share a household with a human, a robot must be able to travel autonomously throughout the living quarters, see and interpret needs, and provide materials and services with a gentle and delicate touch. "A robot with these tools will probably first see duty as a companion to the elderly and the handicapped," Joseph Engelberger wrote in 1995. "It would give ambulatory aid (offer an arm), fetch and carry, cook, clean, monitor vital signs, entertain, and communicate with human caregivers located elsewhere." However, human intervention will still be necessary for personal hygiene, dressing, grooming, and "invasive administration of medicine," and artificial intelligence will

---

[57] Ibid.

[58] Maes, *loc. cit.*

[59] Engelberger, "Robotics in the 21st Century," 166. Often called the father of robotics, in 1995 Engelberger was Chairman of a company seeking to develop personal-service robots.

not provide satisfying conversation.[60] Japanese officials have predicted that "humanoid" robots will be in mass production by 2010.[61]

Virtual Reality

The popularity of computer games has increased in concert with the sophistication of computer graphics. Interactive displays on a monitor are called virtual reality, but the application includes much more than games. Virtual reality permits people to behave as if they were somewhere they are not, such as a computational fiction or a re-created environment form another place or time.[62] Virtual reality is a common tool for training operators to perform complex, delicate tasks in hazardous environments such as space or the inside of nuclear reactors. Pilots, astronauts, and locomotive engineers train in VR cockpits that merge three-dimensional graphics with a view out the window and sound systems offering cues about the surroundings. Architects and home buyers walk through the environments they have in mind before the design is completed, and factory planners evaluate shop-floor movement of personnel and materials before the layout is finalized. Tele-robotic surgery is already being done (see chapter 2). In achieving these advances VR may transform our understanding of computers from "severed heads" to extensions of our whole selves.[63] The social consequences of computer games are discussed in chapter 6.

Designed Insects

Genetically engineered insects may help eradicate diseases and plagues. Malaria, for example, afflicts 300–500 million people each year, killing more than 3 million of them. Efforts to eradicate the disease were spurred by simultaneous publication of the genomes of the mosquito and malaria parasite in 2002. Using this new information, a professor at the University of California at Irvine is attempting to synthesize a gene that boosts the mosquito's immune system, giving it the means to fight off the malaria parasite. Another professor is seeking to genetically modify the crop-killing pink bollworm so that it cannot reproduce. The idea is that biotech bugs would mate in the wild, passing on a lethal gene instead of child-creating genes to the offspring. Efforts are underway elsewhere to make silkworms mass-produce spider silk. Silk is stronger relative to weight than steel and

[60] Ibid.

[61] "Easy on the Starch, I, Robot."

[62] Laurel, "Virtual Reality," 90.

[63] Ibid.

tougher than the artificial fibers used in body armor worn by troops in Iraq. Other researchers are engineering honeybees to be more resistant to pesticides and diseases, Mediterranean fruit flies to be less damaging to crops, and even mosquitoes that are capable of delivering vaccines instead of disease with every bite.[64]

Despite the good intentions of such research, other scientists are alarmed that few safeguards exist to keep unintended consequences from harming humans or the environment. Fast reproducing insects such as bees anchor food chains around the globe. Yet the impact that genetically engineered bugs could have on ecosystems is only now being explored, even as researchers push to release biotech insect experiments into the wild. Biotech crops or livestock are at least *designed* to be controlled, whereas the goal of much of the insect research is to introduce genetically engineered traits into natural insect populations. In principle, the genetic modifications in these insects would not be much different than techniques already deployed. Control programs have sometimes released millions of male insects, sterilized by radiation as a way of limiting population growth in pests. But rendering mosquitoes immune to malaria could make them ecologically fitter, and thereby more likely to transmit other diseases.

In January 2004, the Pew Initiative on Food and Biotechnology called on the federal government to adopt strict regulations regarding biotech insects. "Usually, biotechnology seems to move more quickly than the regulations," says Michael Fernandez, Pew's science director. "But in this case we have the time."[65] So far, most environmental groups have been categorically opposed to the research, saying the effects of such large-scale tinkering would be impossible to predict.[66] The scope and extent of the possible negative outcomes from genetically modified insects suggest the exercise of considerable precaution.

Advanced Materials

Researchers are also working on "intelligent" materials that will be able to anticipate failure, repair themselves, and adapt to the environment. In essence, they will modify their behavior—or properties—to suit the circumstances. Examples include aircraft wings that change shape to adapt to environmental conditions and thereby eliminate the need for flaps; sub-

---

[64] Elias, "Bioengineered Bugs Alarm Some Scientists," D3; Gillis, "And Now, Designer Insects," 31.

[65] Elias, *loc. cit.*

[66] Gillis, *loc. cit.*

marine materials that can change stiffness to fool sonar; and materials that can signal the presence of microscopic fatigue cracks. The materials will have significant impact on engineering design, because engineers will not have to resort to "overdesign" to ensure safety and reliability. According to one researcher: "We will soon have the chance to ask structures how they feel, where they hurt, and if they have been abused recently. They might even be able to identify the abuser."[67] Taking the illustrations one step further, "smart" clothing may contain sensors to detect the presence of chemical weapons on a battlefield, or may dispense deodorant when sensors in a garment detect a certain level of perspiration.[68]

High temperature superconductors offer promise of reducing the 15% of our electricity bill that is caused by electrical resistance, and might also advance options for efficient direct storage of electrical energy. Superconducting Quantum Interference Devices (SQUIDs) will scan and detect weak magnetic signals from the heart and brain. Such devices will permit Doctors to non-invasively pinpoint the areas of the brain responsible for focal epilepsy. SQUIDs will also become standard for nondestructive testing of infrastructure components, such as oil pipelines and bridges, because fatigued metal produces a different magnetic signature.[69] Given recent experiences with worldwide terrorism, sensors for surety of infrastructure components and systems may offer another promising application.

Miniaturization

The technology used to design and produce miniaturized devices will bring about completely different ways people and machines interact with the physical world. Devices called micro-electro-mechanical-systems (MEMS) with manufactured features ranging from a few to a few hundred microns in size are finding applications in optics, electronics, medicine, bio-technology, communications, and avionics. MEMS devices include fuel cells, power generators for wearable computing, electronics cooling, pumps, valves and mixing devices for chemical reactors, medical implant devices, holes for fiber optics, and many more.

As Moore's Law predicts, electronic devices continue to get smaller, but there are physical limits to what can be achieved using traditional lithography on silicon crystals. By moving to extreme ultraviolet, then

[67] Rogers, "Intelligent Materials," 154–57.
[68] Rennie, "Custom Manufacturing," 160–61.
[69] Chu, "High-Temperature Superconductors," 162–65.

perhaps X-ray lithography, the physical size limits for silicon chips may be postponed until the Year 2020.[70] But even these advanced methods cannot fabricate devices so small that their characteristic features are measured in atomistic terms. The next generation of manufacturing technology may be based on machines and materials that virtually make themselves, like biological systems. "Called self-assembly, it is a process . . . in which atoms, molecules, aggregates of molecules and components arrange themselves without human intervention into ordered, functioning entities."[71]

The idea of designing materials with a built-in set of instructions that will enable them to mimic the complexity of life is immensely attractive. All forms of life issue from simple sub-units communicating among themselves. The kind of self-assembly characteristic of living organisms is called *coded self-assembly* because instructions for the configuration of the system are built into its components. This approach will allow fabrication of non-living materials having novel properties and will eliminate the errors and expense associated with human labor. Some day a microelectronic memory device might be able to build itself by the crystallization of smaller parts, thus ushering in a new era in manufacturing. Ultimately, the idea is to cultivate biological molecules that can actually grow and assemble electronic materials on the nanoscale while acting like enzymes and self-correcting as necessary. As the molecules grow the materials mistakes would be corrected automatically.[72] Beyond that, the next step may be to make computers based upon DNA itself.[73]

Nanotechnology—the science of shaping the world atom-by-atom—represents the extreme in miniaturization.[74] Nanoscience started off as little more than a clever means of making very small things (less than one thousandth the thickness of a human hair). IBM scientists made headlines in 1990 by arranging 35 Xenon atoms to spell out the company's three-letter name, creating the world's smallest corporate logo. Cornell University scientists followed with an invisibly small "nanoguitar." Its strings, just a few atoms across, could be plucked by laser beams to play notes 17 octaves above the range of a conventional guitar, and well above the range of human hearing. These feats were novelties, but they proved that with

---

[70] Patterson, "Microprocessors in 2020," 62–67.

[71] Whitesides, "Self-Assembling Materials," 146–49; Flatow, "Micro Biochemical Processors."

[72] Belcher, "Viruses Put to Work to Make High-Tech Materials."

[73] Winfree, "The DNA and Natural Algorithms Group: Research Perspective."

[74] At least until we figure out how to make useful devices from sub-atomic particles.

the proper tools, scientists could arrange atoms as methodically as masons arrange bricks, and in the process make materials not found in nature.[75]

Today nanotech applications are envisioned in just about every industry, from medical science to biotechnology to sports equipment. Smaller computers, lighter and stronger materials are promised, even "nanobots" able to cruise through people's blood vessels to treat diseases. Indeed, products with science-fiction-like properties are already beginning to hit the market. Microscopically thin sheets of tightly woven carbon atoms are being wrapped around the cores of tennis balls to keep air from escaping. New fabrics endowed with nanofibers keep stains from penetrating. New sunscreens have ultraviolet-absorbing particles that are too small to reflect light, making them invisible. Tennis rackets and airplane structures are being made with nanomaterials whose atoms have been arranged to provide new levels of strength.[76] A National Science Foundation brochure lists many other promising examples:[77]

- lightweight materials for more fuel efficient cars
- new classes of pharmaceuticals
- materials that last longer
- artificial photosynthesis systems for solar energy production
- tiny robotic systems for space exploration
- selective membranes that can remove toxics or valuables from industrial waste
- blood substitutes
- coatings for airplanes containing nanoscale pigment particles that can instantly reconfigure to mimic the aircraft's surroundings, making the airplane invisible

Optimism for nanotechnology rivals or exceeds that lavished upon the steam engine, the automobile, and the computer. The NSF brochure contains claims such as these:[78]

---

[75] Weiss, "The Fears and Hopes Offered by Nanotech," D1.
[76] Ibid.
[77] "Nanotechnology: Shaping the World Atom by Atom."
[78] Ibid.

- "Scientists . . . suspect nanoscience and nanoengineering will become as socially transforming as the development of running water, electricity, antibiotics, and micro-electronics" (p. 1)

- "Nanotechnology will have a major impact on the health, wealth, and security of the world's people" (p. 2)

- "If present trends in nanoscience and nanotechnology continue, most aspects of everyday life are subject to change" (p. 8)

- "The possibilities to create new things appear limitless" (p. 1)

- "Nanotechnology may provide humanity with unprecedented control over the material world" (p. 1)

Under the umbrella of the National Nanotechnology Initiative, federal expenditures for nanotechnology rose from $463 million in 2001 to more than $700 million in 2003. [79] In 2003 President Bush signed the Twenty First Century Nanotechnology Research and Development Act, directing $3.7 billion over four years for nano research and development. As reported in the nano news site, the bill gives nanotech "a permanent place in the federal government."[80] Government officials have hailed nanotechnology as "the next Industrial Revolution," worth trillions of dollars in the next decade. "This technology is coming," said the Department of Commerce's undersecretary for technology, "and it won't be stopped."[81]

But some experts are raising a caution flag. In 2001 Bill Joy, cofounder of Sun Microsystems, published a chilling warning that nanotechnology in combination with genetic engineering and robotics will lead to "self-replicating machines," some of which are bound to escape the laboratory.[82] The most pathological of these could eventually overwhelm the human race and digest the living world into a mass of "gray goo." Many scientists dismiss Joy's pessimism. Joy and his followers are also concerned about tailored pathogens. "We are on the cusp of the further perfection of extreme evil . . . a surprising and terrible empowerment of extreme indi-

[79] "National Nanotechnology Initiative."

[80] *Small Times.*

[81] Weiss, "The Fears and Hopes Offered by Nanotech," D1.

[82] Joy, "Why the Future Doesn't Need Us."

viduals," he wrote.[83] We already know that nanoparticles can act as poisons in the environment and can accumulate in animal organs; diesel soot and asbestos fibers provide well-known examples. The first two studies of the health effects of engineered nanoparticles have documented lung damage more severe and strangely different than that caused by conventional toxic dusts.[84]

Sir Martin Rees, Britain's astronomer royal, broadens Joy's warning to include micro-robots that could reproduce out-of-control and devour the Earth's surface.[85] Nanobots—super-small robots that replicate like viruses—might have useful purposes, Rees admits, for example, patrolling the body for cancer cells. But "after 2020," he cautions, "nanobots could be a reality; indeed, so many people may try to make nanoreplicators that the chance of one attempt triggering disaster would become substantial. It is easier to conceive of threats than antidotes."[86] "The odds that our present civilization on earth will survive to the end of the present century are no better than 50–50," he believes.

If Rees is right, society should consider restricting certain types of research to prevent the sort of scenario that he and Bill Joy envision. Even if the odds against such cosmic disasters are vanishingly small—one estimate is 50 million to one—Rees questions whether the potential benefits of the experiment are worth risking the worst-case outcome, namely the annihilation of the habitable Earth. "No decision to go ahead with an experiment with a conceivable 'Doomsday downside' should be made," he says, "unless the general public (or a representative group of them) is satisfied that the risk is below what they collectively regard as an acceptable threshold."[87] During the Manhattan Project, some nuclear scientists feared that the first atomic explosion could "set the world on fire." It is interesting to imagine a public process like Rees urges, where the affected citizens could have debated the advisability of continuing the Manhattan Project.

Technology assessment by technical experts is one thing; but democratic participation in the process would be a paradigm shift in our culture.[88] I will return to this subject in chapter 11. But at the very least, if biotechnologists belittle public fears or blunder into a health or environ-

---

[83] Ibid.

[84] Weiss, "The Fears and Hopes Offered by Nanotech," D1.

[85] Rees, *Our Final Hour*. Quoted in Keay, "Saving the Universe by Restricting Research," A6.

[86] Ibid.

[87] Ibid.

[88] Howard, "Toward Intelligent, Democratic Steering of Chemical Technologies."

mental mishap, the nanotechnology industry could become mired in a costly public relations debacle even worse than the one that has caused GMO crops to be labeled "frankenfood."[89] Woodhouse and Sarewitz point out that today's scientists and engineers working on nanotechnologies have received no more training in the social aspects of their work than had the physicists who introduced nuclear weaponry and nuclear reactors, or the chemists who blithely synthesized millions of tons of chlorinated chemicals without regard for their ecological and health effects.[90]

Medicine

In 1995, key technologies in medicine expected to have an impact in the twenty first century included gene therapy, artificial organs, and new contraceptives. But medical science has advanced far faster than even the futurists could imagine. A growing list of science fiction-like technologies must be included now, such as thought-controlled prosthetics, clones, and trans-human species.

Surgeons have been re-attaching severed appendages for several decades, and transplants of organs such as the heart, liver and kidney have become commonplace. So common, in fact, that the major obstacle to transplantation lies not in surgical technique but in a shortage of organs.[91] This problem is pushing researchers to experiment with the fabrication of artificial organs. Advances in cell biology and polymer manufacture have enabled researchers to construct artificial tissues that look and function like their natural counterparts. Genetic engineering may produce universal donor cells for these engineered tissues that do not provoke rejection by the immune system. Human skin has been grown on polymer substrates and grafted on to burn patients and the ulcers of diabetics. Some experts predict that it is only a matter of time before whole organs will be designed, fabricated, and transferred to patients. Similarly, engineered structural tissue will replace the plastic and metal prosthetics used today to repair joints and bones. Eventually tissue engineers will be able to produce customized shapes such as noses and ears, and ultimately complex body parts such as hands and arms.[92]

---

[89] Weiss, "The Fears and Hopes Offered by Nanotech," D1; Woodhouse and Sarewitz, "Small is Powerful," 63–83.

[90] Woodhouse and Sarewitz, *loc. cit.*

[91] Langer and Vacanti, "Artificial Organs," 130–33.

[92] Langer and Vacanti, *loc. cit.,* 132.

So far no one has succeeded in growing human nerve cells. But until they do, innovative microelectronic and nano devices may substitute for implants of engineered nerve tissue. But medical science is becoming increasingly effective in interfacing implanted devices that interface with tissue and nerve cells. I noted in chapter 2 that degenerated retinas already are being replaced with silicon devices, and amputees are able to control prosthetic limbs from electrical nerve signals. Recently, four epilepsy patients have been able to play chess on a computer just by using their thought processes. The movements were executed by electrical signals in their brains, picked up by electrocortiographic grids placed directly on the surface of the brain.[93] Surely this represents a step toward the development of human-machine hybrids.

In one researcher's view, gene therapy will soon constitute a fourth revolution in our ability to prevent and treat diseases. Public health measures and sanitation created the first revolution; surgery with anesthesia was second; introduction of vaccines and antibiotics was third. Gene therapy will cause another revolution because delivery of selected genes into a patient's cells can potentially cure or ease the vast majority of disorders, including many that so far have resisted treatment.[94] More than 4000 medical conditions, such as severe combined immunodeficiency (SCID) and cystic fibrosis are caused by inborn damage to a single gene. Many other ailments—cancer, AIDS, heart disease, arthritis, and senility—result to some degree from an impairment of one or more genes involved in the body's defenses. Physicians will be able to apply gene therapy by inserting a healthy copy of a gene into the patient's cells in order to compensate for a defective one, or they may introduce a purposely altered gene in order to give a cell a new property.

The military wants any technology that promises to assure the success and safety of its soldiers on the battlefield. Research programs at the Defense Advanced Research Projects Agency (DARPA) are seeking to modify the metabolism of soldiers to allow them to function efficiently without sleep or even food for as much as a week. For shorter periods, they might even be able to survive without oxygen. Another program seeks to enable soldiers to stop bleeding by focusing their thoughts on the wound; and a program called Restorative Injury Repair is aimed at allowing regrowth of a severed hand or a breast removed by mastectomy. The process would be carried out using a mass of undifferentiated cells called a blas-

---

[93] Technology focus: Think It, Move It," 22.

[94] Anderson, "Gene Therapy," 124–28.

tema, also called a regeneration bud. If it gets the right signals, the bud has the capability to develop into an organ or an appendage.[95]

Enhanced Human Beings

Cyborgs, technosapiens, or *robosapiens* are operative terms for the products of the marriage of robotics, AI, and neural interfacing. "Advances in the capabilities of the human species are inhibited by the ponderous nature of natural selection and by the laboriousness of the learning processes that endow our progeny with their forbears' wisdom," Engelberger wrote. "In contrast, every new robot can rapidly incorporate the best physical and intellectual capacity available. Within seconds, all prior robotic experience can be downloaded. Robotics may very well determine how human activity evolves in the twenty first century."[96] Engelberger was introducing the language of transhumanism.

In 2001, the 2001 National Science Foundation report entitled *Converging Technologies for Improving Human Performance.*[97] The book includes reports of experiments that are attempting to combine genetic, robotic and nanotechnologies to improve human performance in all areas. Gregory Stock of UCLA sees such pursuits as the inevitable outcome of the decoding of the human genome. "We have spent billions to unravel our biology," he says, "not out of idle curiosity, but in the hope of bettering our lives. We are not about to turn away from this."[98] But Christopher Hook—director of bioethics education at the Mayo Clinic—views the NSF document as a manifesto for government sponsorship of nanotechnology, biotechnology, cognitive science, and cybernetics to enhance human beings. In an article entitled "The techno sapiens are coming," Hook warns that—if not constrained—the procedures inevitably will move beyond therapy into augmentation or enhancement, of "normal" persons.[99] Troops going to battle in Iraq in 2003 were required to receive vaccinations for anthrax. Eventually, Hook predicts, members of the armed forces will be required to undergo other forms of augmentation.[100] "The report sporadically acknowledges that there may be ethical and social concerns with implementing these technologies," he writes, "yet nowhere does it

---

[95] Garreau, "Evolution of Our Species," 6–7.

[96] Engelberger, *loc. cit.*

[97] "Converging Technologies for Improving Human Performance."

[98] From at a 2003 conference at Yale University. Quoted in Garreau, *loc. cit.*

[99] Hook, *loc. cit.*

[100] Ibid.

specifically articulate them . . . But is there really anything wrong with enhancing our attributes? Each of us engages in various forms of augmentation. We go to school. We train to improve our endurance and agility. We take vitamins. We use corrective lenses, false teeth, and hearing aids. But none of these items and activities seeks to transcend our species' normal capabilities. They are accepted because they merely optimize performance within the natural constraints of *homo sapiens.*"[101]

Any of us who wears a pacemaker, uses a computer, a pen, or drives an automobile is already a hybrid of flesh and machine at one level. We supplement our brains with the use of computers, but the interface—keyboard, mouse, and monitor—is slow and cumbersome. Calculators and computers augment our ability to obtain, store, retrieve, and process vast amounts of information, more than our brains ever could. Why shouldn't we bypass the interface and "hard wire" the connection? And if it takes genetic, cybernetic, or nanotechnologies to assure the success and safety of soldiers, who could argue with that objective? Because having access to technologies that are separate from ourselves and that we can turn off is quite different from permanent implants, or structural or genetic modifications that potentially can be passed on to subsequent generations.

Transhumanism is the belief that someday we will re-engineer our natures to such an extent that a post-human species, or several new species, will emerge. The supposed new species are to be superior to human beings. "Biology is not destiny," says University of Southern California professor of electrical engineering Bart Kosko. "It was never more than a tendency. It was just nature's first quick and dirty way to compute with meat. Chips are destiny."[102] UCLA Professor of English, Katherine Hayles, adds: "Humans can either go gently into that good night, joining the dinosaurs as a species that once ruled the earth but is now obsolete, or hang on for a while longer by becoming machines themselves. In either case . . . the age of the human is drawing to a close."[103] I might be more inclined to listen if either of these faculty had training in biology and genetics.

Thus far, gene therapy has been applied only to somatic cells, but can in theory be applied to reproductive or "germ" cells as well. Modification of germ cells would affect all descendents of the original patient. Some bioethicists argue that genetic engineering should be banned unconditionally because future generations could be harmed by wrongful or unsuc-

---

[101] Ibid.

[102] Kosko, *Heaven in a Chip.* Quoted in Hook, *loc. cit.*

[103] Hayles, *How We Became Posthuman.*

cessful modifications. To others, the very idea of aspiring to such godlike powers is blasphemous.[104] In the words of W. French Anderson, director of the Gene Therapy Laboratories at the University of Southern California School of Medicine, says: "Deliberate application of germ-cell gene therapy would open a Pandora's box of ethical concerns. When we have the technical ability to provide a gene for correcting a lethal illness, we also have the ability to provide a gene for less noble purposes. There is real danger that society could slip into a new era of eugenics. It is one thing to give a normal existence to a sick individual; it is another to attempt to 'improve on' normal—whatever 'normal' means. And the situation will be even more dangerous when we begin to alter germ cells. Then misguided or malevolent attempts to alter the genetic composition of humans could cause problems for generations. Our society went into the age of nuclear energy blindly, and we went into the age of DDT and other pesticides blindly, but we cannot afford to go into the age of genetic engineering blindly."[105] Anderson issued his warning in 1995. It is not obvious that it has had any effect.

Reflection: Technology and Progress

Every new futurist reaffirms the adage that the technological genie is out of its bottle. "History flows only in the direction of technological progress," said theologian Emil Brunner. "It is true of course that knowledge is moving forward in *one* direction . . . The history of technique . . . is the history of an indubitable march forward. One generation makes use of the discoveries and inventions of another. There arises a cumulation [sic] of technical possibilities which 'develops' in an almost unbroken line from the first stone tool to the modern technique of steel and concrete, on the analogy of the development of a child to a man. But where will the next century be?"[106] "Progress is a one way street," echoed physician and trend analyst Richard Swenson. "There is no turning back . . . [Progress] has only been taught to go in one direction, always giving us more and more of everything faster and faster. [But] This is precisely what we have asked and expected of progress. Who in their right mind would expect progress to give us *less and less, slower and slower?*"[107]

---

[104] Garreau, *loc. cit.*

[105] Ibid.

[106] Brunner, *Man in Revolt*, 183, 455.

[107] Swenson, *Hurtling Toward Oblivion*, 41–42.

In 1970, Alvin Toffler warned "We cannot and must not turn off the switch of technological progress. To turn our back on technology would be not only stupid but immoral."[108] According to historian Hermann Kahn, "Any concerted attempt to stop or even slow 'progress' appreciably . . . is catastrophe-prone.[109] In 1980 Toffler added "rather than lashing out, Luddite fashion, against the machine, those who genuinely wish to break the prison hold of the past could do well to hasten the . . . arrival of tomorrow's technologies [because] it is precisely the super- industrial society, the most advanced technological society ever, that extends the range of freedom."[110]

As technological systems become larger and more complex, interconnected and interdependent, and we become more dependent upon them, the notion of irreversibility gains force. But sociologists argue that "the social impacts of technology are far too great to be left entirely to technologists."[111] This school of thinking maintains that the pace at which technology is introduced into the economy must be slowed enough for society to forecast implications and introduce proper controls. It might seem prohibitively expensive to abandon complex systems—such as nuclear power—for simpler ones. But given the political will it is not impossible.[112] However, this is a very large "given." It would require strong and visionary national leadership and popular support of a sort that have not been seen in recent times. U.S. dependence upon the private automobile provides another example, arguably more problematic and even more difficult to redirect than nuclear power because of the social and psychological needs that automobiles fill. Social writer Michael Shallis notes that the Chinese discovered gunpowder, but chose not to develop the gun.[113] Did this decision help the Chinese economy in the short run, or the fate of mankind in the long run? It did not, because other nations rushed in to exploit the Chinese restraint. Similar predicaments abound today as the pace of technological innovation rises.

Thomas Malthus and biologist Paul Ehrlich reasoned that human population growth must eventually be limited by exhaustion of resources

[108] Toffler, *Future Shock*. Quoted in Swenson, *Margin*, 41.

[109] Kahn et al., *The Next 200 Years*, 165. Quoted in Swenson, *Hurtling Toward Oblivion*, 42.

[110] Toffler, *Previews and Premises*. Cited in Chandler, *loc. cit.*, 9.

[111] Winner, *Autonomous Technology*; Winner, *The Whale and the Reactor*; Woodhouse and Nieusma, "Democratic Expertise," 73–96.

[112] Toffler, *Previews and Premises*.

[113] Shallis, *The Silicon Idol*.

(especially food) or by environmental catastrophe (from the toxic by-products of human activity). The recent advances in biology, agriculture, medicine, and nanotechnology have produced a new cadre of technological pessimists who are driven by new concerns such as the emergence of pathogenic substances as an unintended consequence of biotech experimentation. According to physician-futurist Richard Swenson, population growth and progress are certain to unleash one or more lethal outcomes. He isn't just talking about a few negative harmful unintended consequences. He is talking about lethality to the entire global life support system.[114] Whether or not one is convinced by Swenson's apocalyptic forecast, the ever-increasing pace of technological innovation does embody serious implications of "nasty surprises."[115]

But optimists remain undaunted. The successes of science and technology in forestalling limits fueled the optimists' expectation that *all* limits are illusory. Bill Joy's frightening prediction of the threat from autonomous technologies was initially greeted with interest, but soon thereafter the technology community "closed ranks to skewer him."[116] Ray Kurzweil served up the optimists' refrain that technology will be able to solve any problems created by technology. "Technologies may appear alarming when considered in the context of today's unprepared world," he said. "The reality is that the sophistication and power of our defensive technologies and knowledge will grow along with the dangers. When we have 'gray goo' we will also have 'blue goo' ('police' nanobots that combat the 'bad' nanobots)."[117]

The Arrow of Technology

How do we know that we are moving "forward?" How do we measure "forward," "progress," "faster," "knowledge," "profusion," "and more"? Many measures of change indicate exponential growth, or at least growth in highly nonlinear fashion.[118] But most proposed measures deal with impacts rather than the elusive variable called progress. Is "standard of living" or "quality of life" determined by speed or accumulation of mate-

---

[114] Swenson, *Hurtling Toward Oblivion.*

[115] Howard, *loc. cit.*

[116] Woodhouse and Sarewitz, *loc. cit.*

[117] Kurzweil, "Promise and Peril of the 21st Century."

[118] Swenson, *Margin;* Swenson, *Hurtling Toward Oblivion;* Brooks, "The Other Exponentials," 33.

rial goods or by the number of discoveries and innovations?[119] The Gross Domestic Product measures total economic activity; and it is an article of faith (or economic philosophy) that rising GDP means better lives for the populace. *Per capita* GDP is a better measure, but only if the distribution of wealth was equitable to begin with. The "Genuine Progress Indicator" seeks to adjust per capita GDP to reflect quality of life. Costs like those associated with crime, commuting, family breakdown, pollution, and deletion of natural resources are subtracted, and benefits like the value of volunteering and parenting are added. The resulting indicator has barely risen since 1950.[120]

Many discussions about technology and progress either directly invoke an "arrow" concept, or employ terms that imply the existence of a direction of cultural evolution. In the 1995, *Scientific American* special issue editor Lucky wrote: "Although [science and technology] cannot in themselves make life better for everyone, they create a force that I believe has an intrinsic arrow, like time or entropy, pointing relentlessly in one direction, toward enhancing the quality of life."[121] This is more than the irreversibility notion discussed above. An arrow has direction, mathematically speaking, a *vector*. A vector entity not only has *magnitude*—which in the present context is the rate of change of social and physical variables—but also *direction*. Swenson's many plots of exponentially growing entities reveal growth in magnitude, which he calls *profusion*. From the standpoint of resources used and waste generated, profusion by itself is making Western industrial civilization physically unsustainable. But the *character* of our culture is becoming spiritually, socially, and aesthetically unsustainable. Hence study of profusion by itself is insufficiently discriminating. The direction of growth must be considered in addition to its magnitude.[122] Three possible trajectories can be imagined for the future of Earth's human population: sustainable growth, deliberate (managed) decline, or catastrophic decline.[123] The possibilities are depicted in Figure 3.2.

[119] Sarewitz, *loc. cit.*, 117.

[120] Redefining Progress Institute home page.

[121] Lucky, "What Technology Alone Cannot Do," 204–5.

[122] Sarewitz, *loc. cit.*, 102, 117; Borgmann, *loc. cit.*, 84.

[123] Graedel and Allenby, *Industrial Ecology*, 70.

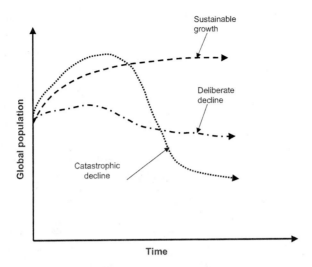

Figure 3.2. Human population scenarios suggested by different technology-society interactions. The starting point is the present global population of approximately 6.5 billion (after Graedel and Allenby[124]).

The futurists whose work I have drawn upon to write this chapter are attempting to discern trends. Although most are assessing trends at a much more detailed level than global population, the variables that they are studying are essential for quality of life on the one hand, and the health of Earth's life support systems on the other. Trend analysis implies extrapolation, estimating destination, assessing direction. The effort invokes questions such as: Where are we going? Will the future be better than the past or the present? Is the future predictable to any degree from study of past and present trends, or is it utterly unpredictable? A person's response to these questions will be determined by his/her worldview, especially his/her perspective on technology. Julian Simon argued that human beings represent intellectual capital that is fungible, i.e., interchangeable with natural capital.[125] Natural capital is our inheritance from nature, i.e., the physical resources of planet Earth, plus energy income from the sun. If intellectual capital really could substitute for natural capital, the declining trajectories in Figure 3.2 need never occur.

[124] Ibid.

[125] Simon, *The Ultimate Resource.*

But what if the course of technology is ultimately unpredictable? Is "climb on and enjoy the ride" the best we can do?[126] Industrial ecology teaches that the present trajectory of industrial civilization is unsustainable, but that we can redirect the arrow; we can select the curve of Figure 3.2. The descriptor for the redirection process is *guided evolution of complex systems*.[127] Ray Kurzweil acknowledged much the same thing when he said "People often go through three stages in examining the possible impact of future technology: awe and wonderment at its potential to overcome age-old problems; a sense of dread at a new set of dangers that accompany the new technology; and realization that the only viable and responsible path is to set a careful course that can realize the benefits while managing the risks.[128]

The Bible not only assigns a vector quality to culture, it also charges the Church (God's people) to pursue cultural transformation. Of course, this mission requires discernment of the direction of progress. Are we headed toward biblical norms of justice, righteousness, and peace?[129] My study of the evidence leads me to identify five components (direction and magnitude) of the arrow of Western cultural development at the present time:

1. Increased presence and influence of technology; that is, Western society is becoming increasingly technological

---

[126] cf. Sarewitz, *loc. cit.*, 122–30.

[127] Graedel and Allenby, *loc. cit.*, 69, 78.

[128] Kurzweil, *loc. cit.*

[129] One of the thorny problems associated with assessment of technology derives from the different measures for physical and social variables. Most of us in technological cultures believe that the physical (i.e., measurable) benefits of technology far outweigh the costs. Along with the technological optimists, I agree with this assessment. Some Christian sects of the Anabaptist tradition disagree, however, as do deep ecologists. Islamic fundamentalists are also conflicted about technology. Although Muslim civilization once led the world in science and technology, today they are angry about the hedonism and materialism in Western culture that is exported into their cultures through the media, and which they believe entices Muslims to become religiously lazy and morally corrupt (Colson, "The Moral Home Front," 152).

Several of the "soft" impacts of technology are also under-valued by technological optimists. In part this may be just a consequence of a naturalistic worldview that disdains things that cannot be measured scientifically. That is not quite the same as saying that immaterial entities do not exist, but when scientists and engineers make physical measures the only basis for making decisions, the result is a worldview of *scientism* or *technicism*. Jesus assigned higher value to some of the "soft" variables than the physical ones. "A Man's life does not consist in the abundance of his possessions," and "What good is it for a man to gain the whole world, yet forfeit his soul?" (Luke 12:15b; Mark 8:36).

2. Increasing dependence upon technology, which may or may not be making us safer and less vulnerable

3. Increased pace of innovation and change, reinforcing and augmenting the magnitude of the arrow. Correspondingly, less time is available to forecast and assess impacts of new technologies

4. Profusion

5. High levels of consumption, with the four-fold non-sustainable impacts described in chapters 5 and 6

Because the Bible assigns high importance to the social, aesthetic, and spiritual impacts of technology, and because I believe that current physical impacts to Earth's life support systems are unsustainable, I find it easy to turn pessimistic—at least in the short term. Things may have to get worse before people determine that radical changes are necessary. But I have not abandoned hope, because the Bible promises substantial healing—even transformation—if God's people put His principles to work. Such optimism is consistent with a *theology of hope*[130] rather than escapism or despair.

---

[130] Cf. Moltmann, *Theology of Hope.*

Chapter 4

The Myth of Morally Neutral Technology

WHEN I was an engineering student I gave little thought to the ethics or philosophy of my profession. My fellow students and faculty alike assumed we were learning to develop things that society needed and wanted. By making more goods available and providing for the defense of the country, we were confident that we would improve people's lives. My first permanent engineering job involved designing automation equipment. We developed automatic, in-motion weighing systems for filled containers (coffee, for example). The purpose of our system was to make sure that the customer received 100% of the advertised product and the producer didn't give any away. Neither the ethical implications for the producer nor the social consequences of replacing workers with machines interested me at the time. As far as I was concerned the technology would avoid USDA fines and maximize corporate profits.

After four years in industry, I returned to graduate school for further study in mechanical engineering and materials science. The Vietnam war protests were in full swing and marches and demonstrations were frequent, especially when recruiters came seeking engineers to work on defense projects. Engineering graduate students accused the protesters of the foolishness of being either humanities majors or hippie dropouts. After completing my doctorate I accepted a research position at Sandia National Laboratories in New Mexico, where I studied the behavior of materials under extreme conditions. I worked on materials for nuclear weapons, nuclear power reactors, and solar energy, and later assumed responsibility for an advanced-weapons concepts group. We developed earth-penetrating weapons and technologies for finding Soviet submarines that might be hiding under the Arctic ice. This experience qualified me for an assignment to the Office of the Secretary of Defense as Scientific Advisor for Arms Control.

Working in a nuclear weapons laboratory gave me no particular pause, because first-class research tools were available and the Soviet nuclear threat had to be deterred. I thought that the anti-war protesters who occasionally demonstrated at the Lab were naive.[1] But I also began to question some of the unabashed technical optimism of my science peers. It seemed to me that social and spiritual approaches needed more say in the solutions. And I began to wonder what others—especially people in the "subcultures" that I participated in—were thinking about the ethical issues posed by technology. That curiosity continued throughout my tenure in the nuclear weapons community, including the time I spent in arms control and dismantlement.

Eventually, I moved to a university teaching position, but my pursuit of the topic was mostly confined to posing questions whenever opportunities would present. Numerous opportunities did arise in classes that I was teaching; and, as one might predict, the engineering students were optimistic about technology, although most were eager to learn more about ethical issues pertaining to their profession. When I posed the same questions to our small group Bible study, the first response was from a distributor of hearing aids and former B52 pilot during the Viet Nam war. One might anticipate that he would categorize technology as beneficial, and so he did: technology to assist hearing is good and technology for war fighting is necessary. An engineer employed in truck manufacturing echoed the sentiment. Collectively, the group members felt that technology is not only beneficial and morally neutral; they also did not think the issue merited discussion in a Bible study. It was not, to them, an important social issue, and certainly not a biblical topic.

Those responses have become distressingly familiar. Westerners devote relatively little thought to the ethical and moral dimensions of technology, in spite of the fact that that our cultures are essentially technological in form and function. Most of us believe that technology is morally neutral and only the user—by selecting the use—can create a moral situation. In order to begin an effort to persuade people to think more deeply about the topic, I compiled a list of technologies and technological procedures that do not seem free of moral consequences, even if the product is never used (Table 4.1). But assessing the moral potential of emerging technologies is seldom straightforward. Weapons development is a technological endeavor that results in destructive outcomes more often than constructive ones—although *relative* moral superiority can be argued for the case of combating evil. Weapons of mass destruction (WMD) are problematic simply because they are so immensely destructive to human life.

---

[1] I thought likewise of our son, who had gotten involved in the protest movement on his college campus.

Procedures	Products
Amniocentesis	Land mines
Abortion	Weapons of mass destruction
Artificial life support	Napalm
Hydrogenation of vegetable oils	D-238 armor piercing rounds
Design with scarce materials	Urban assault weapons
New factory in greenfield	Tetraethyl lead
Carpet bombing	MTBE
Identity theft	Malicious software ("malware")
Overconsumption	Biotech crops
Counterfeiting	Zyklon-B
Scorched earth warfare	Shoddy and unreliable products
Terrorism	Products dangerous to workers
Graffiti	Products dangerous to users
Surrogate parenting	V-chip
Exhaustion of resources	Psychoactive pharmaceuticals
In vitro fertilization	Recreational drugs
Cosmetic surgery	Progesterone: the contraceptive pill
Human cloning	RU 486: the "morning after" pill
Eugenics	Viagra, Cialis, Levitra
	"Date rape" drug

Table 4.1. Examples of value-laden technologies

Disparate groups have opposed or resisted technology over the years, and some of them have implicated Christianity (or Christians) for the problems or threats that they perceived. Ted Kaczynski—the "Unabomber" of the 1990s—vilified technology for destruction of human and natural environments. Although he did not implicate technology *per se*, historian Lynn White assigned blame for environmental degradation to the "Christian dogma" of transcendence of, and mastery over, nature.[2] The Amish, on the other hand, perceive technology as a threat to authentic Christian faith. Each of these positions has a piece of the truth, but each is seeing only a part of the whole; the "elephant in the room." Increasing human capability is one of the primary purposes of technology. Technology has provided humans with a degree of mastery over nature, but at the same time vastly intensified the human "footprint" on the planet. And as we shall soon see, some technologists expect that technology will provide transcendence.

---

[2] White, "The Historical Roots of our Ecological Crisis," 1203–7.

Technology Is a Human Activity

Modern technologies are obviously not limited to "labor-saving" devices. Like an automated farm implement or a pick-and-place robot, a labor-saving device replaces repetitive or arduous human acts. Alternatively, the device might replace intermittent acts that are considered drudgery, such as washing dishes and clothes, waxing floors, grinding coffee, or whipping potatoes. The intended function of a new technology—or product, process, or facility—may be moral or it may be immoral. But much contemporary technology is distinguished by replacement of human action in a moral sense, substituting *technique* for *praxis*.[3] For example, the policy of Mutually Assured Destruction (MAD) during the Cold War supplanted diplomacy to a considerable degree;[4] contraceptives and the "morning-after" pill supplanted chastity; television and movies supplant reading and physical recreation; managerial and propaganda techniques replace older practices and virtues of loyalty, and so on.[5]

That technology shapes culture comprised the arguments of chapters 1–2. But the reverse is also true: just as they do in all human endeavors, cultural and personal biases influence science and technology. Science, engineering, and technology are done by people who have specific *intentions* and who operate according to certain *worldviews*. Thomas Kuhn's oft-cited article about the structure of scientific revolutions called scientific objectivity into question by showing how resistant to change established paradigms are.[6] Postmodernists in the humanities have used Kuhn's observation to argue that science is merely one way of knowing, no more or less useful in learning objective "truth" than any other endeavor.[7]

The postmodernists are partially correct: our worldviews do shape our values and the choices we make. In spite of the foibles of its practitioners, however, the methodology of science "works" because the results can be measured and either verified or refuted. The scientific method differs in this regard from most other human endeavors. The built-in correction process is not merely an exchange of opinions and personal preferences; it is the result of submitting one's calculations or measurements to the

---

[3] Hittinger, "Christopher Dawson on Technology and the Demise of Liberalism, Christianity and Western Civilization," 73–95.

[4] More precisely, MAD is (was) doctrine, not technology, but it was a doctrine inseparable from the technology upon which it was based.

[5] Hittinger, *loc. cit.*

[6] Kuhn, *The Structure of Scientific Revolutions*.

[7] Rorty, "Science as Solidarity," 38–52.

community for independent validation. This *inter-subjective verifiability criterion* is a key difference between science and the humanities—that is, science requires reproducibility of experimental results. There is always a consensus best theory in mainstream science. No equivalent is to be found in the humanities; one practitioner's thesis is as good as any other. Hence peer review in the humanities reduces to a set of opinions and assessment of what is "relevant" rather than unbiased testing.

Although engineering is often viewed as applied science, engineering and technology are separate professions from science and have their own methodologies.[8] Design—whether of products, processes, or facilities—is an engineering activity; some argue that it is the *essence* of engineering. Engineering design may be more intuitive than basic research in the physical sciences, but the results still can be tested against design objectives.[9] Thus engineering also operates by the inter-subjective verifiability criterion. Science and engineering alike, however, are affected by the worldviews of the participants. Engineering design projects *cannot be value-neutral* because they are developed with integral values, principles, and goals in mind.[10] In other words, the worldview of the designer influences the design. Specific ways that ethics and worldviews enter in to the design process will be described in chapter 7.

One's positions are often influenced by perceptions of economic impact or threats to cherished lifestyles. Economic attitudes frequently are determined by one's financial position. Many farmers oppose the Endangered Species Act because it restricts farming of wetlands and along stream banks. Real estate developers and many land owners favor "private property rights." Political conservatives and free market enthusiasts discount global warming—or at least its anthropogenic origins—and oppose the Kyoto Accord on carbon dioxide emissions, as do groups with vested interests, e.g., the National Association of Manufacturers (NAM) and the petrochemical industry. Perhaps as a result of their affinity for the Republican Party, Evangelicals have embraced many of the same views. But that may be slowly changing.[11]

Inter-subjective verifiability eventually exposes most such biases. A few years ago a news note in an engineering journal asserted that 23% of collisions between trucks and passenger vehicles are head-on, where an

---

[8] Dieter, *Engineering Design*, 5–6.

[9] Aesthetic qualities may be an exception.

[10] Wauzzinski, *Discerning Prometheus*, 54.

[11] Harden, "The Greening of Evangelicals."

auto crosses into the truck's path; and that occurs eight times more often than a truck crossing into the path of an auto. The note also asserted that passenger vehicles are six times more likely to sideswipe trucks going in the opposite direction and four times more likely to rear-end them. The conclusion was that truckers are mostly in the right in highway accidents.[12] Some months later a letter appeared in response. The responder wrote that the article failed to note what the expected rate *should* be. Trucks accounted for 7.4% of all vehicle miles in 1977. If we assume that vehicles and trucks have the same crossover rate and normalize for the vehicle miles traveled, we would expect that passenger vehicles would be 12 times more likely to cross over into a truck's path, because they account for 12 times the traffic. It appears the first author was trying to support the conclusion that trucks and truckers shouldn't bear the responsibility for improving highway safety because it isn't their fault. Then the responder dropped his *coup de grace*: the sponsors of the original report were Freightliner Corp., Volvo-GM Heavy Truck Corp., Navistar, Insurance Institute for Highway Safety, Owner-Operator Independent Drivers Association, and American Trucking Association, Inc.[13]

Unintended Consequences and Emergent Properties

Before the orchards were replaced by housing developments, a farming region not far from our home in Livermore, CA grew wonderful "U-Pick" stone fruits and pears. My family and I got into the practice of picking boxes of fruit and drying it in a homemade solar dryer. The process assured us of year-round treats, but the fruit darkened while drying and lost visual appeal. A little research revealed that pre-treatment with sulfur dioxide (SO_2) would prevent the darkening. So I fabricated a smoking chamber from a "wardrobe box" and a stack of plastic nursery flats. Burning pure sulfur in a pan at the bottom of the enclosure filled the box with SO_2, which eventually exited at the top. The process worked to perfection, except that one evening the doorbell rang and our neighbor—who was a very friendly fellow—stood at our door and said (or perhaps he gasped; I don't recall) "Something terrible is happening in your back yard!" Of course, SO_2 is extremely noxious because it forms sulfuric acid when it contacts the mucous linings of the nose and esophagus. And so my urban fruit drying enterprise ended because I could no longer use a key tech-

---

[12] "Truckers Mostly In the Right," 16.

[13] Bee, "Highway Numbers," 8.

nology. We also tried lemon juice and sodium metabisulfite but neither performed very well.

This short story serves to introduce the subject of unintended and/ or unanticipated consequences. Sulfur Dioxide is used commercially for drying fruit, but the emissions are removed by commercial gas scrubbing equipment. It was only when I released SO_2 in a residential neighborhood that its consequences became offensive. I had no intention of harming my neighbors, and I had assumed that the SO_2 would dissipate unnoticed. But on that particular evening the wind was calm and the humidity high, and I managed an operation that inadvertently and unintentionally became noxious to my neighbors.

This outcome might have been predicted if I had done more homework. The "what if" analysis—had I conducted one—might have been called technology assessment. All human actions have consequences beyond those that were intended, and technology multiplies the impact. Every product, process, or facility that emerges from engineering design carries with it the seeds of consequences beyond the design intent, consequences that extend way beyond the "canonical" purposes of engineering such as advances in material and physical well-being, labor saving, defense, and public safety. When the outcome is a happy surprise we call it *serendipity* and we rejoice. But three additional outcomes are possible: the intended one; adjunct consequences anticipated and mitigation procedures planned; and consequences not anticipated and thus no mitigation measures planned—or worse—none are known. The first option can be dismissed because, as I have shown, adjunct consequences *always occur*. The more serious negative outcomes have been called "nasty surprises."[14] Fortunately, unanticipated consequences are usually benign, at least for a single unit or a technology that remains rare. But when they present hazards to people or the environment an ethical dimension emerges.

Sometimes the unanticipated consequences become apparent only after the technology is widely diffused into the economy. Following the lead of physical science, I will call these types of consequences *emergent properties*—or, as industrial ecologist Braden Allenby prefers—emergent *characteristics*.[15] Emergent properties are not a function of our ability to detect them; they are literally unpredictable from any characteristic of a single unit. Thus emergent properties do not emerge just because the number of units grows. Let's re-examine some of the most prominent technolo-

[14] Howard, "Environmental 'nasty surprise' as a window on precautionary thinking," 19–22.

[15] Allenby, *Industrial Ecology*, 18.

gies from the National Academy of Engineering's top eighteen innovations of the twentieth century (chapter 1) for some consequences that were not anticipated at the time of innovation. I have listed some in Table 4.2.

Technology is not inherently more likely to serve evil purposes than good ones, nor is technology *per se* uniquely dangerous compared to all other human endeavors. However, among human endeavors only technology has the capability to extend human life and make it less laborious, but at the same time to extinguish species (including humans), decrease self-reliance, destabilize the planet's life support systems, and invade our privacy and security without our consent. Ecosystem collapse, species extinction, creation of the ozone hole, and global warming occurred when man-made substances were released into the environment. We were surprised

Table 4.2. A century of innovation and unintended consequences

Category	Examples	Unintended Consequences
Electrification	kidney dialysis life support machines elevators traffic lights factories computers	vulnerability to power outages dehumanizing automation coal and natural gas consumption 20 Quads per year
Automobile	private automobiles trucks buses military vehicles other vehicles	deaths and injuries, sprawl, petroleum dependence, pollution, congestion lifestyle diseases, road rage
Airplane	jet transport	noise pollution aircraft as WMD
Water Supply and Distribution	waterborne diseases eliminated Chicago River reversed LA Aqueduct	Chicago pollution to the Mississippi, Owens Valley dustbowl aquifer depletion
Electronics	transistor PWB microchips microprocessors	heavy metal and solvent pollution scarce mineral consumption distraction
Radio and Television	news and entertainment deep space pictures	propaganda social impacts of TV lifestyle diseases

Table 4.2. (*continued*)

Category	Examples	Unintended Consequences
Agricultural mechanization	Tractor/ PTO implements self-propelled machines sprinkler irrigation no-till cultivation	soil depletion and erosion pesticides and herbicides toxic runoff salinization of farmland monoculture
Computers	computation communication private networks	Internet pornography cyber crime social isolation hacking
Telephony	digital transmission fiber optics cell phone	telemarketing interruptions
Air Conditioning and Refrigeration	frozen perishables home and auto A/C	population shifts to hotter regions increased auto use increased electricity use ozone shield damage
Highways	interstate highway system	social and economic changes bifurcation of cities sprawl $125 B construction cost railroad bankruptcies
Spacecraft	rocketry guidance systems moon landing Hubble space telescope Space Shuttle Satellites	ICBMs space based weapons space clutter
Internet	ARPANET e-mail TCP/IP www Internet browsers	pornography proliferation spam hacking ephemeral archiving identity theft
Imaging	color photography holography 3-D imaging moving pictures digital imaging and CDCs Television X-Ray, MRI, CAT, NDE	entertainment culture invasion of privacy

Table 4.2. (*continued*)

Category	Examples	Unintended Consequences
Household Appliances	appliances electronic servants programmable appliances	packaging waste energy consumption disposal problem
Health Technologies	EKG, EEG, X-Ray, MRI pacemaker prosthetics dialysis antibiotics designer drugs endoscope operating microscope laser surgery	drug addiction unaffordable health care dependence on specialists super pathogens
Petroleum and Petrochemicals	catalytic cracking plastics/ polymers synthetic fibers	toxic byproducts non-biodegradable compounds carcinogens
Lasers and Fiber Optics	welding, cutting, drilling, trimming surface treating positioning and measuring cauterizing, tumor destruction barcode scanner comm. tech.	laser weapons retinal damage
Nuclear Technologies	Manhattan project nuclear medicine nuclear power Nonproliferation Treaty	arms race radioactive waste 3-Mile Island, Chernobyl terrorism
High Performance Materials	Super strong/ hard alloys composites conducting polymers superconductors metal-ceramic joints	weapon components scarce mineral use embedded energy toxic and hazardous materials

because we didn't anticipate the durability and toxicity of chlorinated hydrocarbons in nature. We were surprised when chlorofluorocarbons (CFCs) damaged the earth's ozone shield, and that we could produce enough greenhouse gases to warm the planet. Other examples of emergent properties include:

- Acid rain
- Mercury in large fish (via aerosols from coal-burning power plants)
- Dolphins in tuna nets
- Addiction and other side effects of pharmaceuticals
- Dehumanizing effects of assembly-line work
- Sprawl and gridlock as a consequence of automobiles
- Lifestyle diseases
- Poisoning from lead paints and leaded gasoline

The nuclear arms race developed when more than one nation became nuclear armed. This outcome was emergent in the sense that the first nation to deploy nuclear weapons might have hoped to hold its adversaries as nuclear hostages. What other reason could have there been for secrecy? But the technology could not be contained. In contrast to weapons, modern "industrial" agriculture is a technological endeavor whose contribution to human welfare is readily apparent in that it produces good outcomes more often than not, although it has its share of bad results. In this case, the expectation for emergent properties is opposite that for weapons: newer and more powerful technologies bring *increased* potential for good. Yet even in this case there can be unanticipated results. The near certainty that bio-tech crops will cross-pollinate with natural crops in neighboring fields may produce long-term consequences that we don't want. Sport utility vehicles (SUVs) provide another example. Although these vehicles are dangerous to small sedans, this danger doesn't qualify as an emergent property because it was predictable from the relative masses of the SUV and the small sedan. *Not* predictable was how popular SUVs would become and how their size would tend to make their drivers more aggressive.[16]

Emergent properties can lead to secondary effects of their own, in a chain of consequences. The obesity epidemic, for example, has consequences beyond direct health. A recent government study shows airlines have to worry more about the weight of their passengers than their suitcases. Through the 1990s, the average weight of Americans increased by 10 pounds, according to the Center for Disease Control. The extra weight caused airlines to spent $275 million to burn 350 million more gallons of fuel in the year 2000 alone, just to carry the additional weight.[17] The extra fuel burned also had an environmental impact, as an estimated 3.8 mil-

[16] The psychology and sociology of SUVs are explored in chapter 9.
[17] "Obese fliers weigh down planes."

95

lion extra tons of carbon dioxide were released into the atmosphere. The lively debate that followed this article led to the suggestion that airlines should sell tickets by the pound. Maybe it isn't altogether a bad idea. After all, productivity of trucks and trains is measured by ton-miles per unit of labor or fuel.

Emergent properties in the medical field include antibiotic-resistant pathogens in the food supply and in hospitals. Overuse of antibiotics by humans is a big part of the problem. But consumer advocates point to the routine use of antibiotics in animal agriculture as daily therapy to prevent disease. Cattle growers first started using antibiotics decades ago. "Back then, says the director of the Center for Veterinary Medicine at the U.S. Food and Drug Administration, "resistance to antibiotics was something that nobody had even thought of."[18] Yet we have produced antibiotic-resistant bacteria in animals, which get into the meat, or into plants and water via waste runoff.

Noise from autos and trucks on a multi-lane freeway can best be described as a "roar." Which maker or buyer of a "horseless carriage" would have foreseen such an emergent characteristic? Freeway sound walls also have emergent properties. State departments of transportation (which mostly means highways) have taken to building high concrete walls alongside freeways as sound barriers for nearby residences. But this plan has led to additional consequences for which additional remedies have been devised. First, the walls provide no escape from catastrophic incidents like a burning tanker truck. So exit openings are added at about half mile intervals. Second, the walls tend to deflect sound upward, only to have it focus at some more distant site. No remedy for this consequence has been identified. Finally, the walls force a trade-off between aesthetic variables: nearby residents are pleased with the noise reduction, but the walls create a claustrophobic tunnel sensation for motorists. While I was working on this chapter the California Department of Transportation (CalTrans) removed three hundred large redwood trees from alongside Highway 101 near my residence city of Santa Rosa in order to provide room for new sound walls. Most of the letters to the editor were furious because "we are looking more like Los Angeles every day," but CalTrans promised to "plant three trees for every one removed." Only one letter supported the removal.

The reader may be wondering—as I am—why emergent properties or unintended consequences seem dominated by negative outcomes and surprises. Examples of *serendipitous* outcomes ought to be easy to identify,

[18] Pressler, "Building a Better Burger," 10–11.

but not all positive outcomes qualify as serendipitous. In many cases the benefits were the intended goals of the design or development project. Curiously, when I sat down to compile a list of serendipitous outcomes of technology I could only think of a few examples.[19] Here's one: the hydroelectric dams built on the Columbia River provided such cheap electricity in the Pacific Northwest that a large bauxite (aluminum ore) reduction industry sprang up, even though the bauxite was shipped from Jamaica or elsewhere. Another serendipitous outcome was the creation of "slack water," thereby permitting grain barges to travel inland as far as Lewiston, Idaho. The discoveries of penicillin, Teflon, and Post-its™ might qualify, but these are better characterized as inventions than serendipitous outcomes. Is my difficulty in generating serendipity examples a result of a personal mind set that is focused on negative surprises rather than positive ones? Have I been conditioned by years of "environmentalist propaganda"? Or is my struggle just an encounter with the facts, i.e., that there are more negative unanticipated consequences than serendipitous ones? This might be a worthy study for an historian of science (or a psychoanalyst).

Engineers of Armageddon

Historian David Noble argued that science and technology in the Western world have long been understood as means to pursue the biblical millenarian promise of restoring creation to its original God-like perfection. According to Noble, the Manhattan Project team members were the first twentieth century proponents of this "religion of technology." "Endowed from the outset with authority and limitless largesse of the state," he wrote, "[these scientists and engineers] have devoted their energy and imagination to an enlargement of state power; and their counterparts in

---

[19] Writer Tim Stafford suggests that this phenomenon has to do with what we notice. We take offense at unpleasant surprises, as though some evil spirit had messed up our nice project. We tend to take in pleasant surprises with sublime self-satisfaction, as though we always intended that it would be so. For example: agriculture produced the beauty of the English countryside as we know it. Beauty was surely an unintended consequence, but we tend to take it as a given. The ugliness of nineteenth century industry was also an unintended consequence, but from the very earliest days it was bitterly noted and regretted.

space exploration have done likewise."[20] Noble calls them "engineers of Armageddon."[21]

Except for the Manhattan Project, no weapons made the Academy's list of most significant innovations. But many of the other entries led directly to significant advances in war-fighting capability, and (as in the 9/11/2001 terrorist attacks) some "peaceful" technologies have been turned from plowshares into swords. The Manhattan Project achieved its objective: a working nuclear device, detonated on July 16, 1945 at Trinity Site, New Mexico. The demonstration of nuclear capability did not persuade Japan to surrender, so Hiroshima and Nagasaki were destroyed by nuclear bombs. But when the USSR detonated its first nuclear weapon in 1949, the U.S. monopoly ended and the nuclear arms race was underway.

Nuclear weapons were less prominent in the headlines after the Cold War ended, but several events after 2000 put them back on the front pages. The second Bush administration withdrew the U.S. from the Anti-Ballistic Missile Treaty and announced plans to deploy a missile defense system.[22] The administration also signaled its intention to resume developing new nuclear weapons, with a "hard target penetrator," a "mini-nuke,"[23] and a robust multi-application device. The specter of nuclear terrorism, either with a WMD or a radioactive "dirty bomb," grew enormously after the 9/11/2001 terrorist attacks, such that the U.S. invaded Iraq with the announced intent of stopping Saddam Hussein's suspected WMD programs. India and Pakistan rattled their nuclear sabers, the U.S. government determined that Iran was operating an illicit nuclear weapons program, and North Korea conducted missile launches into the Sea of Japan and carried out an underground announced nuclear test. The lone exception was a surprise: in 2003 Libyan President Gadhafi decided to dismantle his

---

[20] Noble, *The Religion of* Technology, 205. What was the ultimate objective of NASA's successful project to land a series of rover vehicles on Mars in December 2003 and January 2004? According to NASA representatives on the January 5, 2004 TV network news broadcasts, the mission was to search for evidence of life on Mars "in order to shed light on the origins of life on earth." Interestingly, the rovers were named "Spirit" (signifying the nature of the mission) and "Opportunity'" (suggesting the technological imperative). Thus this mission has theological implications and quite possibly a spiritual vision after the pattern that Noble identifies.

[21] Ibid. 224.

[22] The rationale was to provide protection from "rogue" nations. But the outcome is liable to be just what the ABM and Defense and Space treaties were designed to prevent: the militarization of space.

[23] Plans to resume plutonium production were revealed in 1995, with the announced purpose of powering surveillance platforms.

theretofore clandestine nuclear weapons program and admit international inspectors.

In the wake of the destructive global wars of the twentieth century and a nuclear arms race that threatened unimaginable destruction, the concept of a *just war* underwent considerable development and refinement. The roots of the concept can be traced to Greek and Roman thought and the writings of theologians Augustine and Thomas Aquinas.[24] The concept includes *jus ad bellum*, morally defensible reasons for going to war, and *jus in bello*, the requirements for moral conduct of war. Different "nonviolent" groups—including secular as well as religious pacifists—have condemned nuclear weapons as immoral under *jus in bellum*. Four reasons are given. First, they are non-discriminating; that is, their explosive yield is too great to preclude harming non-combatants. Second, their great destructive power means that they cannot deliver a proportionate response to any conventional weapon. Third, they leave radioactive debris that renders the land unproductive. Fourth, the doctrines of nuclear deterrence and of retaliation (MAD) rest upon a real threat of using the devices. Hence, the detractors say, nuclear weapons are immoral even if they are not used.[25]

Not surprisingly, designers and producers of nuclear weapons have a different view. Their views should be compared to (or contrasted with) Noble's criticism of engineers engaged in the design and development of nuclear weapons. During the Cold War, most of the developers believed they were saving Western civilization from the real and godless threat of communist ideology. They also believed that the U.S. public was unwilling to pay the price in armaments and casualties—of defending Europe from a Soviet invasion by means of conventional forces. Nuclear weapons offered "more bang for the buck." Broadly speaking, the weapon developers were inclined to see themselves as providing one more technical tool for national policy objectives (in this case, national security).

Most arms developers resist the notion that their technologies help *make* defense policy. However, as new weapon capabilities emerge, the U.S. Defense Department is unlikely to ignore the new capabilities in its war planning efforts. During the anti-war protest movements in Livermore, California, and elsewhere, when the activists attempted to block the gates, lab workers said that the protesters ought to carry their grievances to Washington DC where policy is made.[26] When I went to the Pentagon

[24] Johnson, "Just War, As It Was and Is," 14–24.

[25] Swearengen, "Arms Control and God's Purpose in History," 25–35; Johnson, *loc. cit.*

[26] Swearengen and Swearengen, "Comparative Analysis of the Nuclear Weapons Debate," 75–85.

in 1998 to work on arms control, protesters were there, too. But ironically, some Pentagon employees said "we don't make policy; we just follow orders."[27] That response parallels the defense employed by officers of the Third Reich at the Nuremburg trials. I do not insinuate that the U.S. defense employees were comparable to Nazis; they (and I) believed that the U.S. was *relatively* more moral than the Soviet Union. In a world that has fallen from grace, it may be that relative moral superiority is the best we can attain. But even the best is absolute immorality. In 1948, J. Robert Oppenheimer, reflecting on the first test of the new atomic weapon he had just led his team to develop, used a line from *the Bhagavad-Gita*: "I have become death, the destroyer of worlds." Following the atomic bombing of Hiroshima and Nagasaki, he added "In some sort of crude sense which no vulgarity, no humor, no overstatement can quite extinguish, the physicists have known sin, and this is a knowledge they cannot lose."[28]

Some analysts have attempted to distinguish between offensive and defensive nuclear weapons. Under this scenario, missile defense, the "Star Wars" anti-ballistic missile (ABM) system, and all monitoring of adversaries (including, for example, tracking of Soviet submarines) would be defensive and therefore moral. But how are standoff weapons, stealth and multiple independently targeted re-entry vehicle technologies to be classified? Their objective is to penetrate the adversary's defenses and increase the likelihood of reaching the target. During the Cold War, they were considered "de-stabilizing" technologies. So also were cruise missiles, because they could be easily converted from conventional to nuclear versions without detection. How should the "neutron bomb"—the nuclear artillery that was designed to kill combatants and minimize collateral damage—be classified? Public outrage over that system was palpable, but actually the weapon could comply better with *jus ad bellum* criteria because it would inflict less damage on the civilian infrastructure. Since U.S. nuclear policy was to use tactical nuclear weapons in Europe if NATO forces were losing a conventional war, the weapons were more likely than strategic weapons to be used in wartime. In other words, policy makers assumed that deterrence could fail. At the same time the USSR maintained the doctrine that any use of nuclear weapons by the West would lead to a strategic nuclear response on the U.S.

But technology also helps satisfy *jus in bello*. Consider the technical advances that have produced "smart" weapons and "guided" systems.

[27] Ibid.

[28] www.brainyquote.com.

Target recognition, precise trajectories, course correction, and terminal homing devices permit "surgical" hits and thereby enable target destruction using smaller warheads with correspondingly less collateral damage. In this sense, one might concede that technology is making weapons more moral, or perhaps less immoral. But WMD, land mines, incendiary weapons, ballistic artillery, "dumb" bombs, and anti-personnel munitions remain a major part of world military arsenals.

Antipersonnel Land Mines

Approximately two hundred million antipersonnel land mines have been deployed worldwide, and many of them are still in place. The emergent outcome is gruesome. Land mines were responsible for 500,000 deaths in the twentieth century, most of them resulting from accidental encounters with mines left behind after military hostilities ceased. Land mines presently claim 15,000 to 20,000 victims each year, and half of them die. Eighty percent of these people aren't fighters at all, but civilians and a third of them are children.[29] Nevertheless, as of 2005 the U.S., Russia, and China—the world's major producers and suppliers—had not endorsed the ban on land mines that 130 other countries have signed. New types of mines are still being developed and deployed. Moreover, some mines are designed with a built-in booby trap that causes them to detonate upon any attempt to remove or disarm them.

The good news—if there is any—is that research is being conducted with the goal of making mines that self-destruct after a pre-set passage of time. Also, in November 2003, a new initiative was introduced in the United Nations requiring warring nations to remove all mines after war ceases. This high-minded concept would have to be imposed on the vanquished by the victor, but, in any case, the warring nations would be required to keep detailed records of where the mines were planted in order to facilitate later recovery. But neither of these developments relieves the ongoing gruesome unintended consequences from the millions of mines already laid.

Artificial Intelligence and Bioengineering

Noble indicts the pioneers of artificial intelligence (AI) for their "pursuit of the immortal mind." The goal of AI is not only to regain Adam's pre-fall thinking ability, he says, but to create super-intelligent brains that can sur-

[29] "Modern Marvels: Landmines"; White, "Landmine Survivors' Network"; "Hunting Buried Danger," 19.

pass human thinking and to which the developers can download their own knowledge. Replication of these *techno-sapiens* then will assure immortality of the originator, in mind if not in body. Nobel extends his assessment to include engineers of artificial life, cyberspace, and virtual reality. "As they have trained their minds for transcendence, they have contributed enormously to the world arsenal for warfare, surveillance, and control."[30]

Noble next turns his critique to bioengineering (or biotechnology): the engineering, or redesign, of biological life. Biotechnology belongs under health technologies category of Table 4.2. He writes "Genetic engineers, supported by the state, have laid the foundations for an Orwellian future . . . The long range eugenic implications of this knowledge and technology, viewed in the light of twentieth-century experience, are neither obscure nor unimaginable."[31] Noble calls the human genome project "the biggest engineering project of all time" and argues that the creation of transgenics blurs the distinction between species.[32] He is correct about the latter point. Traditional hybridization produces new variants within species, but the goal of biotechnology is to transfer genes from one species to another.

Some bioengineers are so caught up in the religion of technology, Noble believes, that they imagine themselves as co-creators with God, with the vision of creating defect-free, morally superior humans, geniuses, and prodigies. Some of his concerns do seem to be reinforced by recent comments from the biotechnologists themselves. In a recent interview James D. Watson, co-discoverer of the double helix DNA structure, said "Only with the discovery of the double helix and the ensuing genetic revolution have we had grounds for thinking that the powers held traditionally to be the exclusive property of the gods might one day be ours." With regard to genetic engineering and cloning, Watson said "If you thought every plant was the product of a god who put it there for a purpose, you could say that you shouldn't change it. But America isn't what it was like when the Pilgrims came here."[33]

Many critics of biotechnology—and some biotechnologists—argue that bioengineering must be regulated because of its great potential for negative outcomes. Noble warns that: "The profit-spurred acceleration of genetic experiments has made health, safety, ecological integrity, and bio-

---

[30] Noble, *loc. cit.*, 206.

[31] I think he meant Huxley's *Brave New World*.

[32] Noble, *loc. cit.*

[33] Quoted in Rennie, "A Conversation with James D. Watson."

logical diversity mere secondary considerations, and the routine, unregu-lated production and utilization of human genetic information has added yet [another] new means to the arsenal of social discrimination."[34] How are we to choose between Watson's advocacy and Noble's warning? Should we be persuaded by the optimism of the technologists, or the pessimism of the humanitarians? How is one to assess the potential for good and evil from biotechnology? Is a risk-benefit assessment sufficient? Unfortunately, theological input to the discussion either arrives too late to have any effect, or is co-opted by advocates of a particular worldview. For example, when ecologist Philip Regal conducted a search for a theological basis to support regulation of biotechnology, he concluded that Christian theology sup-ports unregulated experimentation and opposes regulation.[35]

Nanotechnology

Nanotechnology is too recent to have made the list of innovative twenti-eth century technologies. Besides, the field is thus far more promise than actual accomplishment. But expectations are high—nanotech is already being touted as "the next Industrial Revolution." Physical scientists are excited by the prospect that nanotech will recapture the excitement (and government funding) that the field has yielded to the biosciences. "The field is now taking off," Rick Weiss observed in 2004.[36] Phillip Bond, Undersecretary for Technology in the U.S. Department of Commerce, said: "This technology is coming, and it won't be stopped."[37] Undoubtedly Mr. Bond was embracing the new technology, confident that any unan-ticipated consequences will be manageable.

Technology Cannot Be Uncoupled from Its Uses

The National Rifle Association (NRA) says that guns don't kill people; people kill people. Applying the same logic, cars don't kill people, people do; and people, not CFCs, destroy the ozone shield. A particular value system underlies the NRA slogan, a view that demands neutrality of tech-nology in general, and guns in particular. Consequently, any negative outcomes must be the fault of the user alone. Neutral tools can be used for good or evil: guns can be used for robbery or hunting, computers

---

[34] Noble, *loc. cit.*

[35] Regal, "Metaphysics in Genetic Engineering," 25.

[36] Weiss, "The Fears and Hopes Offered by Nanotech," D1.

[37] Ibid.

for spreadsheets or hacking, autos for transportation or personal image enhancement. Indeed, we would have to exclude automobiles from contributing to smog and suburban sprawl, as if these things would have happened without them. According to this view, the person using the tool is subject to questions of morality, not the tool itself.

Engineering Professor Steven Vanderleest responds that the *inherent functionality* of any technology removes its neutrality. "Guns, by design, are made for certain tasks: you wouldn't use a gun to paint a house nor would you use a paintbrush to fire bullets. The use would be impossible or at least much more difficult without the object. The answer to the question of whether a gun or a person kills is that they both do because the killing act requires the presence of both."[38] Even if we argue that technology is a means and not an end, technology still cannot be neutral because the choice of means always carries consequences that are not identical to the original intent. Carroll Purcell adds: "As the material manifestations of social relations, tools are concrete commitments to certain ways of doing things, and therefore certain ways of dividing power. It is a mistake to think that, like black and white marbles, the 'good' and the 'bad' effects of technology can be sorted out and dealt with. In fact, one person's white marbles are another's black: labor saved is jobs destroyed . . . my loss is your gain . . . Technology remains a very human tool, used by some against others."[39]

Purcell and Vanderleest do not dispute that a gun or tool can be used in both good and bad ways. Nor do they claim the potential—both known and unforeseen—of certain technologies to be used for evil should necessarily condemn them. "The value of technology," Vanderleest says, "is [to be] assessed by how likely (due to its specific design) it is to be used in ways that are ethically appropriate."[40] Let's examine some additional illustrations of this point.

Surveillance

Not long ago a column in my local newspaper proclaimed "Petaluma's downtown parking scofflaws are soon going to have it a lot tougher."[41] Because too many downtown workers park on the street rather than using the parking garage, city officials say, shoppers can't find convenient places

---

[38] VanderLeest, in *Connection*.

[39] Purcell, *White Heat*, 218–19.

[40] VanderLeest, in *Connection*.

[41] Sanchez, "Council Approves parking System," B1–B2.

to park. Scofflaws have been playing a cat-and-mouse game with enforcement, erasing chalk marks from tires and moving cars from spot to spot to avoid tickets for exceeding the two-hour parking limit. The City Council approved the purchase of two Auto-Vu GPS systems, at $68,000 each, for the City's "meter maid" scooters. The devices are already used in other California cities, such as Los Angeles, San Diego, Monterey, and Napa. Each device consists of video cameras, a Global Positioning System and a computer. As an enforcement officer drives around, Auto-Vu records the time, license plate number, and location of parked vehicles. When the officer drives by later, an alarm identifies vehicles that have exceeded the time limit. The new system can replace the current method of chalking tires by hand and monitor 12,000 vehicles per hour. The devices can be programmed to identify repeat offenders so that their vehicles can be towed. City officials say the outcome will be more curbside shopping for shoppers, profits for downtown businesses, and sales tax for city coffers. The system can also be used to enforce the 72-hour limit on RVs and other large vehicles parked on suburban streets. Some merchants, however, believe that any crackdown on parking will drive shoppers away. "There has been an element of gamesmanship" on the part of downtown parking scofflaws, said one City Councilman, "but this is an opportunity to change the culture."[42]

*Mal*isicous soft*ware* (*Malware*) was listed with the "inherently immoral" technologies in Table 4.1. Viruses, worms, and spyware most certainly qualify, but what about cookies, spam, "phishing" pop-ups, and "data mining"? When I log on to Amazon.com I find that all my recent activity "pops up" for my recollection. If I look a particular book I learn that "Others who purchased this book also bought the following other titles . . ." That my buying habits are being studied is of mild concern, but when I use my credit card for e-commerce I worry about identity theft. And I should; it is a large and growing problem. In fact, every visit that I make to a web site is being recorded in an on-line database somewhere. No sociopath is necessarily sifting through these records, but the information is accessible to a skilled hacker. I subscribe to an antivirus and Internet security software program, but on-line solicitations are growing ever more clever and sinister. Hardly an email session passes without the arrival of an offer to invest in a banking scam, or to "check my credit union account because a recent attempt has been detected." Some of these seem so authentic that I have taken to regularly warning my wife—who uses the computer much less frequently—of the nature of the latest phony solicitation.

The foregoing vignettes are examples of the broader subject of *surveillance*, another outcome of advancing technology. Identity numbers, camera images, fingerprinting, retina scans, DNA samples, customer fidelity cards, credit cards, mailing lists, consumer groups, Internet activity, software cookies—the lives of citizens and consumers—are monitored and examined by databases as we participate in contemporary society. Governmental and corporate interests are collecting personal data from us all the time whether we know it or not and often without our permission. But since 9/11/2001, consumer data are being merged with data obtained from policing and intelligence activities. Most of us agree that a parking lot under the watchful eye of a surveillance camera or on-street parking under the Auto-Vu system are good things. They help protect individuals and property and promote lawful behavior. But many of those being watched and those who put high priority on civil liberties perceive stealth devices as enabling "bugging," "spying," and "snooping," by bosses on employees,[43] governments on activists,[44] parents on children,[45] and voyeurs on private activities.[46]

Recent advances in miniaturization of sensors add *stealth* to the concern. An Internet search on terms like "surveillance" or "spy tools" will turn up numerous vendors peddling everything from pepper spray to anti-bugging devices, covert video cameras, and night vision equipment. Advocates tout benefits such as intercepting destructive behavior, exposing workers who misuse company resources, tracking truant pupils, and even identifying restaurant workers who fail to wash their hands. One sociologist asks "It may be legal, but is anyone questioning whether a society that spies on itself is moral?"[47] Such watchfulness is not only an intrusion on personal privacy; it may also be used to sort people into social and political categories. As surveillance techniques become more sophisticated and stealthy, more people and populations are counted as "suspicious." Sociologist David Lyon questions the power that surveillance places in the hands of individuals.[48] He worries that intensifying surveillance will have

[43] Jackson, "Is the boss watching?"; Hendren, "Detection system gets the dirt on employees who fail to wash hands."

[44] Epps, "The prying eye of government."

[45] O'Keefe, "Parent's dilemma."

[46] Rule, *Private Lives and Public Surveillance*, 330–58.

[47] Sleeth, "Watching your step," G1–G2.

[48] Lyon, *Surveillance After September 11*. Also see Lyon, *Surveillance Society*.

social consequences that could undermine social trust and democratic participation.[49]

As surveillance devices are becoming ubiquitous, so are technologies for detecting or defeating them. There is a real potential for the security equivalent of an arms race in which each technical advance stimulates matching attempts at countermeasures or evasion, a chain of consequences. As more employers require drug testing, technologies to avoid detection appear.[50] A cheating industry has been born. Smoke detectors in public places now need tamper-resistant technology.[51] Digital access cards for satellite TV are being stolen, reprogrammed, and re-sold on the Internet, so that the TV providers must develop electronic countermeasures.[52] Efforts to evade surveillance need not be based on criminal intent, however; perhaps some cases may be driven by a relatively basic human instinct for freedom.[53] As one hacker says, "it's largely about the challenge. You always have to be one step ahead. I believe in the free flow of information, [and the authorities] can't do anything, it's America."[54] Is this a noble human aspiration, or part of Adam's sin of presumption, i.e., rebellion against all limits?

What Would Jesus Consume?

Overconsumption is an emergent outcome of material progress. British economist F. Bodfield Hooper coined the term in 1879 as part of an economic argument about the causes of recession.[55] In effort to get my junior-level engineering students to consider whether designing commodities for consumption has ethical implications, I gave them a draft journal article[56] to critique as a take-home final exam problem. Aside from complaining, the students reported they had never considered that engineering might contribute to materialism and overconsumption.

---

[49] Lyon, *Surveillance After September 11.*

[50] Payne, "Drug testing gives birth to cheating industry."

[51] Burkdoll, *Eavesdropping on cops doomed by technology*; Payne, *loc. cit.*

[52] Anderson, "Black Market Spreads in Sales of Illicit Access Cards for Satellite TV," B1, B6.

[53] Rule, *loc. cit.*

[54] Anderson, *loc. cit.*

[55] Hooper, *Reciprocity, Overproduction v. Overconsumption.*

[56] Swearengen and Woodhouse, "Overconsumption as an Ethics Challenge for Engineering Education," 15–31.

Hooper believed that for economic growth, consumers must consume as much as industry can produce. Consistent with this idea, producers have learned how to stimulate consumption through advertising. In 1999, $215 *billion* was spent in the U.S. on advertising, and $450 billion on packaging of which perhaps $200 billion is to make items more appealing.[57] Manufacturers introduced 33,681 new products to the U.S. market in 2003, 53% more than 10 years earlier; and spent $249 billion to advertise them.[58] "You have to find ways to get your product into the hands of consumers," says the president of a Boston communications firm, "because if you don't create the demand you have almost no chance of getting on the shelves."[59]

What motivates manufacturers to spin out so many new products? Ultimately, of course, the motive is profit. But proliferation is an inherent outcome. Companies try to gain store shelf space at the expense of their competitors and defend the "turf" they already control. New flavors and sizes and variations on existing brands are relatively quick ways to gain market share. Opportunism—such as the "Atkins diet" fad of 2003–2004 that contributed to a plethora of "low-carb" food items on supermarket shelves—also plays a role. All of this leads to rapid turnover; the average life of a "durable goods" consumer product is about three years, with some expensive items such as computers being useful for less than five. Innovative features provide a market advantage, but only until competitors catch up; hence there is pressure on design teams to bring products to market ever faster. Today's features quickly become standard, a new "quality" level is sought via further innovation, and the cycle repeats. "The cycle gets shorter and shorter," says the president of a market research firm, "and so again, that feeds the new-product process."[60] But much of the stuff winds up in landfills.

When people have no choices, life can be almost unbearable. But, on the other hand, neither increased choice nor increased affluence necessarily increases our sense of well-being.[61] Author Jean Chatzky says that "People who *overwant* tend to believe that money equals happiness.[62] Sociologist Barry Schwartz believes that overabundance of choices is a major contrib-

[57] *Statistical Abstracts.*

[58] Pressler, "New products flooding market, but few care," E6.

[59] Quoted in Pressler, *loc. cit.*

[60] Ibid.

[61] Myers and Diener, "The Pursuit of Happiness," 70–72.

[62] Chatzky, *You Don't Have to be Rich.*

utor to Western dissatisfaction. As the number of choices rises, he says, the variety at first brings a sense of autonomy, control, and liberation. But if choices keep multiplying, negative effects emerge.[63] Eventually we become overloaded, at which point choices no longer liberate, they tyrannize. If one visits a large drug store or superstore today he or she will be confronted with more than 360 types of shampoo, conditioner and mousse, 80 kinds of painkillers, and 40 toothpastes. We also have to make choices in areas that until recently offered few options: telephone service provider, retirement and college savings plans, types of cosmetic surgery, and even alternative lifestyles.[64] Which is the root problem—*Overwant, overabundance of choice*, or *overconsumption*? The question focuses on different parts of the product life cycle. The real issue is that too many units of stuff are being designed, produced, advertised, sold, and eventually discarded.[65]

Overconsumption is not unique to industrial economies. Many tribes, nations, and societies consume more than the local environment can support. Overconsumption may actually have played a role in the sudden decline and disappearance of Sumer and other early civilizations as a result of resource exhaustion or poisoning of the environment.[66] Historically, nomadic tribes just moved to greener pastures when local resources could no longer support them, and so did the homesteaders on the U.S. frontier. But in modern developed economies, consumption levels are far above any required for survival or even, in many cases, a comfortable existence. Sustainability was not part of the vocabulary in Hooper's day. His definition is not adequate today because it does not consider sustainability. But one cannot "over" consume until a measure of desirable—or adequate—consumption is established. Paul Hawken's measure is that the present system is extraordinarily inefficient, especially if eight to twelve billion people are going to aspire to live "American lifestyles."[67] Hawken included environmental and social impacts in his measure, but did not consider spiritual limits. In later chapters I argue that U.S.-style consumption is also unsustainable aesthetically and spiritually.

Still, not everyone would agree that the tangible and intangible problems cohere into an overall problem that deserves to be labeled over-

---

[63] Schwartz, *The Paradox of Choice*.

[64] Ibid.

[65] Schor, *The Overworked American*; Schor, *The Overspent American*; Orr, "The Ecology of Giving and Consuming," 137–54.

[66] Morrell, "Tomb of key Maya ruler found," 1067; Lord and Burke, "America before Columbus," 22–37.

[67] Hawken, "Natural Capitalism," 44ff.

consumption. The real problem, some say, is one of distributive justice, because many have too little while others have too much. Others believe that appropriate technology and other changes can substitute for natural resources in short supply, cut down on pollution, and otherwise allow much higher levels of production and consumption than now are occurring.[68] In fact, the latter is the dominant view behind most discussions of sustainability by government officials and business executives, in which the emphasis is rarely on limiting consumption. Whereas some intellectuals and environmental advocates speak of sustainability as including a reduction in consumption per capita together with population stabilization, the focus is usually limited to greater resource efficiency and less pollution per unit of production.[69] During his final month in office, President Clinton endorsed this boundless technocratic approach to sustainability: "People are not going to be willing to give up becoming wealthier—and they shouldn't."[70] Bishop John Taylor of Winchester has offered a contrasting view. He suggested that "blind worship of growth" in Western economies is symptomatic of "second degree materialism," by which he means we are hooked not only on *having*, but on *getting more*.[71] Thus, the stock market responds not to earnings, or even earnings growth, but to the *rate* of earnings growth. Taylor believes the biblical model is an *equipoise society*, economic equity combined with balance between human and natural systems.

Idols of Our Time

However significant the environmental impacts of consumption may be, a chain of aesthetic, social, and spiritual outcomes are equally important. These outcomes may be less tangible than environmental problems, but are no less real. The chain begins with the ideology of continuous economic growth, moves through the three intermediate stages of production, overconsumption, and materialism, and emerges with an idolatrous outcome. Dependence on things and a system that determines how we live and act is the result. Most of the biblical critiques of materialism in modern industrial societies are based upon cautions about dividing loyalties between God and possessions.[72] Some of them also appeal to biblical

[68] Simon, *The State of Humanity*; Allenby, *loc. cit.*

[69] "Green Products by Design"; Reijnders, "The Factor X Debate," 13–22.

[70] "60 Minutes."

[71] Taylor, *Enough is Enough.*

[72] Ibid.; White, *The Golden Cow*; Sine, *The Mustard Seed Conspiracy*, 83; Foster, *Freedom of*

teachings about distributive justice.[73] Jesus warned repeatedly that material well being has *inexorable propensity* to distract believers from wholehearted pursuit of God. Because anything that does this is idolatry, materialism in Western culture may qualify.[74]

Noble argued that the system to which "the scientific and technological elite" give obeisance is not only religious, it is also contagious.[75] His thesis is persuasive, but his solution—to rid technology of any religious basis—is disappointing and misdirected. He does not discuss technology in the context of any religion other than Christianity, and he believes the relationship is negative. Yet he does not discuss mysticism, Luddism, Gaia or deep ecology, nor does he consider the likely outcomes if all biblical foundations were removed from the technological enterprise and replaced with, for example, the naturalistic philosophies of Carl Sagan or Edward Teller. The Bible does encourage the use of technology. But it explicitly cautions against worship of either the means or the ends. About seven hundred B.C. the prophet Isaiah wrote about mixing technology and idolatry:[76]

> "The blacksmith takes a tool
> and works it with it in the coals;
> he shapes an idol with hammers,
> he forges it with the might of his arm . . .
> The carpenter measures with a line
> and makes an outline with a marker;
> he roughs it out with chisels
> and marks it with compasses.
> He shapes it in the form of man,
> of man in all his glory,
> that it may dwell in a shrine.
> He cut down cedars,
> or perhaps took a cypress or oak.
> He let it grow among the trees of the forest,
> or planted a pine, and the rain made it grow.
> It is man's fuel for burning;
> some of it he takes and warms himself,
> he kindles a fire and bakes bread.
> But he also fashions a god and worships it;

Simplicity; Sider, *Living More Simply*; Sider, *Rich Christians in an Age of Hunger*.

[73] Taylor, *loc. cit.*; Sider, *Living More Simply*; Sider, *Rich Christians in an Age of Hunger*.

[74] Materialism is idolatry in any culture. It is just easier to attain in affluent countries.

[75] Noble, *loc. cit.*, 207–08.

[76] Isa 44:12–17.

he makes an idol and bows down to it.
Half the wood he burns in the fire;
over it he prepares his meal,
he roasts his meat and eats his fill.
He also warms himself and says,
'Ah! I am warm; I see the fire.'
From the rest he makes a god, his idol;
he bows down to it and worships.
He prays to it and says,
'Save me, you are my god.'"

In pursuit of prosperity, salvation, health, security, and so forth, people and societies sooner or later place their faith in things and forces that their own hands have made.[77] Invariably the moment comes when those things or forces gain the upper hand; they control their creators as idols do, as gods who can betray their makers. According to Bob Goudzwaard " . . . persons or things whose help we need to reach our goal become uncommonly important. Gradually we become dependent upon them and because of our dependence they gain power over us. If they wish they can manipulate us or make humiliating demands. If for the sake of our goal we comply, then those persons or things have become our gods."[78] Driven by (Goudzwaard says "possessed by") the goal of material prosperity, various forces, means, and powers in our society rule over us. In particular, the material prosperity goal dictates continuous economic and technological expansion. Goudzwaard develops a convincing argument that the means to progress—the economy, technology, science and the state—have become such forces today. His thesis is consistent with Noble's *religion of technology* and Jacques Ellul's *technique*. Ellul believed that members of our technological society are no more independent than "slugs in a slot machine."[79]

The idea that dependence on material things can become idolatry is not new; hunter-gatherers may have worshipped their material things too. What Goudzwaard is arguing is, I think, the sort of materialism that Jesus warned against. I believe that we are dangerously close to this kind of idolatry today in the West, and in this regard the church is not distinguishably different from the secular culture. "The expectation of ultimate salvation through technology has become the unspoken orthodoxy, reinforced by a market-induced enthusiasm for novelty and sanctioned by a millenarian

[77] Goudzwaaard, *Idols of Our Time.*
[78] Goudzwaaard, *loc. cit.,* 26.
[79] Ellul, *The Technological Society,* 135, 138.

yearning for new beginnings. This popular faith, subliminally indulged and intensified by corporate, government, and media pitchmen, inspires an awed deference to the practitioners and their promises of deliverance while diverting attention from more urgent concerns."[80]

Synthesis

I have been constructing three arguments for why technology cannot be viewed as morally neutral. First, technology is a human activity, carried out by fallen creatures whose motives and reasoning are suspect.[81] Second, all technology has consequences that were not intended by design. Most technologies were developed with beneficial intent, but some have been co-opted for antisocial purposes. Some were designed with malevolent intent, and for many others unintended outcomes emerged after the technology was diffused into society. Third, technology cannot be disassociated from its uses. We might even say that technologies are *defined by* their uses. One additional argument remains to be developed. In the next two chapters I show that the course of technology is putting us on a collision course with physical, social, aesthetic, and spiritual limits.

Monsma summarizes the arguments in the following way:[82]

> "It is simply a fact that technology has carried and will continue to carry, with it and within it, the valuing decisions that people have inevitably—even if unconsciously—made in doing technology. Obscuring this fact with the approach of declared neutrality has been very costly. It is one of the chief contributors to the extent to which technology seems to be out of control. In presuming that technology has its own inner logic, its own wisdom independent of human beings, society has neglected to deal with the value-ladenness of technology, and has thus granted technology a kind of autonomy."

None of this means that we would be better off with less technology; but neither does it mean that we can blithely pursue technology with the expectation that a better future will follow. Instead, it means that we must assess technology just as we must assess other human endeavors. Whether emergent properties are attributable only to the user, to the technology

---

[80] Noble, *loc. cit.,* 207–8.

[81] The theology of the fallen state of creation and its application to technology are developed in chapter 10.

[82] Monsma, *Responsible Technology*, 34.

itself[83] or a combination of the two is arguable. Emergent properties are inherent, but the morality of the outcome cannot be predicted any more than the outcomes themselves. They can be assessed fully only after they are realized. We have seen enough "nasty surprises," however, that we should anticipate that there will be surprises and proceed with caution, especially with high-consequence technologies. Surely biotechnology is one of these. To assume an uncritically optimistic stance regarding a new technology may be naive, but to brush aside all voices of caution in the pursuit of power or profit is immoral. Unanticipated consequences are possible for other fields of human endeavor besides technology, of course, such as politics, religion, and perhaps even literature. Humans are inevitably tempted by evil, but beneficial objectives for human endeavor are possible even if never fully realized. However, technology can affect the global environment more directly and more irreversibly than do other human endeavors; and evidence indicates that modern technologies and the proliferation of technology have increased the risk. What is the optimist's response? *Full steam ahead*, because the benefits will outweigh the risks and negative outcomes can be remedied by additional technology.

Social critic Neil Postman insisted the question that *ought* to be asked about technology is "what has it *undone?*"[84] I propose the question be subdivided into six, namely, what has technology undone—or might it undo—in:

- earth systems (discernable by satellite)
- physical and biological systems
- literacy and imagination
- social, public, and family life
- happiness, civility
- community activities and celebration

Applying Postman's broad question to the analysis presented thus far leads to the four-fold grouping of the impacts of technology displayed in Figure 4.1: environmental, aesthetic, social and cultural, and spiritual. The environmental category includes impacts to earth systems and impacts on biological life. The categories are roughly comparable to the four impact categories in the literature of industrial ecology,[85] except that the "non-

---

[83] Hittinger, *loc. cit.*

[84] Postman, *Technopoly.*

[85] Graedel, *Streamlined Life-Cycle Assessment*; Allenby, *Industrial Ecology.*

technical" impacts are given more emphasis here. I will explore each category separately in subsequent chapters. The questions that I examine for each category are: "is the present paradigm sustainable?" and "is it biblical?"

Figure 4.1. Four categories of impacts of human activity.

Environmental

- Destabilization of natural systems
- Toxicity, species extinction
- Global warming

Aesthetic

- Damage to the commons
- Loss of the pastoral
- Noise
- Light

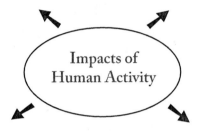

Impacts of Human Activity

Social & Cultural

- Spatial, economic, temporal inequities
- Opacity of systems
- Sociopathic uses
- Infrastructure dependence
- Lifestyle illness

Spiritual

- Divided loyalties
- Technicism
- Loss of community
- De-personalization
- Experimenting with human life

Chapter 5

Impacts in the Physical Realm

I F ASKED on short notice to identify a negative consequence of technology, most U.S. citizens would probably mention *pollution*. Among the four impacts of technology portrayed in Figure 4.1, the preponderance of contemporary criticism focuses on environmental impacts. Perhaps this is because—through labor laws, occupational health and safety regulations, and technological codes and standards—we have made so much progress in humanizing the workplace. Progress of this sort would be listed with social impacts in Figure 4.1. After viewing before-and-after photos of nineteenth-century London or Pittsburg in the first half of the twentieth, we might conclude that we have made equivalent environmental progress as well. But in discussing environmental issues we frequently wind up comparing apples and oranges. Is the environment getting better, or worse? Do recent improvements in urban air quality offset the depletion of aquifers? Is urban sprawl a free society benefit or a bondage to the automobile? Is species extinction an insignificant cost of progress? And for that matter, are environmental impacts a necessary and unavoidable adjunct to progress? Are they merely impediments, or do they portend an ominous limit to technological progress and to the well being of the planet?

New technologies for solving problems seem to appear with regularity, sometimes just when they are most needed. Is necessity the mother of invention? Or does human ingenuity—coupled with technology—know no limits? Environmental impacts have been reduced by catalytic converters and biodegradable packaging. Global shortfalls in food supply were allayed by industrial agriculture, and hybrid or fuel-cell powered automobiles seem to offer hope of accommodating limits to petroleum supply. Combine these solutions with the aforementioned progress in resolving the worst excesses of the Industrial Revolution, and only a small step of faith is needed to conclude that any problems associated with technology can be solved by the clever use of additional technology. If byproducts and unintended consequences are inherent, however, will not multiplication of technology inevitably bring more byproducts and unintended consequences? A holistic assessment must consider all four of the impact categories. Progress in one category can bring regress in one of the others. If the pessimism of Richard Swenson holds, at least one lethal ingredient will be unleashed by the multiplication.[1]

Under the broad title *Tragedy of the Commons?*, Science Magazine in December 2003 published a special issue on problematic outcomes of human activity.[2] *The Commons* are the resources of this finite planet that all living species share, and the reference is to Garrett Hardin's famous article that appeared in the December 1968 issue of the same magazine.[3] In 2004, the senior scientist in charge of renewable resource programs for developing countries at the U.S. National Renewable Energy Laboratory (NREL) used the 12/03 *Science* issue and supplemental materials to derive "the nine critical global issues generated by human activity."[4] The nine are summarized here, arranged in order of their potential to impact human life. Some of these were discussed in preceding chapters; the rest provide the framework for the present chapter.

1. *Energy: increasing demand, dwindling supplies.* Industrial economies run on fossil fuels. But as figure 3.1 showed, the projected global demand for energy will soon exceed the combined production from all fossil fuels, and the gap will only widen. Oil will decline first, followed by natural gas, and finally coal.

2. *Need for clean, fresh water.* Fresh water constitutes only about 2.5% of all the water on Earth, and two-thirds of this is locked in glaciers and ice caps.[5] Just 0.77% of all water (~10 million km3) is held in aquifers, soil pores, lakes, rivers, plant life and the atmosphere. Only fresh water flowing through the solar-powered hydrological cycle is renewable. Non-re-plenishable groundwater can be tapped, but such extraction depletes reserves much the same way as extractions from oil wells. As of the year 2004, 27 countries—such as those in Southern Sahara—are water stressed. Agriculture and urban

---

[1] Swenson, *Hurtling Toward Oblivion.*

[2] "The Tragedy of the Commons?" 1861–1928.

[3] Hardin, "The Tragedy of the Commons," 1243–48.

[4] Touryan, "ASA in the 21st Century," 82–88. It is interesting to compare Touryan's list with the 1998 forecast by engineers in a nuclear weapons lab (see Table 2.2).

[5] Postef et al., "Human Appropriation of Renewable Fresh Water," 785–88; "The Tragedy of the Commons?"

sprawl have strained the water supply in the U.S., draining underground aquifers beyond their replenishment rate and paving over land that once absorbed surface water.

3. *Food production and distribution.* In the presence of dwindling energy resources and insufficient fresh water, severe strains will be placed on food production (on a global scale), biotech crops notwithstanding. Crop yield recently has fallen in many areas because of declining investment in research and infrastructure, as well as increasing water scarcity. Additionally, climate change and the HIV/AIDS pandemic are crucial factors affecting food security in many regions. Loss of agricultural land to urbanization will be discussed later in this chapter.

4. *Environmental Overload.* Technological advances can ameliorate the shortages mentioned above, but at what price on the environment? Atmospheric pollution, global warming, and degradation of the biosphere and lithosphere continue to plague the planet. Full cooperation on an international scale, such as the Kyoto Protocol of 1997, will be required to avoid irreversible impacts. Technological innovations no doubt can develop some substitutes, assist conservation and recycling, and design benign chemicals to replace some toxic ones. Technological and economic optimists believe that human ingenuity will permit us to overcome *all limits* to growth.

5. *Increased poverty, increase in world population.* Although some estimates claim that Earth can sustain more than twelve billion people, unequal food distribution—exacerbated by the crises in the availability of new energy resources and renewable fresh water—could leave 20% of the world's population in extreme poverty. Every year the global population increases by 88 million—equivalent to the population of Mexico in 2002. Most of the increase is occurring in less developed countries.

6. *Pandemics and Chronic Diseases.* One unintended consequence of *globalization* is the spread of diseases that are affecting millions throughout the world. HIV/AIDS has infected 40 million people, worldwide, with 3 million deaths annually. World Vision estimates that by 2010, AIDS will cause 20 million children to be orphaned, mostly in Africa, a potential catastrophe unequaled in human history. In 2003

Sudden Acute Respiratory Syndrome emerged as a global health threat; in 2004 an outbreak of avian influenza in Asia alarmed epidemiologists. Many fear that this virus could mutate into a form infectious to humans, leading o a worldwide epidemic like the Spanish influenza epidemic of 1917. These and other emerging infectious diseases are occurring at the same time as unparalleled breakthroughs in the medical sciences; yet often when they occur in less-developed countries they are not addressed by Western medicine, or addressed only as publicity issues and not as serious human tragedy that could be helped. Lack of medical care is one of the biggest reasons why millions in the developing world die of preventable and treatable diseases. In half of the children's deaths, illness was complicated by malnutrition.[6] Yet the pandemic of child and adult obesity and concomitant morbidities is affecting both rich and poor nations.[7]

7. *Technologically driven ethical issues* in biotechnology, nanotechnology, robotics and cyborg technology represent the next critical challenge. Those who glorify human ingenuity call these breakthroughs the next step in human evolution.[8]

8. *Ethnic unrest and terrorism.* If technological advances in communication have increased globalization and interdependence among nations, their polar opposites—fragmentation through ethnic unrest, the rise of militant fundamentalist movements, and the availability of sophisticated weapons— are fueling terrorism that recognizes no boundaries. The second Bush administration is combating terrorism by military means abroad and technological means at home. Equivalent efforts to resolve the poverty, inequity, and injustice that fuels terrorism seems outside the scope of their effort.[9]

9. *Erosion of traditional moral values.* Not surprisingly, this crisis was outside the scope of the 12/03 issue of *Science*. The biblical teaching that the fundamental problems of humankind arise from corruption of the human heart has always produced

---

[6] World Health Organization (WHO). Cited in Kidder, "Because we can," 4–6.

[7] Mascie-Taylor et al., "The burden of chronic diseases," 1917–19.

[8] In the preceding chapter I extended the scope of this argument by arguing that *all* technology is value-laden.

[9] See, for example, Wallis, *God's Politics.*

confrontation between secular and Judeo-Christian values; and the Christian claim that Jesus is the only way to God is producing confrontation with postmodernism and other world religions. These two issues of the faith, combined with the global tendency to identify Christianity with the excesses of capitalism, are leading to relentless persecution, especially in third world countries. One estimate puts martyrdom of Christians in the twentieth century alone at 26 million.[10]

Can technology provide solutions for all these problems? An optimist would say "yes," whereas a pessimist would point out that that many of the problems themselves have technological causes. The technological imperative compels us to seek technological solutions. But these nine issues are interdependent, greatly complicating the search for solutions. With the West's sense of responsibility before God growing dimmer, says the NREL author, all this could eventually lead to worldwide loss of human dignity, human freedom, and democracy. Western civilization is far from sustainable, but we are not without means to address the problems.

Sources, Sinks, and Limits

Humans were living within Earth's resources when we were hunters and gatherers. Of course, this was a consequence of our small numbers and hand tools rather than a deliberate plan by human strategists and primitive environmentalists. Human populations remained small because life was short and conditions harsh. If and when local resources declined, tribes moved on and the natural systems recovered. Human activity occasionally exhausted local resources—usually harvestable timber or soil nutrients—so that cultures either disappeared or moved to virgin territories.[11] The invention of agriculture permitted a quantum leap in human population, but we began consuming the fertility of the soil, and wasting some of the soil itself. The ancient Romans and Greeks caused enormous environmental problems, including deforestation, overgrazing, erosion, wildlife depletion, and urban problems such as sewage disposal.[12] Did they have an environmental ethic? There were sacred groves and gardens, but it is unclear whether this was the norm, or whether these groves functioned

---

[10] Marshall, *Their Blood Cries Out*, 3–14.

[11] Lord and Burke, "America before Columbus," 22–37; Morrell, Virginia, "Tomb of Key Maya Ruler Found," 1067.

[12] Hughes, *Pan's Travail.*

as something comparable to national and regional parks in our culture. However, relatively modest areas were involved. A grove at Daphne was ten miles in circumference but most were much smaller. The vast majority of Greek and Roman trees and animals enjoyed no divine association so could be chopped down or killed with impunity.[13] Many passages in the Hebrew Scriptures admonish God's people to respect and cherish the land. The prophets even wrote that some of God's displeasure with sin is visited upon the land. Nevertheless, it would be difficult to show that the Hebrews ever developed an environmental sustainability ethic.

The Industrial Revolution resulted from the confluence of technology, fossil energy, and the metallurgy of iron and steel. But subsequent industrial civilization depends upon continuous extraction of essential minerals from the earth's crust, and a search for places to isolate the durable and toxic wastes that seem to be inherent to these civilizations. Extraction, refining, and fabrication of engineering materials from ores require energy—often large amounts of it. Since so much energy is required to create such goods, throwing manufactured items away at the end of their lives instead of refurbishing them or recovering materials represents irrecoverable loss of *both* energy *and* materials. The problem of sustainability has evolved from finding food and warmth to assuring reliable sources of raw materials and energy in addition to managing the byproducts of industrial society. Any of these new problems has the potential to become the critical one for sustainability.

One consequence of the fable that technology is morally neutral is that the technological community has been insulated from the ethics discussions. I have tried to highlight the many benefits of technology, but, as far as I am concerned, the problems that have emerged along with the benefits make the moral content of technology undeniable. Perhaps it is unfair, or at least unbalanced, that Figure 4.1 was cast in terms of variables that are likely to be interpreted as negative impacts. The reason that I find it easier to forecast negative outcomes than positive ones probably results from my engineering study of limits. For me, limits aren't simply an abstract concept; they are real and discernable, at least in the physical realm. But Western civilization is beginning to encounter limits in the social, aesthetic, and spiritual realms. The variables in these dimensions are less quantitatively measurable, but evidence indicative of approaching limits is accumulating. Whether the limits will be encountered first in the supply side (resources) or in the impact side (impacts) is a matter of conjecture.

[13] Coates, *Nature*, 31.

Engineering students encounter the concepts of resources and impacts in abstract terms such as virtual infinity and real finiteness. Virtual infinities provide useful analogs to certain physical situations, so that problems become analytically tractable. Electrical circuit "ground" is one example. But virtual infinities exist only in textbooks. Eventually, the student encounters "real" problems, where *sources* deplete and *sinks* fill up, processes called exhaustion and saturation. Key sources include arable land, energy, fresh water, and minerals. Essential sinks include the global ecosystems and their ability to accommodate the solid, liquid, and gaseous wastes from human activity.

Providentially, many technologically useful minerals are concentrated in "deposits" or ore bodies, from which materials can be extracted economically. Sources of stored energy include fossil fuels, fissile materials, geothermal energy, and—on a much shorter cycle—biomaterial. From a geophysical perspective, these stores were and are developed and preserved by the sun's action, such that the sun is the "ultimate" source. Energy that is not stored (at least not on geologic time scales) includes direct solar, wind, hydro and ocean (tidal, wave, thermal, and chemical) energy. The latter result directly or indirectly from incoming solar radiation and thus—as long as the sun lasts—are inexhaustible. All of these energy sources can be used to drive engines (harnessed by waterwheels and hydraulic turbines, windmills and sails), or converted from solar to thermal, electrical, or chemical forms. Tidal energy and fissile materials for nuclear reactors represent additional sources.

The nineteenth century British economist Thomas Malthus predicted that resource exhaustion on a global scale ultimately would limit growth of the human population. Malthus' prediction—along with others like it—has not been realized because technologists have learned to substitute one resource for another and to find new sources.[14] These successes have bolstered optimists' arguments that human ingenuity can overcome all limits. In January 2004, flush with NASA's success at landing two rover vehicles on Mars, President Bush announced a national initiative to send astronauts to the red planet. His vision included a refueling station on Earth's moon, with the fuel to be extracted from the material of the moon itself. Absent hydrocarbons on the moon, he must have been thinking about some other form of propulsion than contemporary ones. NASA scientists have not discovered fissile materials there or any other useable source of stored energy. Perhaps Mr. Bush was thinking about a nuclear

---

[14] Hollander, "Introduction by the editor," xv–xxvi.

reactor or solar collector. In any case, one must ask: are such technological advances merely postponing the day of reckoning on Earth, or will human ingenuity continue indefinitely to avoid ultimate encounter with limits?

Perhaps our ultimate encounter with physical limits won't have to do with resources at all, but will pertain to Earth's sinks—the ability of natural systems to absorb the detritus of human activity. Since the Industrial Revolution, population growth combined with the great increase in productivity provided by technology has multiplied the "footprint" of human activity, with one of the impacts being byproducts and waste. Pollution is not simply the deposition of waste into the three realms—air, water, and soil—of Earth's environment; it is deposition at a rate that is greater than the repository (*sink*) can assimilate, so that negative changes occur. The negatives can be merely unpleasant, unsightly, and temporary such as odors and smog, or they can be hazardous and permanent. When the rate of deposition exceeds the regenerative capacity of a sink for an extended period the sink can become biologically dead and also unfit for human contact. Examples of places that are no longer safe because of pollution include Love Canal near Buffalo, NY; Chernobyl, Ukraine; many former U.S. and USSR nuclear weapon fabrication sites; and Environmental Protection Agency (EPA) "Superfund" sites.

Most arguments about economic growth, environmental policy, and sustainability reduce to conflicting suppositions about limits.[15] Limits are not discussed much within neoclassical economics because it is assumed that market economics will drive the creation of substitutes as needed. However, it should be kept in mind that the market system does not deal with rates of approach to limits, or the time required for development of alternatives. Because we humans tend to think linearly, the implications of exponential growth escape most of us. Those who discount concerns about limits have to believe either that Earth's sources and sinks are both inexhaustible, or the potential of human ingenuity is unlimited. The possibility that we might transcend the physical limits of planet Earth thus far belongs in the realm of science fiction, so I shall confine my arguments to what the Earth and Sun have to offer. Given this operational constraint, all of Earth's residents must live within our inheritance—the resources that exist on the planet—supplemented with solar radiation, our only useful income.[16]

---

[15] Swearengen, "Brownfields and Greenfields," 277–92.

[16] Cosmic radiation and mass accumulation from meteors offer negligible income.

The rates of extraction of non-renewable materials from the earth's crust and the loss of materials as waste provide measures for the degree of civilization's departure from sustainability. Global warming, species extinction, deforestation, and fisheries collapse are additional measures. In a purely natural system all the planetary substances cycle continuously, from source to sink and back again, supporting biological life in the process. Change occurs, but always near equilibrium rates (except for lightning and other "acts of God"). But lightning "fixes"[17] atmospheric nitrogen, and volcanoes recycle elements from the earth's crust. This characteristic of nature provides the vision for sustainable civilization and is the goal toward which the young discipline of industrial ecology (IE) strives.

Critical Minerals

Fossil fuels are a crucial, but finite, source for industrial civilization. Unfortunately, we may be approaching the limits of this energy source. But there are other critical and finite sources. Consider *non-fuel* minerals—metals in particular—that are essential for technology. Table 5.1 shows the relative global abundance or scarcity of the mineral elements (those that occur in rock and soil near the surface of the planet).[18] The ratings refer to availability rather than total abundance in the crust. That is, an element that is abundant but not concentrated in ore bodies would be expensive or impossible to recover. Hence elements lost to dissipative use—

Table 5.1. Global supply of mineral elements

Unlimited supply	A, Br, Ca, Cl, Kr, Mg, N, Na, Ne, O, Rn, Si, Xe
Abundant supply	Al, Ga, C, Fe, H, K, S, Ti
Adequate supply	I, Li, P, Rb, Sr
Limited supply	Co, Cr, Mo, Rh, Ni, Pb, As, Bi, Pt, Ir, Os, Pa, Rh, Rn, Zr, Hf
Highly limited supply	Ag, Au, Cu, Te, He, Hg, Sn, Zn, Cd, Ge, In, Th

for example, zinc (Zn) in galvanizing, cadmium (Cd) in tires and batteries, Cd and chrome (Cr) in metal plating, various metals in paints and

---

[17] Converts it to a chemical form that biological organisms can use.

[18] Graedel, *Streamlined Life-Cycle Assessment*, 197.

coatings, copper (Cu) in fungicides and marine coatings, and ammunition—are lost forever.

It is important to note that the essential metals for electronic devices appear mostly in the "limited" or "highly limited" categories. In the case of chromium and the platinum group metals, the supply is adequate, but virtually all is from South Africa and Zimbabwe. This geographical distribution makes supplies potentially subject to cartel control. For cobalt and nickel, maintenance of supply will require mining seafloor nodules.[19]

Finite Sinks

Consumer electronics offers a graphic illustration of a problem where the flow of materials from sources to sinks is not sustainable. Critical metals—especially members of the platinum group—are being extracted from limited or highly limited sources (Table 5.1) and not retained in the economy. They are ultimately lost as toxic wastes. The problem of obsolete electronics disposal is large enough that the descriptive term "e-waste" has been coined for it. Why? The notion of progress demands ever newer, faster, and more advanced products. Thus the computer industry continues to introduce new technological advances and "upgrades" on the average of every 18 months, and the average life of a personal computer has shrunk from four or five years to a mere two.

Personal computers contain over 700 different materials, including a veritable laundry list of toxic components such as: lead (Pb), lead oxide and barium (Ba) in CRT monitors, lead and cadmium (Cd) in circuit boards, mercury (Hg) in switches and flat screens, beryllium (Be) and flame retardants on printed circuit boards, cables, and plastic casings.[20] Along with electronic products, U.S. households discard three billion batteries each year.[21] Some household batteries contain trace amounts of mercury (Hg); others contain nickel (Ni), cadmium, and zinc (Zn). Seventy percent of the heavy metals in landfills, including mercury and cadmium, is from discarded electronic products.[22]

---

[19] Graedel and Allenby, *Industrial Ecology*, 232.

[20] Vogtner, "Recycling Your PC," 8; "Electronics Waste: A New Opportunity for Waste Prevention, Reuse, and Recycling"; Kenyon, "New design thinking can minimize electronic waste," 22–24; Puckett et al., "Exporting Harm."

[21] Goodman, "Where Old Computers Go."

[22] Smith, "Health Concerns and Electronics Products"; Rosenblith, "Fact Sheet—Electronics Waste."

A summary of the current situation for e-waste follows:[23]

- More than 300 million computer monitors were sold in the USA between 1980 and 2002.

- One computer becomes obsolete for every new computer put on the market.

- In the U.S. alone, 40 million computers became obsolete in 2001, but only 11% of those were recycled.

- In 2000, 9.2 billion pounds of e-waste went to U.S. landfills, including a billion pounds of PC hardware.

- Each cathode ray tube (CRT) computer monitor or television display contains 4–8 pounds of lead.

- CRT glass contains about 20% lead by weight. When this glass is crushed in a landfill, the lead leaches into the soil.

- By 2007, as many as 500 million computers will have been discarded in the United States, resulting in 6.32 billion pounds of plastic and *1.58 billion pounds of lead.*

- The newer flat-panel monitors, the first of which will be recycled in a few years, contain mercury and other metals.

Although cell phones are much smaller than computers and TVs, their sheer numbers present a similar disposition problem:

- There are at least 200 million cell phones in use around the US and at least 500 million older models stockpiled in drawers awaiting disposal.

- Americans discard about 130 million cell phones per year. This translates to approximately 65,000 tons of e-waste.

Outmoded items mostly go out with the trash. Simply designating e-wastes for recycling does not alleviate the problem, because the U.S. has been shipping over half of its e-waste to China, India, and Pakistan, where environmental standards are less strict. In order to recover precious metals, salvage workers without any personal protective equipment disassemble the devices by hand, put the parts into an acid bath, and dump the liquid waste into a river.[24] Unscrupulous recycling companies lull others into thinking their old computers will be put to good use in some of the world's

---

[23] Gawel, "Groups Aim to Make Molehill Out of Mountain of Electronic Trash," 34.

[24] Goodman, *loc. cit.*

poorest countries. An estimated 400,000 such computers arrive each month at the Nigerian port of Lagos. Unfortunately, only a small portion is repairable; the rest is dumped and often burned.[25] U.S. regulations allow export of used electronics destined for recycling, but the government does nothing to distinguish between true re-use and dumping. We remain the only developed country that has not ratified the Basel convention, a treaty designed to control international trade in hazardous waste.[26]

Toxic materials in landfills are a problem only if the landfills leak. Modern landfills are designed with impervious liners that do not leak, at least for decades. If liners degrade in the future, our children or grandchildren will have to deal with it. This reason alone should provide motive for recycling. Under a new law in California, retailers collect a fee of $6 to $10 with any new television or computer purchase. The State uses the fee to reimburse local manufacturers for the cost of setting up sites where people can drop off old equipment without fee. The law also requires computer manufacturers who ship overseas to ensure the recycler meets international environmental standards.[27] Although manufacturers opposed the law, it is a good beginning. But California is only one state, and the law does not address e-waste other than conventional TVs and computers. Nor does it consider the fact that other nations already have environmental laws that are simply bypassed.[28] The cost of actually dismantling and reusing the materials in a computer monitor in the U.S. is about 10 times as high as the cost of shipping it overseas, which explains why the practice flourishes despite attempts at regulation.[29] In 2006, California also became the first state to declare obsolete flat panel displays and laptops hazardous waste.

Rating Environmental Impacts

It seems part of human nature to dismiss our personal actions as insignificant even while we express concern over cumulative impacts. Certainly driving our automobiles is a case in point. But consider a much smaller item. In early spring 2004, I asked my physician for a refill prescription of a nasal inhalation aerosol for my hay fever. He informed me that the product was no longer available because it contained HCFCs as a propellant.

[25] Puckett et al., "The Digital Divide."

[26] Grossman, "A Digital Dumping Ground," 35.

[27] Gallagher, "Computer, TV Recycling Ordered," E1-E2.

[28] Goodman, *loc. cit.*; Coursey, "How Recycling Your PC Just Got Easier"; Gallagher, *loc. cit.*

[29] Goodman, *loc. cit.*

Sure enough: I read on the label that each pressurized canister contains Cl_3FCH_4 and $Cl_2F_2CH_4$. Each of these compounds is damaging to two of Earth's life-support systems: the ozone shield and the temperature control "blanket." How shall I dispose of the partially full leftover canister? My prescription contains only a small amount of HCFCs, but how many canisters were manufactured over the lifetime of the product? In every case, the propellant was released into the atmosphere. But the story doesn't end there. My wife uses an inhaler for her asthma. And what is the propellant? Cl_3FCH_4 and $Cl_2F_2CH_4$! How can one product be banned and the other permitted? My confusion was resolved when I read that the replacement for the nasal inhaler is manufactured in Canada. Evidently economics trumps environmental management.

Consider another example at the level of personal actions. "Disposable" diapers can take 500 years to decompose in landfills, and more than *20 billion* of them were sent to U.S. landfills in 2000.[30] A California state senator introduced legislation that would add a quarter-cent tax on each disposable diaper sold in California to pay for local recycling programs. Assuming eight changes per 24 hours, it would cost families $12 to $15 per child by the time the child was potty trained.[31] That is not a large amount, but this cost was used to argue that environmental protection is a tax that we don't want to pay.

Is each of these individual actions insignificant? Three points must be emphasized before we can make an environmental assessment. First, some human impacts on the natural realm are no longer local or regional, but have become global in scale, with estimated recovery times *measured in centuries.* The spatial extent and natural recovery times of several human impacts are plotted in Figure 5.1 along with some large natural "acts of God." Impacts near the upper right-hand corner of the figure are more worrisome than those in the lower left. In terms of scale and recovery times, human impacts now match and even exceed natural events. The 500 years required for disposable diapers to degrade in landfills positions them above slash-and-burn agriculture.

The anthropogenic effects plotted in Figure 5.1 are not outcomes of single events (like nuclear war) or single categories of activities (like air conditioning) that can be changed by political will. They represent

---

[30] I am reluctant to ask how many were simply tossed out of car windows. But I have heard that disposable diapers represent one of the biggest items of roadside litter.

[31] "Measure to tax diapers introduced."

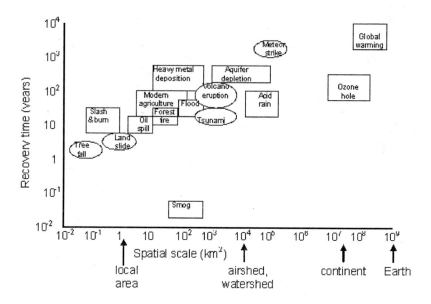

Figure 5.1. Spatial extent and natural recovery times of various environmental events[32]

cumulative effects of many technological activities that are distributed throughout the world. But most of the major anthropogenic impacts are contributed by industrial economies. Ozone depletion, for example, results from the use of chloroflurocarbons (CFCs) and hydrochloroflurocarbons (HCFCs) in refrigeration and air conditioning, metal cleaning, propellants and foaming agents; halons in fire extinguishers; and other halide compounds used as preservatives, fumigants, solvents, and paint strippers. As a result of the 1987 Montreal Protocol, release of these compounds has decreased in industrialized countries. However, the ozone hole—although it changes seasonally—has yet to show a definite trend toward shrinking. Additional large-scale human impacts not plotted on Figure 5.1 might include changes in the earth's *albedo* due to deforestation, desertification, urbanization and paving; noise, and loss of night-time sky from light pollution.[33] Light pollution is well illustrated by NASA's famous satellite photo of the earth at night, Figure 5.2.

[32] Graedel, *loc. cit.*, 196.

[33] Lewis and. Wang, "Geothermal evidence for deforestation induced warming," 535; Schoch, "Fading Glory," D1–D2.

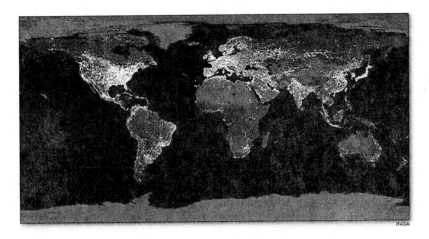

Figure 5.2. NASA's composite image shows what Earth looks like at night. City lights reveal developed areas of the planet.[34]

The second point about the physical significance of human activity concerns the effects of industrial activity on natural cycles. Geoscientists understand that elements and naturally-occurring compounds circulate from the earth's crust, oceans, and biosphere (folia, humus, microorganisms, organisms), through the atmosphere and even stratosphere and back again, borne by water and wind and carried by living organisms. Each cycle has characteristic flow rates, sources, and sinks. Cycle times range from days to thousands of years. Industrial chemicals may create their own cycles or perturb natural ones. Such impacts may not be a problem if the chemical forms are similar to naturally occurring ones. Calcium sulfate (the major component of gypsum) and aluminum oxide (an industrial abrasive and ceramic) being examples. If the form is alien to the natural environment, however, substances introduced by human activity may destabilize the natural cycles.[35] One example is the increasing concentration of materials such as: mercury, estrogen, antibiotics, and pesticides in seawater.

From a biological standpoint, the most important natural cycles are carbon, nitrogen, phosphorous, and sulfur. These elements are called the grand cycle elements, because biological life would not be possible if they did not circulate continuously from soil to atmosphere to living organisms, and back again. Hence industrial activity that perturbs these cycles

[34] Makew and Simmon, "Earth at Night."
[35] Graedel and Allenby, *loc. cit.,* 142–48.

could be expected to have significant implications.[36] The evidence provides cause for concern. For example, by converting atmospheric nitrogen to chemicals and fertilizer and burning fossil fuels, mankind is now fixing as much nitrogen as nature does. The global cycles of virtually all metals and metalloids (except iron, silicon, and calcium) are also dominated by industrial activity. Overall, mankind's demand on the biosphere from agriculture, forestry, fisheries and fossil fuels used 70% of the earth's regenerative capacity in 1961, 100% by the mid-1970s, and more than 125% since 1999.[37]

In similar fashion, fossil fuel combustion and land use changes have doubled the atmospheric concentration of carbon dioxide (CO_2) since the Industrial Revolution. Presently CO_2 is entering the atmosphere 50 times more rapidly than it does from natural sources.[38] Global warming has already caused a major shift in habitats, and, at currently predicted rates, this phenomenon will drive 15 to 37% of all living species toward extinction by mid century.[39] The scale of extinctions could climb much higher because of mutually reinforcing interactions between climate change, habitat destruction, invasive species, and other factors. Dissolution of CO_2 from the atmosphere is making the oceans more acid than they have been for many millions of years. Continued rise will seriously damage marine organisms that contain calcium carbonate in their bodies or shells—corals, planktons, and tiny marine snails—impairing their ability to form shells and skeletons.[40]

Biodiversity provides the source of ecological goods and services that make life on Earth possible and satisfy the needs of human societies. The fossil record shows that biodiversity originally increased (albeit not steadily), and that the average extinction rate was one species every 500–1000 years. In recent times, however, the rate of extinction of mammals and birds is far higher than the natural or "background" rate. Since 1600, the extinction rate has been 50–100 times the "natural" rate; since 1970, 58 fish, nine bird and one mammalian species have gone extinct; and the rate is projected to grow to by another factor of ten to a hundred. The present

---

[36] Graedel and Allenby, *loc. cit.,* 103–04.

[37] Wackernagel et al., "Tracking the Ecological Overshoot of the Economy," 9266–71.

[38] Caldiera and Wickett, "Ocenography: Anthropogenic carbon and ocean pH," 365–69.

[39] "Global Biodiversity Outlook 2002"; Thomas et al., "Extinction Risk from Climate Change," 145–48.

[40] Caldiera and Wickett, *loc. cit.*

extinction rate for all species is estimated at more than one per day.[41] In 2004, the World Conservation Union reported that 15,589 species are threatened with extinction. This figure probably greatly underestimates the true number because only a fraction of known species have been assessed.[42]

The third point about anthropogenic impacts pertains to dynamic stability. Some of my evangelical friends—engineers no less—dismiss human causes for global warming because, they say, human activity must be insignificant compared to global processes. But this argument is based upon relative *amounts* (rather than *flows*) of anthropogenic emissions. The argument is flawed because it is a static assessment. More sophisticated assessments may still be flawed if they assume that natural systems are stable and will recover naturally following a perturbation. Some natural systems are likely to be *meta* stable and thus subject to catastrophic and irreversible upset, a state of affairs that the media have been calling "tipping points." Global climate may well be a case in point. For example, shrinking of the polar ice caps and expansion of deserts would decrease the earth's reflectivity and thereby increase its rate of warming. But optimists emphasize possible offsetting forces. Increase in ocean surface area due to sea-level rise, increase in cloud cover due to increased evaporation, and northward march of agriculture all might increase reflectivity and thus impart cooling. If tipping point theorists are correct, however, a wait-and-see approach seems highly imprudent.

Additional Anthropological Impacts

Consider an example for the "Heavy metal deposition" box in Figure 5.1. Extensive industrial and commercial use of the metal lead (Pb) resulted in worldwide deposition of the metal. Elemental lead in the sediments of Swedish lakes parallels worldwide production dating back to the beginning of metal smelting about 3000 BC.[43] Lead aerosols apparently traveled great distances from their sources at smelters and production sites for utensils and coins.[44] After the Industrial Revolution the deposition increased even more, especially with the use of tetraethyl lead in gasoline.

---

[41] United Nations Environmental Programme, *loc. cit.*

[42] Cropley, "More Than 15,000 Species Facing Extinction."

[43] Renberg et al., "Pre-Industrial Atmospheric Lead Contamination Detected in Swedish Lake Sediments," 323–26.

[44] A contemporary analog is occurring with mercury (Hg). The metal is being dispersed globally in the fly ash from coal-burning power plants.

In 1925, Frank Howard, the President of Ethyl Corporation, hailed the development of tetraethyl lead as "an apparent gift of God."[45] If Howard was correct, God was not being environmentally sensitive at the time. We soon discovered that lead was accumulating in sediments at the mouth of the Mississippi River. The rate of accumulation began to decline, however, when use of lead in U.S. gasoline and paint was banned in 1970.[46] By developing a substitute and ending its use in gasoline, the accumulation of lead in the environment has decreased (although not reversed). Technology and political action combined to create an environmental success story in this case, but the story also shows how technology was required to solve a problem created by technology.

As a result of atmospheric pollution, the amount of sunshine reaching the surface of the earth declined 10% from the late 1950s to the early 1990s, 2 to 3% per decade. In the U.S. and Europe the percentage drop was greater, and Hong Kong experienced a 37% decrease.[47] How does this happen? Some incident sunlight reflects off soot particles in the air and back into outer space. Pollution also causes more water droplets to condense out of the air, leading to thicker, darker clouds that block more light. CO_2 is a greenhouse gas, but SO_2 and ash in the atmosphere (from autos and power plants) may cause cooling. The SO_2 forms sulfate aerosols, droplets which collect in a haze that reflects sunlight away from the planet. Volcanoes and other natural sources also produce significant amounts of atmospheric CO_2, SO_2, and ash. The earth cooled for three years following the last eruption of Mt. Pinatabu in 1991. By itself, global dimming might be co-located with the "Volcanic eruption" box in Figure 5.1.

Dust and ash from volcanoes travel great distances, but in contrast to anthropogenic sources, volcanoes are highly infrequent. The decline in incident sunlight from 1950 to 1990 is an emergent outcome of industrialization and desertification. Both processes are anthropogenic, the first direct and the second indirect. Dust from the growing deserts in China, combined with ash from their coal-burning power plants, now dim the skies over the U.S. The "Climate change" box in the figure combines the warming effect of the greenhouse gasses, principally methane and carbon dioxide, with the global dimming effect of soot and dust.[48] An optimist

---

[45] "Proceedings of a Conference to Determine Whether or Not There is a Public Health Question in the Manufacture, Distribution, or Use of Tetraethyl Lead in Gasoline," 105–7.

[46] Trefy et al., "A Decline in Lead Transport by the Mississippi River," 439–41.

[47] Chang, "Scientists find less sunshine reaching Earth," A6.

[48] Plus other possible contributors such as changes in Earth's albedo due to urbanization, cultivation of land, and shrinkage of the polar ice.

might propose that relaxing controls on SO_2 and ash emissions from power plants could offset the warming effect of CO_2.[49] Unfortunately, SO_2 also produces acid rain, and sulfate aerosols have been linked to ozone layer depletion.[50] Technical fixes usually bring new surprises.

Commercial fishing has become so efficient that it typically takes just 15 years to remove 80% or more of any species that becomes the focus of a fleet's attention. As a result, populations of virtually all of the world's major marine fish species have fallen to 10% of their natural levels. Shrimp trawlers in the Gulf of Mexico alone capture an estimated 10 million to 20 million juvenile red snapper every year, nearly three quarters of all the recently born red snapper in the region, hampering recovery of that struggling species and pitting shrimpers against local fishermen. Bottom-scraping trawling nets have seriously scarred coral-rich areas and other sensitive environments at the bottom of the oceans. Tens of billions of pounds of marine life and seabirds are unintentionally hooked or entangled every year and thrown back into the sea injured or dead. Patagonian long-line fishing boats killed more than 250,000 seabirds in the period 1996–1999. And every year, 20,000 acres of coastal wetlands and river outlets—critical spawning grounds and nurseries for many of the faltering ocean fish species—are lost to coastal development.[51]

Coastal wetlands that have escaped development around the globe are increasingly polluted with agricultural runoff and toxins, rendering them biologically less productive. Paved surfaces have created pathways for transport of oil, grease, and toxic pollutants into coastal waters. To emphasize this point, I asked the students in my industrial ecology class to estimate the amount of oil dripped on impervious surfaces in the U.S. and the world in one year. After certain assumptions, such as drop size and leak rates, the estimates varied from 470 million gallons per year in the U.S. to 5 billion gallons per year worldwide. Obtaining the "correct" answer was not important compared to the experience of considering cumulative impacts. The Pew Ocean Commission estimated 16 million gallons of oil (the equivalent of the Exxon Valdez oil spill) run off U.S. streets and driveways into our waters.[52]

[49] Wigley, "Could Reducing Fossil Fuel Emissions Cause Global Warming?" 503–5.

[50] "Global Warming, Ozone, and Acid Rain."

[51] Weiss, "The Last Buffalo Hunt," 35; Weiss, "Fish Out of Water," 35; "America's Oceans in Crisis"; Myers et al., "Rapid worldwide depletion of predatory fish communities," 280–83.

[52] "America's Oceans in Crisis," *loc. cit.*

According to the National Marine Fisheries Service (NMFS), the government office most responsible for protecting U.S. oceans, American fisheries have been experiencing steady improvement. In fact, they maintain that some species once in trouble are now "fully rebuilt" and scores of other species are "recovering."[53] But experts question the meaning of those terms. They have asked "restored in reference to what?" Is it fair to call a population "rebuilt" when it has been restored to the level of a decade ago—a level already 90% below what it was before large-scale fishing emerged in the 1950s?[54] Perhaps NMFS's position is biased by the organization's location within the Department of Commerce.

Noise: The Acoustic Environment

When our son was young, I had an enchanting "LP" record entitled *Steam railroading under thundering skies*. We could listen to wind, thunder, and the sounds of a small steam railroad in rural Mississippi. Perhaps this record is not what led to his sound recording endeavor, but in any case during college he became very interested in the "acoustic landscape." Among other things he made some recordings over background sounds from the city and country—garbage trucks, industry, and animals. He called the result "industrial music," and as far as we know he was the first to use the term. Now my wife Nancy and I live in an urban environment, and we can hear the sounds of the city. In contrast to industrial music, we have some tapes and CDs that record sounds from nature—birds, whales, and a tropical rain forest. The freeway is a mile distant as the crow flies, and on weekday mornings it manifests itself with a low roar. We also hear nearby neighbors depart for their morning commutes, and school buses and garbage trucks in the 'hood. We live under the flight path of the county airport, and small airplanes, business jets, and helicopters add to the cacophony. One neighbor has installed a hot tub and a fountain in his back yard, and while we occasionally hear the gurgling fountain, more often at night I hear a 60-HZ "hum" from the pump motors. On the other hand, the city limits and the urban growth boundary are nearby and sometimes we can hear roosters crowing. Normally we don't give the sounds a second thought; we have gotten used to them. But when I get into the forest and just *listen*, sometimes the quiet seems like a loud roar!

Audio technologies, like personal phones and stereos, have effects way beyond entertainment and communication. Some are unintended,

[53] Weiss, "Fish Out of Water," 35.
[54] Ibid.

others are deliberate, such as audience stimulation and propaganda. In 1938 Adolph Hitler allegedly wrote in the Manual of German Radio that without the loudspeaker, we (the Nazis) would never have conquered the country.[55] The U.S. military is very interested in generating sound signals, listening for signals, and developing quieter submarines. The Navy's interest results from its undersea warfare mission. Every U.S. war ship and submarine has an "acoustic signature" recorded for purposes of subsequent identification by sonar. Only the most powerful sonar can detect the new super-silent subs; but unfortunately, an unintended consequence has again emerged. These sonar signals are apparently very painful to marine mammals (whales and porpoises). When in the vicinity of powerful sonar signals they try to get out of the water, and in doing so often strand themselves on a beach. The Navy has officially acknowledged responsibility in only one case, a beached whale in the Bahamas, but evidence has accumulated for similar effects in Puget Sound and elsewhere. The Navy has agreed to scale back its testing in Puget Sound, but the effects in the open ocean are still of concern.[56]

The Platform for Human Activity: *Land*

Earth's "skin"—the outermost one-tenth of 1% of its diameter—contains all the essential stored energy and minerals that make industrial civilization possible. The top few feet are especially critical because soil fertility—including carbon, nitrogen, minerals, and humus—is essential for biological life. But the topmost portion also provides the *platform* for most human activity. All land-based biological organisms share the space, although they are not necessarily co-located. Thus buildings, impervious surfaces, riparian areas, open spaces, wilderness, topsoil, and fresh water all must be included in an assessment of sustainability because human activity is steadily increasing its use of all these resources. Even non-arable land is a resource, because it participates in the global cycles of energy, minerals, and water. And land is used as a *sink* for the detritus of civilization. Although the discussion that follows is restricted to North America, it is important to re-emphasize that the scale of human activity is great enough to affect global cycles.

The eighteenth and nineteenth centuries provided citizens of the developing U.S. with many reasons for optimism. They won their indepen-

---

[55] These days a computer connected to the Internet is more effective as a bullhorn ever was.

[56] Moffett, "Whales."

dence from European masters, and the vast emptiness of the land and abundant natural resources seemed to offer unlimited opportunity for human initiative. Resources were plentiful: water for navigation and the water wheel, forests for building and charcoal, wildlife for food and hides, and virgin soil for crops. More land for "Manifest Destiny" was acquired by purchase (e.g., the Louisiana Purchase from France and Alaska from Russia) and military appropriations (from British, Mexican, Canadian and Native American interests). The supply of natural resources grew with the discovery of large coal, oil, and natural gas fields; in arid regions windmills pumped water from shallow aquifers and irrigation water was brought from the hills. That this abundance became available during the Industrial Revolution only reinforced the optimism. A tacit belief emerged that Earth's resources are immeasurably greater than the requirements of human activity, and thus can support such activity essentially without limit. An "exploit and move on" land use ethic emerged—endless virgin land lay over the next hill.

During the first half of the twentieth century, industry concentrated in large cities to be near to labor pools, markets, and transportation. Larger cities flourished as a consequence, but small towns struggled. In the latter half of the century, the movement shifted into reverse. Infused with optimism at the end of World War II, middle and upper class people began abandoning cities for new communities where they could be free from the crime and pollution of the urban cores. Sub-urbanization was underway. That these new communities were racially, economically, and culturally homogeneous was probably more a consequence of economics than deliberate individual choice. Nevertheless, with a few noteworthy exceptions, urban regions which once functioned as vital communities began a long process of economic and social decline.

Urban Brownfields

By the 1960s, it was common to hear about "America's Rust Belt" in reference to cities where heavy industry—especially steel making—had abandoned factories and departed. Rust Belts are vaguely associated with former industrial areas of the Northeast and the Chicago, Illinois–Gary, Indiana region. If a suburbanite travels only by air and interstate highways he or she may never encounter these sites and may not be aware of the ongoing nature of the problem. As a frequent Amtrak passenger, I have seen the problem nation-wide, because railroads enter cities through former industrial regions. California—the "Golden State" where growth and economic prosperity once seemed limitless—had a significant problem with abandoned industrial sites. During summer breaks from college, I worked in California at a corrugated box factory in Emeryville, a "tin-can" plant in Fullerton, and a cannery in Hayward. Those factories and most of their former neighbors closed during the de-industrialization process, and some of the former factory sites lay unused for years as contaminated lots and derelict buildings known as "urban brownfields." Several other former industrial cities in California—Oakland, Richmond and South San Francisco in the North; Compton, Vernon, Norwalk, and Los Angeles in the South—encountered difficult economic times when their tax bases departed or closed.

Brownfields are defined by the EPA as "abandoned, idled, or underused industrial and commercial facilities where expansion or redevelopment is complicated by real or perceived environmental contamination."[57] In 1995, the General Accounting Office estimated that there were 450,000 such sites in the U.S., meaning that the ground was contaminated and required cleanup before the property could be returned to economic productivity.[58] In mid 1996, the Emeryville City Council announced their intent to define the entire city a toxic waste zone.

Associated with these sites, and the exodus of commercial enterprise which created them, are numerous contingent effects: unemployment, loss of community (the sense of place and belonging where people work, play, and live); segregation (both economic and racial); polarization between urban and suburban regions; and increased use of petroleum for commuting to and from the suburbs. Prior to the environmental legislation of the 1980s, departing industrial organizations had zero accountability to the city or the abandoned community. Even with present legislation, they have minimal accountability, or none if they declare bankruptcy. Local governments seemed resigned to this business "churn" as just an inevitable manifestation of the market economy. Suburban communities where new factories open nearly always welcome the new jobs, but they certainly do not perceive any obligation to the former host city. After all is said and done, cleanup of abandoned sites often falls on public agencies, especially the federal "Superfund" program.

The brownfields issue never made it to the "front burner" of U.S. environmental problems. When addressed at all, it was viewed as more of an economic rather than an environmental issue. The problem has been

---

[57] "Brownfields Glossary of Terms"; Swearengen, *loc. cit.*

[58] "Brownfields Major Milestones and Accomplishments."

pushed a little further off stage by the economics of globalization of manufacturing jobs. These traditionally well-paying industrial positions are not
just moving to ex-urban areas, they are moving "off shore," i.e., to other
countries where wages are lower and regulations weaker. For a while, the
North American Free Trade Agreement (NAFTA) drove U.S. manufacturing jobs to Mexico, but more recently globalization is driving Mexican
manufacturing jobs to Asia and Africa. Most recently, many service sector
jobs that can be done by telephone and Internet are moving to India and
other developing nations. Now engineering development jobs are following. Globalization of manufacturing may multiply urban brownfields in
the U.S., but at least it is not associated with the companion land use
problem described next—the consumption of greenfields.

Greenfields

In the 1990s, the exodus of commercial enterprise from U.S. cities entered
a second phase: industry began moving again, away from the suburban
communities that grew in the preceding four decades. Industry began to
ruralize itself; cities *and* their suburban rings experienced population decline. And the trend is still accelerating. Since 1950 more than 90% of
U.S. metropolitan population growth has taken place in the suburbs;[59]
since the 1960s America's metropolitan areas have been consuming land
at a rate four times faster than population growth.[60] The population of
metropolitan Pittsburgh has declined by 8% since 1980, but as people
spread out, the amount of developed land in the area increased by nearly
43%. The population of Atlanta increased by 22,000 during the '90s, but
the expanding suburbs grew by 2.1 million.[61]

The new development has swept into forest, agricultural, recreational,
and grazing lands. Former greenfields are being consumed at ever-greater
distances from cities. Families moved even from the relatively young metropolitan areas of California. One-half million acres of prime agricultural
land in the Central Valley of California were converted to housing and
industry during the period 1982–1987;[62] at this rate over a million acres
of land in the San Joaquin Valley will be urbanized by the year 2040, triple
the current amount.[63] Nation-wide, 4.3 million acres of farmland were

[59] Kotkin, "Reinventing Suburbia," G1, G8.

[60] Lassila, "The New Suburbanites," 16–21.

[61] Brooks, "Our Sprawling, Supersize Utopia," 38.

[62] "Beyond Sprawl"

[63] "Model forecasts four choices in Central Valley," 30.

lost to development between 1982 and 1992, nearly 50 acres every hour of every day.[64] Over the same interval, Washington State lost 743,671 acres of farmland to development, and Oregon lost 130,285.[65] In 1962, Arnold Toynbee wrote: "It used to be that cities were protected by walls against the danger of being reabsorbed into the countryside. In the last 100 years, open countryside is being counterattacked and overrun by cities in a headlong career of territorial aggression."[66] The trend has only accelerated since. Consistent with Toynbee's view, today the greenbelts (wetlands, parks, forests, wilderness and agricultural preserves) need to be fenced off. The ultimate contradiction may be gated rural communities, which have arisen like modern re-enactments of the ancient walled cities.

If land were an infinite resource, there would be no need to manage the process that has just been described. In fact, land use management is hotly controversial, whether we are talking about mining, cattle ranching, landfills, recreational sites, or subdivisions. The American frontier experience led to a tacit conviction that Earth as a resource is immeasurably greater than the requirements of human activity, and thus can support such activity essentially without limit. The contemporary manifestation of the struggle is the "property rights" of private owners vs. the regional or local plans for management of growth. No matter what the vested interests, land *is* a finite resource, especially in the presence of a numerically expanding human population and a spatially expanding civilization. Demographers forecast that world population will eventually stabilize at between two and five times present levels, but either number requires far better land use than we presently practice.[67] The increment in worldwide food production produced by the "green revolution" has peaked, so that absent a technological breakthrough—such as by agricultural biotechnology—that leads to a new green revolution, agricultural land must be preserved for food production.[68]

But the greatest constraint, or limit, to the de-urbanization process (suburbanization, ex-urbanization, and ruralization) may be indirect—namely, energy use. In addition to promoting sprawl, highway-based transportation is much more energy-intensive than other transportation modes. Larger houses and increased reliance on automobiles means that

---

[64] Sorenson et al., "Farming at the Edge."

[65] Ibid.

[66] Toynbee, "Cities in History," 12–28.

[67] Holdren, "Energy Agenda for the 1990s," 378–91; Toynbee, *loc. cit.*, 336–60.

[68] More recently, competition for arable land has begun to include biofuel crops.

suburban dwellers use 33% more energy per capita than urbanites.[69] For now, and into the foreseeable future, this means there will be an increasing need for fossil fuels: coal and natural gas for electricity, petroleum for transportation. The same study also reported that suburban tracts of land with between one and four families per acre cost more in municipal services than the taxes they pay. A much more secure future would be achieved if we were to manage land as the finite resource it is and utilize it efficiently.[70] Concentration of people and commerce in cities preserves greenfields and reduces energy use.

Brownfields and greenfields are clearly linked aspects of the larger problem of land use. Indeed, one way or another, all of the environmental issues discussed in this chapter are linked. Unfortunately, we continue to address each problem without relation to the others, without regard to the fact that the solution to one problem may intensify others.[71] Borrowing a phrase from Robert Wauzzinski, the problem is one of "micro solutions to macro problems."[72] If no account is taken in the board room of the macro economy's dependence on nature—on nature's limited resources, on its adaptability to change, and on its capacity to absorb the wastes of our technological activities—then no account will be taken by designers, engineers, and manufacturers when they decide on materials, energy supplies, production sites, and waste disposal.[73] Where does the social impact on the companies' former communities, or the loss of farmland or riparian habitat, enter the decision to move to greenfields?

By the time that they have worked their way through the factors involved in selecting a new plant site—whether they intended to or not—company decision makers, utilities, local governments, and the local work force have become involved in the issue of land-use ethics.[74] However, local and regional governments usually lack a unified methodology for planning and making decisions. Christian educator Ruth Conway suggests that industrial firms should conduct a social analysis, or audit, of the impact of their activities on the lives of the people affected: suppliers, employees at all stages and all levels of manufacturing and marketing, investors, clients, or users. The audit should also investigate possible impact on

[69] Rickles, "Suburbia Isn't What It Used to Be," 27.

[70] Minkin, *Future in Sight;* Minkin, "A More Shocking Future," 47–52.; U.S. Bureau of Census, *loc. cit.;* Hayward, "Broken Cities."

[71] Conway, *Choices at the Heart of Technology,* 73.

[72] Wauzzinski, *Discerning Prometheus,* 126.

[73] Conway, *loc. cit.,* 11.

[74] Swearengen, *loc. cit.*

both the natural and the built environments. The social accounts would then be published alongside the financial accounts together with a report on the actions proposed in response to the findings.[75]

Closure

I have used numerous illustrations to argue that Western industrial civilization is not physically sustainable in its present *modus operandi*. Our demands for raw materials, land, and energy and our generation of wastes are exhausting *sources* and saturating *sinks*, not just within the confines of our borders, but globally. The impending decline of fossil fuels (Figure 3.1) may present the next strategic source exhaustion; and critical metals may be close behind (Table 5.1). Fish, plant, insect, and animal species as well as minerals and arable land must be included on the list of limited sources. The global extent and extreme persistence of many environmental impacts (Figure 5.1) quantifies the severity of the problem of saturated sinks.

Even with compelling evidence, mobilizing a national response is anything but easy. We have an enormous capability for avoidance or denial, especially when the alternative requires difficult choices. An optimist whose outlook is rooted in the Enlightenment and the American frontier spirit might argue that human impacts on Earth are either benign, reversible, or insignificant compared to natural events. He/she might also believe, like the late economist Julian Simon, that human ingenuity can overcome all limitations.[76] In the recent past, materials scientists have succeeded in structuring polymers that have electrical conductivity and can replace solders in some applications on printed wiring boards. Superconducting compounds already are being pressed into engineering applications. Nanotechnology is being heralded as the next Industrial Revolution. Biotechnology is hailed as the answer to world hunger and disease. Molecular semiconductors offer hope for the next leap in computing power. In light of the wondrous contributions of science and technology, why not be optimistic?

Realism requires that we place all the facts on the table and consider them thoroughly. The process will require dialog among engineers, physical and life scientists, economists, social scientists, behavioral scientists, politicians, and theologians. Sustainability initiatives are appearing at local and even regional levels. But they aren't having much effect nationally. In

---

[75] Conway, *loc. cit.*, 82.

[76] Simon, *The State of Humanity*; Simon, "Earth's Doomsayers are Wrong"; Simon, "Finite doesn't fit here."

fact, polls have shown that Americans may be *losing* interest in environmental problems. The percentage of Americans who call themselves environmentalists dropped from 76% in 1989 to 50% in 1999.[77] Redirecting our civilization toward sustainability demands a national effort that is not in evidence today.

[77] Alden, "Reducing Demand for Lumber."

Chapter 6

Impacts in the Social, Spiritual, and Aesthetic Realms

THE EFFECTS of industrialization on families, demographics, and the environment, and the dehumanizing nature of assembly-line jobs—as described in chapters 1 and 2—all could be termed social and spiritual impacts. The picture is familiar from history and sociology texts. But here I shall focus on more contemporary social and spiritual impacts. When I make presentations on technology and culture my audiences are generally ready to acknowledge environmental impacts. Discussion tends to focus not on the existence of the problem, but how severe it is and what should be done about it. But making a case for social, spiritual, and aesthetic impacts is much more difficult. One reason is that the effects are difficult or impossible to study quantitatively (except by statistical methods). Spiritual impacts especially lie outside the domain of scientific inquiry and thus are not included in secular efforts to assess impacts. Although people may disagree about the best response to environmental impacts, at least those can be measured. Oceanic dead zones, global warming, species extinction, fisheries collapse, urbanization, salinization, erosion, turbidity, and deforestation—all are amenable to quantitative assessment.

One way to begin meaningful discussion of the less tangible impacts is to compare technology-enabled progress and regress—undones, as Neil Postman called them.[1] Some contrasting pairs are listed in Table 6.1. The pairs do not all have the same degree of contrast, and each regress variable could be disputed—in part due to the measurement difficulty—but also (and especially, I think) because listing them as indicators of regress implies criticism of certain cultural customs and norms. One way or another, the variables are implicitly anthropocentric, because they pertain to human life and civilization. The list is worldview-dependent; a pantheist might include some different variables.

---

[1] Postman, *Technopoly*.

Table 6.1. Indicators of progress and regress

Progress	Regress (undones)
economic growth	overconsumption
agricultural biotecnology	species extinction
leisure time	stress
information	surveillance
life expectancy	bioethics
home ownership	civility and community
stuff per household	happiness
labor productivity	demeaning work
mobility	sprawl
live births	out-of-wedlock births
literacy	imagination
communication	tranquility
calories per capita	lifestyle diseases
antibiotics	superpathogens
repeatable experience	distraction
entertainment	boredom

By most Western measures, progress has run way ahead of regress; the benefits of technology greatly outweigh the costs. But such a conclusion amounts to placing all the progress and regress indicators on a pan balance as in Figure 6.1, and expecting it to tilt toward happiness. This utilitarian

Trade off the benefits — Scale of Happiness — and impacts?

Food production
Medicine
Communication
Leisure
Mobility
Safety

Environmental
Social & Cultural
Spiritual
Aesthetic

Figure 6.1. Assessing the total impacts of technology

methodology works for simple problems where the variables are clear-cut, measurable, and uncoupled from the others. But it fails when the variables are not measurable, are measured in different units, or are subject to personal preferences. The latter cases are the norm, unfortunately; progress and regress usually reside in different domains. Rationalists (a category that includes most engineers) are inclined to view social, spiritual, and aesthetic variables as "soft" and nothing but individual preferences. Although the need to consider "human factors" has entered engineering design (and made it more complex), many engineers struggle when it comes to making tradeoffs that pit measurable variables such as efficiency and productivity against less measurable entities. So do economists. And whenever metrics for impacts are elusive it is difficult to obtain consensus or galvanize public action, unless the issues are cast in terms of injustice (e.g., "David vs. Goliath") or a violation of individual rights. The movie "Erin Brockovitch"[2] typified the latter—pitting a lone heroine with an environmental ethic against an establishment whose only ethic was profit.

Even in the physical realm some variables are less quantitative than others. For example, the loss of night sky due to light pollution mentioned in the preceding chapter lacks a benchmark. My professor colleague from Wyoming is adamant that night sky is still intact there, but his position is based more on affection for his home state than on measurements. Global warming provides another example. It is difficult to extract the warming trend "signal" from the "noise" of annual and geographic variations in Earth's temperature. But perhaps the embedded social variable is even more significant. Some people believe that an anti-capitalist, anti-growth agenda drives the global warming issue, and who is to say it is not being used by deep ecologists to advance their social agenda?

The concept of sustainability—or sustainable development—emerged in the 1980s from the confluence of environmental and energy studies. The first definition was "development that meets the needs of the present without compromising the ability of future generations to meet their own needs."[3] This wording implicitly includes the ethic of temporal social justice. Examples include the present generation exhausting nonrenewable resources, permanently damaging global systems, or—by living beyond our means—creating large public debts that must be paid by our children. A commentator on a National Public Radio "talk show" recently quipped "Future generations should be obligated to pay for Cold War federal defi-

[2] ©Universal Studios, 2000.
[3] *Our Common Future.*

cits, because they are beneficiaries."[4] The beneficiaries, however, were not provided opportunity to participate in the decision. Was this taxation without representation?

From the standpoints of sustainability and quality of life, soft impacts of technology may be as important—and possibly more important—than physical impacts, even though the latter receive the vast majority of our attention. Although great progress has been made in neuroscience and psychopharmacology, spiritual and psychological ills are not yet accessible to technological repair.[5] Western youth are rebelling against unseen and little understood de-humanizing impacts, and so are some other societies that are feeling the advance of technological culture. Islamists want the things listed under progress in Table 6.1, but not the undones. But separating benefits from the social and spiritual impacts that accompany technological development will require a different paradigm than the present one.[6] In the remainder of this chapter, I shall use case studies to create a picture of the social, cultural, and spiritual impacts of technology. The studies are grouped into three levels: personal impacts, interpersonal impacts, and effects on social systems and structures. Few environments affect only the individual psyche while having no effect on social or group function. But considering the impacts at various levels provides structure to the discussion. Aesthetic impacts were discussed briefly in the preceding chapters and they are included indirectly in what follows. I believe that, *on balance*, social and spiritual impacts of technology may be less sustainable than environmental impacts.

Impacts at the Personal Level

Our three grandchildren are a source of great delight. This year (2006) they are ages five, seven, and nine. Over the past year the youngest morphed from a toddler into a small boy. In San Francisco, California, where the family lives, the older two attend one school and the youngest attends a different school in a different part of town. Each child must be delivered and picked up each day. After-school and weekend activities include one or more of swimming and violin lessons, basketball, soccer, "tee" ball, ballet,

[4] National Public Radio, 2002.

[5] See Science Magazine special issue on Cognition and Behavior, October, 2004.

[6] This assessment about radical Islamists is unquestionably controversial—especially to the Evangelical Christian Right, who often argue that the U.S. is hated essentially because of our Christian virtues. A recent book reveals how little Westerners understand about the alienation (Pearse, *Why the Rest Hates the West*).

art, and/or playground time. Unsupervised outside play is unfortunately not safe in the city, so the children have an afternoon sitter. The struggle to make ends meet occupies a very large part of their parents' lives. They cannot readily move to a cheaper area because mom helps run her family's hotel business, and dad works long hours in the intense and rapidly changing "dot com" world. "How are you doing?" I asked my son, Peter, during a recent telephone call, even though we often talk twice per week and get together at least twice each month. "We are surviving," he replied, to which I responded, "Is it sustainable?" He said "Physically, probably yes. I imagine that we can keep up this pace indefinitely; but spiritually, probably not. There is a cost for this lifestyle."

Physician Richard Swenson has attempted to assess the spiritual and psychological impacts of modern life. "While most of the *progress* we boast of is found within the material and cognitive environments," he says, "most of the *pain* we suffer is found within the social, emotional, and spiritual."[7] As a medical practitioner, Swenson sees a steady stream of exhausted, hurting people coming into his office. He believes that a majority of them are suffering from an uncontrolled societal epidemic that he calls living without *margin*. Margin is the space that once existed between our current condition and our psychological or spiritual limits. According to Swenson the pursuit of progress has pushed many of us against and beyond our limits. "Progress has limits." he writes. "Some limits are external (for example, environmental, material, economic) while others are internal (for example, psychological, social, spiritual). Since we are impinging on many of these limits, much of our life experience is now traveling through uncharted territory."[8] He argues for the existence of a natural "law of limits" in the spiritual realm, analogous to the one in the physical realm.[9] He even suggests that that the familiar "S-curve" from biology (Figure 1.1) also applies to the human psyche and spirit. When human beings are operating at capacity (the inflection in the S curve), limiting factors begin to produce the phenomenon known as saturation. At this point the margin is zero. If at the saturation point we take on more, our lives can become overloaded; any perturbation may cause breakdown.

Studies of affluent societies in the second half of the twentieth century indicate that happiness has not increased with standard of living. Up to a point, affluence succeeds. There is much less physical misery than before,

[7] Swenson, *Margin*, 36.

[8] Swenson, *loc. cit.*, 46.

[9] Swenson, *loc. cit.*, 74–77.

and most people are better off. Yes, more money can bolster the happiness of people living in poverty. But more money makes surprisingly little difference for the safe and warm and fed. In fact, it appears that happiness has *declined* in recent decades.[10] Physicians, psychologists, and public health officials have provided statistics demonstrating widespread and prolonged stress, coupled with too little sleep for adults and children alike.[11] Rates of depression are high, and children are not exempt. The use of antidepressants and other psychiatric drugs in children and adolescents more than doubled from 1987 through 1996.[12] Prescriptions for SSRIs—the class of antidepressants that includes Prozac® and Paxil®—have been rising dramatically. In the 5-to-10-year-old age group Prozac was prescribed or recommended 61,000 times in 1992 and 220,000 times in 1994.[13]

From 1995 to 2004, inflation-adjusted median family income rose 14.3%, to $43,200. But people feel "squeezed" because their rising incomes often don't satisfy their rising wants for bigger homes, better health care, more education, faster Internet connections. Only about 9% of U.S. adults feel they have attained the good life. Most said the good life means having good health (87%), free time (66%), and spiritual well being (64%). Yet the same people placed owning a car ahead of having children and a well-paying, interesting job that contributes to the welfare of society. Fifty-two percent said owning a car is essential to the good life, up from 30% in 1975. Forty eight percent said a vacation home would be necessary, up from 19% in 1975.[14]

Jean Chatzky says that people who "overwant" tend to believe that money equals happiness.[15] Advanced societies need economic growth to satisfy these multiplying wants. But the quest for growth unleashes new anxieties and conflicts that disturb the social order. Symptoms of the dis-

---

[10] Myers and Diener, "The Pursuit of Happiness," 70–72; Lane, *The Decline of Happiness in Market Democracies;* Frank, *Luxury Fever;* Blanchflower and Oswald, "Well-being over time in Britain and the USA," 1359–86.

[11] Brindle, "GPs Report Rise in Stress," 3; Gleick, *Faster;* Robinson, "The Time Squeeze," 30–33; Schor, *The Overworked American;* Swenson, *Margin.*

[12] Roeburn, "A childhood epidemic."

[13] Brophy, "Kindergarteners in the Prozac nation."

[14] Singletary, "Study Finds More Money Doesn't Make People Much Happier," E2; Singletary, "Materialism At Heart of American Dream Kills Contentment," E2. However, important aspects of a satisfying life such as self-esteem, personal development, and a sense that one is valued as a person can be enhanced by certain job roles (cf. Lane, *The Market Experience.*

[15] Chatzky, *You Don't Have to Be Rich,* ch. 3.

ease that social economist Juliet Schor called "affluenza"[16] include over-work, necessitated in part by credit card debt and patterns of spending intended to keep pace with the lifestyles depicted on television. Affluence liberates people to pursue self fulfillment, but the promise is so extravagant that it preordains disappointments and sometimes choices that have anti-social consequences.[17] At some point, our boundless desire for things runs headlong into the fact that we can only work so hard to pay for them; then we begin depriving ourselves of time at home. Maintaining large homes, yards, and other material possessions also requires many hours of unpaid work. Further exploration of the social and political impacts of material consumption is available in several recent books.[18]

Opacity and Disengagement

Recently the "check engine" light on my 1997 Mazda turned on. I checked under the hood for obvious things—disconnected wires, cracked vacuum lines, etc.—but found nothing. So for $90 my mechanic's computer de-termined that my catalytic converter was failing. Years ago I would have replaced the converter with a straight pipe section; but not today. A rebuilt converter cost $500 after installation and certification by a licensed smog station. "What if the diagnostic is wrong?" I asked. "What if some other part, such as a sensor, is giving the reading?" He shrugged. Both of us were at the mercy of the diagnostic equipment.

Science writer Bernard Dixon identified a whole list of technological devices that—like the emission control system on my Mazda—are *opaque* to the users. They function as "black boxes." The user neither knows nor cares how they work, or how or where they are made. If they break, we replace them and discard the old one. We also become dependent upon experts who in turn depend upon opaque diagnostic equipment. Edward Tanner, author of *Why Things Bite Back: Technology and the Revenge of Unintended Consequences*[19] said "I wouldn't turn back the clock even if I could . . . yet I'm no longer sure that the shift toward complex systems is as benign as Dixon suggested. America's technophilia is a love of consump-tion, not necessarily of understanding."[20]

[16] Schor, *loc. cit.*; Schor, *The Overspent American.*

[17] Offner, *The Challenge of Affluence.* Quoted in Samuelson, "Affluence and Its Discon-tents," 26.

[18] Frank, *loc. cit.;* Putnam, *Bowling Alone;* Lane, *The Market Experience;* Chatzky, *loc. cit.*

[19] Tanner, *Why Things Bite Back.*

[20] Tanner, "Beware Our Diminishing Curiosity," 28. Tanner believes that the more ordi-

Author Sven Birkerts broadens the indictment. "The explosion of information, along with general societal secularization and the collapse of what theorists call the 'master narratives' (Christian, Marxist, Freudian, humanist . . .), has all but destroyed the premise of understandability," he says. "Instead of trying to discover the 'truth' of things we redirect our energies into managing information." In a thought-experiment, Birkerts peels off the layers of technology from culture one-by-one, first taking away all things "tele-," then airplanes, plastics, synthetic fibers, efficient sanitation, asphalt, wristwatches, ball-point pens, and so forth. The experiment led him through a "progressive widening of space and an increase of silence." "As I move more deeply into the past," he said, "I feel the encroachment of place; the specifics of locale get more and more prominent as the distance to the horizon increases. So many things need to be reconstituted: the presence of neighbors; the kinds of knowledge that come from living a whole life within a narrow compass; the aura of unattainable distance that attaches to the names of faraway places—India, Ceylon, Africa . . . And what was it like to live so close to death? And what about everything else: the feel of woven cloth, the different taste of food, drink, pipe and tobacco?"[21]

"Technical creations foreshorten our existence into an opaque, if glamorous, surface," writes Albert Borgmann, "and replace the depth of tradition and rootedness of life by a concealed and intricate machinery of techniques and therapies."[22] Borgmann illustrates the concept by reading the ingredients on the label of Cool Whip® topping, none of which seem even remotely associated with dairy cows. Neither, for that matter, do they sound like food. [23] Something significant has been displaced by this "technological universe of opaque surfaces," which differs from the time when the world underlying things was more apparent:

> "A modern woman sees a piece of linen, but the mediaeval woman saw through it to the flax fields, she smelt the reek of the retting ponds, she felt the hard rasp of the hackling, and she saw the soft sheen of the glossy flax. Man did not just see 'leather,' he saw the

nary people understand about their infrastructure and its hazards, the more accountability they will demand from utilities, public agencies, and legislators. But perhaps they won't. The numbness of postmodern culture is extensive. I wonder if Tanner is not a '60s idealist who still believes that if only people "knew" what is going on, they'd pour into the streets to protest.

[21] Birkerts, *The Gutenberg Elegies*, 17.

[22] Borgmann, *Power Failure*, 86–87.

[23] Birkerts, *loc. cit.*, 16.

beast—perhaps one of his own—and knew the effort of slaughtering, liming, and curing."[24]

The loaf of sliced bread that we take from the supermarket shelf does not concretely recall and reveal a wheat field, a harvest, a miller, an oven, a hand that blesses and cuts the bread. "I know that there is some sort of technological substructure to this opaqueness, presumably some agribusiness in the wheat belt and an automated bakery in the metropolis." Borgmann says. "But my grasp of this machinery is as vague as my knowledge of its existence."[25]

"The compound of commodity and machinery is the technological device," he continues, "and the distinctive pattern of the division and connection of its components is the *device paradigm*."[26] The paradigm damages our ability to think for ourselves, locks us into the technological way of life, and invites to try to fill our inner needs by purchasing a commodity instead of participating in community activities. "We are surrounded by devices we can only purchase, not maintain, which produce commodities we can only consume, not create . . . our contact with the world is reduced to effortless and inconsequential consumption." [27] The more technology we can afford, the more perfectly disburdened—and disengaged—we become.[28] Technological culture has replaced *engagement* of our world with mere *consumption* of it. Commodities by their very structure tend to lull and dull our senses and talents. And they distance us from nature.

Respect for Nature

Despite increased access enabled by all-terrain-capable recreational vehicles, more roads, and ultra-light backpacking gear, our estrangement from nature is growing. Ever more complex and efficient technological systems are being interposed between the individual and the harsh constraints of nature.[29] Of course, some of this separation is positive, for example by providing protection from weather, wild animals, inset-borne disease, and in-

---

[24] Hartley, *Lost Country Life*, 5. Quoted in Borgmann, *loc. cit.,* 17.

[25] Borgmann, *loc. cit.*

[26] Borgmann, *loc. cit.*, 18.

[27] Borgmann, *loc. cit.*, 17.

[28] Borgmann, *Power Failure*. Quoted in Crouch, "Eating the Supper of the Lamb in a Cool Whip Society," 26–27; Conway, *Choices at the Heart of Technology*, 109.

[29] Birkerts, *loc. cit,* 215.

creased agricultural productivity. But one cynic is rather blunt: "For most Americans, environmentalism is a relationship with their TV set."[30]

Perhaps many urban dwelling citizens do experience "nature" only through a television screen. Although the optimistic intent of some TV producers may be to increase appreciation for nature, loss of direct contact leads to its unavoidable devaluation.[31] There is a significant urban-rural divide in our society, exemplified in the 2004 presidential election as "red" vs. "blue." The Republican red states are more rural and less populous, the Democratic blue states more urban and industrial. Urban folk are much more immersed in—and surrounded by—technological civilization than are rural and small-town folk. Many farmers believe "urban environmentalists" are misguided idealists who know very little about the natural environment they are fighting to preserve. Conversely, urban dwellers think that their country cousins do not understand the impacts of technological civilization.

Undaunted innovators believe that technology can bridge this divide by reconnecting consumers with nature through a technology called "identity preserve" (IP). Consider this excerpt from an article entitled "Buy food, feel the farm":

> "Imagine an apple. You bought it home from the supermarket, and now you're removing the little sticker on the fruit. You scan the tiny code on that sticker and your computer screen instantly fills with blooming orchard a-buzz with bees, and then you watch happy apple pickers up on ladders, and then you see how the apples get packed in a shed, and then the farmer family happily appears, man and wife and ruddy-cheeked kids against the backdrop of snowy Cascade mountain peaks."[32]

Will the apple taste better when the consumer views the idyllic where, when, by whom, and how it was raised? Fran Pierce, director of the Center for Precision Agriculture Systems at Washington State University, thinks so. He believes that high-tech traceability promises boundless opportunities, including new marketing aspects. Pierce hopes IP will save American agriculture.

---

[30] Stokes, "Environmentalists Work Harder, Smarter at Communications than Natural Resource Users," 10–11.

[31] Borgmann, *loc. cit.*

[32] Featherstone, "The Frame around WAWG," 31.

How much wilderness, if any, should we preserve? The Psalmist wrote of wilderness as a place of inspiration, solitude, and refreshment[33] where "the trees will sing for joy" at Jesus' return.[34] As mentioned above, Jesus made retreats to places of solitude a regular practice.[35] But couldn't this be a county park or a well-tended banzai garden? Americans have covered vast areas of open country and seacoast with homes, highways, malls, and business parks. Forests are clear-cut for lumber and paper, and demand for energy leads to additional strip mines and power plants—which consumers wish to be located far away from them. New roads are carved into remote areas to provide access to virgin timber and commerce follows: ski resorts, golf courses, vacation homes and lodges, plus the essential supporting services and infrastructure. Airplanes over-fly the parks and wilderness areas, carrying sightseers and commercial travelers. The Grand Canyon is frequently veiled in a blanket of haze, and Yosemite Valley smells of vehicle exhaust.

Incremental replacement of the pastoral and peaceful is another example of "the tragedy of the commons."[36] Each new development brings immediate tangible rewards to the developers and the first few occupants while the aesthetic losses are shared by everyone. Inexorably, the very peace, beauty, and solitude that drew people in the first place disappear. Inspiration and solitude are much harder to find today than when the Psalmists sang and Jesus sought solitude to pray.

Entertaining Ourselves to Death[37]

Our grandchildren love Disneyland. Is a visit to the "Magic Kingdom" *nothing but* wholesome entertainment? Or is something else being subtly taught by the series of vicarious experiences? What are we to make of the physical virtual realities that we are constructing—theme parks, wild animal parks, video games, and Bellagio-style casinos? Are zoos and national parks sufficient for encountering nature and creating respect for it? Does electronic entertainment promote isolation, depersonalization, and desensitization, or does it bring people together and facilitate communication?[38] Our present state of understanding in the "soft sciences" doesn't

---

[33] Pss 23, 65, 68, 121.

[34] Pss 95, 96.

[35] Mark 1:35–38; 6:46; Luke 22:39.

[36] Hardin, "The Tragedy of the Commons," 1243–48.

[37] The title is borrowed from Postman, *Amusing Ourselves to Death*.

[38] Is cosmetic surgery acceptable on biblical grounds? What about cosmetic psychiatry,

yield quantitative answers to most of these questions, but the fact that they are questions at all reveals how far technology has progressed. And it reinforces the fact that technology has social, cultural, and spiritual impacts. Following his analysis of the effects of mass-produced entertainment on individuals (especially children), Birkerts concludes "We have created technology that not only enables us to change our basic nature, but that is making such change all but inevitable."[39]

Like other technologies, the impact of recorded entertainment cannot be separated from the electronic equipment that reproduces it. Acquiring and operating sophisticated electronic devices requires time and energy. Chat rooms, video games, surfing the web, e-commerce comprise a major portion of the time spent on PCs at home. In the month of January 2003 alone, 27 million "hits" were made on pornographic web sites. But time management alone does not account for the impact of entertainment. When my son, Peter, said there is a spiritual price to pay for his family's lifestyle, I didn't ask whether he was referring to a loss of spiritual awareness due to busyness, or to a spiritual impact upon his children from the content of the television programs they see. When parents are "stressed out" by the fast pace of life and urgently need some home time to pay bills, fix meals, prepare their income tax return, talk to adults, or do laundry, electronic entertainment often seems like a "godsend." But have you tried to get the attention of a five-year-old who is watching cartoons on TV? Parents, teachers, or coaches seldom see that kind of focus. Regardless of the particular variant—television, DVD, computer game, or personal video player—mass-produced entertainment exerts a powerful hold on children. That should not surprise us, because the experts who create the material have learned how to control the children's attention, and the medium requires no self-discipline from the consumer. No "pass-fail" grading system operates.

The significance of mass-produced entertainment results as much from what is displaced as what is provided. "Today as never before in human history," according to Birkerts, "a child in the U.S. lives in an entertainment environment, where no space is available for the concept of 'vertical awareness.'" He believes that these "omnipotent media systems" are contributing to widespread loss of cultural literacy and imagination. These technologies have changed the way people experience the world: reading has been replaced by watching/listening, letter writing by telephone and email, face-to-face communication by "chat rooms," "blogs," forums and

wherein antidepressants are prescribed to make life "better than well?"

[39] Birkerts, *loc. cit.*

text messaging. A reader is compelled to call up images from his/her own experience to interpret written text; thus active mental effort is invoked. The reader becomes like a traveler in a foreign land who picks up bits of information about the customs, practices, and attitudes of the people and then must try to order that information into a whole; or like a detective who finds clues, some clear, others opaque, some perhaps misleading, from which the reader must reconstruct what has happened. Unlike electronic media, reading "keeps alive the dangerous and exhilarating idea that life is not a sequence of lived moments, but a destiny."[40]

More than 45 million U.S. homes have video game consoles. Yet many parents and teachers hate video games because they believe them to be the enemy of learning. But the games do teach something—probably several things. Unlike humans, the machines never lose patience. And they have become second nature to many kids. Young soldiers in Iraq say virtual reality games help hone their shooting skills. "Soldiers in this generation probably feel less inhibited, down in their primal level, pointing their weapons at somebody," says the director of the technology division at Quantico Marine Base. "That, in effect, provides a better foundation for us to work with."[41] In 2006 the Federation of American Scientists called for federal research into how the addictive pizzaz of video games can be converted into serious learning tools. The theory is that games teach skills that employers want: analytical thinking, team building, multitasking, and problem solving under duress. According to federation President Paul Kelly, what's needed is research into which features of games are most important for learning—and how to test students on the skills they learn.[42]

The Marines and the Federation of American Scientists wish to use video games to teach soldiering and employment skills, but nothing is said about the associated moral learning. Parents and teachers really do have cause for concern, however, because most video games are violent and often misogynist. Consider *Forward Command Post Playhouse*, a bombed-out dollhouse for 5-year-olds complete with smashed furniture, broken railings and bullet holes in the walls; or a video racing game for six-year-olds called *Burnout 2: Point of Impact*, which features gruesome crashes, like a man's head smashing through a windshield. *Grand Theft III* is part of a series where all boundaries of civilized behavior have vanished. You get to shoot whomever you want, beat women to death with baseball bats,

[40] Birkerts, *loc. cit.*, 75–76, 85.

[41] Vargas, "A Substitute for War," 20–21.

[42] Feller, "Video games get respect," A5.

or have sex with prostitutes and then kill them and retrieve your money.[43] Media and video game producers protest their innocence, but connections have been found between time spent playing violent video games and aggressive behavior and delinquency—especially among young males, and especially among "individuals who are characteristically aggressive."[44] In laboratory studies, exposure to graphically violent video games increases aggressive thoughts and behavior in some studies, with men having more hostile views of the world than women exposed to the same stimuli.[45] Would it be to the common good if such "entertainment" were outlawed? It is hard to believe that such laws would somehow *reduce* civility, as libertarians would have us believe.

Impacts on Socialization and Community

When Nancy and I moved to Santa Rosa, California, our neighbors organized a Labor-Day "block party" to get acquainted with us (although the cynic might say to inspect the newcomers). Even moving over a dozen times before, we had never before experienced such a welcome. Nor, as far as I can recall, have we ever organized a block party. But our block party was the exception. Several analysts think that neighborhood gatherings and other community celebrations may be waning in America.[46] And they warn "groups are vital structures for social orientation and functioning."[47] Home fireworks may be an example of replacing public celebration with a commodity; but to the extent that they bring family and neighbors together for celebration, they may not be altogether negative. In 2004, the Santa Rosa City Council banned home fireworks after a destructive Independence Day fire. But the gain in safety was offset by loss of one more neighborhood celebration.

Technology is damaging to community because it divides the world into public production and private consumption.[48] This division is displacing many "focal practices" that are essential to family and community

---

[43] Horbert, "Violent toys take a sad toll on Youth." The article refers to Lion & Lamb Project "Dirty Dozen 2002."

[44] Karr-Morse, *loc. cit.*; Getlin, "Our violent nature"; Rhodes, *Why They Kill*; Bingenheimer, et al., "Firearm Violence, Exposure, and Serious Violent Behavior," 1323.

[45] Anderson and Dill, "Video Games and Aggressive Thoughts, Feelings, and Behavior in the Laboratory and in Life," 772–90.

[46] Ibid.; Carter, *Civility*; Borgmann, *loc. cit.*

[47] Baal-Schem and Shinar, "The telepresence era."

[48] Baal-Schem and Shinar, *loc. cit.*, 61.

but whose benefits cannot be procured. [49] Technologies such as telecommunications, home entertainment centers, and air conditioning make it possible and comfortable for us to work and shop at home. But they also reduce face-to-face encounters between people in the workplace and marketplace. Remote garage door openers enhance personal safety and comfort, but they also reduce encounters with our neighbors. Gated communities, houses with acreage, and second homes are increasingly popular with those who can afford them. The "McMansions" or "starter castles" on the affluent fringes of America's big cities allow each family member his or her own bathroom, television, computer, telephone, and individualized schedule. [50] Advances in telematic (voice) and telepresence (video) services are exacerbating these tendencies toward reduced face-to-face contact, to the extent that some futurists predict that within a generation up to half of all interpersonal interactions will be via "tele-living." [51] The result, according to Albert Borgmann, is "lives of distraction that are isolated from the environment and from other people." [52] He proposes that we deliberately redevelop "communities of celebration" to recover lost focal practices.

On one level or another we shrug off the undones and bow to progress; but with each capitulation we are drawn more deeply into the web. The more deeply we are implicated, the more we forfeit in the way of personal initiative and agency. [53] Bierkerts suggests that only three places of sanctuary remain free from technological impacts: churches, therapists' offices, and art, which he defines as "anything that can grant us true aesthetic experience." [54] This hope of sanctuary sounds rather weak, buried as it is among the enormity of the concerns that Birkerts raises. Churches are not technology-free, but they are one of the remaining places in our culture that consciously focus on developing and nurturing *community.*

Since 1965, Moore's Law has dictated not only the pace of product obsolescence and innovation, but also the pace of life in California's "Silicon Valley." One entrepreneur said "the Valley's designers and engineers took a wrong turn by adopting lifestyles that emulated the machines they were creating." In the words of another, "the skill sets and people's

---

[49] Borgmann, *loc. cit.*, 22.

[50] Baumgartner, *The Moral Order of a Suburb*; Lynch, *A Cry Unheard.*

[51] Baal-Schem and Shinar, "The telepresence era," 28–35.

[52] Baal-Schem and Shinar, *loc. cit.*, 33.

[53] Baal-Schem and Shinar, *loc. cit.*, 28–29.

[54] Baal-Schem and Shinar, *loc. cit.*, 75–76.

lives didn't adjust as fast as the stock market ticker."[55] In other words, the "dot com" lifestyle leads to a decline in socialization and "civility." But the problem is not restricted to Silicon Valley. One airline agent broadened the diagnosis beyond simple travel stress: "As a society our manners are simply getting worse."[56] Fifty four percent of employees in the travel industry cite passenger rudeness as the top cause of job-related stress. The decline in civility correlates with the increase in passenger loads that began with deregulation, fare wars, and consolidation; and post-9/11/2001 security measures have intensified the problem.[57] But "the fabric of social interaction was a lot less frayed when it had a lighter traffic load running over it."[58] A California Highway Patrol officer remained hopeful: "People seem a lot busier and more concerned with their own business; but when there's an accident you still see good Samaritans."[59]

Solitude and Silence

I would add the symphony hall to Sven Birkerts' list of places of sanctuary that can grant true aesthetic experience. Nancy and I purchase season tickets (peanut heaven seats) to the nearby symphony every year. We love the experiences, always finding ourselves inspired by the rousing pieces and lulled nearly to sleep by the soothing ones. Sometimes there are soloists and other times choirs. Last season a children's choir accompanied the orchestra and they were great! Because watching the performers is much of the experience, listening alone to a symphony on even the best sound reproduction system cannot match the live performance. But sitting quietly and listening is difficult for me because I have a learned need to be *productive*.[60]

Although Jesus spent most of his public ministry accompanied by his disciples and interacting with people, he prepared for and recovered from major events with times of solitude:

- just before His public ministry (Matt 4:1–11)
- before choosing the twelve apostles (Luke 6:12)
- after John the Baptist's martyrdom (Matt 14:13)

[55] Markhoff, "Some Voices in Silicon Valley Speak Out for Slowing Down."
[56] Estabrook, "A Paycheck Weekly, Insults Daily," 5, 11.
[57] Manserus, "Turbulent Manners Unsettle Fliers," 5, 11.
[58] Sciano, "Honk if You Think I'm Rude," 5, 11.
[59] Ibid.
[60] Productivity and efficiency as societal norms are discussed separately in chapter 9.

- after feeding the 5,000 (Matt. 14:23)
- after working all night (Mark 1:35)
- retreating with the apostles (Mark 6:31–32)
- after healing a leper (Luke 5:16)
- at the transfiguration (Matt 17:1–9)
- in the Garden at Gethsemane (Matt. 26:36–46)

During these retreats Jesus prayed, meditated, and sometimes fasted. Those who wish to follow the Master's practice likewise need to create spaces in their lives where communication with God is unimpeded. Because God seldom speaks loudly, silence must accompany the solitude. Although engineering is predominately a team activity, I have learned to enjoy the solitude that is available riding on a train or walking in a forest. In addition to the symphony, the seashore or a waterfall could serve that purpose. Silence, however, requires more: it demands relinquishing efforts at control, because much of the time that we are speaking (or acting, for that matter), our hidden agenda is to shape others' opinions of us.[61] According to theologian Richard Foster, a day of noise and voices can also be a day of silence, if the noises echo the presence of God.[62]

The development of recording technology in the twentieth century affected both solitude and silence. To begin with, the listener no longer has to be in the presence of musicians. He or she can listen to music not only in a concert hall, but also the living room, the kitchen, the car, anywhere. More than just providing remote access to the performances, the technology has enabled "repeatable experience."[63] Today's listener can do something that Bach or Beethoven could not, namely, experience a musical work performed identically many times. The capability also applies to video, popular photography, and instant replay. In a different domain, refrigeration also enables repeatable experience by permitting menus to be prepared from perishable foods, far from their place of origin, long after harvest, as often as one can afford.

But a large part of technology's impact on socialization and community results from its intrusion into solitude and silence. We try to surround ourselves with sounds that give us pleasure. In other cases we try to mask or drown out sounds that displease us. But sometimes we may be

---

[61] Foster, *loc. cit.,* 101.

[62] Foster, *Celebration of Discipline,* 98.

[63] Boorstin, *Technology and Democracy,* 152–66.

intentionally subjected to sounds without our consent. This might be just lack of consideration (as in a neighbor's loud and late party), but it could be a deliberate attempt to influence us. Music clearly does influence our moods, psyches, and spirits. But musical ambience is used to affect everything from intimacy ("mood music") to shopping habits.[64] Now we find ourselves surrounded by music most of the day whether we wish to or not. Youthful drivers equip their automobiles with high power bass systems that literally shake the occupants and everybody within range. In the culture of youthful rebellion, this is a mark of individuality and significance. Muzak—sometimes called "elevator music"—is another example. Muzak in elevators, supermarkets, and when we are put on hold. Music historian Joseph Lanza offers a positive perspective on the phenomenon:[65]

> "A world without elevator music would be much grimmer than its detractors (and others who take it for granted) could ever realize. This is because most of us, in our hearts, want a world tailored by Walt Disney's 'imagineers,' an ergonomical 'Main Street U.S.A.,' where the buildings never make you feel too small, where the act of paying admission is tantamount to a screen-test—and where the music never stops."

But isn't this actually escapism, reflecting a culture that prefers the superficiality of artificial environments over the harshness of reality?

Akio Morita, Sony's CEO at the time the Walkman® was introduced, feared that personal stereos would foster isolation—to a degree that would wreck modern society. Like bass boosters in autos, portable digital players or personal stereo devices are most often used by younger people, especially singles. With the advent of the Walkman, many of them began to include music as part of their environment almost continuously, albeit voluntarily. The trend might have begun as an effort to displace Muzak—which none of them consider music—with recordings of their own choosing. But isolation is an adjunct outcome. "Since the Sony Walkman arrived in the U.S. in 1980," says *N. Y. Times* reporter Warren St. John, "New Yorkers have been using gadgets to tune each other out. They provide opportunity for total, uninterrupted isolation from one's surroundings for long periods of time."[66] IPods hold a record store's worth of music for people who want to be "corked off by their ear buds," he says.[67]

[64] DeNora, *Music in Everyday Life*, 109–50.

[65] Lanza, *Elevator Music*, 233.

[66] St. John, "The World at Ear's Length," 9.1–9.2.

[67] St. John, *loc. cit.*

Executives at Apple (the maker of the iPod) disagree. "A few antisocial types might use an iPod to turn off the world, but such people are a small minority," they say. "City dwellers can live life in a bubble in other ways. Just by remaining behind the wheel of a car they can avoid interaction with others and tune in to whatever environment they wish to be in."[68] Rather than providing private cocoons, it is conceivable that youths might be using their Walkmans (and iPods) to establish community and share ideas and values in a world of fragmented families and communities.[69] But a potentially more serious unintended outcome has also emerged. Headsets shut out background noise, but the focused sound they deliver in its place causes irreversible hearing loss.[70]

Nearly a third of adults label cell phones the invention they cannot live without but hate the most, edging out alarm clocks (25%) and television (23%).[71] Do cell phones promote socialization, or are they replacing face-to-face encounters with electronic ones? They enhance connectivity and personal safety, but they also cause accidents, invade privacy, and disrupt solitude. In a survey conducted by the psychology staff at Mississippi State University, 20% of call phone owners use their phone in heavy traffic, even though 80% think they are being unsafe in doing so.[72] According to a California insurance company, 6,000 crashes per year in the state can be attributed to cell phone use while driving. As I reported in the Prologue, Nancy became one of them.

Cell phones have turned into coming-of-age markers for teenagers. Newer models come with color screens, digital cameras, and Internet access for sending and receiving pictures and downloading "ring-tones." One-third of teens and preteens ages 11 to 17 owned cell phones in 2003, and the figure is expected to reach nearly one half by 2007. At the end of 2004, youths aged 11 to 24 generated $21 billion in revenue for wireless service providers, nearly a quarter of the total market. According to the president of a company that specializes in marketing teen brands: "It's become the most important thing before the driver's license . . . they feel they've been given more freedom and respect because they have been given the ability to be reached . . . It's a badge, it's a reflection of who they are,

---

[68] Ibid.

[69] Thanks to Denis Haack of Ransom Fellowship for this insight.

[70] Kosko, *Noise.*

[71] Ho, "Jammers Quash Cell Calls in Public," D1, D8.

[72] Schwartz, "Does Your Seat Mate Have a 'Mute' Button?" 5, 10.

and how they are perceived by their peers."[73] The impact for teens is not just status, of course. Safety has been a strong selling point; parents want to know where their kids are. The kids know who's calling because of caller ID, and they answer or call back because they don't want their parents to take the cell phone away.

Among the millions who have embraced the freedoms that mobile communications offer, some people insist on using their cell phones in inconsiderate ways. According to columnist John Schwartz: "Cell phone conversations fill public space with private minutiae. But additional technology is enabling people to fight back with detectors, jammers, and other gizmos to defend privacy, security, and sometimes sanity."[74] A British firm sells a portable jammer disguised as a cell phone that can disrupt cellular communication up to 45 feet away. "You will be able to silence those anti-social types who insist on using their cell phones in the most indiscreet way," says an Internet ad for the product. "The beauty is that they will not know it is you who has switched them off!"[75] Jamming cell phones is illegal in the U.S., but with pocket-sized jammers sold online by foreign companies and even on eBay, and the military and government already using such devices, the wireless fight is here. "It's like the battle between the radar detector and jammers. It keeps on escalating." says Jeff Kagan, an independent telecommunications consultant. "The inventor of the cell phone never thought about the fact that people would be using them constantly and impeding on other people's privacy; the inventor of the camera phone never thought about the fact that they would be used in locker rooms and other inappropriate places."[76]

Even "video voyeurism" is being fought with technological countermeasures. A product being rolled out will disable the camera portion of a cell phone while leaving its other functions alone.[77] And countertechnology has reached television. Although a lot of people love TV, apparently some have had enough of it, especially in public places. The gadget lets people turn off most TVs anywhere from airports to restaurants. Orders for the TV-B-Gone® poured in after the gadget was announced in Wired Magazine and other online outlets in 2004. With a press of a but-

---

[73] Noguchi, "Teens: Gold mine for cell-phone industry," D8.

[74] Ibid.

[75] Ho, *loc. cit.*

[76] Quoted by Ho, *loc. cit.*

[77] Ho, *loc. cit.*

ton the gizmo goes through a string of about 200 infrared codes that control about 1,000 TV models.[78]

One final illustration demands telling; specifically, the deliberate use of sound to influencing feelings—and in this case, shopping behavior. A new technology called *Whispering Windows* permits retailers to reach potential customers by audio signals that supplement window shopping. An advanced "smart metal" inconspicuously transforms a pane of glass or solid surface into an audio speaker, thereby giving retailers the ability to attract customers using sound as well as sight. The system makes use of two small chrome-plated devices, each about the size of a hockey puck, attached to a pane of glass or other smooth surface. Unlike traditional speakers, which often project distorted and inconsistent sound, Whispering Windows allows solid surfaces such as glass, steel, plaster, wood and other solid materials to produce spoken words, music or both.[79] Sound-emitting walls are the next commercial application although the first scenario that enters my mind is a haunted house. Military applications are secret.

Technology to Produce Morality

In chapter 2 we discussed the increasing use of technology for public, private, and individual safety and security. Some of the applications are attempts to affect what we might call "private morality," such as using cameras to record traffic light violators or to provide surveillance in stores, drug testing, "v-chips," software filters, and now a truancy detector card.[80] Technical means are even used to guard against irresponsibility, e.g., programmable switches to turn on the dishwasher and sprinklers or turn off the lights, warning lights when it is time to change fluids or filters, and a thermostat that automatically changes the temperature set point to save energy.

Once introduced into complex social situations, however, technologies never do just one thing. They are what Richard Sclove terms "polypotent"—accomplishing several things at once, many of them un-

---

[78] "Gadget puts TV haters in control," A2.

[79] 78 Baker, "Electronic Device Converts Windows into Speakers."

[80] Andern, "Black Market Spreads Sales of Illicit Access Cards for Satellite TV"; Auster, "Striking Back at Terrorism," 16–21; Jackson, "Feds Put Billions into Terrorist Fight"; Jewett, "V-chip? What V-chip?"; Kozlowski, *High-Tech Surveillance*; Parker and Kasindorf, "Schools Taking Security to Heart"; Paula, "Crime Fighting Sensors," 66–68; Snyder, "High-Tech Student ID Card Sounds Alarm if Class is Cut"; Wayne, "Developing smart weapons."

intended.[81] How are we to measure the overall effectiveness of the social control achieved by technologies? Where technological innovators take direct aim at thwarting the behavior of a target group, they usually succeed to some degree. Although a skilled professional thief can defeat most security systems, less competent and determined burglars will be deterred. This is not news. What is interesting is that when technologies induce behavioral conformity to other people's norms without actually persuading the would-be violator to change his moral stance, there is an excellent chance that the un-persuaded one will find an alternative outlet for his antisocial behavior. In other words, technologies may more easily be used to *displace* immoral or socially unacceptable behaviors than to actually *quell* them. Those purchasing the technology may be buying themselves increased safety or whatever, but trouble for someone else. Technologies thereby may manipulate more than once: first in dissuading a perpetrator from undertaking the original action, but second by re-targeting the perpetrator toward another victim. This is the simple version of the transfer phenomenon. Where the manipulation in question is less obvious, so also will the displacement be less obvious.

"Technology can be embraced as simply a more rapid means of bringing ancient wisdom to modern folks" says the editor of *The Christian Science Monitor*. "But it carries the risk that as it dominates human activities, it can foster a myth that it is a source of answers, rather than just a tool."[82] The Director of the University of Louisville's National Crime Prevention Institute says he feels discomfort because "everywhere I go somebody wants to take my picture." "We probably should have had a national conversation," he said, "before diffusing the surveillance technologies so widely."[83] He is calling for some form of *technology assessment*. Without this "national conversation," the trend is toward technocracy, technicism, or the specter of Ellul's *technique*.[84]

Unfortunately, the threat of terrorism, the rising price of gasoline, and the pace and stress of contemporary culture are drowning out calls for technology assessment. Theologian Francis Schaeffer believed that we will voluntarily relinquish much in order to gain, or maintain, "personal peace and affluence." The silent majority will give up their liberties inch-by-inch as long as their own personal peace and prosperity are not challenged, as

[81] Sclove, *Democracy and Technology.*
[82] Van Slambrouck, "From the land of high tech comes a human connection."
[83] Quoted in Sleeth, "Watching your step," G1–G2.
[84] Ellul, *The Technological Society.*

long as the goods are delivered. When civility decreases, good people often clamor for more law and order, or governmental control, because only the state is capable of enforcing such order. The market economy offers only technological approaches; but using technology to manage human behavior moves a social problem into the scientific and technical arena.[85]

Effects on Social Systems and Structures

There is no hard break between impacts at this level and the preceeding one—socialization and community; the difference is more a matter of focus. Technologies that affect systems and structures are likely to affect individuals as well, but perhaps with smaller impact (although there may be exceptions where the reverse is true). In the following, we consider the effects of automation, globalization, and information technology on the workforce and the more system-level issues of social justice and export of cultural damage.

Automation and Globalization

Companies pursue automation to remain competitive by reducing labor costs and, in some situations, by improving product quality. Unlike humans, machines don't get bored and make mistakes (unless they wear out), and modern machining centers are capable of achieving finer tolerances than the most skilled human machinists. Measured as product produced per labor dollar, automation has raised U.S. labor productivity, but also eliminated many well-paying manufacturing jobs. Yet the gains have not been enough; manufacturing jobs continue to move overseas. *Globalization* is also enabled and propelled by technology—the Internet, telecommunications, air transport, and containerized freight. According to classical economic theory, productivity gains and cheaper goods and services must raise the nation's standard of living. If social costs are not considered, automation and globalization must be judged as positive.

But consistent with the now-familiar format of unintended consequences, there are reasons for concern. Globalization is creating new competitors for U.S. industry; and many would-be purchasers of cheaper goods and services are the same persons whose jobs have been eliminated by automation or shipped overseas. Traditional economic theory maintains that manufacturing is one of three bases for generation of wealth (mining and

[85] Sarewitz, *Frontiers of Illusion*, 164.

agriculture are the other two).[86] Agricultural productivity in the U.S. has been rising for a long time, primarily due to petroleum-driven machinery, petroleum-based fertilizer, and petroleum-based pesticides. More recently, information technology (IT) and GMO crops are being introduced in effort to continue the productivity growth. Mostly due to coal mining, U.S. mineral production also is high. But physical limits are beginning to constrain productivity growth in both mining and agriculture. [87]

The National Association of Manufacturers is trying to save U.S. manufacturing jobs by pushing legislation and regulatory changes that would reduce business taxes, health care costs, product liability judgments and the cost of complying with government regulations. In other words, rolling back some of the protections against social and environmental impacts of technology. But jobs lost to productivity gains will not come back regardless of what U.S. policymakers do. Importing manufactured goods for sale in the U.S. can save consumer dollars—but does not generate domestic wealth in the traditional sense because retail sales do not increase value per se. But some predict that information technology (IT) will supplant the losses in manufacturing. The optimism of the economists reads: ". . . globalization of software and IT services, in conjunction with diffusion of IT to new sectors and businesses, will yield even stronger demand in the United States for IT-proficient workers."[88] It remains to be proven that IT can replace manufacturing as a wealth generator. In any case, retraining of factory workers into IT professionals is going to generate significant social upset. The economic impacts of automation and globalization cannot be separated from the social impacts.

Technology and Cities

The Industrial Revolution and its offspring—mass production and automation—fostered the urbanization of Western civilization. But some suggest that the combined forces of mobility and communications technology are making cities unnecessary.[89] Because people and machines can now communicate electronically, it is argued, commerce is becoming distributed such that people no longer need to assemble at integrated central

[86] Berry, "Doing More With Fewer Workers," 19.

[87] Previously we explained how "mad cow" disease was a result of the quest for productivity.

[88] Mann, "Globalization of IT Services and White Collar Jobs," 6.

[89] Guilder, *Life After Television*; Hayward, "Land-Use Planners Don't Understand Urban Complexities," 3B; Kotkin "Beyond White Flight," 26–27; Siegfried, "The Inner City in the 21st Century," 19–30.

worksites. Manufacturing organizations are evolving into "virtual enterprises" wherein different aspects of product development (design, cost estimation, procurement, testing, fabrication, and assembly) are carried out at geographically (including globally) dispersed sites. Futurist Ray Kurzweil argues that in addition making cities obsolete, decentralized technologies are also enabling a more secure future because distributed technologies such as the Internet tend to be flexible, efficient, and relatively benign in their environmental effects.[90]

In my view, Kurzweil is at best half right. Large losses occur when high voltage electricity is transmitted long distances from large "centralized" generation sites. From the perspective of material, resource, labor, and economic productivity, modern electric power plants far surpass the cumulative productivity of small, distributed systems. I think he is completely wrong on the other points—especially with respect to transportation systems, a subject worthy of a separate chapter. With the obvious exception of agriculture, cities, in principle, offer the most efficient structure for production and consumption.[91] Examples of this efficiency include reduced energy use for transportation and space heating; better use of space (spatial organization); reduced consumption of materials for building; efficient use of time (for commuting and shopping); and specialization in skilled trades and professions. But the social and cultural advantages that cities offer over rural life may be even more important. Cities offer the basis for development of culture and community: performing arts, diverse and vibrant neighborhoods, medical centers of excellence; even zoos are part of the cultural richness available only in cities. The idea that cities are obsolete discounts their social, economic, and environmental benefits and the social costs of their loss. The "trump" issue, however, is the inescapability of physical limits. We cannot forever expand into greenfields.

Of course, cities must be attractive places to live. Unfortunately, the decline in civility in U.S. culture is stimulating just the opposite, and this decline in civility produces a self-reinforcing cycle. In pursuit of peace and quiet, city dwellers fled first to the suburbs, and subsequently to the country; but once there they must go everywhere by automobile. Driving is at best an asocial—and increasingly an antisocial—practice. Arnold Toynbee wrote that: "close settlement does not constitute a city unless the inhabitants...are conscious of having a corporate social life...a genuine

[90] Kurzweil, "Promise and Peril of the 21st Century."
[91] Toynbee, "Cities in History," 336–60; Doxiadis, "The Coming World City," 12–28.

community...at least the rudiments of a soul."[92] Jane Jacobs argued that heterogeneity and variety in cities will produce vitality if these variables are understood and nourished.[93] The Netherlands has one of the highest average population densities in the world, yet no area of the country *seems* overcrowded, certainly not when compared to Hong Kong, New York, or Rio de Janeiro. The Dutch have studiously pursued "a lighter mode of urbanism" using the three spatial dimensions in a creative way that links economy with ecology.[94] The results demonstrate that the claustrophobia of the city can be avoided even as large-scale densification proceeds.

I close this section with reference to the biblical City of God—the New Jerusalem.[95] The city is to be fashioned in the form of a cube a thousand miles on a side, with the seat of government located therein. As much as I love pristine nature and desire to preserve greenfields, God has decided to dwell for eternity in a city. Well, maybe He will vacation on the restored Earth.

Social Virtues and Democracy

Social means of control, such as regulations, progressive insurance rates, and "sin taxes" are difficult to impose in a democracy. But social means of managing risk are actually more common than we might realize. We require motorists to wear seat belts and motorcyclists to wear helmets. Seat belts and helmets save lives and reduce the number and severity of injuries, and the laws that require them reduce medical costs for everyone. Because drivers using cell phones are four times more likely to be involved in an accident, some states have banned their use while driving. Headsets apparently don't help because it is the distraction of the conversation that is the problem.[96] So why should those who take care of their physical condition and avoid high-risk lifestyles share costs with those not so inclined? If we were to remove the principle of shared risk, all people whose lifestyles make them higher risk would be uninsured or face much higher rates. What would be the impact on community? The vision of community requires a number of social virtues that transcend the individualism so highly valued in our culture. These are the kinds of difficulties that en-

[92] Toynbee, *loc. cit.*

[93] Jacobs, *The Death and Life of Great American Cities.*

[94] Maas et al., *Fairmax.*

[95] Rev 21–22.

[96] Granelli, "Study: Headsets don't reduce accident rate for drivers on cell phones," A1, A13.

hance the appeal of technological solutions, if such can be found. But the paradox that hopefully is becoming clear is that technological solutions bring new problems.

Steven Carter believes that democracy requires self-discipline in place of self-indulgence, i.e., discipline of individual passions for the sake of living among others. Therefore declining civility is placing democracy at risk. Population growth and greatly expanded impact of human activity enabled by technology mean that we impact each other much more frequently and in myriad more ways than before. We are long removed from the frontier society where a person could exercise whatever "freedoms" he or she might choose without impacting another person's rights. Individual liberties cannot be unlimited. Absent voluntary self-restraint, however, these limitations must be attained via laws and regulations.

Russell Hittinger, Chair of Catholic Studies in the Department of Philosophy and Religion at the University of Tulsa, believes that our technological society cannot be understood until we appreciate the extent to which it is a "package deal."[97] Neither liberalism nor secular religions of progress are the chief enemies of culture, he argues; *technology* is. Hittinger writes about emergent social and cultural impacts, exactly paralleling the concept of emergent physical outcomes that was discussed in the preceding chapter. He argues that the social and cultural impacts of modern technology are a moral consequence of many individual choices that in themselves seemed innocuous or amoral.[98] Today's technological order requires strong central government, because the state mobilizes the forces necessary for constructing, maintaining, and protecting the necessary sophisticated infrastructure.[99] In current terms, this infrastructure includes energy supply, air traffic control, highways, national and homeland security, interstate commerce, the Internet, stem cell research, etc.

There are legitimate fears about such a "statist" position. It invites comparison to specters of technocracy.[100] But the inescapable fact remains that the more technically complex our society becomes, the more we become dependent upon the services of authorities and experts. Early Western ideals of progress emerging from the Enlightenment defined progress in individual terms such as enlightenment, liberty, justice, and rights.

[97] Hittinger, "Christopher Dawson's Insights," 93. Hittinger has the broad definition of technology in mind. More than machines, it is the systematic application of tools to culture.

[98] Ibid.

[99] Hittinger, *loc. cit.* 79–80.

[100] Bell, *The Coming of Post-Industrial Society.*

But according to Hittinger, "technological order" is now the real basis of secular culture.[101] In the new cultural pattern, tools are either deliberately designed to replace the human act or have the unintended effect of making the human act unnecessary or subordinate to the machine. The old liberal ideals of limited government, individual creativity, and an autonomous private sphere more or less immune from centralized planning are violated whenever the technological imperative dictates otherwise.

Inappropriate Technology: Exporting Cultural Damage

Hittinger suggested that technology can be transferred from culture to culture, "working just as well in Cambodia as in Cleveland."[102] Presumably he meant physically transferable—assuming the locale has, for example, electric power sufficient to operate a motor, or with the quality and reliability to avoid damaging a modern computer. But there is a problem when we export technologies that have greater negative impacts on indigenous cultures than they do on our own. "Of course modern technology is not neutral," Hittinger added, "because it goes as a 'package deal' or an ensemble of choices. Thus it is more than the moral problem of individual choices. Wherever modern technology goes, the technological order follows." With the exception of the fundamentalist Islamic states, traditional cultures have succumbed to the technological order. Hittinger thinks the verdict is still out on the Islamic states, who are attempting to preserve a traditional religious culture even while embracing the necessities of modern technology.[103] But he penned these thoughts in 1995. Perhaps today the verdict is in.

There are many examples. The settlers of the new world completely destroyed a flourishing native "American Indian" culture. Disease: smallpox, measles, and syphilis was the first "tool" of destruction. Technology: the buffalo rifle, iron horse, and plow represented the second tool. Technique: treaties, privatization of land, and forced resettlement on reservations was the third. Nestle Company's promotion of infant formula in place of breast-feeding was intended to liberate nursing mothers. But it caused widespread disease among infants in the undeveloped world because the water from which the formula was mixed was not sanitary.[104] In the 1960s, the Skolt Lapp people of Finland decided to change their method of herd-

---

[101] Hittinger, *loc. cit.*, 82–83.

[102] Hittinger, *loc. cit.*, 84.

[103] Hittinger, *loc. cit.*, 92.

[104] Broad and Cavanagh, "The Corporate Accountability Movement," 12, 30.

ing reindeer by replacing their dogsleds and skis with snowmobiles. But the very nature of the snowmobile resulted in the breakdown of traditional Skolt society.[105] In Tanzania, women and young boys thresh maize, corn, and other grains for eight to nine hours a day. A group of Taiwanese consultants proposed the introduction of electric grain grinders to help with this difficult and arduous task. The entire harvest could have been ground in minutes, but the critically important social groupings and interactions in that culture would have been destroyed. The solution was a variety of hand grinders that would reduce the strenuousness of the grinding while maintaining the social groups.[106] The American and Canadian governments provided computer software and training to the Indian and Inuit peoples of the Arctic regions to enable them to use computer models for resource management. But the relationship among humans and animals became based on computer print-outs—fast-paced, objective, abstract, quantitative. Objective, scientific, and quantitative computer management systems rarely improve upon native conservation and management systems. In fact, the modern systems often prove disastrous.[107]

Technological Distraction

I close this chapter on social and spiritual effects by focusing on *distraction*. Although it could be discussed under personal impacts of technology, the distraction phenomenon is sufficiently profound that it provides a fitting capstone to the chapter. Some of my colleagues argue that technology is driving human evolution in a way that modern youth are becoming more capable of multitasking than their parents' generation was. If this is so, then young people should be exempt from the forthcoming California law that bans hands-on cell phone use while driving. However, I am skeptical of this application of evolutionary theory. I think *partial tasking* is much more descriptive than multitasking. Partial tasking correlates better with the societal phenomena of decreasing attention spans and decline in self discipline.

Nevertheless, partial tasking per se is a comparatively minor problem. Many of us have become so fascinated by technology that we dedicate substantial amounts of time and energy to acquiring more and more technological objects. Not all of this can be explained by the instrumental value of the devices, i.e., the capabilities that they provide. For many of us,

[105] Winner, *Autonomous Technology*, 87. Quoted in Monsma, *Responsible Technology*, 34.

[106] Papanek, *Design for Human Scale*, 9. Quoted in Monsma, *loc. cit.*, 71–72.

[107] Mander, quoted in Conway, *loc. cit.* 74.

technology has taken on *intrinsic* value.[108] In the extreme, this can become idolatry, as in the case of technology for safety and security. Long before that extreme is reached, however, technology requires our time and attention. We must learn about its functionality, do comparison shopping, set up the devices and learn to operate, maintain, and eventually dispose of them. But the most difficult problem that we must wrestle with is that the salience of technological objects and the urgency that they so often impart to our lives tend to draw our attention away from the highest good and replace them with activities directed to things of lesser value. "Perhaps the greatest danger of technology," says engineering professor Ken Funk, "is its capacity to distract us from God and His kingdom." Funk calls this a *profound* distraction.[109] Rightfully so.

[108] Funk, "Technology and Christian 'Values.'"
[109] Ibid.

Chapter 7

Ethics and Values in Engineering Design

HOPEFULLY BY now the reader is convinced of four points about technology and culture. First, Western culture has been powerfully influenced by technology. Second, technology is neither ethically neutral nor free of values. Third, present-day industrial civilization is physically, socially, aesthetically, and spiritually unsustainable. And fourth, although most of them didn't set out per se to change human civilization, technology developers have become the primary agents of change in contemporary culture. When I make these claims I am using a broad definition of technology, incorporating "applied sciences" such as biotechnology, agricultural and life sciences, and engineering. I am also including *technique*: the application of scientific and engineering methodologies to structures and processes in the social, cultural, and spiritual realms. Technique is Jacques Ellul's term for the "autonomous social process" that amounts to a step-by-step procedural way of living. Technique is ubiquitous—standard practice—in marketing, politics, business administration, public relations, education, evangelism, and church growth. It can be seen in factories, bureaucracies, RandD teams, city planning, and other rational methods of one kind or another.[1]

I believe the distinction as the primary source of progress and change belongs more to technology than science, because it is through technology that new products and processes enter culture. Moreover, most of the products and processes we enjoy today began as engineering projects, not scientific investigations. The boundary between science and technology is not abrupt, however. "Pure" science or "basic research" seeks knowledge for the sake of knowing—such as cataloging the human genome, unraveling the origin of the cosmos, or searching for the unifying theory of matter and energy. As soon as this knowledge is utilized to solve a problem, such as curing diseases of genetic origin, creating new sources of energy,

[1] Wauzzinski, *Discerning Prometheus*, 63.

175

or managing global warming, the science gets applied via technology. Still, problem solving per se is not the purpose of science.

On the other hand, it isn't always straightforward to define engineering and technology as "problem-solving." I explained previously that science *qua* science tries to remove human values and influence from its conclusions, and as far as possible, from its procedures as well. Technology makes no such claim. In fact, as a "problem-solving" endeavor, engineering *consciously and deliberately* incorporates values of sponsor, user, and other constituencies. In this chapter I examine how and where ethics and values enter into the design process. I use engineering design to illustrate the concept because I am familiar with this field and because the process is more "proceduralized" than, say, biotechnology. That may be only because engineering is an older discipline than biotechnology and other emerging fields. But I believe that the conclusions apply to the range of technology disciplines and to *technique*.

Infusion of human values into technology is quite general: one way or another, stakeholders inject their values into the development and application of technology. All designs are sponsored either by a person or an organization, but always with an objective in mind. Most often the objective is profit, so that rapid development of the new product is necessary to beat the competition to market. Economic determinists—those who believe that the price system sets the best course for society—might dismiss this point. But those who agree that economic activity is value-laden will admit that the economic motives of the sponsors actually add another value layer to the motives of designer, user, and material suppliers. Consider the concept of *quality*. A high-quality product works as it should, lasts a long time, and is easy to maintain. For many years in the U.S. we believed that products higher in quality cost more to design, develop, and produce. Eventually, however, we have learned that higher quality and lower costs can go hand-in-hand.[2] Extra effort invested in the design process may indeed cost more up front, but the costs are more than recouped during production and use. Better designs mean not only that fewer defective units have to be scrapped during production, but fewer defective units will have to be recalled.

I reviewed numerous candidate textbooks for "Manufacturing Planning" and "Systems Design," two junior-level courses that I taught in the manufacturing engineering program. Most of the books taught the Total Quality Management (TQM) philosophy of engineering design and

[2] Ullman, *The Mechanical Design Process*, 4–5.

production. This comes as no surprise, because TQM returned the U.S. manufacturing sector to global economic competitiveness in the final two decades of the twentieth century.[3] The first principle of TQM is that the customer defines quality, and the customer's needs are *the* top priority.[4] More generally, the methodology attempts to ensure that the values of the designer, the sponsor, and the customer all are captured—or at least considered—in the design process, and reflected therefore in the design itself.[5] However, the TQM perspective does not consider unintended consequences, emergent properties, or sustainability.

Some of the textbooks that I reviewed argue that ethics can be derived from TQM. Although this claim may seem crass, it is consistent with a worldview that emphasizes economic growth, and with a strictly utilitarian ethic. In their textbook on quality, authors David Goetsch and Stanley Davis assert that "ethical behavior begins with values," "values lead to peak performance," and "ethical behavior in the long run, is the *profitable* thing to do."[6] In her textbook on the subject, Donna Summers argues that TQM draws ethics into engineering practice because it offers a systematic way for creating responsive social structures.[7] But Summers' ethics are in service to productivity and the economic growth that she believes will follow. Authors Roberta Russell and Robert Taylor note "Quality is determined by what the consumer wants and is willing to pay for." But on another page they are forced to acknowledge that "Each year Americans dispose of 350 million home and office appliances (30 million of them hair dryers) and more than 10 million PCs."[8] Norman Gaither's textbook states that some companies see environmental work as a business opportunity, but also that "the quality of a product is a customer's perception of the degree to which the product meets his or her expectations"; "quality drives the productivity machine"; and "quality management programs are viewed by many companies as productivity improvement programs."[9]

In chapter 3 I introduced the idea of emergent properties and serendipitous—that is, unanticipated but beneficial—impacts of technology. I also mused on the apparent tendency of unforeseen consequences to be

[3] In the recent past "Lean/Six Sigma" [LSS] methodology has become the buzzword, but the two quality processes are similar.

[4] Russell and Taylor, *Operations Management*, 85.

[5] Summers, *Quality*; Goetsch and Davis, *Quality Management*, chapter 4.

[6] Goetsch and Davis, *loc. cit.*, 107, 109.

[7] Summers, *loc. cit.*, 52–57.

[8] Russell and Taylor, *loc. cit.*, 77, 200.

[9] Gaither, *Production and Operations Management*, 40, 652, 658.

negative more often than serendipitous. Now we can see some procedural reasons for this tendency. First, TQM seeks lowest cost to consumer and maximum economic return to producer. The costs of physical impacts—such as exhaustion of natural resources, pollution, conversion of agricultural and riparian land, etc.—are not considered unless the consumer demands it or the producer is forced to pay for it. Second, unforeseen consequences often are social, spiritual, or aesthetic in nature. Examples include: spatial and temporal inequities, loss of privacy, damage to the commons and to cultures, dependencies that approach addiction among consumers, materialism, idolatry, and technique. Because the problem of unanticipated outcomes is outside the scope of TQM, engineers don't spend much energy thinking about them, especially the more subjective, non-technical consequences.

But even where physical impacts can be measured, various groups disagree on the economic value to assign to them. What economic value do we assign to species preservation? What is the value of the tiger salamander that is endangered by development in Sonoma County, California where I live? Developers cite the hundreds of millions of dollars of economic activity that development would bring, and ask whether saving the salamander can be worth that much. Is it fair—or even meaningful—to bargain this way? The problem for social, aesthetic, and spiritual effects is even more difficult. These impacts tend to go on undetected until they are large and irreversible, because they are not measurable in the way that physical impacts are. All too often in the design process this means that aesthetic, social, and spiritual impacts are either assigned much lower significance than economic ones, or are excluded from consideration altogether.

The TQM process is utilitarian to begin with. Taken to its logical extreme, it leads to naturalism, or technicism—the technological equivalent of scientism. Naturalism and scientism maintain that nothing exists beyond the discernable physical universe. *Methodological* naturalism maintains that because supernatural domains are inaccessible to the methods of scientific inquiry, they must remain outside the scope of rational investigation. Of course, prior to the development of appropriate detection technology, these belief systems would have required the rejection of much of modern physics as well. But as sensing technology progressed, the domain of naturalism and scientism shrank.[10] The roles of rational methodology

---

[10] This is parallel to the "god of the gaps" problem, wherein all things that science cannot explain are attributed to god. In this belief system, god is continually shrinking. In scientism, the physical world continually expands as science progresses, but nothing else exists.

in the engineering design process are discussed in the following section. A Biblical framework for technology development and use is the subject of chapter 10.

Risk, Risk Management, and the Precautionary Principle

Risk is the probability of realizing harm from a hazard. The probability of the harmful event can be characterized mathematically from the results of testing or experience, but the outcome that actually will be realized in any selected event is *not* known. For example, the likelihood that we will die in an auto accident on the way to the grocery store can be quantified statistically, but we might still decide to go if the risk is acceptable to us in lieu of the benefit. Alternatively, we might decide to travel by bus or order online. Whatever our decision, if we are acting in response to the probability distributions associated with this activity, we are doing risk management. We are making informed decisions in response to a risk assessment. Risk assessment is value-neutral, but risk management is value-based, because human judgment is involved.

Uncertainty is a lack of knowledge concerning the kind of impact, or the probability distribution of the impact variable. The theoretical possibility exists that there is no impact variable because there is no impact. However, experience has taught us that although impacts may be small, there are no zero impact technologies. Even if you receive a gift that you never use, it still had impact during its manufacture, packaging, and shipping, and it eventually will be discarded or recycled. In life, uncertainty is more of a problem than risk, because risk can be managed to some extent by purchasing insurance or hedging. One form of hedging would be to delay or cancel development of a new technology or product until a means to manage the risk is developed, or alternative approaches can be studied. But decisions of that sort are much more likely to be taken in a "boardroom" than in any sort of public action.

Risk management is especially pertinent to technologies and engineered systems that create the possibility of high-consequence accidents such as those that might occur at nuclear power plants or in chemical reactors. In 1976, an explosion at a chemical factory in Seveso, Italy, released clouds of dioxin (a toxic chemical), exposing hundreds of residents and ultimately killing thousands of animals that had consumed contaminated food. In 1978, it was discovered that the Love Canal housing development in New York State was built on a former chemical waste dump;

the development was eventually declared uninhabitable. The world's worst industrial accident to date occurred in 1985 at a Union Carbide pesticide plant in Bhopal, India. Twenty seven tons of methyl isocyanate, and a like amount of toxic reaction byproducts, escaped from a reactor, killing over 2000 people and injuring more than 200,000. Two decades later the site remains toxic and the groundwater contaminated. In 1986, a meltdown accident at the nuclear reactor near Chernobyl, Ukraine demonstrated the dangerous contamination effects of large uncontained radiological disasters, and it severely reduced public confidence in nuclear power.[11]

Other technologies have produced a social benefit upon application but are toxic to touch or taste, or require toxic materials in their manufacture. Some utilize highly scarce and irreplaceable material resources, yet are introduced into the economy without plans for recovery of these materials at the end of the product's operational life. Still other technologies—such as galvanizing, protective plating, ammunition, sacrificial anodes, fireworks, and brake pads—*require* material dissipation to accomplish their intended purpose. Some technologies are morally controversial but pursued nonetheless because, it is argued, if we don't, less altruistic societies will pursue them and either use them against us or gain a market advantage over us. The U.S. government pursued nuclear weapons because the Nazis were trying to do so. With regard to GMOs, human cloning, and stem cell research, the U.S. is competing economically with Europe, South Korea, and other technologically advanced nations. Medical and agricultural biotechnologies hold promise of great benefit to human health and welfare, but also dangers.

Technology and technique could almost certainly reduce the probability of many accidents, but of course, only those that we can foresee. As described in chapter 2, requiring breathalyzer ignition interlocks on every automobile would help manage the DUI consequence of intoxication. The cost-benefit tradeoffs of this risk management approach could be evaluated quantitatively. The benefit could be predicted statistically because intoxication is a well-studied social phenomenon, and the relative frequency of DWI is also well characterized. Risk and uncertainty would both be reduced, because all potential intoxicated drivers could be intercepted before they do damage—not just the ones that officers happened to observe driving erratically. But legislation to mandate the technology has not been enacted, because it is viewed by some as another infringement on liberties, and because the "technology" can be easily defeated.

---

[11] "Pollution," *Microsoft® Encarta® Encyclopedia 2000.*

Some safety technologies have been legislated, but only after a disaster or series of accidents. Automobile air bags were introduced to reduce the risk of fatalities in head-on collisions—the most lethal of automobile accidents. On July 11, 1984, then-Transportation Secretary Elizabeth Dole signed an order requiring all new vehicles sold in the U.S. to have driver's side air bags or automatic seat belts by 1989, and passenger-side air bags soon after. The rule required bags to deploy with enough force to protect unbelted adult male crash test dummies in a 30 mph crash.[12] The rule was implemented only after fierce debate between air bag advocates and the auto industry. Industry opposed the rule because it would add cost to vehicles—consistent with my foregoing claim that costs not forced on the producer are excluded from the TQM process. To get the industry to acquiesce, Secretary Dole promised that the law would be rescinded if states that comprise two-thirds of the population passed laws requiring seat belt use. Tying seat belt use to air bags made sense in an era in which the national seat belt use was just 13%, compared with 79% today.

According to government estimates, air bags saved 15,000 lives in the twenty-year period after the law was enacted.[13] But there was an unintended consequence. The explosive filling of the bags caused 224 deaths—many of them children and small women. The auto industry had warned that the devices deployed with such force they could harm more people than they protected. However, researchers were hampered because there were no child or female crash test dummies that might have shown the dangers of air bags to smaller passengers.[14] Automakers paid out millions to settle lawsuits, and in 1997 began installing less forceful devices. That action, combined with increased seat belt use and placement of infants in back seats, led to a rapid reduction in deaths from automobile accidents.

Technology for aviation safety provides another illustration of legislated application. In many instances, the technology was available long before the accident that prompted the legislation, but resisted by the pilots and the airlines until a crash prompted the legislation. Examples include the Traffic Alert and Collision Avoidance System (TCAS), Terminal Doppler Weather Radar and the fuel tank inerting system. TCAS was developed in the 1960s, and, if deployed earlier, it would have prevented the mid-air collision over Los Angeles on August 31st, 1986 between an Aeromexico DC-9 approaching LAX and a Piper PA-28. Eighty two

[12] Durbin, "15,000 saved by air bags," A5.
[13] Ibid.
[14] See Prologue for a personal account.

people died. Likewise, the fuel tank inerting system that would have prevented the explosion that brought down TWA flight 800 had been in existence since 1983.[15]

Decisions to delay the adoption of safety technologies are often determined by simple cost-benefit analyses. Airlines weigh the cost of installing new technologies against what they determine the cost of a crash would be. The inerting fuel tank, for example, cost less in terms of added weight than the in-flight entertainment systems that were chosen instead. An assisted recovery system (ARS) is available to detect the presence of mountains or buildings and override the pilots, potentially preventing terrorists from steering the plane into harms' way. But pilots are reluctant to give up control to automated systems.

The foregoing analysis reveals one of the more thorny aspects of technology for health and safety. Without assigning a dollar value to human life, airlines and auto manufacturers alike must hope that their gamble does not result in injuries or death that might have been prevented. If they were to assign a dollar value to human life, what figure should they choose? Anything less than millions would engender public outrage.[16] But adopting such a value would probably bankrupt the airlines, because either they would pay prohibitive sums in compensation to families of accident victims, or they would have to adopt every conceivable safety technology. Some of the technologies would increase the weight and fuel use of the airplanes, and decrease their performance.

Consider the numbers for automotive air bags. If on average eight million new vehicles are sold each year in the U.S., and the average cost for including air bags is $500 per vehicle, then over the twenty year period after the law was enacted we spent eighty billion dollars to save those 15,000 lives. That turns out to be more than $5 million per life saved. Distributive justice makes the cost hard to rationalize, because many more lives could have been saved simply by spending the same amount to provide immunizations and food aid to people in the Horn of in Africa or South Asia. Nevertheless, beginning in 2006 every new vehicle in the U.S. was required to have sensors that reduce air bag inflation if the seat occupant is small. Side air bags, which will be required by 2009, will save

---

[15] Barlow, "Crash Site Secrets."

[16] This has been done in the past, and the airlines (or their insurance companies) are paying and are still in business. Another example is the government payouts to families of 9/11/2001 victims based on quantitative life-value analyses.

additional lives; but automakers say they will add $500 to $1,000 to the cost of every vehicle.[17]

The common thread that ties these diverse examples together is perception, assessment, and management of risk. Risk management supposes that any threat can be addressed by technology and a rational methodology. Some technologies generate controversy because they pose immediate threats to human life. In the long run, however, non-sustainable cultural practices may affect human lives more than high visibility accidents involving high-consequence technologies. Risk assessment, risk management, and managing uncertainty are important parts of the engineering design process. Of course some design procedures—especially those involving low-consequence systems—are "determinate" and not probabilistic. But all fit the scope of "rational methods and procedural way of living" that Ellul calls technique.

Social scientist Jeff Howard believes that the "risk paradigm" is not capable of delivering on its promise. He is referring to the effort to reduce risk by technical means, underpinned by risk analysis.[18] Howard perceives that the risk paradigm—and the worldview of rationalism that underlies it—cannot address the social and cultural consequences of existing and proposed technologies. In part this is because risk assessment is carried out by technical experts rather than by a democratic process. As a case in point, industrial ecologists Thomas Graedel and Braden Allenby suggest that the risk assessment methodology developed for human toxins and carcinogenesis can be extended to provide a "comprehensive" domain that could include, for example, aesthetic and global damage.[19] Consider regional degradation of scenic vistas due to atmospheric pollution. To quantify the risk, experts first estimate the exposure, which in this case is the number of people for whom visibility degradation represents loss of quality of life. Then they calculate impact as the product of the dose, the probability of effect, and the exposure (the population that is exposed to the dose). Dose-response relationships have been established for such impacts as sulfur gas emissions and visibility degradation, or acid rain and carbonate stone loss. The impacts have to be multiplied by a weighting factor less than 1 to account for the fact that, to most people, aesthetic risks are not as important as carcinogenesis. According to Graedel and Allenby the actual value of the

---

[17] Durbin, *loc. cit.*

[18] Howard, "Eight tenets of precaution"; Howard, "Environmental 'nasty surprise' as a window on precautionary thinking," 19–22.

[19] Graedel and Allenby, *Industrial Ecology*, 59–60.

weighting factor would have to be determined by social consensus.[20] But as I said before, Howard argues that the risk paradigm cannot determine a social consensus.

In the case of global impacts, e.g., damage to planetary systems, the whole population of the planet is involved, but dose-response relationships and weighting factors are not at all established. Graedel and Allenby believe that weighting factors should be high for serious and irreversible impacts where the sustainability of global life support systems is at risk. They attempt to incorporate intergenerational justice by noting that since the risk of global impacts often extends for several generations, integration (summation) over time is necessary. They view this process as a complex but tractable technical problem. At this point I must agree with Howard's criticism: such exuberant technological rationalism is tantamount to *technicism*. Although they do not directly say so, one assumes Graedel and Allenby believe that cultural and spiritual impacts are also amenable to the methodology. If their rationalism were appropriate, all four impact categories of Figure 4.1 could be traded off by adopting different/multiple technical processes for each category, balancing the benefits and costs in the manner shown in Figure 6.1. But a problem with priorities would immediately arise. Many religious persons would assign a larger weighting factor to spiritual sustainability than to physical sustainability.

The problem of managing unforeseen outcomes seems a contradiction of terms. To err on the side of caution or try to pursue a less uncertain world, we can think up hypothetical risks—risks that have not been shown to exist but rather may plausibly exist. We can define a test that will reveal whether the imagined outcome can occur. If it can be made to occur during the test, and the impact can be measured, then risk methodology can accommodate the new risk. But why not apply the method to hypothetical or imagined events, and mitigate the risk *before* damage is realized? Risk analysis, the scientific approach to managing hazards, stumbles at this point because it requires data—sufficient in quantity and collected over sufficient time—upon which risk management decisions can be based. In other words, there has to be an impact before a means can be implemented to mitigate the impact. "Unknown risks" exist in the region that lies beyond scientific knowledge, and it is in this region that the *precautionary principle* (PP) (also known as the principle of precautionary action) has been designed to operate.

---

[20] Graedel and Allenby, *loc. cit.*, 60.

The "wingspread version" of the PP states:[21]

> "When an activity raises threats of harm to human health or the environment, precautionary measures should be taken even if some cause and effect relationships are not fully established. In this context the proponent of an activity, rather than the public, should bear the burden of proof. The process of applying the precautionary principle must be open, informed and democratic and must include potentially affected parties. It must involve an examination of the full range of alternatives, including no action."

Careful reading reveals four points:[22]

- people have a duty to take anticipatory action to prevent harm
- the burden of proof of harmlessness of a new technology, process, activity, or chemical lies with the proponents
- before using a new technology, process, or chemical, or starting a new activity, people have an obligation to examine a full range of alternatives including the alternative of doing nothing
- decisions that apply the PP must be open, informed, and democratic and must include affected parties

The PP operates presently in the world of pharmaceuticals. Proposed pharmaceuticals have to be demonstrably effective in double blind clinical trials. New medicines are not approved for market until they have been thoroughly tested, not only for effectiveness in the intended application but insofar as possible, tested for possible side effects. The FDA will not approve a new drug until the producer satisfies the FDA that the risks are known and manageable. For the most part, except for terminally ill patients who are often willing "guinea pigs," this is how we want it. Of course, even that amount of conservatism isn't always sufficient to prevent tragedies, as exemplified by the effect of Thalidomide on fetuses or Ephedrine on blood pressure.

In discussing the differences between the "scientific" and the "precautionary" approaches to managing risks, Howard summarizes each as follows:[23]

---

[21] *Science and Health Network Home Page*; Tickner et al., "The Precautionary Principle in Action."

[22] Ibid.; Howard, "Environmental 'nasty surprise' as a window on precautionary thinking"; Apel, "Are Risk Assessment and the Precautionary Principle Equivalent?"

[23] Howard, *loc. cit.*

In the *risk paradigm*, an individual chemical can be regulated only if reasonably well established evidence demonstrates that this specific substance is harmful.

In the *precaution paradigm*, biological relationships are assumed so complex as to be effectively indeterminate. Risk assessment itself is seen as suffused with values. Late-modern industrial culture is seen as capable of wreaking major biological devastation even before it recognizes it is doing so.

Because it is seemingly weighted so heavily in favor of the consumer, some consumer advocates would like to see the PP applied to the whole of the economy—chemicals, GMOs, consumer goods, agriculture, forestry, etc. Under this scenario, before any new technology, process, or chemical could be marketed, precautionary measures would have to be taken. These measures would be taken even if some cause-and-effect relationships were not fully established scientifically. The sole pretext would be novelty: if it is novel, it is likely to contain emergent properties and present unknown hazards, so the PP should apply. The burden of showing that a risk does *not* exist would belong to the proponents of the new technology.

But what company (or military, for that matter) can afford to wait for the results of tests for hypothetical hazards, or pay for such tests, when product demand and perhaps adversaries or foreign competitors are racing onward? If the consumer products industry—cell phones are an example—were subject to the precautionary principle in the same way that pharmaceuticals are, an entire industry would have to re-invent the way it does product development, marketing, and product retirement. No regulatory agency oversees the effectiveness of consumer electronics, but we'd probably have to create one.

Despite Graedel and Allenby's optimism (or technicism), it would be even more difficult to attempt to use risk analyses to manage the aesthetic, social, cultural, and spiritual consequences of technology, because—as I discussed above—in most cases these impacts lack measurable characteristics. Yet it is precisely these impacts upon which the issue turns. Engineers, scientists, economists, and biologists tend to favor use of the risk paradigm for making decisions about impacts. Sociologists, environmentalists, and humanists tend to support the precautionary approach. Decision-makers from the "hard" sciences tend to discount or discredit "soft" impacts because they cannot be measured. The attempt to gain a hearing for soft impacts via the precautionary paradigm seems to have failed. This is probably because the consumer is too busy consuming to realize they should have a voice in these matters. But soft impacts are just as un-measurable as ever; and the sides are aligned according to their worldviews.[24] Before finally accepting or rejecting the precaution paradigm, let's first consider an alternative formulation. Industrial chemist Andrew Apel argues that the wingspread statement should be recast as follows:[25]

> "When an activity has the potential to benefit human health or the environment, it should be implemented with due caution, knowing that some cause and effect relationships cannot be established scientifically. In this context the opponent of the activity, rather than the public, should bear the burden of proof."

But this re-statement inverts the process, in essence replacing the PP with the risk paradigm. Placing the burden of proof on the opponent will have the effect of removing their teeth. The PP simply seeks to reduce uncertainty before the product is released, as is the situation for pharmaceuticals today, but in doing so it provides the opponents with a very big trump card.

Some social scientists have called for "Intelligent Trial and Error" (ITE) as a third approach that lies between the risk paradigm and the precaution paradigm.[26] ITE calls for:

- wide, early debate about a proposed technology;
- initial precautions that err on the side of caution (e.g., reversal of burden of proof; containment of adverse impacts);
- built-in flexibility to facilitate modification when errors are detected;
- pre-manufacture testing, pilot projects, and other means of accelerating detection of errors;
- diverse, multi-partisan monitoring;
- well-funded means of interpreting results of testing and monitoring from diverse ideological and knowledge perspectives;
- gradual scale-up as learning occurs;
- strong incentives for error correction.

---

[24] Sandin et al., "Five Charges Against the Precautionary Principle," 287–99.

[25] Apel, *loc. cit.*, 3.

[26] Morone and Woodhouse, *The Demise of Nuclear Energy?*; Lindblom and Woodhouse, *The Policy-Making Process;* Howard, "Environmental 'nasty surprise' as a window on precautionary thinking."

Whether ITE provides an approach that is agreeable to producers, consumers, and critics of technology awaits further study. It is clear enough that sudden imposition of the PP on all of commerce—pharmaceuticals, chemicals, manufactured goods, and whatever—would remove U.S. industry from global competitiveness. If it could be adopted for all the producing and exporting nations, however, through the auspices of the UN or the World Trade Organization, the PP could become a real savior for the biosphere.

Engineering Ethics

Few design textbooks incorporate discussion of ethics, no doubt because design and ethics both are topics worthy of full volumes.[27] Nevertheless and to the authors' credit, a few modern engineering design textbooks do incorporate short treatments of ethics.[28] Product safety, reliability, patent and copyright infringement, and protection of proprietary information are considered to be ethical concerns that the professional engineer is most likely to face. The subject of ethics is somewhat more likely to be incorporated in texts on systems engineering than texts on component design.[29] Goetsch and Davis, for example, include an entire chapter on "Quality Management and Ethics," including an explanation of the meaning, bases, and purpose of ethical behavior.[30] Their compilation of ethical issues found in corporate-sponsored ethics training programs is shown in Table 7.1.

[27] For example, Martin and Schinzinger, *Ethics in Engineering*.

[28] Dieter, *Engineering Design*; Hyman, *Fundamentals of Engineering Design*.

[29] Blanchard et al., *Systems Engineering and Analysis*, 535–54; Gaither, *loc. cit.*; Goetsch and Davis, *loc. cit.*; Russell and Taylor, *loc. cit.*; Summers, *loc. cit.* For purposes of this study, *systems engineering* also incorporates systems analysis, production and operations management, and quality management.

[30] Goetsch and Davis, *loc. cit.*, chapter 4.

Table 7.1. Ethical issues in corporate-sponsored ethics training programs

Drug and alcohol abuse	Receiving excessive gifts and
Employee theft	entertainment
Conflicts of interest	False or misleading advertising
Quality control	Giving excessive gifts and
Misuse of proprietary information	entertainment
Abuse of expense accounts	Kickbacks
Plant closings and layoffs	Insider trading
Misuse of company property	Relations with local communities
Environmental pollution	Antitrust issues
Methods of gathering competitor's	Bribery
information	Political contributions and activities
Inaccuracy of books and records	Improper relations with government
Inaccurate time charging	representatives

The new criteria (beginning in 2000) for accrediting engineering education programs in the U.S. require engineering schools to develop in their students "an understanding of the professional responsibilities for the practice of engineering in the contemporary, global, corporate context including social, economic, legal, ethical, and environmental issues."[31] Article I of the Code of Ethics of the Institute of Electrical and Electronics Engineers (IEEE) is a mandate to "make engineering decisions consistent with the safety, health and welfare of the public, and to disclose promptly any factors that might endanger the public or the environment."[32] The American Society of Mechanical Engineers (ASME) International, of which I am a member, has a Technology and Society Division (of which I am also a member), within which there is a Committee on Ethics and Professionalism (E&P). The mission of the E&P Committee is to "motivate every engineer to actively think about and behave in a highly ethical and professional manner."[33]

But engineering practice includes some built-in contradictions. Engineering educator George Dieter notes an inherent conflict between the engineer's desire to gain a maximum profit for the employer (and thus achieve recognition and promotion) and the desire to adhere to a standard of ethics that places the public welfare ahead of corporate profit.[34] He also

[31] Criteria for Accrediting Programs in Engineering in the United States.

[32] *IEEE Code of Ethics*. Reprinted in Dieter, *loc. cit.* 68–69.

[33] Technology and Society Newsletter (ASME), 1993.

[34] Hyman, *loc. cit.*, 66.

discusses the issue of "whistle blowing" and the conditions under which engineers would be morally justified in reporting unethical behaviors of their employers.

Design for X

Engineering design has become more complex than when I first studied the subject as an undergraduate mechanical engineering student. As I recall, I took design in the first semester of my senior year, followed by a "projects" class where we built and tested the device that we had designed. The engineering program at Washington State University, Vancouver, Washington, where I recently taught, includes an introductory design course in the freshman year, Systems Design and Machine Design in the junior year, and in the senior year, a full year project called Capstone Design. Some of the topics that I studied in different courses as an undergraduate were repackaged into the expanded design program, but other topics, especially systems design, are new.

Systems design includes consideration of the whole life cycle of the product including production, packaging and shipping, use, maintenance, and retirement. The process requires defining what the product will be used for, how it will function, what its performance will be, the range of probable cost, and the user interface. The designer must consider many things that may, in the end, determine the product's success or failure.[35] The paradigm for these considerations is called "Design for X" (DFX), where X may be any or several attributes from the following list:

- Cost (life-cycle cost)
- Compliance (C)
- Manufacturability (M)
- Fabrication (F)
- Assembly (A)
- Testability (T)
- Serviceability (S)
- Reliability (R)
- Safety and Liability Prevention (SL)
- Environment (E)
- Logistics and Component Applicability (LC)

[35] Graedel and Allenby, *loc. cit.*, 186–87.

Design for environment is a rather recent addition to the DFX list, and it includes energy use and emissions during operation, maintenance, and disposal. Driven by the terrorist phenomenon, the newest "X" is *sabotage*.[36] When I studied engineering as an undergraduate, consideration of sabotage as something to design against did not enter our minds. Air transports had not been used as weapons of mass destruction and wars were fought by armies. Although one could argue that WWII Japanese fighter pilots on suicide missions were prototype terrorists, they differed in at least three major respects from the 9/11/2001 attacks. They had not commandeered peacetime aircraft, the targets were military, and the attacks were under the control of a national sovereign authority. Solutions that have emerged thus far for preventing commercial airliners from being hijacked include airport screening, plain clothed air marshals, bars on cockpit doors, and arming pilots. Future considerations include the ARS system described earlier.

Someone lacking engineering experience (but having considerable mathematical prowess) might suggest the DFX list be managed as a mathematical multivariate optimization problem. Multivariate optimization seeks to minimize the variance of a dependent parameter in the presence of variances of the independent or control variables. If that seems overly complex, consider a pressure vessel, where the control parameters might be dimensions and material strength, and the dependent parameters would be dimensions (vessel size and shape), volume, or energy stored in the vessel. The mathematical optimization method is limited to problems having quantifiable variables and a known relationship among dependent and control variables. In other words, the designer has to be able to write an equation among the variables in order to apply the method. In the "real world" design process, however, one often seems to be trading off apples against oranges. It might be even closer to the true picture to say that we must trade off apples and shoes.

The simple and unavoidable truth is this: no design can simultaneously maximize all the "X"s. Tradeoffs and compromises will have to be made. The first reason is that Design for Cost (DFC) is either an explicit design objective or it is understood that DFC is always an objective when designing products for the marketplace. Explicitly or implicitly, for consumer products DFC often is weighted more heavily than any of the other DFXs, most notably Design for Environment (DFE). The unavoidable ethical issue for design engineers is that as they wrestle to prioritize the

[36] Smith, "New "X" in DFX.

DFX objectives, *most solutions tend to add direct costs*. And if costs rise, the product's chances for success shrink. Creative breakthroughs that permit simultaneous optimization of two or more Xs are rare. However, as the list of DFXs becomes codified, guidelines for each DFX objective are becoming available. Some companies are marketing software for DFM, DFA, DFE, and perhaps others. EPA offers DFE information, and professional societies, such as Society of Manufacturing Engineers (SME), ASME, and IEEE, have produced monographs of DFX guidelines.

QFD

One of the popular methods for turning "customer wants" into design specifications is called Quality Function Deployment (QFD). One of the tools of TQM, QFD was developed in Japan in the 1980s and introduced in the U.S. in the late 1980s. It involves use of matrix diagrams that force the designer to consider correlations between variables, two by two. When painstakingly applied, QFD enables quality to be defined by the customer, designs to be driven by "needs," and a time-to-market short enough to assure economic return to whoever is paying the designer. Unlike the mathematical process of multivariate optimization, QFD is semi-quantitative. But it provides a process of optimization for the very common situation of less-measurable characteristics. Judgments and tradeoffs take the place of mathematical manipulations. Nevertheless, someone's values will influence the judgments. The process forces collection and clarification of all the necessary information needed to develop design specifications. Several distinct steps are involved. The customers (by no means limited to the end user) must be identified and their requirements determined (these aren't always well thought out beforehand). The competition must be assessed: how is the need presently satisfied? Measurable specifications must be developed to guide the design, so the designers will know if they have succeeded, or how far they have missed the objectives.

The methodology is worked out in a "House of Quality" (HOQ) as shown in Figure 7.1.

House of Quality

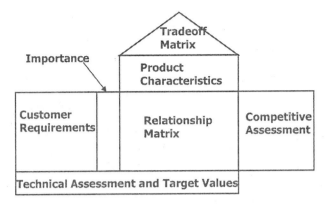

Figure 7.1. The house of quality, also known as a QFD diagram

If thoughtfully pursued, the procedure will extract or reveal key information, thereby assuring the customer's delight.[37] The figure is only a silhouette. In an actual HOQ, each "room" is a matrix containing either data or interactions where product attributes must be traded off against one another. Without going into all the details, the process can be illustrated by a simple example, a fender-like accessory called "Splashguard" for a mountain bicycle.[38] Its purpose is to keep water off the back of the rider. In this case the customers include not only the end users, but also marketing people and mechanics who might install the Splashguards. Their respective desires can be collected by various means, such as polls and interviews.

The results are grouped into categories called "functional performance," "human factors," and "interface with bike." The relative importance of each customer's set of requirements, or desires, is defined by assigning a weighting factor to each. Riders valued price and looks highest, marketing people valued performance and price highest, and mechanics valued performance and looks highest. Unspoken, but implicit, is the requirement that the new product be profitable. Competition for the new Splashguard was determined to be a raincoat and two competitors' products. Each competitive alternative is scored in the categories extracted from the three customer groups. For more sophisticated products than the Splashguard, reverse engineering may be necessary before the competition can be fully characterized.

---

[37] Ullman, *loc. cit.*, 100–101.

[38] Ullman, *loc. cit.*, 103.

Design specifications are derived from the customers' requirements. The requirements must be cast in measurable terms before the process can proceed. When this step is completed, then the designer must deal with the fact that improvements to one specification may impose a positive or negative effect on others. Values of customer, user, salesmen, and mechanics were already noted. Examination of the QFD methodology reveals several areas where the designer's values could influence the design. Such opportunities occur whenever designer preferences or judgments are invoked as they must be in prioritizing and making tradeoffs. Designer values are in operation when weighting factors are assigned. When tradeoffs are made, the designer's worldview will influence the result. The customer can help with these tradeoffs, but the customer will press for the impossible task of simultaneous optimization of all the parameters—or maybe seek a less quarrelsome supplier.

Clearly, design is not a purely objective and rational process. It is not intended to be, and it cannot be. According to TQM philosophy, a design is good only if the customers think so. The customer's desires, therefore—not the engineer's vision of what the customer should want—drive the design. Unlike the scientific method, design methodology intentionally incorporates the values of the constituencies. And just as in the risk paradigm, individual preferences and expert judgment play major roles. For example, industrial ecologist Thomas Graedel showed how design decisions can be derived from one's views on economic growth vs. conservation, the primacy of human life, the problem of global warming, etc.[39] But what if some of the designer's values conflict with the customers' values? According to some ethicists, designers' beliefs about what the customer *should* value must be excluded from the design process. Attempts to teach the customer about sustainability and an equipoise society,[40] for example, are not part of the TQM process, and actually might be construed as a violation of the implied contract between engineer and employer. On this point, it is evident that contemporary engineering practice contrasts sharply with medicine. Ethical medical doctors do not just prescribe what the patient wants, but prescribe what is *needed*, including diet and exercise.

What if the designer has information that either is not known, or has been discounted by the customer? What if the designer's information concerns hazards, scarce materials, or disposition problems? What if the designer's concerns pertain to aesthetic, social, cultural, or spiritual issues?

[39] Graedel, *Streamlined Life-Cycle Assessment.*

[40] The term "equipoise society" was coined by Bishop John Taylor of Winchester (Taylor, *Enough is Enough*). It calls for equity plus balance.

These problems are benign for the innocuous example chosen here, but it is a simple exercise to suggest a handful of technologies that are not benign. If no measurable engineering parameters for a customer's specific requirement can be identified, QFD suggests that the requirement is not well understood.[41] In these situations, the requirement must be re-addressed or perhaps omitted. But the unfortunate outcome for almost all "soft" variables is exclusion from consideration in the design process.[42]

The Splashguard example falls a little short of the noble idea of engineering work being "problem solving for the betterment of society." The only problem to be solved here is how to beat the competition with a particular consumer product. It even represents a rather watered-down version of designing to fill a market need. There is nothing to suggest that customers came up with the statement of need and brought it to the designers. The latter does occasionally occur, of course. Sometimes a customer is prepared to sponsor the solution, (e.g., the U.S. Department of Defense), but usually not (as in the occasional visit by an entrepreneur to the engineering department at a local university, seeking help with bringing a concept to reality).

Engineering and Overconsumption

The design textbook from which I extracted the Splashguard illustration does an excellent job of introducing the concepts of systems design. However, the classic ideal of engineering as a "problem solving" and "needs-meeting" profession is running into some ethical paradoxes. At least that is true if one accepts the concept of limits. In a previous chapter I introduced the engineering concept of sources and sinks, and the physical limits they invoke, i.e., source exhaustion and sink saturation. Analogous problems are emerging in the social, psychological, and spiritual arenas, as an increasing number of specialists are writing about the effects of Western lifestyles, material consumption, and cultural impacts of technology. So what problems are we engineers mostly solving these days, and what needs are we mostly meeting? Are we part of the solution, or part of the problem?

One can readily argue that clean water supply, sanitation, transportation, communication, mobility and security all qualify as needs to fill or problems to solve. And every activity that produces economic return is

---

[41] Ullman, *loc. cit.,* 115.

[42] Soft variables are not always excluded. For example, "sexiness" of a product might be included as a design objective. But a lively debate might ensue when it came time to assess the variable.

counted toward the GDP. But what about consumer goods and services, which account for two-thirds of GDP? Somebody has to purchase all the stuff we engineers design in order for the economic gains to be realized! Consumer goods require raw materials, production, packaging, advertising, shipping, operational energy and materials, maintenance, repair, and disposition. Much of this is reflected in the ever-increasing need for clean water, sanitation, transportation, communication, mobility and security that engineers are working to supply. The process is self-reinforcing.

As one of the "seven deadly sins" of the Christian faith (and also condemned by many other religions), materialism has provided subject matter for many writers over many centuries. Social Scientist Ned Woodhouse and I chose to write about overconsumption rather than materialism because we wanted to reach engineers with the message.[43] The term served our purpose better than materialism because its characteristics are more measurable and less directly invoke personal morality. But the term gains and retains meaning only in concert with the concept of limits. Overconsumption increases the rate of source exhaustion and sink filling; or in other words, increases un-sustainability.

Environmental measures that indicate overconsumption were provided in chapter 5. At the socio-cultural level, overconsumption goes hand-in-hand with the invisible metasystem that Borgmann calls the *device paradigm*.[44] But is it really an ethical issue? Materialism, for example, has never been included as a topic in engineering ethics texts, and little mention of the subject is found in the aesthetic design literature.[45] A search of the literature of technology and society reveals only sparse analyses of the association of materialism with technology per se, and *no* analyses specifically focused on the contributory role that engineers play. Perhaps not surprisingly, the proliferation of stuff results from engineers doing their jobs well—by designing and producing for low cost, plus clever design features and appealing packaging. In effect, engineering—as presently taught and practiced—enables and even abets overconsumption. The drivers are the endless quest for speed to market, quantity, and productivity. If, as futurist Edward Barlow claims, engineers have become "the enablers, the agents

[43] Swearengen and Woodhouse, "Overconsumption, Engineering Design, and Christian Ethics," 1–12; Swearengen. and Woodhouse, "Cultural Risks of Technological Innovation," 15–28; Swearengen. and Woodhouse, "Overconsumption as an Ethics Challenge for Engineering Education," 15–31.

[44] Borgmann, *Power Failure*.

[45] Whiteley, *Design for Society*; Papanek, *Design for the Real World*; Papanek, *The Green Imperative*.

of change, and de facto social experimenters in industrial society,"[46] then engineers are also agents of overconsumption.

As noted above, in the TQM context a design is good only if the customer thinks it is good.[47] The definition of "customer" was broadened to include sales and maintenance personnel, but why only these? What about the rest of culture who share the common resources—such as air, water, and land? A clash between the TQM philosophy and the existence of limits seems inevitable unless sustainability is incorporated. And I mean four-fold sustainability as I have defined it, not "economically sustainable" as some economists would interpret the term. Engineers are taught about physical limits because they must master the concept in order to do engineering calculations. But how can a design be *good* if it accelerates a collision with social limits, *regardless of the short-term delight of the customer?* More generally, how can an engineer fulfill his/her ethical obligations if the product or solution exacerbates a problem with limits? Should the engineer warn the customer? And if he/she did, wouldn't that be a little like biting the hand that feeds us (engineers)?

It seems unthinkable that engineering could be done differently; yet it is hard to deny that consumption as now practiced has come about partly because engineers have been very successful at their work. Innovative features provide a market advantage to newly introduced products, but only for a time until the competitors catch up. Hence, there is pressure on design teams to accelerate the design process and bring new products to market ever faster. Today's innovative features quickly become standard. A new "quality" level is sought, leading to further innovation. The cycle repeats. The resulting abundance of technology, unquestioned production of goods, and unlimited consumption of resources is consistent with an optimistic view of technology. Technological optimists do not see the self-reinforcing cycle as a concern. I am reminded of Oppenheimer's rationale for working on the Manhattan project "because it was technically sweet." It was much later—after the consequences were realized—that he became introspective.[48]

Overconsumption is equivalent to Richard Swenson's term "profusiuon."[49] Thus there is an implicit connection between overconsumption and the *lethality* that Swenson describes. Should engineers recognize any

---

[46] Barlow, "Creating the Future."

[47] Ullman, *loc. cit.*, 112.

[48] Long, "Robert Oppenheimer."

[49] Swenson, *Hurtling Toward Oblivion.*

special responsibility here? Even if they are implicated, do they have special insights into the risk of lethality? The answer is definitely yes with respect to weapon systems, homeland security, energy supply and possible environmental impacts. Even those who do not find this argument compelling may acknowledge a *risk* that consumption, as now practiced, *may* lead to serious and undesirable outcomes that are both tangible and intangible. Just as nuclear power reactors posed a risk of catastrophe and therefore merited precautionary design, might there be ways to protect against the "maximum credible accident" from consumption?[50] Is it an engineer's professional responsibility to contribute to such protections—perhaps especially a Christian engineer's responsibility?

Broad interpretation of the ABET criteria and other professional codes might be seen as including—or at least admitting—overconsumption as one of the abuses against which engineers might be expected to speak out. But outside of a select group of religious publications, materialism does not get much press as an ethical issue, and it receives essentially none in the engineering texts. Materialism is not on the list in Table 7.1, nor do I find emergent properties, justice, damage to cultures, and a number of other issues that were introduced in the preceding chapters. One might argue that materialism is implicit in the "environmental pollution" entry of the table, but more likely the entry refers to illicit dumping or other releases of contaminants. Overconsumption or "second degree materialism" are not likely meanings.[51] It is almost as if the profession of engineering, and the benefits that it delivers, are held in such esteem that the "dark sides" are forgiven a priori. Limited coverage of environmental ethics in general, and total omission of materialism in engineering textbooks, are hardly surprising given that the foundational thesis in modern treatments of TQM and engineering design is that *economic growth is the essence of progress.* The inevitable collision with limits is also not discussed in the same works.

Nevertheless, there is some stirring about overconsumption in the engineering community. Scholars in the fields of environmental ethics have begun dealing with some aspects of the phenomenon, especially sustainability.[52] Engineering educator Joseph Herkert argues in favor of includ-

---

[50] Morone and Woodhouse, *loc. cit.*

[51] "Second degree materialism" was also coined by Bishop Taylor. The concept emerges when we observe that the stock market responds neither to earnings nor earnings growth, but to the *rate* of earnings growth!

[52] Boylan, *Environmental Ethics*; List, *Environmental Ethics and Forestry*; Wenz, *Environmental Ethics Today*; Yaffee, *Judaism and Environmental Ethics.*

ing environmental sustainability among engineers' ethical responsibilities, and Kevin Hallinan and colleagues assert that designers have an ethical responsibility to develop products that live up to their advertising, provide durability, and efficiently utilize the diminishing supply of nonrenewable energy.[53]

Industrial Ecology and Life Cycle Design

If overconsumption is a real concern that cannot be wished away by supply-side optimism, just three possible options present themselves for avoiding mass starvation or some other calamitous future caused by energy and material shortages. These are: to reduce human population; to reduce per-capita consumption continuously and sufficiently so that total consumption declines even as population rises; or to shift to an economy that has cyclic material flows and renewable sources of energy. I foresee little possibility of achieving either of the first two options without catastrophes such as war or pestilence. But a promising approach for moving toward sustainable civilization—and simultaneously addressing overconsumption during the engineering design process—comes from the nascent field of industrial ecology (IE). Practitioners of IE view themselves as engaged in the "engineering of sustainability."

The first goal of IE is to minimize anthropogenic perturbations to natural cycles, especially cycles of the key elements (carbon, nitrogen, phosphorous, and sulfur) of biological life. A corollary goal is to avoid creating new cycles by introducing substances that are not found in nature and thus, because they are unfamiliar, are not readily assimilated or broken down by nature. Most often this process translates to toxicity. The second goal is to move away from the present throughput of raw materials in the economic system. Only cyclic flows of materials—sometimes called *biomimicry* because it mimics what the biota does—would be entirely sustainable. Thus the amount of extraction, e.g., mining, of raw materials from the earth's crust provides a measure of sustainability. The less mining, the closer we approach sustainability. In a near-sustainable economy, raw materials would be extracted only to replace the small amounts of material lost to unavoidably dissipative uses.

IE offers designers a methodology for assessing overall impacts of alternative designs that are under consideration. First we must recognize that every product in the economy is, in final analysis, a result of extract-

---

[53] Hallinan et al., "Balancing Technical and Social Issues," 4–14; Herkert, "Sustainable Development, Engineering and Multinational Corporations," 333–46.

ing raw materials from nature and transforming them by application of energy into tools and machines for human empowerment or pleasure. The approach is based upon the idea of establishing "budgets" for materials and energy. This entails measuring the energy and resources *in to*, and products, energy, and wastes, *out of* each stage in the life of the product. Entities with value and entities that are potential liabilities are all included.[54] In theory, zero discharge means greater efficiency and profitability at the same time. Not only would no energy or raw materials be wasted, but no pollutants would be emitted. But even more fundamental question should be asked. Can the "need" be met by a service instead of a product? If not, and the product "must" be developed and produced, can a product-take-back system be implemented to reduce waste and facilitate recovery of elements that are potentially in limited supply? Better yet, can the need be met by upgrading an existing product rather than by introducing an entirely new one?

The principles can be introduced into the design process via DFX—especially Design for Environment, Maintainability, Disassembly, and Recycle. Product longevity should be maximized through design for durability and serviceability. Modular designs that permit component or subsystem upgrades would become the norm. Consistent with the second law of thermodynamics, any material usage is dissipative to some degree—a result of oxidation and corrosion, friction and wear, and losses during extraction and production. Environmentally sensitive designers will minimize such losses through judicious materials selection and will especially seek to avoid intentionally dissipative uses of scarce elements. But when IE principles drive the process, DFE will also require designing for retention of embedded utility at the end of the functional life of the product.

The concepts can be clarified by considering Figure 7.2, and the life stages of the materials that go into a product. As raw materials are extracted, refined, formed into shapes, and incorporated into products, the progressively rising price (i.e., added value) in each stage reflects the energy and labor that it took to get the product to its present stage of utility. Most of the impacts—whether environmental, social, spiritual, or aesthetic—are concentrated in the extraction, use, and waste stages.

---

[54] Graedel and Allenby, *loc. cit.*, 109.

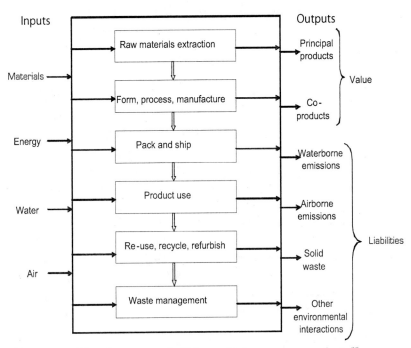

Figure 7.2 The elements of a life-cycle inventory analysis[55]

The "Potential liabilities" of figure 7.2 include not only liquid, solid, and gaseous wastes created during extraction, manufacture, packing and shipping, use and disposition; but also secondary wastes, such as by-products, packaging materials and shipping, solvents and lubricants during manufacture and use, and dissipative losses during use or disposition. Discarding the product after end-of-life not only fills up Earth's sinks, it also wastes all the "embedded" energy and effort required to transform minerals in the earth's crust into useful products.[56] To preserve the embedded energy and utility, products or components should be refurbished and re-applied in the same function that they were designed for. A product should not be labeled "green" until its entire life cycle is green. For example, pollution prevention in the manufacture of automobiles (i.e., a "green factory") is a desirable objective, but does not begin to address the major environmental impacts of the automobile, which occur during raw materials extraction, vehicle use, and eventual disposal.

---

[55] Graedel and Allenby, *loc. cit.*, 110.

[56] Graedel and Allenby, *loc. cit.*, chapter 19.

Accomplishing design objectives with less material, replacing scarce materials with substitutes that are plentiful, and making products last longer is called *dematerialization.*[57] Dematerialization provides a second measure of progress toward the goal of reducing raw material use and moving toward sustainability. It involves achieving design objectives with less material, replacing scarce materials with plentiful materials, and making products last longer. In DFX parlance, this could translate to design for durability, serviceability, disassembly, and recyclability. Another way of looking at this is to think in terms of increased productivity per unit of material used in the product, i.e., increasing the material dwell time in the economy. Dwell time can be increased by recycling materials at the highest possible level, i.e., refurbish and re-use should take precedence over recovering materials as scrap.

The pulp and paper industry has made progress that other industries might emulate. Of course the industry is based upon a renewable resource—wood chips. But increasingly these chips are being obtained from fast-growing cultivated trees like hybrid poplar. Moreover, the hybrids are of lighter color than pine and fir and thus require less bleach to produce "bond" paper. High quality letter paper is produced from new wood; lower-quality print paper includes some recycled letter paper. Brown wrapping paper, corrugated boxes, and newsprint contain progressively greater amounts of recycled paper; and at the end of the line—toilet paper. In each recycle the wood fibers get chopped shorter and the quality of the paper degrades, but, in the end, the fibers are short enough to compost effectively. At the same time, chlorine bleach is gradually being phased out, as is the foul-smelling sulfite digestion process.

The impact assessment phase of the life cycle analysis in IE actually seeks to include social and political impacts. Principal concerns identified thus far include regulatory and legislative status, impacts on labor and community, inequities, and "significant externalities."[58] Externalities are attributes that are outside the price system; they have not been assigned an explicit economic value. As an example of external social impact, consider that the time value of money in the current price system encourages exploitation of raw material deposits rather than long-term preservation for future generations. In the nearer term, after ore bodies are exhausted, mining towns become ghost towns—accompanied by major damage to families, communities, and local economies. A major thesis of this book is

[57] Bernardini and Galli, "Dematerialization," 431–48.
[58] Graedel and Allenby, *loc. cit.*

that social, aesthetic, and spiritual consequences of technology and its uses must be included in impact assessments, irrespective of the fact that these impacts are usually less tangible than physical impacts. Depersonalization, materialism, dependency, and distraction are some of the major ones, but a host of potential socio-cultural risks are exacerbated by the rapid technological innovation that drives consumer society. Inadequate time for learning gradually from experience is a consequence, as is a tendency to try solving problems by technological fixes rather than by a judicious balance of methods. Social and spiritual impacts such as these are beginning to receive acknowledgement from the sociological community, but have not yet been discussed in the IE literature. Nor, with a few exceptions, have they been discussed by the Church.

Closure

The premise of this chapter is that technology is neither ethically neutral nor free of values. I have shown how personal and group values enter into the engineering design process. Technology is "done" by human agents who have agendas, few of which are as utopian as the aphorism that engineering is "problem solving for the betterment of human lives." The fact that engineering and technology have done so much good for humans is attributable as much to serendipity, the hand of God, and the benefits of the market economy and the capitalist system as it is to the benevolence of engineering as a discipline. Moreover, engineering successes also have created a state of overconsumption that is not physically, socially, or spiritually sustainable.

Most professionals acknowledge that they have responsibilities to society that go beyond competent behavior in performing procedures for clients. That is to say, the public good sometimes requires that professionals take a broad view of what the world needs from them, as when physicians worry about poverty and hunger rather than merely trying to cure sick people who come into their offices. Are environmental, social, aesthetic, and spiritual impacts of technology an engineering problem? Or are they a social problem, a problem with corporate culture, or a spiritual problem? I would affirm every one of these. The problem is the fault of suppliers, corporate executives, designers, and consumers. The root cause is greed. Like malnutrition, overconsumption is an example of an ethical issue that cannot be solved solely by improvements in individual engineers' moral reasoning. A realistic understanding of the ethical obligations of engineers must take into account the web of incentives and constraints within which they work.[59]

Professional organizations are well positioned to publicize the need and lobby for improvements. Professionals in the computer and consumer electronics industries could develop guidelines for handling and disposing of obsolete products. Although businesses are beginning to dismantle and recycle old PCs, markets for used materials need government stimulation and oversight to be successful. Professional associations should address the issue; and contemporary computers must be designed for recycling. Some computer company executives gradually will yield to pressure, and design employees can help bring the pressure. IBM's introduction of a program in November 2000, in which the company will buy obsolete computers (and not just those made by IBM) for recycling, seemed to open the possibility of life cycle design. Unfortunately, in 2004 IBM sold its personal computer division to a Chinese company. The Chinese record on recycling is fraught with human and environmental abuses.

Whatever they can or cannot do at work, engineers and other designers also have lives as consumers and as citizens, and there may be ways to exert influence in those spheres. As consumers, design professionals purchase homes, and fill them with stuff. They might be able to exert influence disproportionate to their numbers if they were to come to see consumption as an avenue for influencing social change. Since many people still do not know about re-use/recycling opportunities and others lack the motivation to take advantage of them, proactive engineers could be key for the publicity and success of these programs by using them when they are functioning as consumers.

Industrial Ecology offers the designer a methodology for dealing with overall impacts of a product, process, or facility. The discipline seeks to make consumption sustainable by re-engineering the way industry and the consumer use materials and energy. Absolute sustainability remains an idealization to date because we depend upon non-renewable energy, and we use scarce materials in dissipative ways. However, IE focuses on reducing impact rather than consumption.[60] Notwithstanding my support for the principles of IE, I have grave doubts that sustainability can be achieved without reduction of per-capita and total consumption, especially by Western economies. If "impact" in IE were to include social, cultural, aesthetic, and spiritual aspects as I have described them, overcon-

[59] Allenby, *Industrial Ecology*.

[60] Lave et al., "Recycling Decisions and Green Design," 18A–24A; Graedel and Allenby, *loc. cit.*

sumption and materialism would necessarily be incorporated in the engineering design process. I believe such a result can be achieved without a reduction in our standard of living. But standard of living must be assessed in broader terms than the materialistic measures of per-capita income or consumption.

Chapter 8

The Spirit of the Age

"PROVIDENTIAL FORCES" enabled U.S. culture to evolve to its current configuration. Natural resources were favorable for development: mid-latitude climate, fuel and non-fuel minerals, domesticated livestock,[1] navigable waters, deep water ports on three seacoasts, forests, and rich agricultural lands. Political and religious freedom enabled the populace to exploit these resources for economic gain. But the *ethos* of the people (at least of the group in power) or the prevailing *myth* were as important as any of these factors. The way we viewed nature, constrained government, used market economics, rewarded enterprise, and understood our destiny—these were the sorts of concepts that unleashed human initiative. Some very fundamental philosophical and theological questions were embedded in the myth. For example, was the bountiful land a gift from God? If it was, then to whom was the gift directed—Native Americans, European settlers, African slaves? What was our responsibility toward the land? How important was the notion of continuous progress? Are science and technology the chief instruments of progress? Is the mission of science mere *knowledge*, or is it Godly wisdom? Is human welfare the domain of technology rather than science? Must science and technology be naturalistic endeavors, or is a supernatural dimension allowed?

During the Middle Ages, answers to questions like these automatically considered God's purposes for His creation. But the myth of a divinely ordained, purposeful creation began to fade during the Enlightenment. Today such questions are seldom asked, because a particular worldview has come to dominate Western culture. Contemporary Western attitudes toward technology have Christian origins, historian David Noble argues, but they have been supplemented by Enlightenment thinking.[2] According to sociologist and theologian William Stahl, the modern world rejected

[1] Most of the domesticated herbivores originated in the Middle East. They were brought to North America by European immigrants.
[2] Noble, *The Religion of Technology*.

the earlier myth but created a new one based on science and technology. He says "Today, faith in the universal efficacy of technology is the one faith that pervades Western culture at all levels."[3] Philosopher George Grant calls technology "the essence of modern society" and "the ontology of the age"[4]; and professor or religion David Hopper believes the ability of technology to offer and inculcate another definition of what it means to be human is today's chief challenge to theology.[5] Dutch Christian economist Bob Goudzwaard dubbed Western culture idolatrous, as did the American culture critic Neil Postman.[6]

All of these writers refer to "Western" culture in the singular. Postman, however, argued that despite similarities in appearance, European and American cultures are driven by very different ideologies. "The success of twentieth-century technology in providing Americans with convenience, comfort, speed, hygiene, and abundance, was so obvious and promising," he wrote, "there seemed no reason to look for any other sources of fulfillment or creativity or purpose."[7] Postman believed that this historic idealism led to the present state of U.S. culture and our religious devotion to technology. He invoked the term *technopoly* to distinguish U.S. culture from its European cousins. Postman made an important point: North Americans and Europeans do differ in their approach to land use, environmental protections, and conservation, and for that matter, to religion. But he should have included geographic factors in his list of contributing causes.

Most of the works cited above were produced by practitioners in the humanities, especially philosophy and social science. Technologists have much to learn from them; things that the technological community either hasn't discerned or has discounted. Perhaps the reason is that technologists are likely to be optimistic about their profession. Or perhaps they are simply too involved in their work to pause and reflect. (After all, the terms "geek" and "nerd" have some operational basis.) For reasons like these, philosopher Carl Mitcham prefers philosophies of technology written by the humanities community because, he says, humanities is by definition *broader* than engineering.[8] Postman suggests that natural scientists *cannot*

---

[3] Stahl, *God and the Chip*, 13.

[4] Grant, *Technology and Empire*; Grant, *Lament for a Nation*, 133.

[5] Hopper, *Technology, Theology, and the Idea of Progress*, 112.

[6] Goudzwaard, *Idols of Our Time*; Postman, *Technopoly*.

[7] Postman, *loc. cit.*, 52–54.

[8] Mitcham, *Thinking Through Technology*, 89*ff.*

offer moral judgments regarding their work, because to do so would compromise the objectivity of science. "The very principles of natural science, with its requirement of an objective stance toward what is studied," he wrote, "compel the natural scientist to abjure in his or her role as a scientist such moral judgments or claims."[9] I think it is amazing how Postman can absolve science of responsibility while decrying its impacts. He fails to recognize that the scientific enterprise is conducted by humans. But his absolution definitely does not apply to technology which, as I described in chapters 4 and chapter 7, *intentionally* incorporates human values.

In 1985, after searching through two centuries of philosophical literature, Langdon Winner concluded that a philosophy of technology had not been written.[10] The bibliography in the philosophy of technology at the time included well over a thousand books and articles in several languages, but Winner believed that little was of enduring substance. He offered two possible explanations for this state of affairs. First, "despite the fact that nobody would deny its importance to an adequate understanding of the human condition, technology has never joined epistemology, metaphysics, esthetics, law, science, and politics as a fully respectable topic for philosophical inquiry." Second, "engineers have shown little interest in filling this void . . . [they] appear unaware of any philosophical questions their work might entail."[11] A decade later, Mitcham reached a similar conclusion.[12] But in noting that science concerns itself with what *is* and technology with what *is to be*, Mitcham was saying that the need for a philosophy of technology is more poignant that a philosophy of science.[13]

A satisfactory philosophy of technology must raise the fundamental questions about technology and provide the founding principles of the endeavor, according to Winner. He believes the fundamental *question* is: "as we make things work, what kind of world are we making?" whether the founding principles that guide the endeavor permit practitioners to assess their role in shaping society.[14] To Winner's fundamental question I have added: "is it four-fold sustainable?" and we shall search the scriptures for the founding principles. But we needn't start from scratch. The works

---

[9] Postman, *loc. cit.*, 160.

[10] Winner, *The Whale and the Reactor*, 4.

[11] Ibid.

[12] Mitcham, *loc. cit.*, 10, 94, 106, 112, 142, 154.

[13] Mitcham, *loc. cit.*, 249.

[14] Winner, *loc. cit.*, 17.

of Monsma, Schuurman, Stahl, Hopper, Borgmann, and Wauzzinski[15] indicate to me that a philosophy of technology is beginning to take shape. Palmer and Eastern Seminaries are developing a "theology of informational technology" to better equip Pastors and church leaders to serve as "messengers of the Gospel in a technologically obsessed, fast-paced, ever-changing world."[16] All these works by Christian philosophers and/or theologians might be properly termed theological philosophies of technology. Meanwhile, the secular community is still searching for a durable secular basis for technology and culture.

Sampling Attitudes about Technology

In late 2001, the Environmental Communications Commission (ECC) of ASME International randomly invited 2000 members (1000 inside and 1000 outside the U.S.) to take part in an online survey designed to reveal people's perception of the connection between the engineering profession and the environment. The basis for the survey was explained in the following terms:[17]

> "The engineering profession is continually involved in a massive redesign of the environments that we live in. Our homes, our work places, the stores we shop in, the way we get from one place to another . . . all that is the 'stuff' of engineering. Of course, there is also the natural environment to account for. The air we breathe, the water we drink, the unspoiled countryside that we expect to be there for recreation. That too can be influenced by modern society and, as engineers change the face of the modern world, there is a concern that they may also be effecting undesirable changes in the natural environment."

Over 90% of the respondents characterized the effects of engineering on society as positive, and more than 85% believed that engineers fulfilled their responsibility to ensure public safety. The numbers for environmental protection were not quite as optimistic: only 72% believed that engineers were fulfilling their responsibility to safeguard the environment, and 66% personally felt either highly- or well-informed about the effects of engineering on the environment. However, only 9% of the engineers who responded believed the average person was either "highly able" or

---

[15] Monsma, *loc. cit.*; Hopper, *Technology, Theology, and the Idea of Progress*; Borgmann, *Power Failure*; Wauzzinski, *Discerning Prometheus*.

[16] Rodin et al., "A theology of Technology."

[17] Edelson, "EED Member Survey results," 3.

"able" to make decisions on technological matters. Looking at the results, survey administrator Martin Edelson remarked "To achieve the ECC goal of fostering dialog between engineers and the public it seems that, first, engineers must be convinced that the public can actually be engaged in such discussions." This result portends problems for social scientists' desire for a more democratic process of technological decision-making.[18]

For the past several years, the American Scientific Affiliation has distributed a questionnaire at *Congress 200X,* a winter gathering in Boston of several thousand Christians from all over New England (in 200X, "*X*" = 1, 2, 3, . . . , corresponding to the particular conference year). The questionnaire for Congress 2003 pertained to environmental stewardship. One of the questions asked how Christians should view the development of genetically modified (GM) foods. Twenty responders thought GM foods had great potential for benefiting humankind; fifteen felt that it was okay to deploy them as crops and foods as long as they were clearly labeled; seventeen said that countries should ban them because of the potential harm to people and the environment; and eight didn't know what to answer. Next was the familiar question about what would Jesus drive if he were in the U.S. today. There were many responses—"a pick-up truck" garnered the most votes, but the largest group (37 votes) said that it was "a silly question."[19]

Additional questions asked what the most risky activity is (among six choices) for human health, and what did the survey takers think of the Endangered Species Act. Most thought smoking tobacco was the most risky behavior, while being overweight and consuming alcoholic beverages were second and third respectively. These perceived risks were followed by driving an automobile, air pollution from power plants, and living near a nuclear power plant. Thirty-four respondents thought the Endangered Species Act provides important protection for species that are part of God's creation, while 19 thought it should be revised because it goes too far and infringes on property rights. Two thought it should be abolished.[20] This survey provides interesting insights into evangelical Christian attitudes about the environment, but unfortunately no demographic information about the respondents was obtained. Were there differences depending upon occupation, level of education, male vs. female?

[18] Sarewitz, *Frontiers of Illusion*; Howard, "Eight tenets of precaution"; Howard, "Environmental 'nasty surprise' as a window on precautionary thinking," 19–22; Morone and Woodhouse, *Averting Catastrophe.*

[19] Munro, "The Executive Director's Corner," 2.

[20] Ibid.

I have conducted my own survey, with the goal of discerning evangelical Christian views of technology. I distributed the questionnaires at church seminars, classes, and workshops; and—for purposes of comparison—also in college classes. My sampling is not statistically rigorous because the populations that I desire to characterize are not as large and not as diverse as the U.S. Population as a whole. Most of the respondents were white, college educated, and urban (as opposed to rural)—primarily because they are the most readily accessible to me at present. The most meaningful outcomes of the sampling are first, a take on the urban/suburban evangelical perspective on technology; and second, gender, occupation, and age group differences.

The results are compiled in Table 8.1, entered as the percent of the affirmative vote relative to the number of respondents in each category (column). Question 1 asked the responder's profession, age, religious tradition, and sex. Statement 2 asked for a ranking of the top five influences on Western culture from the following list:

- literature
- philosophy
- art
- technology
- democracy
- weapons
- music
- language
- religion
- capitalism

All the sectors agreed that our society is technological (statements 2, 7, 8). The majority appears to believe that technology is morally neutral and only the user—by selecting the use—can create a moral situation (Statement 3). Technical students are optimistic about the beneficence of their chosen profession. Liberal arts students, on the other hand, are not so sure that the benefits of technology outweigh the risks (statement 5) or that more technology is the answer to the negative impacts of technology. I interpret this to mean that—while they readily embrace new technologies (especially consumer electronics)—they are suspicious of "big science" such as nuclear energy, genetically modified organisms GMOs, and industrial research.

Table 8.1. Attitudes toward technology, by sector and percentage

#	Question	Non-technical Students	Technical Students	Male Evangelicals	Female Evangelicals	Silicon Valley Evangelicals
2	Technology in top five in influence on Western culture	82	100	76	82	70
3	Technology is neutral; only the user creates morality	70	100	89	80	81
4	Technology should be pursued wherever it leads	26	80	42	18	40
5	Benefits outweigh risks on the whole	45	90	84	71	92
6	Technology can remedy unanticipated consequences	43	80	55	55	44
7	Technology has enabled Earth to support larger population	82	100	93	86	96
8	I can opt out whenever I choose	18	20	18	18	11
9	Nature's value is as a source of material and energy	36	30	67	57	63
10a	The future looks brighter Thanks to technology	34	100	62	43	74
10b	The future looks darker Because of technology	21	0	13	18	7
11	There is an area of my life untouched by technology	70	20	67	84	30
	Number of respondents	46	10	55	49	27

More often than not their apprehensions revolve around real and potential environmental impacts. Except for statement 11, responses among male evangelicals living in Silicon Valley, California, the "birthplace of the high-tech industry," were the same as their peers everywhere.

Some interesting differences also appear. Among evangelicals, females are much less optimistic about technology than males. Statement 4 concerns the technological imperative, and number 6 refers to "the technological fix." Most responses to these two questions were guarded; only the technical students voted affirmatively. The response to statement 9 indicates that the "creation care" ethic is not widely embraced by evangelicals. However, technical students rejected the utilitarian view of nature. This result suggests that young engineers (at least the ones that I taught) are bringing an environmental ethic into the profession.

As many as a quarter of evangelicals declined to fill out the questionnaire. They wrote or stated that technology is not only beneficial and morally neutral, but the topic does not represent a social problem worth discussing—certainly not a biblical one. Of those that responded, evangelical Christians tend to view technology with favor, males more than females. Some of the responses were pessimistic, more so among liberal arts students and female evangelicals. Fewer than half of the respondents thought that the future looks brighter because of technology, and a significant fraction thought it looks darker (statement 10). Nature does not derive its value from what it *does*—i.e., supplying raw materials. It has value because of what it *is*: God's magnificent creation.

Statement 11 generated several clever responses, mostly by the liberal arts students (Are they less reverent?). Some of them argued that at least one area of life remains untouched by technology. Here are some of the best answers:

- Love
- "Sleep, although my dreams contain images of technology at times and the shrill sound of my alarm clock awakens me in the morning"
- "I hate technology so much that I am moving to a farm in Oklahoma"
- "There is no area; we are slaves to technology"
- "Final death; the moment in which the brain ceases to function"
- Sex
- "My relations with my daughter"
- "My relations with my cat and bird"

- "My breasts"
- "I cannot think of one aspect of my life that has *not* been influenced by technology—unfortunately"

Other responses included: faith, beliefs, philosophy, spirituality, prayer, emotions, feelings, affections for others, family, reading, reading the paper to relax, my garden, understanding of right and wrong, thought processes, and hobbies. I would debate with those who wrote that their faith was unaffected by technology. They must have overlooked the influence of the Reformation on the Christian faith. If they had considered it, they would have acknowledged that the new technology of the printing press enabled Luther to publish his ninety-five theses.

The Roots of Technological Worldviews

Where did the attitudes revealed in the surveys come from? Are they original with the respondents of my survey, or are they culturally determined? In other words, do they mirror norms of the larger culture? Each response reflects a *worldview*: an interpretive framework or set of commitments by which we manage reality and pursue a place within it. Whether or not we are aware of them, our worldviews motivate our actions and govern our outlook and choices.[21]

"Christians are all too little aware of the obvious connection between the gigantic scientific-technological development and the process of secularization," says Egbert Schuurman [and] "When people fail to take into account the history of ideas in the background of current developments, they quickly look for an easy solution to the problems with which they are confronted. Without taking account of the causes, they opt for a shallow and shortsighted solution. By paying attention to the historical-intellectual background, we have a better chance of meeting the challenges of our time."[22] Once we know what technicism is, for example, we will recognize it frequently in everyday life. More often than not, however, personal worldviews remain unexamined; at least they are not often explored as part of an ongoing process of personal growth. This indictment applies to evangelical Christians as much as it does to agnostics, because the issue of technology and culture is largely absent from the list of important things Christians are expected to master.

[21] Conway, *Choices at the Heart of Technology*, 27.

[22] Schuurman, *Faith and Hope in Technology*, 72.

David Naugle—a professor of philosophy at Dallas Baptist Seminary—examined the development of the worldview concept from an historical perspective. His goal was "to concentrate on how worldview has been treated by a variety of thinkers, including Christians, in the course of its theoretical development."[23] Some historians of science have traced the worldview that underlies modern science and technology to certain features of ancient Greek thought. The first feature was (and is) that the natural universe obeys laws, and is therefore amenable to rational explanation. Thus it became possible to develop a body of knowledge about nature. The second feature was a method of deductive reasoning. Operating on these two concepts, the ancient Greeks produced some remarkable developments in philosophy, logic, and mathematics—and these in turn led to significant advances in astronomy, physics, and biology. Each of these advances then provided essential tools for the eventual development of modern science.[24]

Nevertheless "the imperative force of progress" did not flourish in the grand Greek, Roman, and Egyptian civilizations themselves, because most events were assumed to lie beyond the control of humans. The operative worldview was *fate*—which inhibited any view of progress and promoted resignation instead of revolution, reformation, or betterment. For understanding nature's mysteries, the principal tool was reason; observation and deduction were not considered essential. Consequently, there was no systematic effort to manipulate nature.[25] Moreover, the concepts of democracy and pursuit of happiness did not apply to all people, especially not the slaves or artisans who did much of the work. "Work and the development of the natural world were not viewed in a positive light by the Greeks because this world was shunned for the ethereal world of rational philosophical norms. . . . Mechanical arts like engineering were called 'adulterine arts' and people of inferior heritage occupied themselves with these arts."[26] In effect, the ancient Greeks believed that the world should be *understood*, but there was no reason to try to *change* it. This belief strongly influenced Western culture up to the Renaissance.

The Hebrew-Christian tradition contributed the notion of a progressive, or unfolding, reality. A progressive view means that new possibilities can be realized, and thus improvement is possible. Christianity,

---

[23] Naugle, *Worldview.*

[24] Jeeves, *The Scientific Enterprise and Christian Faith,* 13.

[25] Jeeves, *loc. cit.,* 11; Wauzzinski, *loc. cit.,* 38.

[26] Sambursky, *The Physical World of the Greeks,* 230. Quoted in Jeeves, *loc. cit.,* 12.

in particular, incorporates a "linear" view of history, at least in the sense that history had a beginning (at the Creation) and will have an end (the Consummation). Moreover, Christianity includes a notion of *progress,* because God is reconciling all things to Himself during this present age of *redemption;* the reconciliation will be complete at the end of history, i.e., at consummation. During the age of redemption, Christians (redeemed persons) can grow to become more like Christ and practice His virtues, and in this belief there lies a notion of possible improvement. Judeo-Christian scriptures also contain the concept of the "culture mandate," embodied in the creation narrative and amplified elsewhere in the Old Testament. Wauzzinski identifies three elements of the culture mandate:[27]

1. Creation—as God's handiwork—is intrinsically valuable

2. development is a necessary and essentially good part of human activity, *as long as . . .*

3. "subduing" also entails "keeping or maintaining and preserving the creation"

The cultural mandate is at odds with the Greek concept of a natural realm that is unresponsive to human initiative. But Christian sociologist Steven Monsma pointed out another important aspect. He said: "The linear view of history and the fulfillment of the cultural mandate associated with it may not be represented simply by a straight line. For beginning and end, and everything in between, are dependent upon and oriented toward God as the Creator of all things. Hence the movement of history and the fulfillment of the cultural mandate not only have a horizontal dimension but also a vertical, transcendent one."[28]

Another issue must be considered as we ponder the roots of Western attitudes about technology. David Noble asserts that not only historically, but continuing into the present, technology has been conducted as a religious endeavor. Technology and religion are intimately connected especially in the U.S., he argues, because here an unrivaled popular enchantment with technological advance is matched by an equally earnest popular expectation of Jesus Christ's return. Often both positions are held simultaneously, including by technologists.[29] In Noble's words:[30]

---

[27] Wauzzinski, *loc. cit.,* 34–35.

[28] Monsma, *loc. cit.,* 42–43.

[29] Noble, *loc. cit.,* 5.

[30] Noble, *loc. cit.,* 9.

"The dynamic of Western technology, the defining mark of modernity . . . is actually medieval in origin and spirit. A pattern of coherent, continuous, and cumulative advance in the useful arts, as opposed to a slow, haphazard accumulation of isolated specific inventions, emerged uniquely in the European Middle Ages. This reflected a profound cultural shift, a departure form both classical and orthodox Christian belief, whereby humble activities heretofore disdained because of their association with manual labor, servitude, women, or worldliness came to be dignified and deemed worthy of elite attention and devotion. And this shift in the social status of the arts, if not the artisans, was rooted in an ideological innovation that invested the arts with significance beyond mere utility. Technology has come to be identified with transcendence, implicated as never before in the Christian idea of redemption. The worldly means of survival were now redirected toward the other-worldly end of salvation."

Noble's observation seems borne out by the results of my simple survey.

Augustine of Hippo believed that technology existed—became necessary—only for mankind in the fallen state. Prior to the fall from grace, he reasoned, mankind would have had no need for technology. In this view, technology has nothing to do with transcendence. In the early Middle Ages, however, the relationship between technology and transcendence began to change.[31] Illustrations on calendars circa 830 began to indicate that men regarded advancing technology as an aspect of Christian virtue.[32] The Christian philosopher Erigena argued that the useful arts were part of mankind's original endowment, his *imago dei*, rather than a necessary endeavor of his fallen state. Noble believes that Erigena's concept provided a turning point in the ideological history of technology, because it implicitly taught that mankind's pre-fall powers could be at least partially recovered.[33] Other philosophers and theologians expanded this concept and ultimately it became part of orthodoxy.[34] Thus a major shift ensued at the end of the first millennium, from the mechanical arts understood as efforts to *relieve* the effects of the fall, to the mechanical arts as efforts to *recover* some of the pristine conditions of the original creation. In the thirteenth century, Michael Scot held that "the primary purpose of the hu-

[31] Noble, *loc. cit.*, 12.

[32] White, *Cultural Climates and Technological Advance in the Middle Ages*, 172–73. Quoted in Noble, *loc. cit.*, 13.

[33] Noble, *loc. cit.*, 16–17.

[34] Theologian Francis Schaeffer upgraded the theme in his work, replacing Erigena's "partial recovery" with "substantial healing" (Schaeffer, *Pollution and the Death of Man*).

man sciences is to restore fallen man to his "prelapsarian position"; and the mechanical arts began to provide assistance to the spiritual life.[35]

The term *Middle Ages* was invented during the Renaissance, a period of cultural and literary change in the fourteenth, fifteenth, and sixteenth centuries. It was not meant as a compliment. During the Renaissance, people thought that their own age and the time of ancient Greece and Rome were advanced and civilized. They called the period between themselves and the ancient world "the Middle Age."[36] During the Middle Ages, European society was permeated by Christian presuppositions concerning humankind, earthly life, and the hereafter. The development of technology began to provide some assurance that mankind was indeed on the road to recovery. Accordingly, technological invention was duly incorporated into biblical commentary and Christian history.[37]

It could be argued that the invention of the printing press started the Renaissance in Europe, *circa* 1300, because now ignorance could be addressed by technology.[38] Following the lead of Roger Bacon a good deal of theological reflection of the period focused upon the fall from grace, in the firm belief that the effects could be reversed. God had already granted to fallen man the means to recover his rightful reign. "Contemporary theology thus provided the moral underpinnings for that ascendancy of man over nature which had by the early modern period become the accepted goal of human endeavor."[39] Learned men of the age took seriously the injunction of the prophet Daniel that, as the end approaches, knowledge and understanding will increase; the wise will understand, while the wicked will not. They also took seriously the need to prepare for the glorious days ahead. Their efforts to gain and encourage scientific knowledge, build a new educational system, transform political society, were all part of their millenarian reading of events.[40]

In Noble's interpretation of history, this millenarian milieu decisively and indelibly shaped the Western conception of technology.[41] As the poet Milton insisted, nature would not merely become known to man but "would surrender to man as its appointed governor, and his rule would

---

[35] Noble, *loc. cit.,* 20.

[36] Rosensweig, "The Middle Ages."

[37] Noble, *loc. cit.,* 21.

[38] Wauzzinski, *loc. cit.,* 41.

[39] Thomas, *Man and the Natural World,* 18, 22.

[40] Noble, *loc. cit.,* 45–47.

[41] Noble, *loc. cit.,* 48.

extend from command of the earth and seas to dominion over the stars."[42] Not until the Copernican revolution in the sixteenth century, however, did the notion of progress and the related ideas of autonomy and reason come to prominence. With the publication of the King James Bible, the people of England were able to turn directly to scriptural authority for guidance in their everyday lives and understanding of their role in the divine plan. The monastic and millenarian conceptions of redemption crystallized to incorporate the ideas of transcendence as a recovery of mankind's divine likeness, restoration of Adamic perfection, knowledge, and dominion, a return to Eden, and identification of the mechanical arts as a vehicle of such transcendence.[43]

The Renaissance cultivated a strong current of secularization in Europe that would shape Western society. The philosophy was secularizing because it ignored the church, resurrected affinity for classical Greek civilization, and emphasized human observation and human achievement.[44] The spirit of the Renaissance was to declare humankind's freedom to set its own course, unencumbered by a world structured by Christian belief. At this point people began to "free their minds from the shackles of the church's external authority and traditions, and [shift] their attention to a hopeful future built by science and technology."[45] Francis Bacon argued that humankind should use its powers and skills to conquer and harness nature to meet human needs. René Descartes saw the human mind as autonomous and free to construct its own frameworks. John Locke sought to define a *technotopia*, and Adam Smith freed the political and economic spheres from the need for divine intervention and guidance. One after another, the pillars that had upheld the Hebrew-Christian worldview—which saw God as a moving, controlling, law-establishing being—were removed.[46] It became attractive to believe that human beings, by the power of their own reason and by study of themselves and nature, could fully understand the world and chart a sure path to endless human progress.

[42] Milton, cited in Noble, *loc. cit.,* 48.

[43] Noble, *loc. cit.,* 44.

[44] Wauzzinski, *loc. cit.,* 36; Monsma, *loc. cit.,* 48.

[45] Monsma, *loc. cit.,* 36.

[46] Monsma, *loc. cit.,* 48.

Technological Optimism

What was begun by the Renaissance and carried forward by modern philosophy was completed by the Enlightenment. Beginning in the seventeenth century and continuing through the twentieth, the Industrial Revolution and a series of scientific and technological discoveries gave great impetus to the ideology of boundless social progress on the shoulders of technology.

> "The age of Enlightenment was a term used to describe the trends in thought and letters in Europe and the American colonies during the 18th century prior to the French Revolution. The phrase was frequently employed by writers of the period itself, convinced that they were emerging from centuries of darkness and ignorance into a new age enlightened by reason, science, and a respect for humanity. . . . Of the basic assumptions and beliefs common to philosophers and intellectuals of this period, perhaps the most important was an abiding faith in the power of human reason. The age was enormously impressed by Isaac Newton's discovery of universal gravitation. If humanity could so unlock the laws of the universe, God's own laws, why could it not also discover the laws underlying all of nature and society? People came to assume that through a judicious use of reason, an unending progress would be possible—progress in knowledge, in technical achievement, and even in moral values."[47]

People in Edwardian England looked back on a century of economic progress and social improvement and thought that they had solved all their important problems. Economists argued that growing interdependence and the ruinous cost of modern warfare would make war so prohibitive that no rational nation would engage in it; war would die out.[48] Optimists of the 1800s forecast that the steam engine would transform society; of the 1900s that mass production would transform society; and in the current century biology, nanotechnology, and information science will transform society. Michael Foucault developed the concept of the Panopticon as a framework for ultimate control of society by technical means. In each of these utopian forecasts, transformation is equated with human progress. "Up to the mid-nineteenth century," says British educator Leonard Waks, "technology was primarily regarded as the instrument for fulfilling the dreams of 'eliminating needless toil, creating wealth, and

[47] Tackett, "The Enlightenment."
[48] Mead, "Apocalypse Now-or Soon," 22–23.

shaping a more just and humane society,' the *means* to a good end. But gradually the conception of technological progress became detached from the enlightenment idea of social and political liberation, technology itself becoming the criterion of the good. From being the *means*, it became pursued as the *end*."[49]

The ideas that emerged from the Enlightenment can be distilled into five points that summarize the Enlightenment worldview:

- Human autonomy
- Rationalism or scientism
- Technological determinism
- Continuous progress
- Progress measured by material improvement

Depending upon which historical account one prefers, the biblical worldview was either replaced by the Enlightenment worldview or adapted by the technological utopians to produce a "synthesized" view that combines biblical and Enlightenment concepts, as follows:

- Human beings are more important than other biological life
- The purpose of nature is to provide resources to support human culture
- The value of nature is derived from its role as provider of raw materials
- Technology can be pursued to mitigate the effects of the fall
- Technology can be pursued to restore the Edenic state
- Technology can give humans powers that surpass Adam's powers
- Progress is a spiritual pursuit
- Progress can be measured in material terms

This optimistic view assumes that progress in science or technology automatically translates to progress in human welfare.[50] Technical progress has unquestionably contributed to the betterment of the human condition. Only a fool would want to give away all the wealth and freedoms and powers that technology has given to us (at least to many of us). But several authors caution that uncritical technological optimism leads to the con-

---

[49] Waks, "Value Judgment and Social Action in Technological Studies," 35–47. Quoted in Conway, *loc. cit.*, 38.

[50] Sarewitz, *loc. cit.*

stant expansion of technology and to the ontological place that it presently occupies in our culture.

The great shortcoming of technological optimism is its inability to consider factors other than technological ones.[51] "Optimists believe that technology should occupy the greatest possible space," Wauzzinski writes, "and should be accorded the highest level of importance."[52] Evidently the highest level of importance comes at the expense of the social, spiritual, and aesthetic dimensions. These "soft" variables are usually "external" to the economic valuation system and the engineering design process.

Unquestioning technological optimism causes us to become inundated by modern technology, because solutions to deep problems come to be addressed by predominately technical means.[53] Ruth Conway refers to the process of recasting all problems into technological ones as "the technical fix."[54] Certainly our federal and state governments, in seeking to accommodate pluralistic thinking, often pursue technological solutions first and sometimes exclusively, as exemplified by the technological pursuit of safety and security described in chapter 2. If technology is the key to solving lasting human dilemmas, and if humans can be defined fundamentally as technical creatures, then, according to Wauzzinski, its place *should* grow because technical activity would be essential both for human identity and for deliverance from perpetual human problems.[55] Wauzzinski writes

> "Even if I grant that technology can correct most human problems, and that, as a result, its presence should be multiplied, then doesn't this state of affairs create an increasing imposition of technology on modern life? In fact, isn't this imposition the key problem that results from the deployment of modern technology? If it is, then to grant technology more room to attempt solutions would be only to increase the problem caused by modern technology. Perhaps we need to take a few mental steps back and reconsider our fundamental assumptions."[56]

---

[51] Cf. Postman, *loc. cit.*; Schuurman, *loc. cit.*; WauzzinskI, *loc. cit.*

[52] Wauzzinski, *loc. cit.*, 51–54.

[53] See Borgmann, *loc. cit*; .Conway, *loc. cit.*; Monsma, *loc. cit.*; Wauzzinski, *loc. cit.*

[54] Conway, *loc. cit.,* 61.

[55] Wauzzinski, *loc. cit.*, 50.

[56] Wauzzinski, *loc. cit.*, 50–51.

The Scientific-Technological Worldview

Previously I cited several philosophers, sociologists, and theologians who have argued that the social impact of modern technology is essentially religious. The most outspoken proponents of this viewpoint include William Stahl,[57] George Grant,[58] David Hopper,[59] and historian David Noble.[60] Theologian and editor of *Zygote* magazine Philip Hefner goes even further. He says, "technology is itself a medium of divine action, because technology is about the freedom of imagination that constitutes our self-transcendence."[61] In one sense Hefner's position is representative of extreme technological optimism; but in another he is shifting to a mystical form of postmodernism. Technological mysticism identifies scientific knowledge with power and technology with control.[62]

Such thinking is not limited to theologians. Engineer and Parliamentarian Egbert Schuurman argues that *the scientific-technological worldview* is "the spirit of the age" in contemporary Western cultures.[63] Schuurman believes that the optimistic view of science and technology is religious and should be treated as such by the church. The scientific-technological worldview is Schuurman's descriptive term for the fundamental attitude that seeks to control reality, to resolve all problems with the use of scientific methods and technological methods, tools, and procedures.[64] The *technological imperative*—the belief that whatever technology *can* do it *should* do—is consistent with the scientific-technological worldview. The imperative couples strong technological optimism with an equally strong devotion to market economics. It assumes that the socio-economic process of technological innovation and progress is too complex for humans to understand and to try to manage, so any attempt at direction should be left to the market. In the process, "external" ethical-moral frameworks are subordinated to market forces. The essential characteristics of the scientific-technological worldview are:[65]

---

[57] Stahl, *loc. cit.*

[58] Grant, *loc. cit.*

[59] Hopper, *Theology, Technology, and the Idea of Progress.*

[60] Noble, *loc. cit.*

[61] Hefner, *Technology and Human Becoming*, 88.

[62] Stahl, *loc. cit.*

[63] Schuurman, *loc. cit.*, 56.

[64] Schuurman, *loc. cit.*

[65] Ibid; Monsma, *loc. cit.*, 49–50.

- the mission of science is to free mankind from superstition in all its forms;
- science alone can render truth about the world and reality;
- science and technology are the sources of progress;
- science and technology must be free to go wherever they will;
- the marketplace is the best guide.

Taken to its limit, the scientific-technological worldview would transform all aspects of life into a set of "techniques"—the application of technical methods to solutions for defined problems and a worldview that subsumes all forms of thinking into rationalism. It is but a short step from here to *technicism*: belief in human autonomy and a religious devotion to technology. Technicism reduces everything to the technological; it sees technology as the solution to all human problems and needs. Enabled by science and technology, human minds and hands become sufficient to control the whole of reality and to guarantee material progress. Thus technology becomes a savior, the means to make progress and gain mastery over modern, secularized cultural desires. Technology becomes its own reason for existing. God is out of the picture; mankind becomes autonomous—master of his own destiny.

Revisit, for a moment, the surveys that I discussed earlier. Even as a majority provided responses that are consistent with technological optimism, most respondents distanced themselves from the technical imperative, and I surmise that few—especially evangelical Christians—would admit an attraction to technicism because of its evident spiritual and/or utopian-sounding definition. Most Christians would distance themselves from the scientific-technological worldview as they do from the technological imperative. But for the most part we—secular and Christian alike—are unaware of the scientific-technological worldview and its controlling influence on our culture. Political philosopher Sociologist Langdon Winner dubbed this state of affairs *technological somnambulism*. "We are sleepwalking through the process of reconstituting the conditions of human existence," he wrote, "lulled by the myth of the moral neutrality of technology, the notion of progress, and technological optimism."[66] Wuzzinski adds that we need to begin a dialog about the place and meaning of technology

---

[66] Winner, *loc. cit.*, 5–6, 10, 50.

in our lives if we are to move beyond our current state of being "collective technical sheep."[67]

I believe that the scientific-technological worldview must be included in any list of worldviews that compete today for the hearts and minds of Westerners. Any such list must include the following entries:

- World religions and their cults
- Postmodernism
- Relativism
- Mysticism, neo-paganism, shamanism

- Deep ecology
- Radical feminism
- Tribalism
- The scientific-technological worldview

Technological Pessimism

Technological pessimism is much younger than technological optimism because this worldview could not evolve until technology was diffused into world economies along with its excesses and unintended consequences. In England at the outset of the Industrial Revolution, factories became the site of organized production of textiles, replacing small-scale manufacture in homes. At first, most factories were comparatively small, employing fewer than 100 workers. Initially they allowed families to remain together, husbands weaving, wives spinning, and children fetching and carrying. Ultimately, however, factories disrupted family life. Women and children easily operated the new energy-driven machines, and they worked the same 12-hour days as men. Since factory owners could pay women and children lower wages, men were driven out of the industry. The craft of handloom weaving disappeared amidst great hardship. An occupation that employed about 250,000 men in 1820 sustained fewer than 50,000 by 1850.[68] During the anti-technology rebellion of 1811–1816, displaced workers attacked factories and factory owners in some communities. In others, rioters known as Luddites attacked the machines themselves.[69] The Luddites might be called early, if not the first, technological pessimists. Although they attempted to defend their communities and their way of life, the Luddites were unable to stop the Industrial Revolution.

[67] Wauzzinski, *loc. cit.*, 180.

[68] Kishlansky and Weisser, "Early Stages of Industrialization."

[69] Postman states that the origin of the name "Luddite" is obscure. Other sources associate the label with a social radical named Ned Lud, who destroyed equipment in a Leicestershire village in about 1779.

Thomas Malthus was the first to argue that technological civilization is physically unsustainable. In his famous *Essay on the Principle of Population* he wrote:[70]

> "Population, when unchecked, increases in a geometrical ratio. Subsistence increases only in an arithmetical ratio. A slight acquaintance with numbers will shew the immensity of the first power in comparison of the second."

But Malthus thought humanity would survive anyway, because nature has a natural way to cut population levels—"crime, disease, war, and vice being the necessary checks on population."[71] Of course, the quality of that continued existence was going to be grim. Twenty-two years before Malthus published his work, Adam Smith had inquired into the nature and causes of wealth with his book *The Wealth of Nations*. One might conclude that the Malthus essay was an alternative analysis of the nature and causes of poverty. Instead, the work was more a response to the writers who were expressing optimism and faith in the nature of man, viz., that man might perfect himself through the application of reason and will power.[72]

Any list of notable modern-day pessimists would have to include Stanford biologist Paul Ehrlich, who continues to predict environmental calamity resulting from the seemingly unavoidable consequences of technological society. Ehrlich's public debates with the optimist Julian Simon were intense. These bitter adversaries argued in the "op-ed" pages of major newspapers, and transacted wagers regarding evidences for their convictions. Simon cited historical evidence to argue that human ingenuity will remove all limits to growth, whereas Ehrlich asserted that we are on course to resource exhaustion and ecological catastrophe.[73] Other notables and groups who belong on the list of technological pessimists include consumer advocate and former presidential candidate Ralph Nader; deep ecologists, and radical ecological groups such as Earth First!, Earth Liberation Front, and Animal Liberation Front. Deep and radical ecologists tend to view technology with suspicion, primarily because of the recognized impacts of technology on the environment. Accordingly, the proponents give technology little role in the evolution of a sustainable world; rather, they advocate return to low-technology options such as bicycles for transporta-

---

[70] Malthus, *Essay on Population.* Quoted in Landry, *Thomas Robert Malthus.*

[71] Ibid.

[72] Landry, *loc. cit.*

[73] Simon, "Earth's Doomsayers are Wrong"; Ehrlich and Schneider, "A $15,000 Counteroffer."

tion. According to industrial ecologists, the result of deep ecology would be a forced, and wrenching, reduction in Earth's carrying capacity.[74] The underlying worldview of deep ecologists is that human life possesses no superior claim over any other biological life with respect to its right to existence and the resources of the planet.

I have mentioned how optimist Alvin Toffler viewed technological pessimists. He declared that "rather than lashing out, Luddite fashion, against the machine, those who genuinely wish to break the prison hold of the past could do well to hasten the . . . arrival of tomorrow's technologies [because] it is precisely the super-industrial society, the most advanced technological society ever, that extends the range of freedom."[75] But technological pessimists think that optimists are mistaken to equate economic and technical development with freedom and human betterment. Instead, pessimists point out loss of freedoms that technology can bring when we become dependent upon it.

Technological Determinism and the Technological Imperative

Malthus believed not only that population growth would eventually outstrip man's ability to live on this planet, but also that there is nothing we can do about it. He asserted that any laws aimed at the betterment of society—by alleviating want and misery—are likely only to aggravate the evils they seek to cure.[76] Jacques Ellul, the French sociologist and technological pessimist, insisted "there can be no human autonomy in the face of technical autonomy"; that "technology has spawned a gulag"; and that technological autonomy reduces the human being to "a slug inserted into a slot machine."[77]

The notion that technological developments are unstoppable once under way is *technological determinism*. The forward march of technology is presumed to be inevitable, unavoidable, and irreversible. Some who invoke technological determinism equate it simply with the notion of inevitability, which is more precisely the *technological imperative*. The imperative is common among technological futurists, for example, when they say things like "the information technology revolution is inevitably

---

[74] Graedel and Allenby, *Industrial Ecology*, 68.

[75] Toffler, *Previews and Premises*.

[76] Malthus, *loc. cit.*

[77] Ellul, *loc. cit.*, 135, 138; Also see Wauzzinski, "Technological Pessimism," 98–114.

on its way and our task as users is to learn to cope with it."[78] The doctrine of the technological imperative includes the mandate that because we can do something (i.e., it is technically possible), either this action ought to (as a moral imperative), must (as an operational requirement), or inevitably will (in time) be taken.[79] Referring to the atomic bomb, Jacques Soustelle declared "since it was possible, it was necessary."[80] Fatalists like Swenson might add "since we can now destroy the planet, in time we will." [81]

Technological determinism results when Enlightenment philosophy is applied to science and technology in the way that Adam Smith and Edmund Burke applied it to economics. It assumes that society and persons are inexorably conditioned, influenced, and defined by technology and rationally planned processes. *Strong* technological determinism is the extreme stance that a particular technology is either a sufficient condition to determine social organization and development, or at least a necessary condition requiring additional preconditions. Either way, certain consequences are seen as inevitable or at least highly probable. In its most extreme form, the entire structure of society is seen as being determined by technology. New technologies allegedly transform society at every level, including institutions, social interaction and individuals. At the least, a wide range of social and cultural phenomena is seen as shaped by technology. "Human factors" and social arrangements are seen as secondary. *Weak* technological determinism suggests that the presence of a particular technology is an enabling or facilitating factor leading to potential opportunities that may or may not be taken up in particular societies or periods because other mediating factors intervene.[82]

For *optimistic* technological determinists, a mystical, quasi-religious faith in technological progress prevails; a kind of invisible hand guides technology ever onward and upward, using individuals and organizations as vessels for its purposes but guided by a sort of divine plan for bringing the greatest good to the greatest number.[83] New technologies and processes are not only accepted, they are embraced, mostly without debate and often without awareness of the effects these things are having. Optimistic technological determinists equate technological progress with social progress,

---

[78] Chandler, *loc. cit.,* 9.

[79] Ozberkhan, "The Triumph of Technology."

[80] Quoted in Ellul, *loc. cit.*, 99.

[81] Swenson, *loc. cit.*

[82] Chandler, *loc. cit.*, 16.

[83] Purcell, *loc. cit.*, 38. Italics added.

somewhat akin to the Christian doctrine of election. More fanciful determinists forecast future technologies involving machine consciousness, which will be superior to human consciousness.[84] Such futurists often note our increasing dependence on mechanical devices and machine-like features of current human behavior as evidence of an evolutionary symbiosis of human beings and machines. Chandler refers to this view as *techno-evolutionism*.[85] Techno-evolutionists define progress in terms of successive stages of technological development, frequently portrayed as "revolutions" or "ages"—the "iron age," the "machine age," the "age of automation," the "atomic age," the "nanotechnology revolution," and so on.

Technological determinists can also be pessimistic although not all technological pessimists are determinists. Social scientist Langdon Winner suggested that failure to exercise active choices in the use of complex interacting technologies leads to "technological drift."[86] Determinists implicitly—and sometimes explicitly—believe that neither science nor technology is predictable. [87] But this requires the conclusion that all scientific advances are purely serendipitous, and that no technology is undertaken for problem solving! Some Christian philosophers (e.g., Borgmann and Wauzzinski) warn that we must change the way we view and use technology. Borgmann captures his concern in the *device paradigm*, not unlike Ellul's *technique*; Wauzzinski appeals for *discernment*.[88] "Most of us want the 'good' results of material security, comfort, wealth." he writes. "We want progress; we want the blessings of abundant and cheap energy. What we fail to see, however, is the force with which such principles *direct* society into a macro and micro acceptance of technical deployment and its consequences."[89] Wauzzinski and Borgmann are neither deterministic nor pessimistic; they believe that by applying revealed principles society can be redirected. But for Malthus, Swenson, and many others, catastrophe is inevitable. Their catastrophism could be equated to apocalyptic eschatology, although these particular authors do not explicitly do so.

As discussed in chapter 7, IE takes a pessimistic view of the sustainability of industrial civilization as presently configured, yet optimistically determines that it can be redirected without great upheaval. Practitioners

---

[84] See chapter 3.

[85] Chandler, *loc. cit.*, 13–14.

[86] Winner, *Autonomous Technology*, 88ff. Cited in Chandler, *loc. cit.*, 17.

[87] Sarewitz, *loc. cit.*, chapter 2.

[88] Borgmann, *loc. cit.*,17–18; Ellul, *loc. cit.*, v; Wauzzinski, *Discerning Prometheus*, 68–70.

[89] Wauzzinski, *loc. cit.*, 121.

believe that IE is "the means by which humanity can deliberately and rationally approach and maintain a desirable carrying capacity, given economic, cultural, and technological evolution."[90] This statement sounds very close to Ellul's definition of *technique*, although the redirection process is "deliberately" chosen. But the choices are driven by the actions of technical experts, not via democratic means. Nevertheless, IE acknowledges that techno-evolution has a vector nature, a direction, and that we humans had better choose the direction rather than just letting it happen. Because the proponents admit that other paths and outcomes are possible, IE is closer to a position of *weak* technological determinism.

Utilitarianism and Realism

The pan balance of Figure 6.1 illustrates utilitarian methodology. Admitting that technology has both "benefits" and "costs," utility in this context seeks to achieve the greatest good for the greatest number. The methods that are used to achieve this utility emphasize "rational techniques" such as risk assessment and cost-benefit analyses. We are asked what we are willing to give up or trade off in order to enjoy the benefits; or conversely, how much we are willing to part with to reduce the risk of harm. Wauzzinski describes the process in the following way:[91]

> "Economic rewards, such as products, salary, and consumption, represent key rewards for technological subjugation (of nature). Humanity has wrestled nature, and the winning is tasted in the bite of economic rewards. At this point, instrumental rationality is joined by utilitarian rationality. Acquisitive, calculating, economic rationality takes the specific outcomes produced by technology and labels them by a calculus known as utilitarian. Technology produces discreet and countable bits of economic rationality waiting to be enjoyed. Enjoying these bits results in 'happiness.' Happiness or utility comes from the consuming of economic units. We are believed by economists to be utility-maximizing individuals who seek to weigh, calculate, and amass bits of measurable happiness produced by technology."

To some degree, we often do act as "utility-maximizing individuals." Consider "spare the air" alerts that we have in California on hot summer days. A survey conducted by Bay Area Air Quality Management District following an alert day in September of 2004 revealed that although 70%

---

[90] Graedel and Allenby, *loc. cit.*, 9.

[91] Wauzzinski, *loc. cit.*, 59.

of the people were aware of the alert, less than 15% took any action to reduce their contribution to air pollution. The morning free rides offered by Bay Area Rapid Transit on such alert days increased ridership by 5% the first day and 8% the following day.[92] Although we listen to the appeals, we almost always choose to drive anyway, and to use our large appliances when it is convenient rather than after the heat of the day. The explanation is simple: benefits are immediate whereas costs are delayed and/or shared. The problem parallels the *Tragedy of the Commons,* because personal benefits from technology almost always exceed our share of the public costs. Strict utilitarianism would address the problem by increasing the immediacy of the costs, i.e., by internalizing them.

Although utility methodology might seem to offer a balanced approach to evaluating technology and culture, four reasons disqualify it as an objective process. First, it assumes additive linear systems which means that effects such as toxicity from different sources can be added. Second, it deals only with entities that can be assigned economic value. Things that are assigned no economic value are presumed to have no value. Third, it assumes that all the affected parties are aware of, understand, and have submitted voluntarily to whatever risks they are facing. And finally, the method usually requires the judgment of "experts" and thus is subject to a charge of elitism.[93] At a minimum the outcomes derived from applying this method are influenced by the worldviews of the experts, and most often this worldview is the scientific-technological one. The philosophical problem with utilitarianism is that it is excessively reductionistic.[94] The humanities, social sciences, and religious traditions have given us too much insight into the rich complexity of humanity for us to be considered simply as rational, utility-maximizing individuals.[95]

Trading off implies giving up a little bit of X in order to attain a little more Y. The method is used in the engineering design process, as I showed in chapter 7. But even if the designer could foresee all the adjunct impacts and emergent outcomes, it is not possible to optimize near-term design objectives and minimize long-term impacts at the same time. Some variables must be minimized (most likely those that reduce the profitability of the product) and others maximized. That many of the variables that must be traded off are not measurable in the same frame of reference only com-

[92] Cabanatuan, "Only 15% participate in Spare the Air day," B1, B5.

[93] Howard, "Eight tenets of precaution"; Howard, "Environmental 'nasty surprise' as a window on precautionary thinking," 19–22; Sarweitz, *loc. cit.,* 73, 160.

[94] Wauzzinski, *loc. cit,* chapter 3.

[95] Wauzzinski, *loc. cit,* 179–80.

pounds the problem. Some variables are physical, others social, still others aesthetic. Spiritual variables are ruled out a priori. Finally, it simply isn't true that the same design will be best for all cultures.

Postmodernism

Postmodernism demands separate discussion because it has significantly influenced contemporary Western worldviews. But like the scientific-technological worldview, the "man in the street" is little aware of its presence. Because it developed as a reaction to the scientific and rational approach to understanding known as modernism, postmodernism in most extreme form is rather pessimistic about technology. Some postmodern apologists argue that Thomas Kuhn's classic *The Structure of Scientific Revolutions* reveals that scientific "truths" are culturally determined,[96] and that Einstein's Theory of Relativity proves that reality cannot be objectively measured.[97] The exchange of letters regarding crossover accidents between autos and large trucks (chapter 4) would be cited as evidence that the claims of science are influenced by the values of the investigator.

Extreme postmodernists would argue that *all* conclusions drawn from empirical evidence, and even the process of gathering the data, are hopelessly perverted by the values of the investigator and his lust for power. This presumed contamination leads to a "hermeneutic of suspicion," where hidden values are assumed to underlie any narrative, including scientific ones.[98] Religion is often dismissed as just another personal preference. The scientific understanding of nature is itself a scientific invention no more or less "real" than any other product of the human mind. Because each position is as valid as any other, the methodology boils down to a power struggle between "in favor" and "out-of-favor" positions. But if everything boils down to marketing one's own ideas, there remains no way to choose between positions.[99]

However, scientific results can be measured and tested. One person's opinion is *not* as good as anyone else's. Extending Einstein's theories from the realm of quantum physics to social and philosophical frameworks leaps far beyond the boundaries of the original theory. In light of their view regarding truth, it is paradoxical that postmodernists have such strongly-held convictions. Two are particularly common: the environment must

[96] Kuhn, *The Structure of Scientific Revolutions.*

[97] Rorty, "Science as Solidarity," 38–52.

[98] Larzelere, "Values and Social Science."

[99] Ibid.

be preserved, and any religion that claims transcendent truth must be rejected prima facie. Postmodernists acquire and use the same technologies for communication, transportation, security, sustenance, health care, recreation and comfort as the technological optimists. When new culture-changing technologies enter the economy, they are embraced just as quickly by postmodernists as by technicists. Postmodernists may diverge a little in their choices of companions, their selection of entertainment, and their forms of worship; but as parents, homeowners, consumers, commuters, workers, and vacationers their lives are determined by technology.

Finding a Basis for Steering Technology

I have argued that engineers are the principal, but unintentional, agents of change in technological societies because their expertise helps to create and produce the technologies that both change the way we live and produce the huge environmental impacts we are facing. More and more we are living in a "built environment" and less in a natural one. From a philosophical perspective, the fundamental question for technology is *what kind of world are we making*? Langdon Winner phrased the question this way: "Are we going to design and build circumstances that enlarge possibilities for growth in human freedom, sociability, intelligence, creativity, and self-government? Or are we headed in an altogether different direction?"[100] Our response to this question will be determined not only by our worldviews, but also by our convictions regarding human nature. If we hope to steer technology, our proposed methods also will be determined by our view of human nature. Specifically, do we believe that, in the absence of coercion, humans are capable of morally upright behavior? Do we believe humans will voluntarily relinquish short-term pleasures for long-term benefit?

Thomas Sowell, nationally-known columnist and Senior Fellow at the Hoover Institution, identified two basic views of human nature.[101] The view that he called a *constrained vision* assumes first that humans act only out of self-interest (they are pleasure-maximizing entities). In addition, he asserts that human endeavor is too complex to model or manage. In this model, the mysterious invisible hand yields better outcomes than any individual, economic, or social planners could achieve. Solutions are beyond human reach; tradeoffs are the best we can hope for. The best public policy under this view is *laissez-faire*—a framework of laws under which a systemic (but chaotic) process can operate. Incentives can be added as nec-

[100] Winner, *loc. cit.*, 17.
[101] Sowell, *A Conflict of Visions*.

essary to get the interests of society attended to, but we must not tamper with the process.

Sowell calls the alternative view of human nature *unconstrained*. This alternative assumes that humans are capable of self denial and valuing other peoples' needs above their own. This vision has a high, or unconstrained, view of human moral potential and sense of social duty. In the unconstrained vision, socio-economic processes can be adjusted to achieve outcomes that meet societal needs. The public interest can be specified and pursued rationally, and parties can agree on what constitutes "needs."[102] In essence, the unconstrained view holds that we can achieve much better than tradeoffs. Because of the prevalence of tradeoffs it is tempting to identify the engineering design process—and likewise IE—with the constrained view. But IE practitioners believe that sustainability can be engineered.

In *The Existential Pleasures of Engineering*, engineer Samuel Florman wrote "Engineers derive pleasure from helping others, to the extent that the main existential pleasure of the engineer will always be to contribute to the well-being of his fellow man."[103] But Florman has also argued that "professionals have the task of meeting the expectations of their clients and employers. Professional restraints should be laws and governmental regulations rather than personal conscience."[104] These two statements are contradictory unless morality is relegated to the domain of private beliefs and divorced from public application. The conscientious engineer—Christian or not—must face a certain dilemma because there are no laws or regulations regarding unanticipated outcomes. We only attempt to regulate them after the fact. The precautionary principle offers an exception, but its extension from pharmaceuticals to general industry is highly contentious.

At the secular university, undergraduate education in the professions is dominated by technological optimism and the constrained vision of human nature. Thus students of the professions must take classes outside the professions to encounter an unconstrained view. Yet if he/she does take classes outside the professions, he/she is likely to find that the postmodernist worldview has supplanted the optimism of the unconstrained vision. The dilemma for educators is how to teach corporate competitiveness along with social, environmental, and spiritual responsibility. Advocates of the constrained worldview believe themselves to be socially

---

[102] Sowell, *A Conflict of Visions*, 72.

[103] Florman, *The Existential Pleasures of Engineering*, 147.

[104] Florman, *The Civilized Engineer*, 32.

responsible, but to achieve it they invoke a mystical force that allegedly steers the collective result of individual self action.

Some evidence indicates that the engineering profession is beginning to recognize the multidimensional impacts of its work. Most of the curriculum descriptions published for U.S. colleges of engineering now include sentences in their objectives about preparing socially responsible graduates. The accreditation criteria now stipulate that every graduate must receive a "broad enough education to understand the impact of engineering solutions in a global and societal context."[105] But engineering graduates are going to need a philosophical framework that can "handle" issues as complex as the ones that technological society is now facing.

Harvard developmental psychologist Lawrence Kohlberg identified three levels of moral development: *pre-conventional*, where right conduct is whatever benefits self; *conventional*, which means adopting the norms of family, group, or society; and *post-conventional*, which means acting on principles that are not reducible to self-interest or social convention.[106] Carol Gilligan, one of Kohlberg's students, changed the conventional level to self-sacrifice for the benefit of others, and the post-conventional level to balancing one's own needs with the needs of others while maintaining caring relationships.[107] With these modifications, Gilligan has been credited with developing the "ethics of care" and establishing a moral foundation for environmental care.[108] But the foundation has not been enough. Something more compelling is required.

Martin and Schinzinger identified seven possible ethical frameworks that might be suitable for engineering practice.[109] But they consider religious ethics *least* effective. Divine command ethics "has things backwards," they say, because moral reasons are not reducible to religious matters and "a morally good deity would command on the basis of moral reasons." This rather circular statement amounts to an assertion that they will be the arbiters of how an acceptable deity would perform. Martin and Schinzinger also discount the effectiveness of rule-based ethics, i.e., professional codes. Other educators reason that "professional codes, like religious dogma, are effective primarily at the pre-conventional level of moral development . . . and will restrict our students' ability to reason through their own

[105] "Criteria for Accrediting Programs in Engineering in the United States."
[106] Kohlberg, "Essays in Moral Development."
[107] Gilligan, *In a Different Voice.*
[108] Haws, "Ethics Instruction in Engineering," 223–29.
[109] Martin and Schinzinger, *Ethics in Engineering (3rd. Ed.).*

values and select ethically appropriate courses of action."[110] To each of these secular ethicists, human moral reasoning is superior to revelation as a guide for engineering practice.

However, even as they discount religious bases for ethics and morality, secular ethicists acknowledge that religious convictions have strong motivational qualities. Although he formally rejected the idea of a personal god (or any supreme being), physicist and philosopher Carl Sagan concluded that only religious convictions have a compelling force strong enough to allow us to solve the environmental crisis.[111] God is reduced thereby to *technique*. Designer and educator Victor Papanek and industrial ecologist Thomas Graedel each invoked a "spiritual" dimension ad hoc for industrial design and industrial ecology, respectively.[112] But each carefully avoided any suggestion of *revealed* values. Papanek wrote:

> "If beauty and high utility exist simultaneously and are furthermore clear expressions of the social intent of the designer, it is possible to speak of the spiritual in design."

Papanek's concept of the spiritual lacks substance for Christians because it does not recognize a God who can be known. However, Papanek offers three "elements of the spiritual in design" that should be acceptable to a biblical worldview:[113]

1. The design releases transcendental feelings (hints of the sacred).

2. The designer intends a social good—namely, a service to our fellow humans and/or the planet.

3. The intended use of the product will nourish our soul and help it to grow.

Industrial ecologist Thomas Graedel invoked four "grand objectives for life on earth, its maintenance, and its enjoyment." Graedel believes that these objectives should be universal, i.e. acceptable to most, if not all, religions and worldviews:[114]

---

[110] Haws, *loc. cit.*

[111] Sagan, "To Avert a Common Danger," 10–14.

[112] Papanek, *The Green Imperative*; Graedel, *Simplified Life Cycle Assessment*.

[113] Here Papanek introduces the term "soul" but in the absence of explanation we assume he intends for the term to be interchangeable with "spirit."

[114] Graedel, *loc. cit.*, 5.

- The Ω_1 objective: Maintaining the existence of the human species.

- The Ω_2 objective: Maintaining the capacity for sustainable development.

- The Ω_3 objective: Maintaining the diversity of living things.

- The Ω_4 objective: Maintaining the aesthetic richness of the planet.

Graedel's appeal is akin to C.S. Lewis' description of the *Tao*—the fundamental truths.[115] Graedel reasoned that although the grand objectives framework is an important prerequisite to determining what societal activities would be desirable, they do not ensure progress toward achieving these objectives, nor do they deal with the thorny problem of tradeoffs among the Ω (Omega) objectives themselves.[116] But they do demand that societal activities from agriculture to manufacturing to transportation be evaluated with respect to their impacts on the objectives.

As a test problem, we can examine the grand objectives to see whether they provide a sufficient ethic for the problem of land use. The Ω_1 objective requires minimization of negative impacts on the provision of basic needs—food, shelter, water. The Ω_2 objective requires a dependable supply of energy and the availability of material resources. Ω_3 mandates protection of a suitable amount of natural areas, maximizing biological diversity on disturbed areas, and avoiding large-scale monocultural vegetation. The Ω_4 objective requires control of wastes—minimizing emissions that result in smog, restricting activities that degrade visibility, encouraging farming and agricultural practices that avoid land overuse and erosion, and preserving open spaces. Some impacts of human activity bear on more than one grand objective. Global climate change, for example, is related to both Ω_1 and Ω_3.

Graedel acknowledged that his approach is basically utilitarian, inasmuch as it requires a ranking of the relative importance not only of the grand objectives, but also of specific environmental concerns that are related to them. Nevertheless, he says, "progress results when desirable actions encouraged by some framework of this type occur over and over again."[117] But no utilitarian argument can provide a compelling ethic for sustainable land use. I agree with Carl Sagan that a spiritual motive is

[115] Lewis, *The Abolition of Man*, 18.
[116] Ibid.
[117] Ibid.

238

required. Contrary to Sagan, however, I expect the belief system be objectively true. For the Christian, such utilitarian uses of religious motives are not only empty, but they are tantamount to suggesting that it is acceptable to believe a lie as long as the belief produces desirable results.

Synthesis

Most of the worldviews pertaining to technology and culture discussed in this chapter or the preceding ones are shown in Figure 8.1, where they are arranged according to their relative degree of optimism or pessimism. There seems to be an option to fit every possible perspective. Schuurman substitutes "nature idealism" for postmodernism at the left extreme, but U.S. culture is conflicted in this regard. Technicism—the end state of the scientific-technological worldview—is at the right extreme. Schuurmann contrasts the two extremes by noting that technicists "consistently pursue and put into practice the scientific-technical ideal of control, [whereas the nature idealists] "condemn and even destroy every science and technology." The absolutization of science and technology operates at one extreme, and the absolutization of freedom, spirituality, and nature at the other.[118]

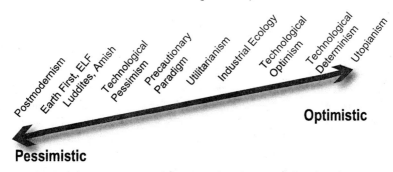

Figure 8.1: The spectrum of philosophical views of technology

Which worldview, ethical framework, or philosophy offers the best hope for answering the fundamental questions regarding the technological enterprise, and for developing its foundational principles and steering technology and culture? The scientific-technological worldview is the spirit of the age in Western cultures, but it has placed us on a course that is environmentally, socially, aesthetically, and spiritually unsustainable. Both nature idealism and postmodernism emerged as reactions to the excesses of modernity that resulted from the scientific-technical worldview. The

---

[118] Schuurman, loc. cit., 148–49.

nature idealist worldview is espoused by a vocal and sometimes violent minority. But the ideals espoused by nature idealism require a great, and possibly catastrophic, reduction in Earth's population, and postmodernism leads to philosophical despair. The foundation of both extreme worldviews is a quest for freedom. Not freedom as liberty in Christ and submission to guidance from God's law, however. Instead, this is a quest for autonomy—absolute independence from God.

To the extent that they value the human condition in addition to nature, more than one religion or worldview may offer the required multidimensional framework for steering technology and culture toward fourfold sustainability. Steven Bouma-Prediger identified the virtues that he thought necessary for an ethic of creation care.[119] Troy Hartley identified four "philosophical" and seven "worldview" frameworks that purport to offer the values required for environmental ethics.[120] Hartley concluded that the concept of environmental justice resides in many ethical systems, worldviews, and religions, but that the seven major religious worldviews lack the dimension of distributive (economic) justice. With respect to the Judeo-Christian tradition at least, this conclusion is unwarranted, because the theology of distributive justice has been well developed.[121] Hartley also failed to recognize an eighth religious worldview: determinism. Rigid adherence to determinism—i.e., the belief that an invisible hand guides the collective outcome of self-interested human initiative to bring about progress—*is a religious perspective*. It consists of tenacious, enduring trust in a benevolent but unknown force.

But very few of the competing worldviews simultaneously uphold all the essential elements of the human condition: life sustenance, equity, justice, dignity and self-worth, freedom, and participation by individuals in the decisions that affect them.[122] Religious systems that value nature above the human condition cannot meet these criteria. Pantheism—the concept that everything is spiritually autonomous and equal in value—cannot because it is obvious that humans really do have a special role in nature that nothing else has.[123] In a biblical worldview, all ethics are derived from

---

[119] Bouma-Prediger, "Creation Care and Character," 6–21.

[120] Hartley, "Environmental Justice," 277–89.

[121] Clouse, *Wealth and Poverty*; Sider, *Cry Justice*; Sider, *Rich Christians in an Age of Hunger*. Spaling and Dekker, "Cultural Sustainable Development," 230–40.

[122] Spaling and Dekker, *loc. cit.*

[123] Schaeffer, *loc. cit.*

theology.[124] Human morality ultimately rests on the unchanging nature of God.

Schuurman concludes that ethics of duty or responsibility will provide the best framework for recovering a responsible approach to technology.[125] As a Christian, he means responsibility to biblical norms, God's law. Secular ethicists discount responsibility or duty ethics, but the anthropocentric alternatives are powerless compared to the scientific-technological worldview. From the ethical platform of responsibility to God, Schuurman develops a set of normative principles for technology.[126] Using philosophical language for the same objective, Wauzzinski concludes that a "structuralist" approach will enable us to make use of the "inherent goodness" of technology while at the same time not falling prey to excessive technological optimism.[127] Although he does not explicitly say, the structure that Wauzzinski proposes is to be derived from Scripture. The essentials include the following:[128]

- Technology must enhance life, not dominate it.
- To enhance life technology must:
  - be affordable;
  - preserve and enhance aesthetic beauty;
  - promote rather than divide family life;
  - be enriching, not depleting of the natural environment;
  - promote an ethically rich, compassionate, less coldly mechanistic view of the universe.

Monsma, Schuurman, and Wauzzinski proceed no further in the development of a theology of technology.

If Christians are to demonstrate responsible (biblical) use of technology, they will have to pay more attention to the scientific-technological worldview and its prevailing influence on our culture. And they must expect to live differently from the dominant trends of Western culture. Unfortunately, the most common approach Christians take is to separate their faith from culture and hence also from its technical develop-

---

[124] Lev 19:1–2.

[125] Schuurman, *loc. cit.*, 186–87.

[126] Schuurman's list is similar to the one developed by Monsma, to which Schuurman was a contributor.

[127] I would prefer to say "potential" rather than "inherent" goodness.

[128] Wauzzinski, *loc. cit.*, 180–82.

ment. Christians distinguish themselves in U.S. culture scarcely, if at all, from non-Christians. Just like the secular culture, Christians are unaware of the influence of the scientific-technical method of control. In their evaluation of culture, they do not view technology as an important factor but as morally neutral, or even as a purely positive thing that can satisfy the human hunger for control and status.[129] I believe that discerning culture and living biblically does not mean becoming anti-technology or dropping out. The necessary changes are not draconian, but they do require commitment and perseverance.

[129] Schuurman, *loc. cit.*, 171, 185.

Chapter 9

Personal Mobility: The Greatest Freedom?

ANTHROPOLOGIST LESLIE White believed that cultural development can be determined by energy use. "Culture advances as the amount of energy harnessed per capita per year increases," he wrote . . . "or as the efficiency or economy of the means of controlling energy is increased, or both."[1] So the U.S., which uses more energy per capita (and in total) than any other nation, must be highly cultured. But perhaps we need to add *liberty* or *freedom* to the criteria. "All men have rights to life, liberty, and pursuit of happiness," asserts our Declaration of Independence. The Preamble to the Constitution says that a purpose of government is to "secure the blessings of liberty"; and the Constitution guarantees certain civil *liberties* and civil *rights*. Some of the freedoms that (in my opinion) Americans have come to expect are compiled in Table 9.1. Technology has long been utilized to help provide and/or assure many of these liberties.

The difference between freedom *from* and freedom *to* is conflicted, however, and new capabilities enabled by technology have increased the confusion. In previous chapters I discussed applications of technology to deliver mankind from threats of nature, hunger, disease, and material want; and to provide safety, security, communication, and information. The utopian promise includes: material and social liberty, disburdenment from physical imperfections and spatial limits, and *transcendence*. But along with these promises we have come to view nature as merely something to be studied, counted, measured, molded, and controlled. In the process, we have dominated, exploited, and damaged nature. Progress is understood as material proliferation in the presence of the liberties of Table 9.1.[2] All this resulted from a symbiotic melding of biblical millenarianism, enlightenment rationalism, and the physical resources of the New World.

[1] Quoted in Nusser, "Leslie Allen White."
[2] Borgmann, *Power Failure*, 120–21.

Table 9.1. Liberty as freedom *from* and freedom *to*

	Freedom from	Freedom to
Social	Disfigurement Risk Immobility Prejudice Confinement	Form relationships Communicate (speech) Escape or isolate Travel Organize and socialize Choose one's career
Political	Search and seizure Injustice Taxation without representation Military aggression	Assemble Make contracts Choose governance Choose where to live
Material	Poverty Misery (discomfort?) Hunger Cold Disease	Choose goods and services Own property Gain wealth Consume Dispose
Spiritual	Insecurity Ignorance Fear Superstition Doubt	Worship Celebrate Choose one's destiny Control nature Respond to God

Even abortion has been cast in terms of reproductive rights and freedom of choice. In its landmark decision of 1973, the U.S. Supreme Court held in *Roe* v. *Wade* that the constitutional right to privacy means that states cannot bar a woman from having an abortion. As a practical matter the ruling reflected the prevailing belief that the Constitution protects people's right to live their lives pretty much as they desire.[3] But privacy is not explicitly mentioned in the Constitution; it is a derived concept. Similar to the struggle to define and delimit "freedom of speech," the constitutional right to privacy is elusive. Human population has increased greatly and the powers of technology have vastly expanded our reach. Whether face-to-face or at a distance by electronic means, encounters between one person's rights and another person's freedoms are much more frequent now. Liberties that could be exercised freely on the "Western frontier" now are

[3] Lieberman, "Constitution of the United States."

likely to affect a neighbor; we simply cannot live our lives "pretty much as we please." The laws and regulations we write to reduce these encounters or their impacts inevitably multiply along with technology and population. Examples range from traffic regulations, covenants, codes, and restrictions for housing developments, licenses (for fishing, hunting, driving, contracting, practicing medicine, etc.), to environmental regulations, occupational safety and health, business practices, truth in advertising and lending, weights and measures, and on and on. Human freedoms, liberties, limits, and responsibilities have become intensely intertwined.

The point I am making is that individual liberties *must* be constrained when population and human impacts multiply. To further the argument, I organized the liberties in Table 9.1 into "social," "political," "material," and "spiritual" categories. The result reveals a certain similarity to the four-fold (aesthetic, social, physical, and spiritual) impacts of technology described in chapter 4. All evidence indicates the constraint will be achieved voluntarily, with *less* governmental laws and regulations. Yet the seemingly endless string of advances provided by technology is causing us to question the very idea of limits. The notion removes many restraints on human endeavor—and also on behavior. On the other hand, numerous writers have warned that technology can also *reduce* freedoms, leading first to dependency and eventually to *enslavement*. Which is it? Edmund Burke proclaimed that the kind of freedom he loved is not "solitary, individual, selfish liberty. It is that state of things in which liberty is *secured by the quality of restraint*."[4] Robert Wauzzinski noted "neither freedom nor determinism . . . is the mark of humanness. Responsibility is."[5]

No single example of technology embodies the conflict between freedoms and limits more succinctly than the private vehicle. Automobiles—together with the immense infrastructure they require—provide a prime illustration of the collision between freedom on the one hand and limits and responsibilities on the other. Considered collectively with the vast array of powered recreational equipment, a case can be made that private vehicles comprise the single greatest threat to sustainability of our planet. The most cherished American freedoms have come to be identified with privately owned vehicles, almost as if prior to the twentieth century Americans were not free. That seems rather ironic considering the myth of the cowboy. At their core, private vehicles represent only the harnessing of energy to provide mobility. Steam power—the first prime mover

---

[4] Burke, "Selected Letters," 542.

[5] Wauzzinski, *Discerning Prometheus*, 90.

of the Industrial Revolution—preceded the internal combustion engine by almost a century. Robert Fulton made his first steamboat trip up the Hudson River on October 12, 1807. Steam engines revolutionized mass transportation via ship and rail, and also changed agriculture and industry. But the external combustion steam engine did not power a revolution in private transportation because it was heavy and inefficient; the absence of a "radiator" severely compromised its efficiency. It was the internal combustion engine that enabled the realization of privately owned vehicles. As we shall see shortly, the species has diversified to include many different types. Internal combustion engines are also used to power portable tools, stationary machinery, and toys.

Spontaneous mobility doesn't explain the grip that private vehicles have on us. After all, horses and bicycles can offer the same spontaneity, of course with more effort and less range. In late October of 2003, Nancy and I took a sentimental journey back to New Mexico where we lived years ago. We traveled through places we had never seen while we lived there: the Vermillion Cliffs, Glen Canyon, Monument Valley. Yes, we traveled by automobile: our four-cylinder compact 1997 station wagon. During one leg of the trip—on Highway 99 through California's San Joaquin Valley— I entertained myself by copying headlines from billboards that, to me, portrayed some of the absurdities of contemporary American culture:

- A 5th-wheel trailer named "wilderness"
- Nissan Frontier pickup truck: *"Instanto de Liberdad"*
- Sonic Drive-in: "Paving the Way to Great Taste"
- Chukchanzi Gold Casino: "Yosemite Finally Has a Night Life"
- Holiday Inn Express: "Deluxe Free Breakfast"
- Housing Development at Chowchilla: "The Lakes at Pheasant Run"
- Dodge Trucks: "Grab Life by the Horns"
- "Litter Cleanup by the Lethal Riders"

Notice that every advertisement directly endorses either autos or the supporting infrastructure. But our culture has attached another layer of benefits to this form of mobility. If we are to believe the advertisements, these technological marvels will satisfy most of life's critical needs. We can select from the following list the benefits that apply to our particular situation:

- freedom (by mobility)
- security (especially the large SUVs)
- image (for the plain person)
- status (for the seeker)
- pride and self esteem (for the lowly)
- assertiveness (for the meek)
- escape (from tedious or threatening existence)
- self expression (for the inarticulate)
- fun and excitement (for the bored)
- satisfaction (for the dissatisfied)
- protection (for the cowed)
- identity (for the lonely)
- power (for the weak)
- attention (for the overlooked)
- companionship (by attracting others)

People may think they chose a car rationally. But consumer psychology expert Charles Kenny of Memphis says it isn't so. "Car choice comes from the right side of the brain," he says; "the emotional, irrational, side. It's driven by psychological needs that most of us don't recognize."[6] "Your car is the best way of advertising who you are and how well you're doing," adds Carleton Kendrick, a psychologist who analyzes auto trends as an indicator of social change. Kendrick notes that "cars are an extension of what we want to be, whether that's successful, cool, or just different."[7] "About 25% of people choose cars that make them feel powerful," says James Hazen, a psychologist who works in the auto industry. Some people want cars that look good and stand out. A sports car hints of the inner James Bond. Still other people find comfort in blending in with all the other white sedans on the road. Parents want vehicles that can get them to soccer games, keep them safe, hold all their stuff—but at the same time tell the world who they are, how the family defines itself.[8] The bottom line, according to Kendrick, is "How does your car make you feel?"[9] Before you can say a word, your car broadcasts the answer.

Are not these the qualities that the Holy Spirit will provide to believers? Jesus taught that *truth* will set us free. The lame man who was healed used his new mobility to praise God (Acts 3:8). "Well, nobody takes these advertising claims seriously," we reply. If that is true, why do producers

[6] Quoted by Hales, "What your Car Says About You," 8.

[7] Ibid.

[8] Hales, "The New Family Car," 8–10.

[9] Quoted by Hales, "What your Car Says About You," 8.

spend *hundreds of billions* of dollars each year on advertising?[10] I submit a simple test: imagine that we were forced to relinquish one or the other of two freedoms—spontaneous mobility and the private automobile, or freedom of religion. Which would we choose to give up? Be honest, now. Which one would win in a popular vote? In fact, both are at risk in contemporary Western culture. Private automobiles are unsustainable because we are approaching encounters with physical limits; and freedom of religion is at risk as postmodernism advances and the courts pursue a totally secular public sector.

Lifestyle Vehicles

While they are telling the world who we are, today's vehicles must also get us to soccer games, keep us safe, and hold all our stuff. According to Ford Motor Company's Director of Lifestyle Vehicles "The family car has become a family room on wheels. It's the hub of all the family energy and excitement. It's a combination breakfast nook, entertainment center, changing area and chat room. The biggest mom-pleasers are features that make life on the road easier: juice-box sized cup-holders, dinner trays, and separate temperature and audio controls for kids. Many see new entertainment options, such as back-row DVD players with pull-down screens and individual headphones as sanity savers."[11] Psychologist Kendrick even asserts that: "whatever form a family car may take, its essential purpose [is] to bring families together[!]"[12]

Because the attributes that attract us to automobiles and create such a strong bond are enabled by technology, they have become more voracious consumers of new technology than any other product in the marketplace.[13] The average car today has dozens of tiny computers inside, controlling everything from gas consumption to gear-shift points. Computers control the devices that make traveling more comfortable, including climate, audio, suspension and fancy seat-back DVD players. Bumper-mounted sonar can help ensure you never back into another tree or tricycle again. New mapping computers communicate with satellites to make asking for directions a thing of the past (phew). And now you can dial-in to a help facility to track your stolen car, unlock the doors or summon roadside

[10] See chapter 4.

[11] Ref.

[12] Hales, "The New Family Car," 8–10.

[13] Constable and Somerville, *A Century of Innovation*, 20–21.

assistance. Even stylishness is created no longer with clay mock-ups, but rapidly and inexpensively using 3-D surface contouring software.

Tomorrow it will be more like a thousand computers per auto. Engineers at IBM are working on a virtual co-pilot to keep us awake on long trips by spritzing us with ice water if we look drowsy. Steering wheels will give us a little shake if we're driving erratically. Phased array radar will track cars around us, ensuring safe separation by warning first, and then automatically braking or speeding up to avoid an accident. A rolling Internet node will help us get around accidents and avoid problems. Wireless technology will automatically and dynamically configure and reconfigure a network using all the cars in, say, a 500-foot radius. High tech road sensors will communicate with the traffic sensors in our car to help identify, and then avoid, traffic jams. If one car spots trouble, all the other cars down the line can be warned. As flat color displays get cheaper, expect them to proliferate throughout the car. Advanced audio technology and noise-canceling headphones will turn every car into a personal home theater customized for each passenger. Most cars will be outfitted with satellite video and audio, helping to make the car at least as connected as the home. And those same networks will also make it easier to find a gas station, hamburger joint or bathroom, just when you need it most.

The foregoing vision of future automobiles came from a description by technophile and auto enthusiast Jim Louderback.[14] I could have placed his rosy forecast in chapter 3, *Transcending all Limits*, but I include it here for its automobile content. This is unabashed technological optimism. In order for this utopian automobile-based future to actually occur, many physical, social, and spiritual limits will have to be overcome.

The High and the Mighty

No more graphic illustration of freedom leading to excess can be provided than sport-utility vehicles (SUVs). Author Keith Bradsher provides an insightful analysis of the SUV phenomenon in *The High and the Mighty: SUVs: The World's Most Dangerous Vehicles and How They Got That Way*.[15] The book is a study of Washington politics and the ways of Detroit, according to reviewer Jay Rosen, but also the politics of our roadways and the social psychology of Americans as drivers.[16] When automotive fuel efficiency standards were introduced in 1975, the rules for so-called non-

---

[14] Louderback, "Cars go High-tech."

[15] Bradsher, *The High and the Mighty*.

[16] Rosen, "Car or Truck?"

passenger vehicles such as minivans, SUVs, and even some cars weren't all that important, because these vehicles accounted for less than 20% of the market. But beginning about 1998 "full size" (an advertising term) SUVs became the "hot" personal and family vehicle, and by 2005 SUVs and large pickups accounted for more than half of all automotive sales. [17] Although these vehicles consume more fuel and produce more pollution, they are subject to much lower fuel efficiency standards than passenger cars. The largest class—which includes the Hummer H2, Lincoln Navigator, and the Ford Excursion, weighing 8,500 to 10,000 pounds—don't have to meet any mileage standards at all![18]

The mileage requirements enacted in response to the Clean Air Act were less stringent for trucks because trucks were assumed to be essential tools for businesses. Then EPA classified SUVs as trucks. Congress slapped a 10% luxury tax on cars with price tags of $30,000 or more. But the excise tax exempted the "light truck" category that included the biggest SUVs.[19] "Getting SUVs classified as trucks was a political feat worth quite a bit to the auto industry," says Bradsher. The Chrysler PT Cruiser was classified as a truck because its back seats are removable. In order to take advantage of that particular loophole Subaru modified the design of its Outback station wagon and sedan so that they too could be classified as trucks.

One of the psychological attractions of the SUV is that the driver gets to perch above other vehicles. Looking down on passing traffic gives some illusion of highway command. But SUVs are more dangerous than other vehicles in collisions with automobiles. As more SUVs hit the road, this argument becomes a self-fulfilling prophecy. In 2003, 55% of SUV fatalities resulted from rollover crashes.[20] The machines are actually "tippy monstrosities with mediocre brakes that block other drivers' view of the road and inflict massive damage during collisions."[21] But some (mostly younger) SUV owners seek still more sense of command. They boost the height of their vehicles by a foot or two, placing the bumpers at eye level of passengers in sedans.

---

[17] Most of the analysis also applies to "4X4" pickup trucks, a less expensive version of the same problem.

[18] DeGaspari, "Retooling CAFÉ," 24–27.

[19] Rosen, *loc. cit.*

[20] Tyson, "DOT Releases Preliminary Estimates of 2003 Highway Fatalities."

[21] Quoted in Rosen, *loc. cit.* The Federal government apparently agrees, because the 2005 Transportation Act, signed into law by President Bush on August 8, 2005, includes mandatory safety upgrades for SUVs. But they don't have to be implemented until 2009.

Bradsher argues that SUVs are not only the world's most dangerous vehicles, but also the most anti-social. He thinks Detroit has conned drivers into believing that bigger, heavier, taller vehicles are safer because they feel strong and intimidating and "look likely to demolish other people's cars in collisions." "The SUV is a vehicle of aggression," says Bradsher, "a machine to menace other people with. It was understood and marketed that way by an auto industry that itself behaved cynically and aggressively in securing loopholes and exemptions that made the SUV so fantastically profitable."[22] According to a Chrysler marketing specialist the Dodge Durango is supposed to look like a savage jungle cat. "A strong animal has a big jaw; that's why we put big fenders."[23] An advertisement for the 2004 Volvo SUV boasted that the vehicle "takes an aggressive stance."

My observation is that SUVs also tend to be driven aggressively. I acknowledge that this observation might be an artifact of their large size and therefore they are more noticeable. People used to say the same thing about VW "Beetles." But because they were smaller than other cars, such aggressive driving placed their drivers at disproportionate risk. For SUVs, the opposite is true. I think that SUV drivers tend to feel less vulnerable and as a result they drive faster. Personal ethics can affect driver aggressiveness or the propensity to park in spaces marked "compact." But they cannot neutralize the fundamental bases of the vehicle design. GM's "Hummer" has a very wide track that reduces its tendency to roll, but this monster fares very poorly in the environmental and social impact categories.

According to a former American Motors Company executive and senior marketer of Jeep, the market is entirely psychological; there is little to no actual customer need for four-wheel drive.[24] But affluent baby boomers like the idea of being able to go off-road even though they will probably never do so. I would suggest three additional motives. First, young parents perceive increased safety for their families. Data showing SUVs to be less stable and quite threatening to smaller vehicles have not dissuaded them, nor have steep purchase price or high fuel consumption. Second, for some—especially young males—a truck or SUV provides an image of masculine ruggedness.[25] The third motive is compensation, for small or shy people or others with feelings of inadequacy. In each of these cases, advertising creates an image that is at variance with highway safety statistics

---

[22] Quoted in Rosen, *loc. cit.*

[23] Ibid.

[24] Ibid.

[25] A new badge of macho among young suburban males is to shower the sides of their "4X4" pickups with mud and then leave it on for their neighbors to admire.

on the one hand, and physical sustainability on the other. So why don't we just outlaw such vehicles—especially the largest ones—and prohibit boosting their height? There are federal and state height restrictions relative to headlights—but they are rarely enforced. Strict enforcement likely would be viewed as another infringement on individual liberties. It wouldn't be infringement on the personal spontaneous mobility that we value so highly, but would be resisted because owning up to the psychological motives is embarrassing to vehicle owners. All sorts of bogus rationalizations are proffered instead, and the real issues receive little honest discussion.

In sum: full size SUVs and pickup trucks are not morally neutral, because they incorporate the following *known and inherent* characteristics:

1) Although rationalized as transportation, their primary role is psychological.

2) They consume more fuel and produce more pollutants than necessary for the transportation service provided.

3) They are unstable and are inclined to roll over during sharp maneuvers.

4) They are likely to cause serious injury to occupants of smaller vehicles.

5) They obstruct the views from smaller vehicles.

6) They obstruct ingress and egress when they are parked in compact stalls.

7) They do not fit in most garages, and when parked in streets and driveways they extend over the sidewalks.

Most of these characteristics are properties of the vehicles themselves, independent of the drivers. And most do not qualify as emergent properties because they could have been predicted in advance.

Fuel for the Fleet

Because petroleum delivers benefits that we value so highly, it will not be easy to reduce its use. Plastics, pesticides, fertilizer, home heating, lawn mowers, leaf blowers, and a myriad other "non-road" uses account for a significant portion of petroleum use, but vehicles consume the lion's share. Gasoline prices at the pump underwent a steady rise beginning in 2003 and continuing into 2006. Angry motorists demanded government investigation into the possibility of "price gouging" by the petroleum companies, and email chain letters argued for boycotts of Exxon-Mobil "to show them that this is a buyers' market and we won't be pushed around." But they were wrong. Repeated government investigations found only supply-and-demand at work, and the boycotts went nowhere. According to the EPA, Americans now confront a situation where supply and demand are in a delicate balance.

For the previous twenty years, U.S. consumers benefited from low energy prices. Adjusted for inflation, prices actually declined during the period. With cheap gasoline readily available, we renewed our enthusiasm for larger, less fuel efficient vehicles, and drove them more. We drove 2.88 trillion miles in 2003, up from 2.86 trillion in 2002. Over the past twenty years, while population grew 27%, on-road vehicle miles traveled increased by 114%.[26] At the same time, refiners decided not to build new refineries in the U.S. due to low return on investment. Instead, increased demand has been met by operating existing refineries at "full throttle." As refineries reach maximum capacity, refiners and marketers began to import gasoline and other refined products in addition to unrefined crude oil.

The fuel supply problem is not as bad as it could be, because technology has provided gains in efficiency—better combustion, lighter materials, and precision manufacturing that permits lighter motor oils. But the gains have not been nearly enough to overcome the supply-and-demand problem created by larger vehicles and more driving. Because there are no short-term substitutes for gas and oil, when demand exceeds supply, prices spike. The two oil crises of the 1970s caused recession and inflation. Efficiency and productivity gains across the whole economy have moderated the near-term impacts of the price run-ups in 2006, but the net effect of our petroleum addiction is that we are mortgaging our future. Because domestic supplies peaked long ago, the U.S. must import more than half of the petroleum we consume, accounting for nearly a quarter of our international trade deficit. Higher prices hit U.S. farmers especially hard because they have to pay more for fertilizer, fuel, and transporting their products to market at the same time that globalization is driving down the prices for their crops.

In August 2005, Transportation Secretary Norman Mineta announced new fuel-efficiency standards for SUVs, minivans, and light trucks, proclaiming that the rules would "save gas and result in less pain at the pump for motorists."[27] Maybe so, but just barely. The proposed

[26] EPA, *loc. cit.*

[27] "Green Light for Guzzlers," 24.

rules would raise average mileage for such vehicles by only 1.8 miles per gallon over the 2008 to 2011 model years. Under current consumption trends, this change would save 10 billion gallons of gasoline over 15 years, about 25 days of national consumption. Considering how closely personal vehicles are bound to our national psyche, the fact that the proposed new standards are minimal and painless should not come as a surprise. Americans will sacrifice many things before they relinquish the tangible and intangible rewards of the automobile. But perhaps market forces can accomplish what government is unwilling to do. In September 2005, industry-wide sales of the largest SUVs were down 43% from a year earlier,[28] and as I write this, car sales in 2006 may surpass sales of SUVs and light trucks for the first time since 1981.[29]

But technological and economic optimists are still willing to argue that conservation isn't necessary. Paul Ballew, GM's chief market analyst, said "the level of consumer interest in small cars is being overplayed."[30] Others argue that petroleum from Canadian tar sands "will help keep American SUVs running for years to come."[31] The tar sands of Athabasca are a huge resource indeed: 1.7 trillion barrels of oil is enough to supply current U.S. consumption for about twenty years. But only 10% of that is recoverable with today's technology, and the environmental impact would likely be staggering. Recovery of petroleum from tar sands is done by strip mining, not drilling. Two tons of earth must be mined and processed to produce a single barrel of oil. Even in the early stages of development, the mine pits literally resemble mini-Grand Canyons.[32]

It is unfortunate that government did not act much earlier to reduce our petroleum dependency by gasoline taxes, tougher fuel-economy standards, and visionary exhortations about the long-term benefits of reducing consumption. If they had, we might have minimized or avoided the petroleum-related environmental, economic, social, and political problems that now occupy much of our national attention.

---

[28] Data from Ward's AutoInfoBank. Reported in Hakim, "SUV sales plunge as gas prices take off," E1, E6.

[29] Durbin, "Car Sales Fall in November," E2.

[30] "Even in Texas, the cars are smaller," A10, A13.

[31] Hall, "Future of U.S. oil flows through Canada," A1, A17.

[32] Ibid.

NASCAR Dads and Monster Jams

The role filled by personal vehicles in the American psyche has profoundly religious overtones. Nowhere is the relationship more evident than when Christianity joins the National Association for Stock Car Racing (NASCAR). NASCAR racing and the Christian faith have worked hand-in-hand for some time. Infield chapel services are conducted for drivers, crewmen, and officials. A retired Baptist minister offers a pre-race invocation. The racing schedule takes a break for Easter. Driver Bobby Labonte advertised Mel Gibson's movie *The Passion of the Christ* on the hood of his racing car, and Morgan Shepherd, who drives for the *Victory in Jesus* racing team, has a Jesus decal on the hood of his racing truck.[33] Humorously, another race car advertises Tim LaHaye's *Left Behind* book series. Maybe these things are not surprising for a sport that grew up in the Bible belt. From one perspective, NASCAR's alliance with the Christian faith gives the sport a wholesome, family-oriented image.[34] But from my perspective the alliance seems a sacrilege; a violent and dangerous secular sport cloaked in a Christian flag. Concerns for driver safety and fuel consumption are swept aside in a rush of adrenaline.

The "monster trucks" cousin of stock car racing hasn't yet packaged itself as a Christian sport, but it nevertheless offers further insight into the American psyche. The United States Hot Rod Association's (USHRA's) monster truck blowouts drew 3.5 million people in 2003, 10% more than the year before. If you have the right cable or satellite package, you can watch Monster Jam showdowns on the Speed Channel. These spectacles appeal to a certain subculture, well-characterized by a reporter for the Santa Rosa (California) *Press Democrat*: "When tire-kicking, big-belt-buckle-toting fans pour in this weekend for the mud fest that is the USHRA Monster Jam at the Santa Rosa Fairgrounds, an oaky, toasty, buttery chardonnay might be the last thing on their minds. Pushing the Bud, [the event caterer] expects to sell "less than two bottles of wine."[35]

Monster trucks are about 11 feet tall and about 12 feet wide; minimum weight is 9,000 pounds. The engines are supercharged and methanol injected; each burns up to 250 gallons of methanol per run (approximately 250 feet). The tires must be 66 inches high and 43 inches wide, and they cost about $2,600 apiece. The average monster truck team will go through eight tires in a year. A crew of eight works 18-20 hours for three days to

---

[33] Newberry, "NASCAR Drives Religion in the Fast Lane," C1–C2.

[34] Ibid.

[35] Beck, "Monster Jam," D1, D8.

construct a monster truck course. It is not uncommon for dump trucks to make more than 200 trips to deliver the dirt to each stadium. The average amount of dirt used per track varies between 700 cubic yards for an arena and 3,500 cubic yards for a stadium. Each year 700,000 cubic yards of dirt are used to put on USHRA events. "Oh yeah," adds driver "Grave Digger" at the end of an interview, "You can go to Wal-Mart and Target and buy [toys] right off the shelf. Hot Wheels has Maximum Destruction. Tyco makes a huge remote-control Maximum Destruction truck."[36]

The Great Dispersion

The problem of land use was analyzed in chapter 5, described with respect to brownfields and greenfields. If one investigates the factors that a company considers when selecting a new plant site, a clear message emerges that today's employees are *expected* to commute by private automobile.[37] Public land use policy occasionally slows, but usually facilitates, the practice. A worldview that reflects unlimited economic progress underpins the process, but the automobile is the key enabling technology. The automobile's contribution is sprawl; more broadly, the *dispersion of society*. After the Industrial Revolution but before the automobile, cities expanded in radial directions, along trolley lines. With the flexibility provided by the automobile, however, they could expand anywhere.[38] And in the U.S., they certainly have.[39] Fifty years ago we thought freeways were the solution to moving people quickly and efficiently. People could live in low population-density suburbs, drive into the city center, and park their cars in large lots near where they worked or shopped. There was traffic, but it was manageable. But the freeways threading past farms and fields attracted developers who wanted to bring shopping closer to the motorized suburbanites. Shopping malls, generally located along metropolitan beltways and surrounded by acres of blacktop, became new traffic magnets. Following the same plan, suburban office parks, created suburb-to-suburb travel. Constructed with public funds, freeways subsidized the flight of industries from cities to countryside.

New York Times columnist David Brooks views dispersion through the lens of economic optimism. "From New Hampshire down to Georgia, across Texas and up through California," he writes, "you now have the

36 Ibid.

37 Swearengen, "Property Rights versus Stewardship," 12–24.

38 Constable and Somerville, *loc. cit.*, 20.

39 Brooks, "Our Sprawling, Supersize Utopia," 38.

booming exurban sprawls that have broken free of the gravitational pull of the cities and now float in a new space far beyond them. . . . These new spaces are huge and hugely attractive to millions of people . . . In these new, exploding suburbs, the geography, the very landscape of life, is new and unparalleled. The reality is that modern suburbia is the latest iteration of the American dream . . . today's suburbs are the products of the same religious longings and the same deep tensions that produced the American identity from the start. The complex faith of Jonathan Edwards, the propelling ambition of Benjamin Franklin, the dark, meritocratic fatalism of Lincoln—all these inheritances have shaped the outer suburbs . . . [But] the truly historic migration," he wrote, "is from the inner suburbs to the outer suburbs, to the suburbs of suburbia."[40]

The problem with Brooks' optimistic view is that he assumes land, atmosphere, water, and energy are infinite sources and sinks for the materials and detritus of human activity. But they are not—although we act as if they are. As reported in chapter 5, a half million acres of prime agricultural land in the Central Valley of California were converted from agriculture to housing and commerce in the interval 1982–1987; without change in policy another million will be developed in the next 40 years.[41] As a result of farmland conversion and other factors—such as the rising cost of petroleum for fertilizer and transporting crops to market—in 2004 the U.S. became a net importer of food. Automobiles are the primary agents of unsustainable land use, petroleum consumption, pollution, and social decline. As we shall shortly see, they are also associated with carnage.

Even at the apex of the Interstate Highway program in the 1970s, the metropolitan freeway systems designed in the 1940s and 1950s were straining to accommodate the new and unexpected travel patterns associated with dispersion.[42] The freeway that was the solution of the 1950's has become a rush-hour parking lot in the twenty-first century. In the view of some, the resulting congestion has become a cancer on the transportation system. Automobiles are becoming unmanageable in some areas, malls and office parks are poorly served by mass transit, and suburb-to-suburb commutes are almost impossible without a car. But building new highways—or expanding the capacity of the ones already built—is only a band-aid solution.

[40] Ibid.
[41] "Beyond Sprawl."
[42] Cornehls, "The Automobile Society," 52–53.

As "developable" land becomes more scarce, debate over the role of the market in land use (played out in local and regional planning meetings and on the forum pages of the local newspapers) grows increasingly strident. The polemics focus mainly on traffic congestion and environmental impacts *versus* property rights, while the other social costs of sprawl are mostly overlooked. That benefits of development accrue locally (and to the developers) while the costs are borne regionally (and, many have argued, disproportionately by the poor) remains outside the scope of the discussions.[43] For the cities that donate people and industry to the dispersion, the debate is different. Departure of industry and the non-poor reduces city government's ability to produce tax revenue to provide services and mitigate inner city troubles. "The process," as one writer phrased it, "makes a mockery of equality of opportunity."[44] The forces driving the economic, environmental, and social consequences of urban flight are systemic, and they will continue to accrue in the absence of incentives to redirect the trend.

Health and Safety

Now we turn to the most troubling of the emergent properties of our automobile-based society: the impact on public health. The first impact is indirectly caused by sprawl. It's not just the land that disappears with each subdivision; it's our body shape. Suburbanites are on average six pounds heavier than their urban counterparts. The number of miles a typical American drives has doubled since 1963 and the number of overweight children between 6 and 11 has doubled since 1973. Kids today spend about an hour a day in cars, not counting the school bus.[45] "One of life's great ironies," according to columnist Ellen Goodman, "is that so many families move to the exurbs for a better lifestyle for the kids. Where upon parents turn into chauffeurs and kids get strapped into car seats whenever we need a bottle of milk. If we don't care that every gallon of gasoline puts 20 pounds of carbon dioxide into the air, maybe we'll care that it puts those pounds on the hips. Instead of lecturing Americans to ease up their driving for the sake of the environment, we could market it as a weight loss activity. Instead of slapping stickers on SUVs impugning the politics

---

[43] Lee, "Environmental Justice, Urban Revitalization and Brownfields."

[44] Fysh, "Expert Predicts Housing Problems for Seattle." Free market advocates argue that liberal policies cause taxes to rise, thereby driving industry from the cities (Hayward, "Broken Cities").

[45] Goodman, "Warning: Your car is making you fat," B5.

of the owners, we could slap warning labels on cars saying 'This Vehicle Will Make You Fat.' We could form Gas Watchers: instead of weighing in on a scale once a week, we'd have to report our odometer. Want to lose six ugly pounds, reduce sprawl and make sidewalks our most important project? Put aside your Safari, park your Defender, trade in your Explorer for walking shoes."[46] To supplement Goodman's proposals, I would add boycotting drive-up services: bank tellers, fast food purveyors, espresso windows, liquor stores, dry cleaners, whatever.

The second health and safety impact of our automobile-based society is more poignant than obesity. It is the rates of death and injury in, or by, automobiles. In 1899, *Scientific American* predicted that the automobile would "eliminate a greater part of the nervousness, distraction, and strain of modern metropolitan life. Apparently they hadn't thought about the ramifications of pedestrian vs. car in cities designed to accommodate walkers, horses, and bicycles. On August 17, 1896, Bridget Driscoll became the first road fatality in the world. She was a 44-year-old mother of two children who had come to London with her teenage daughter and a friend to watch a dancing display. While the driver was reported to be doing 4 mph, witnesses described her as being hit by a car traveling at "tremendous speed." The crash occurred on a terrace in the grounds of Crystal Palace in London. The car was owned by the Anglo-French Motor Car Company, which was offering demonstration rides to the public. The car was driven by Arthur Edsell, an employee of the company. He had been driving for only 3 weeks (no driving tests or licenses existed at that time). He had apparently tampered with the drive belt, causing the car to go at twice the intended speed. He was also said to have been talking to the young lady passenger beside him. After a six-hour inquest, the jury returned a verdict of "accidental death." No prosecution was proposed or brought against driver Edsell or the company.[47] Three years later Henry Bliss was struck and killed in New York City, the first automobile-pedestrian fatality in the U.S.[48]

Pedestrians were clueless about the dangers of cars in the early days. Drivers could barely drive, much less watch out for moving objects; and cities were not engineered for these potential problems. Fatalities soared as cars moved into cities. New York police established traffic rules, noting that if something wasn't done, "only agile pedestrians would sur-

[46] Ibid.

[47] "RoadPeace."

[48] Carpenter, "Hit and Run."

vive." Even without rules, some people felt cars shouldn't be allowed in the cities. The peak year for such anti-auto sentiment was 1905, when rock-throwing mobs regularly attacked automobiles in New York City, smashing and overturning cars in frustration.[49] At the inquest following Bridget Driscoll's death, the London Coroner said "This must never happen again."

But it has happened again, and again. Fast-forward about 90 years. According to the World Health Organization 1.2 million deaths and 50 million injuries occur each year on roads.[50] About 43,000 lives are lost each year in the U.S. in traffic accidents, plus 500,000 serious injuries.[51] In late 1995, Congress abolished the national 55-mph speed limit, even though it was known that highway accidents would increase. And they did—roughly 15% in the states that raised their speed limits after Congress gave permission. In states that maintained the 55 mph limit the rates remained fairly constant.[52] At least for a while. Over a longer term the correlation between speed limits and accident rates is weak. In recent years a trend toward reduced accidents and fatalities has emerged, probably associated with improvements in the safety of cars and roads.[53]

In the UK, five times as many people are killed on the roads than are murdered; road crashes are the leading cause of death and acquired disability for those between 5 and 40 years old. One in 80 EU residents is expected to die 40 years prematurely due to a road crash; over half of all road deaths In London are pedestrians. Ian Roberts, Professor of Epidemiology and Public Health at the University of London, said about the epidemic of road death and injury ". . . it is unusual to encounter a serious analysis of road danger in national news media. [But] by 2020, road crashes will have moved from ninth to third place in the world disease ranking. If we overlook this carnage, it will be the propaganda coup of the new millennium."[54]

[49] Ibid.
[50] "Road Safety: A Public Health Issue."
[51] Tyson, "DOT Releases Preliminary Estimates of 2003 Highway Fatalities."
[52] "Higher speed limits, deaths tied," A10.
[53] See, for example, "Traffic Fatalities vs. Crashes."
[54] Roadpeace, *loc. cit.*

Sacrifices to Molech?

People died in U.S. traffic at the rate of 1.5 deaths per 100 million vehicle miles in 2003, unchanged from the previous year.[55] Of the 43,220 fatalities each year, 972 were children aged seven and under.[56] Worship of the Ammonite god *Molech* involved the sacrifice of children.[57] Old Testament Law demanded the death of anyone who offered his child to Molech. Several other references of child sacrifice not specific to Molech also appear. But Solomon built a monument to Molech on "the hill that is before Jerusalem," i.e., the Mount of Olives. King Ahaz burned his children in the fire, and Manasseh did the same.[58] Samaria was judged for this sin.[59] King Josiah of Judah destroyed the high places of Molech,[60] but the prophet Eezekiel was still condemning the practice early in the sixth century BC. The Diaspora seems to have put an end to the practice among the Hebrews but it lingered into the Christian era among the Carthaginian Phoenicians of North Africa.[61]

On the one hand, hinting that highway fatalities amount to child sacrifice is unfair, even outrageous. The sacrifices to Molech were deliberate, whereas in traffic accidents children's deaths are accidental. But on the other hand, if we make public policy choices that predictably will result in the death of children, we can't exactly view them as being accidental. The fatality rate is predictable. From a biblical perspective, Molech was an idol. Dutch parliamentarian and economics professor Bob Goudzwaard identified five characteristics of idol worship:[62]

1. People sever something from their immediate environment, refashion it and erect it on its own feet in a special place.

2. They ritually consecrate it and kneel before it, seeing it as a thing that has life in itself.

3. They bring sacrifices and look to the idol for advice and direction.

---

[55] Tyson, *loc. cit.*

[56] Ibid.

[57] Lev 18:21, 20:2–5; 2Kgs 23.

[58] 2 Chr 28:3; 2 Kgs 21:6.

[59] 2 Kgs 17:17.

[60] 2 Kgs 23:10, 13.

[61] Douglas, *The New Bible Dictionary*, 836.

[62] Goudzwaard, *Idols of Our Time*, 21–22.

4. They expect the idol to repay their reverence, obedience, and sacrifices with health, security, prosperity, and happiness.

5. They give the idol permission to demand and receive whatever it desires, even if it includes animal or human life, because they see the idol as a savior, as the one who can make life whole and bring blessing.

It is hard to argue that automobiles don't qualify. In chapter 2, I noted that both persons and societies put their faith in things or forces that their own hands have made. In chapter 8, this process was labeled technicism: the spirit of the age in Western societies. When people put themselves in position of dependence on created things, according to Goudzwaard, invariably the moment comes when those things or forces gain the upper hand. "It is conceivable," he wrote, "that the means to progress which our own hands have made—the economy, technology, science and the state—have become such forces today, imposing their will on us as gods."[63] The prophet Isaiah warned about gods who make no demands on their owners but cannot save them.[64]

Our personal vehicles do make demands on us. We often sacrifice in other areas in order to purchase and operate them. Several homes in my neighborhood are poorly maintained but their driveways host one or more shiny new vehicles. In addition to the purchase cost, we spend additional sums to "personalize" our vehicles with accessories, upgrades, and modifications. Then we take them for weekly washing, regular oil changes, and sometimes "detailing." Some people also look to their vehicles for safety and security. "We make room for technology, even if we must sacrifice," Goudzwaard notes, "because we believe that technology gives life meaning."[65]

A Sustainable Alternative

We have seen how centering the U.S. transportation system on private motor vehicles has dispersed society, consumed greenfields, and fostered the decline of urban cores. More than two-thirds of the land area in Los Angeles is devoted to the automobile for streets, highways, parking, sales, service, and other related businesses.[66] Nationwide, the area paved for

[63] Goudzwaard, *loc. cit.,* 13.

[64] Isa 44:9–20.

[65] Goudzwaard, *loc. cit.,* 22.

[66] Yates, "California Dreaming," 31–32.

streets and highways would cover the state of Indiana. In contrast to automobiles, trains are the agent of cities and centralization.[67] As we shall see, they offer many other advantages as well.

The federal government underwrote the first transcontinental railroad in order to solidify the country politically and to move the military about cheaply and quickly. On this basis, the nation gained a very positive financial return on its investment. Subsequent public investment in transportation has been justified on the basis of providing mobility for commerce; to open market opportunities and making it possible for private enterprise to create wealth.[68] With the possible exception of the political objective, these reasons are as valid today as they were when the transcontinental railroad was completed in 1869. In terms of energy efficiency, labor productivity, and land use, rail transportation is more efficient than any other motor-powered mode.[69] However, the government long ago shifted its investment to rail's competition: highways, waterways, and airways. Today the competition for railroads is from private companies that operate on public highways, airways, and waterways. State, federal, and county governments own and maintain the rights-of-way and the control or signal systems for each of these modes—except rail. In many instances, the government also owns the terminals. Nominal user fees are charged, but these fees do not properly reflect taxes and similar expenses that railroads pay.

In 1996, the direct (that is, a budget item) federal subsidy to U.S. highway transportation was $300 billion larger than the defense budget and more than 5% of the GDP.[70] When indirect costs are included, the subsidy to automobiles was estimated at $2000 per auto per year *above* what drivers pay in taxes and other fees.[71] By 2004—when state and local governments alone spent more than $65 billion for new construction and major repairs of highways—the estimated subsidy had risen to between $5,000 and $20,000 per vehicle per year.[72] If routine maintenance is included the total state and local government expenditure topped $118 billion in 2004. The National Automobile Dealers Association reported that total dealership sales of vehicles in calendar year 2004 exceeded $714

[67] Gordon, *Passage to Union.*

[68] Ambrose, *Nothing Like it in the World.*

[69] *Transportation Energy Data Book, Edition 25.*

[70] Durning, "The Car and the City"; Goddard, *Getting There*, 255; Mathews, "Once a Blessing, automobiles turn into a curse." Also see "Taming the Beast," 1–18.

[71] Ibid.

[72] Wilson, "Pedals vs. Fuel Cells."

billion. Meanwhile, capital expenditures for all public transportation in the U.S. amounted to only $13.2 billion.[73]

The foregoing figures include the costs of building and repairing roads, snow removal, traffic control systems, lighting, law enforcement, and emergency services. They do not include parking lots, loss of economic activity due to congestion, illness caused by air pollution, medical care for the victims of two million accidents each year, military protection for our oil supply, program subsidies that support extraction, production, and use of petroleum, and bond interest. These costs are paid by every taxpayer, not just the owners and drivers. Most of the costs are paid straight out of general revenues.[74] In 1989, Congress took $5.3 billion out of the general Treasury to pay for aviation expenses, and in 1990 approximately $7.1 billion—or about $28 per citizen.[75] The congressional Office of Technology Assessment estimated that in 1995 automobile drivers paid directly only about 10% of the costs they incurred.[76]

There is no "profit and loss" bookkeeping in highway parlance, only pavement crumbling under the weight of heavy trucks. The damage done to a roadway by just one pass of a tractor-trailer rig is equivalent to the damage done by 2,000 to 3,000 passenger vehicles. The impact increases exponentially with weight: a 95,000-pound truck does two to three times the damage of an 80,000-pound one.[77] Even the American Trucking Association acknowledges that one 80,000-pound truck can cause the same damage as 800 to 1,000 automobiles.[78] Compare this with the fact that Union Pacific Railroad spent $35 million to repair flood damage in the Feather River Canyon of California after the winter storms of 1996-97, and Southern Pacific Railroad spent $80 million during the floods of 1984-1987 to shore up its Great Salt Lake causeway. Had these damages been to highways, the state highway departments would have done the repairs with public funds. No trucking company operates a civil engineering or construction division.

---

[73] Hutchinson, "Easy on the Gas," 24–33.

[74] Property taxes, appropriations from the general fund and timber revenues made up one-third of Oregon's 1992 road and highway budget (Hagerbaumer, "Make the most of it").

[75] Russakoff, "Chasing After That Pie in the Sky."

[76] Office of Technology Assessment 1994. Cited by Hagerbaumer, *loc. cit.*

[77] Johnston, "Riders are an afterthought in the battle to save or dismantle Amtrak," 61–65.

[78] Lankard and Lehrer, "Axles to Grind," 34–38.

Revenues generated by railroads do not cover the cost of capital; but neither is this true of any other transportation mode.[79] Every other industrial and capitalist nation uses gasoline taxes to support non-road transportation modes. But the U.S. charges only a half to a sixth of the per-gallon gasoline tax of other industrial nations.[80] If the hidden subsidies were included in the cost of gasoline, its cost would rise between $2.20 and $4.26 *per gallon.*[81] Whereas Switzerland spends $228 per person annually for capital investment in railroads, the United States spends $1.64. In this regard, we rank thirty-fifth in the world, between Bolivia and Turkey.[82] The tradition continues even in the face of unprecedented uncertainties about petroleum. The 2005 Transportation Act directed over 90% of the federal funds to roads and highways. Petroleum consumption alone should provide sufficient motive for reassessing the way we subsidize highway transportation, because, at a minimum, U.S. dependence on imported oil severely constrains foreign policy options; and at most it greatly increases the probability of wars for assurance of supply.[83]

Two recent examples reveal how entrenched "highway thinking" really is in the U.S. In 2000, the U.S. government prepared to spend $22 billion over two decades to add just one lane each way to Interstate 81 in Virginia to accommodate truck traffic, while the parallel Norfolk Southern Railway's Shenandoah Valley line languished as a slow single-track railroad. It would cost a fraction of that amount to turn the railroad into a high-speed, double-track intermodal conveyor.[84] In 2004, the plan morphed into building an entirely new highway just for trucks, using a combination of federal, state, and private funds and a proposal to charge tolls. The initiative was seen as a prototype for a national network of new interstate highways for trucks.[85]

An example from the Sonoma-Marin County area of California offers another illustration. Highway 101 is the main (and only) north-south transportation artery through these counties north of San Francisco's Golden Gate Bridge. It is mostly a four-lane freeway built during the freeway-building frenzy of the 1960s, and today it ranks among the most con-

[79] Ellis, "Excess capacity a thing of the past," 16–17.

[80] Teepen, *loc. cit.*

[81] "The Real Price of Gasoline"; "Gasoline Cost Externalities."

[82] Oakes, "Amtrak hopes to keep up with budget streamline," 10A; Hutchinson, *loc. cit.*

[83] Heinberg, *The Party's Over.*

[84] Phillips, "The new millennium," 12–13.

[85] Ginsberg, "How About a Road Just for Trucks?" 31.

gested corridors in the state. A moribund railroad parallels the highway, and in fact extends nearly 300 miles up the coast to Eureka. Sonoma and Marin Counties have been working to initiate a commuter train along the line, and several cities have built stations in anticipation. The train would operate right alongside the most congested portions of highway 101, connecting at Larkspur with the ferry to San Francisco. But unfortunately, opposition has emerged. One opponent is the CEO of the Marin County Chamber of Commerce, who opposes spending public funds for commuter trains. His rationale is "small businesses have a tough time competing in this difficult economy from a bottom-line perspective. It costs money to help underwrite the cost of using transit."[86] Like most U.S. motorists he seems to believe that autos and trucks pay their way. Adding one lane each way to the freeway will cost over $30 million per mile, *five times* the per-mile cost of refurbishing the railroad and establishing commuter service. And the latter figure even includes purchasing the vehicles and maintaining the system.[87]

If we continue doing what we've always done, we'll get what we've always gotten; namely, sprawl, congestion, pollution, ever-increasing reliance on petroleum, and dependence upon an inefficient transportation system. Transit critics miss the essential truth that the present paradigm is not sustainable. The day is approaching where private automobiles *cannot* be the backbone of our transportation system. When the combined effects of sprawl, petroleum dependence, and environmental impact are factored into the equation, the marginal return on additional investment in our system of highways carrying private vehicles begins to turn negative. Few lawmakers seem to grasp this fact or use it to inform their constituencies. The public pays attention to potholes, parking, and the price of gasoline, but the subsidies to transportation are not well known or understood. I suspect this is not only because the data are fragmented and scattered, but also because the majority of us just don't want to know. We want to believe that further investment at the margin will bring positive returns. This seems to represent exactly the stupor that Langdon Winner called "technological somnambulism."[88]

This section would not be complete without brief mention of additional environmental advantages of railroads vs. highways. Reduction in petroleum consumption and air pollution is guaranteed. Each solo auto

[86] Meagher and Seidman, "Slow and go costs jobs," 88–95.
[87] Benefield, "Not so fast," A1, A15.
[88] Winner, *The Whale and the Reactor*, 10.

commuter in the San Francisco Bay Area who switched to public transportation would save the country 500 gallons of gas and keep 9.1 pounds of hydrocarbons, 62.5 pounds of carbon monoxide, and 4.9 pounds of nitrous oxides out of the air every year.[89] As a consequence of fossil fuel combustion, the U.S. is the world's major generator of CO_2 and the greatest contributor to global warming. Each highway transportation unit shifted to rail reduces our contribution of CO_2 in proportion to the reduction in fuel consumption. Indirect environmental benefits also exist. Highways are impervious while railroad roadbeds are porous. Because rainwater can percolate to the subsoil, runoff problems are reduced in comparison to pavement. And railroad right-of-way does not serve as a physical barrier to wild animals as do interstate highways. Finally, land productivity of railroads—ton-miles per acre of land—for rail freight is four times higher than the comparable value from trucks.[90]

Closure

During the furor over the "What Would Jesus Drive?" campaign in 2005, an engineering educator colleague of mine decided to conduct an experiment to obtain some concrete understanding of resource consumption by her fellow church members.[91] To carry out the experiment, she counted the number of vehicles at two services of her church one Sunday, and from the attendance "head count" she determined the number of people transported per vehicle. She then conducted a similar assessment during a Monday evening at a restaurant parking lot. A restaurant was chosen for comparison because people would most likely go there with a family as they do to church, whereas one might use a different vehicle and might not bring the family when shopping for groceries or other stuff. The per-vehicle headcount for the restaurant was assumed to be the same as for the church. By looking up the EPA mileage for each vehicle she produced an estimate of the "per capita gasoline efficiency" of each venue.

Within the accuracy of the study, the transportation habits of the Churchgoers were indistinguishable from those of the restaurant customers.[92] Although the study was not statistically rigorous, my colleague believes that her congregation is representative of most moderate-to-large

---

[89] Johnston, "Commuters may trade cars for trains," 1, 4.

[90] Commoner, *The Poverty of Power.*

[91] Miller, "Gasoline Consumption and Stewardship."

[92] It must be presumed that the people who were counted at church didn't *en masse* go to the same restaurant on the night of the study.

Midwestern churches. I am disappointed by the outcome, but not surprised. I have arrived at a similar—also not systematically studied—conclusion simply by looking at my own church parking lot. I believe that professing Christians should be demonstrating a lifestyle of sustainable consumption, and transportation choice is a high-impact place to begin.

The private automobile provides convenience when its numbers are bounded, but as a mass transportation system it contains the seeds of its own demise. The price of our mobility is counted in traffic deaths, environmental damage, congestion, sprawl, and dependence on imported oil. In order to free ourselves from bondage to the automobile system and achieve a more sustainable world, we will have to seek alternative means to meet the spiritual needs that automobiles provide. The root conflict pits individualistic personal liberties against changing our behavior in order to create a higher good. Unfortunately, so many of us are dependent upon the present system that change will require a major cultural shift. But it can be accomplished. We can build ourselves out of the present predicament even more efficiently than we built ourselves into it, because this time we will be doing it purposefully, with sustainability measures to guide us. Commuter rail offers fast and efficient transportation, and well-planned feeder bus routes enhance flexibility. Many U.S. cities recognized their mistake too late and now are spending billions to re-create the rail transit systems they had torn up in the twentieth century rush to freeways. So are many other metropolitan areas.

In 1975, G.L. Houseman wrote that the pervasiveness of the car and the need to promote, enhance, and protect the right of mobility raise a number of policy questions—the most important of which are as follows:[93]

- Whether the right of mobility should be enacted into law or even into the Constitution.

- How to establish requirements that would provide equal access to shopping, businesses, and public events for those who do not own automobiles.

- Whether 'drive-in' types of business establishments and public facilities should be discouraged, how this can be brought about and whether this is applicable under a large variety of situations.

[93] Buehand, review of "Dead End," 89–90; Buehand, review of "The Death of the Automobile," 89–90.

- How to regulate new construction that might attract large numbers of cars.
- How to articulate and provide for the needs of non-owners of autos.

"Resolution of these issues will imply a new life style." Houseman concluded. Libertarians will decry any attempts to address Houseman's "policy questions" as social engineering, but I think he was prescient. A society using rail as its transportation backbone would not offer the spontaneous mobility of the private automobile, or the flexibility of motor freight. But there aren't many places in Europe that one cannot reach quickly and efficiently by rail. Such a system in the U.S. would conserve land, fuel, environment, and permeable surfaces—and restore a measure of tranquility. And it will reduce the carnage of the highways. Our national dependence on petroleum is a large and growing national security risk. No serious contenders to replace petroleum—biomass, fuel cells, hydrogen, or electric vehicles—are anywhere close to reality.

Rising above the business-as-usual, linear thinking mode has never been more urgent. We cannot pave our way out of congestion and energy dependency. It took us 70 years to build our way into this crisis, and now we must build our way out. Time is no longer on our side. The evidence indicates that we have considerably less than 70 years to accomplish the shift.

Chapter 10

Technology and the Kingdom of God

WE ARE a long way from managing the consequences of technology, or acknowledging its limits. We are falling short because we lack a compelling basis for guiding the effort. Sustainability cautions apparently are compelling only when the impacts are certain to affect the children and grandchildren we play with; and philosophical arguments are restricted to philosophers, theologians, and other academics. Only religious arguments carry enough force to compel ordinary people to change their ways. Unfortunately, the contemporary American version of the Christian faith is infected with enlightenment optimism and technological determinism; the scientific-technological worldview. Once the leaders of the Church understand these things, the correction can begin. The *profound distraction* of technology and the spiritual nature of the scientific-technological worldview must be added to the list of contemporary issues that the laity must be equipped to discern. They can then proceed with the culture mandate as God intended.

The co-existence of positive benefits and negative impacts of human endeavor should not surprise students of the Bible, because scripture portrays a creation where good and evil co-exist. God's creation was good (He said it was); but He incorporated in it a capacity for evil because only creatures with free moral choice can satisfy His desire for fellowship. Prior to creation, Satan fell from grace and was expelled from God's presence as a consequence of his scheme to be equal with God. After the creation, Satan seduced humans to follow the same path. So God evicted them all from the Garden of Eden and imposed a curse on creation. There had to be a curse (a consequence for sin) because in the absence of a consequence, free moral agency would be meaningless. But God has assured ultimate victory; good will triumph at the end of history.

This powerful teaching contains the biblical response to those who reject its message because they cannot accept a God who would allow suffering and evil. It also contains the foundation for a theology of technology. The biblical diagnosis is that the present state of creation is *abnormal*, because the earth and its inhabitants are damaged by the curse. The fallen, abnormal state is the consequence of the sin of presumption—created beings aspiring to be God or to share His powers. The *normal* state is the one that God established in the Garden, and at the end of history the Edenic state will not only be restored, it will be purged of the very capacity for evil.

Biblical History: Creation and Fall

The Bible is not a historical record of man's search for God. Rather, it is the account of God's gradual revelation of Himself by means of His interaction with humans and the rest of His creation.[1] The revelation can best be understood as unfolding in four successive stages: *creation, fall from grace, reconciliation and redemption*, and *consummation*.[2] Creation and the fall from grace are described in the first few chapters of Genesis, with additional perspective added via many other Bible passages. The accounts of the patriarchs, prophets, judges, priests and kings partially communicated God's purposes, but Jesus' life, death, and resurrection revealed the true nature of the things God had been communicating. It is that the future kingdom involves the abolition not of space, time, or the cosmos itself, but rather of that which threatens space, time, and creation—namely, sin and death.[3] Paul, Peter, and the other New Testament writers explained how God's message applies to all nations and taught about living under grace. The early Christian apologists Irenaeus, Clement, Tertullian, Augustine, Francis Bacon, Roger Bacon, Luther and the Reformers added the doctrine of *Imago Dei,* thereby resulting in the five foundational elements of a reformed biblical worldview:[4]

1. Creation: of a cosmos originally good, but containing the possibility of the fall

2. Imago Dei: human beings created as image-bearers of God and sharing fellowship with Him

3. The fall: of the first humans from their privileged state as a result of willful transgression of *limits* placed on their freedoms by God

---

[1] Isa 10:12, 28:29; Moltman, *Theology of Hope*, 77.

[2] Brunner, *Man in Revolt.*

[3] Wright, *Jesus and the Victory of God*, 218.

[4] Brunner, *loc. cit.*, 12, 105, 129, 131, 264, 513.

4. The curse: placed on humans and on nature as a result of the fall

5. Inherited sin: the willful transgression of limits by all humans

When God gave humans dominion over His creation, He not only gave us the ability to modify and shape creation, in effect He directed us to *create culture*; the cultural mandate of Genesis 1–3.[5] Culture is the secondary environment that humans superimpose on nature.[6] Monsma explains the cultural mandate as a call to transform untamed nature into a social environment with the aid of tools and procedures as they are developed.[7] What tools and powers did the first humans have? They were given dominion (rule) over and authority to name (Heb. *shem*) the animals, which to some commentators means taming wild animals, developing a taxonomy, and engaging in the work of animal husbandry. They undoubtedly used their voices to steer the animals, probably supplemented by sticks or "prods." Perhaps they built corrals, pens, and fences. But they didn't need to separate herbivores from carnivores, because before the fall all mammals—including humans—were herbivores.[8] Presumably, both humans and animals ate grains, low-hanging fruit, and roots. Later perhaps they cooked some of the food, meaning that fire, cookware, and utensils were developed. Adam was directed to "work and take care of" the Garden; the first horticulture. But what was there to care for? Were there weeds in the Garden; poisonous plants, pollination problems, aphids, and clay soil? Did fruit trees need pruning, dormant spray, thinning, and fertilizer? Likely not, but we must assume that vegetable matter underwent decay in order to replenish the humus, and hence the existence of the biological grand cycles and a food chain seems to have credence, at least in the biota and humus.[9] Civilization was sustainable: human activity was in harmony with nature and did not threaten to unbalance it.

The first humans, Adam and Eve, refused to limit themselves to act within the bounds set by God. They sought to "be like God" by deciding for themselves what was right and wrong. In so doing they declared

---

[5] Monsma, *Responsible Technology*, 37ff; Wauzzinski, *Discerning Prometheus*, 35.

[6] Niebuhr, *Christ and Culture*, 32.

[7] Monsma, *loc. cit.*

[8] Gen 1:29–30.

[9] Snoke, "Why Were Dangerous Animals Created?" 117–25.

their independence from Him, and the result was the fall from grace.[10] Until this moment they not only had all their needs met, they had God's assurance that they would be met. In chapter 2, I referred to this happy condition as *surety*, which today we attempt to achieve by technical means. But when they were evicted from the Garden Adam and Eve encountered a dangerous and hostile realm. Life became arduous and adversarial; their exercise of dominion began to include an arduousness and drudgery that was unknown before.[11] They became dangerous to the Earth and its creatures, to other humans, and to themselves,[12] and nature became dangerous to humans.[13] Perhaps natural processes passed a "tipping point." Yet these may have been the least of their troubles. Their greatest loss was ready access to the Creator.

The fall was not a one-time simple moral lapse; it heralded complete loss of the state of innocence and the beginning of destruction of the creation by the creature.[14] The fall and curse resulted in a profound four-dimensional alienation:[15]

- theological—humans from God

- psychological—human nature divided against itself

- sociological—humans from humans; damage to godly functioning of community

- ecological—human dominion over nature became exploitative and adversarial

The desire for autonomy began with Satan, seduced Adam and Eve, and infected their descendents. Their endeavors became accompanied by jealousy, arrogance, hubris, and greed, as seen in Cain's attitude and the Babel event.[16] The Bible teaches that every human being since Adam and Eve

---

[10] Gen 3:5.

[11] Gen 3:17–19. This exegesis requires Adam and Eve to have lived full lives before the fall, rather than 12 hours as the young Earth model demands (Fischer, "Young-Earth Creationism: A Literal Mistake," 222–31.

[12] Gen 3:14–19; Rom 8:21–22.

[13] Schaeffer, *The God Who is There*; Schaeffer, *Pollution and the Death of Man*, 67–68.

[14] Brunner, *loc. cit.*, 105, 512–14; Bonhoeffer, *Creation and Fall*, 76; Bonhoeffer, *Temptation*, 76.

[15] Brunner, *loc. cit.*, 129–38, 168, 229–33, 278–88, 409–11; Clayton, *God and Contemporary Science*, 43; Bonhoffer, *loc. cit.*, 76; Schaeffer, *Pollution and the Death of Man*, 67–68.

[16] Gen 11:1–9.

inherited their fallen natures; each one of us independently commits the same sin of presumption.[17] Autonomy or "self law" has become the predominant article of faith, and domination and subjugation our corresponding view of nature.[18] Our Imago Dei has become perverted and defaced. In Emil Brunner's theology we have assumed *solidarity* with Adam in sin.[19] The Apostle Paul calls the fallen nature "man without the Spirit."[20]

Redemption and Reconciliation: the Kingdom of God

Since the fall, and perhaps since Satan's fall in pre-history, God's purpose in biblical history has been *redemption* and *reconciliation*. In an incremental way, redemption and reconciliation restore God's rule over His creation. To re-emphasize its importance, God formally renewed the cultural mandate after the flood.[21] Noah was to set about doing the things that God had wanted Adam to do. God's rule defines His *kingdom*, on this Earth and in Heaven.[22] When Jesus announced the kingdom,[23] He meant that God's kingdom had broken into temporal history. From a theological perspective, biblical history is "not surveyed from the standpoint of the end at which all things stand still . . . it is a future announced from the midst of the process."[24] Regardless of how or when it will be consummated, God's kingdom has begun on this Earth.[25]

Armed with the understanding that God's present work is redemption and reconciliation, the results of which expand His present-and-future kingdom, we are now better prepared to consider the possible contribution of technology to the process. If technology can help restore some lost dominion, it can also help advance God's kingdom. A Bible-based science and technology "should consciously try to see nature substantially healed, while waiting for the future complete healing at Christ's return."[26] What assets that Adam and Eve enjoyed and subsequently lost can be restored to

---

[17] cf. Rom 5:12–14.

[18] Wauzzinski, *loc. cit.,* 29–31.

[19] Brunner, *loc. cit.,* 123, 130.

[20] 1 Cor 2:14.

[21] Gen 9:1–7.

[22] Luke 11:2–4.

[23] Mark 1:15, 9:1.

[24] Moltmann, *loc. cit.,* 133.

[25] Bonhoffer, *loc. cit.,* 25.

[26] Schaeffer, *Pollution and the Death of Man,* 81.

some degree by technology? What aspects of the four-fold alienation can be alleviated by technological means? And what limits should be placed on technology in order to avoid repeating the sin of presumption?

During the early years of the second millennium, and as an adjunct to the millennial movements that periodically surged through Europe, the idea gradually emerged that technology could help recover the pristine conditions that Adam and Eve enjoyed in the garden.[27] Although the envisioned recovery that was to be facilitated by technology was primarily physical, no distinct separation was made between physical and spiritual realms. The Carolingian philosopher Erigena apparently was first to argue that the "useful arts" were part of mankind's original endowment rather than a necessary endeavor of his fallen state. Thus mankind's pre-fall powers could be at least partially recovered.[28] Francis Bacon developed the argument further: "Man by the fall fell at the same time from his state of innocence and from his dominion over nature. Both of these losses, however, even in this life, can in some part be repaired: the former by religion and faith, the latter by the arts and sciences."[29]

The End of History

Jesus' work of redemption and reconciliation will be completed at the *consummation*, marking the end of temporal history. At the consummation all things will be finally reconciled to God[30] and liberated from their bondage to decay.[31] That *all things* will be reconciled means that the kingdom has not only to do with persons, but also with relationships: between humans and other humans, and between humans and nature. The creation will be transformed from its fallen state to a perfect or glorified one.[32] In other words, the four dimensions of alienation will be repaired and creation as a whole will be reconciled to God.[33]

But the final state will not be simply Eden recovered; it will be perfect. That is because the original creation contained the possibility of sin and thus was imperfect, whereas the eternal kingdom will be free from even the possibility of sin. Thus the final state will be better than the initial

---

[27] Noble, *The Religion of Technology*, 16–17.

[28] Ibid.

[29] Bacon, *Novum Organon.* Quoted by Schaeffer, *Pollution and the Death of Man*, 69.

[30] Col 1:20.

[31] Rom 8:21.

[32] Brunner, *loc. cit.,* 416–17, 427.

[33] Moltmann, *loc. cit.,* 204.

one. Apparently we will be given powers exceeding those that Adam and Eve enjoyed. But to presume that this future perfection legitimizes the present use of technology to achieve powers that Adam and Eve could not have had comes dangerously close to repeating the original sin. Because reconciliation is a process that will be completed only at the consummation, in the interim man "must in obedience seek the divine righteousness in his body, on earth, and in all creatures."[34]

In Matthew 24, Jesus responded to his disciples' question "what will be the sign of your coming and of the end of the age?" with a word picture of social, political, spiritual, and physical chaos. "Then the Son of Man will come with power and great glory," he said. How are we to understand this portrayal? The Bible clearly predicts a time of chaos, but the causes and the chronology are not specified. Could this chaos be an emergent outcome of technology and the inevitable end state of our present course? Will the situation be facilitated by technology, or will technology have nothing to do with it? Some theologians and futurists have interpreted the biblical portrayal as nuclear holocaust, others as environmental catastrophe. Could the pestilence of the book of Revelation be biological warfare, or biotech out of control (ala Bill Joy's "omnivorous gray goo")? Will the predicted famine result from soil exhaustion, failure of biotech crops, or insufficient fresh water?

In apocalyptic eschatology normally associated with dispensational theology, consummation is not the eventual overcoming of evil with good, but separation of good from evil including *replacement* of a world under the power of evil with a world of righteousness.[35] Reinhold Neibuhr argued that Jesus' words in Matthew 24 were not meant to be interpreted chronologically because doing so would reduce God's ultimate vindication over history to a point in time, and presuppose an eternity that "annuls rather than fulfills the historical process."[36] Jürgen Moltmann wrote that apocalyptic eschatology "shows signs of non-historic thinking .. a deterministic view of history, a fatalistic dualism not found in the writings of the Old Testament prophets . . . contain[ing] traces of a distant God of Deism."[37]

---

[34] Moltmann, *loc. cit.*, 206.

[35] Moltmann, *loc. cit.*, 134.

[36] Niebuhr, "The Nature and Destiny of Man," 325–26.

[37] Moltmann, *loc. cit.*, 134–35.

Albert Truesdale describes the apocalyptic model as "discontinuous eschatology."[38] The discontinuity arises when God destroys (or allows destruction of) the physical universe, after which He creates a new heaven and new earth. Rather than *re*-creation or *renewal*, this model has more in common with the original creation *ex nihilo*. With the "pre-tribulation rapture of the saints" a discontinuity in human history occurs as well, when believers are removed from Earth during the tribulation only to return later to rule with Jesus during the millennium. The discontinuous eschatological model is often combined with a utilitarian interpretation of Genesis 1–2; that is, intrinsic value of the creation is discounted relative to the value that nature earns through its productivity for the human race.

Even though advocates of discontinuous or apocalyptic eschatology expect inexorable descent into chaos and apocalypse (culminating in destruction), at the same time they are inclined toward an optimistic and deterministic view of technology. This may be because discontinuous eschatology provides no basis for critiquing misguided technological innovation; negative consequences are interpreted as portents of the coming destruction. If environmental degradation and cultural disasters are evidence of the approach of the end times and verification of the trustworthiness of scripture, any proposed ethic of sustainability seems greatly weakened. To be "self-referentially coherent" one would have to cheer the damage! Historian Lynn White's oft-cited article castigating the Christian faith for insensitivity to environmental degradation[39] was based primarily on his (mis-)interpretation of the dominion mandate in Genesis 1–2. Even though White didn't address discontinuous eschatology explicitly, the model seems indicted by his critique.

Purification Eschatology

The culture mandate seems clear enough for Adam and Noah's situations; after all, they were creating culture ab initio. But how are we who were born into already-mature cultures supposed to continue the mandate? Carl Henry, theologian and founder of *Christianity Today*, said that: "The divine culture-mandate means that both in perspective and practice the Christian is to bear witness to the divine spiritual and moral dimension in work and leisure, in learning and the arts, in family and public

[38] Truesdale, "Last Things First," 117–22.
[39] White, "The Historical Roots of Our Ecologic Crisis," 1203–7.

life."[40] According to this view the people of God have a mandate not only to discern contemporary culture, but also to steer it toward Godly norms. Theologian Howard Snyder added: "Now, even before the return of Christ, man in Christ has responsibility for all of culture . . . Our mission is nothing other than bringing all things, and supremely all people of the earth under the dominion and headship of Jesus Christ. If not all come willingly, nevertheless, every knee will bow and every tongue will confess that Jesus Christ is Lord."[41]

Because human understanding became impaired by the fall from grace and because God has placed limits on human knowledge, is it not an act of hubris to claim that one has the definite key to interpretation of biblical eschatology? If we determine that technology is the source of the end-times chaos portrayed in Scripture, do we continue to pursue technology because the outcome is in God's plan? It would be far better—and more biblical—to try to manage it, and especially try to stop technologies with large destructive potential. Even if we decide that technology has nothing to do with the end state, we still are responsible for pursuing substantial healing of the effects of the fall.

An intriguing alternative to the discontinuous model, but one not widely considered in the evangelical church, holds that instead of the creation's destruction and subsequent replacement by an undamaged new heaven and new earth, corruption will be removed. The outcome will be the *whole creation* purified.[42] If the very potential for evil is also removed, the result will be beyond the Edenic state, although this difference is not explicitly explained in the "purification eschatology" literature. Purification eschatology is consistent with amillenial concepts of the kingdom of God on Earth, and it precludes an escape from present responsibility.

Christ and Culture

Extending transformation from individual sanctification to redemption of culture has been controversial in the Church, especially within evangelicalism. But theologian N. T. Wright believes far too many people think the individual is all that matters and the corporate is a diversion. "The great emphasis in the New Testament is that the gospel is not how to escape the

---

[40] Henry, *A Plea for Evangelical Demonstration*, 107. Quoted in Snyder, *The Community of the King*, 26.

[41] Phil 2:10–11. Cf. Synder, *loc. cit.*, 12, 26.

[42] Alcorn, Randy, *Heaven*; Kirk, *Good News of the Kingdom Coming*, 48–58; Reitkirk, *The Future Great Planet Earth*.

world," Wright says, "[but] that the crucified and risen Jesus is the Lord of the world. His death and Resurrection transform the world, and that transformation can happen to you."[43] Instead of thinking about gospel and salvation as something that saved people apart from the world, Wright came to understand the gospel and salvation as being "something which was basically God saving the world. The gospel declared something that was publicly true about the whole world rather then simply opening up an option into which I as an individual and other individuals could step."[44]

In his classic work *Christ and Culture*, H. Richard Niebuhr identified five possible Christian approaches to culture: Christ *against* culture, Christ *of* culture, Christ *above* culture, Christ and culture *in paradox*, and Christ the *transformer* of culture.[45] Although he does not explicitly say, it can be assumed that Niebuhr has Western civilization in mind. Christ *against* culture draws heavily from 1 John. Advocates separate themselves from society and give up all responsibility for the world, shunning material wealth, military service, and political involvement. The Christ against culture position captures Anabaptist doctrine. Christ *of* culture senses no great tension between Christ's teaching and the world; advocates are able to accommodate biblical principles to contemporary civilization. This viewpoint is much in evidence in America today, where some Christian leaders identify "our way of life" with biblical principles. The accommodation may require selective usage of scripture or Gnostic separation of the spiritual and material realms.

The Christ *above* culture view emphasizes the relationship between God and man and discounts the importance of any relationship between God and culture. This group is willing to cooperate with nonbelievers in carrying on the work of the world while attempting to maintain a distinctive Christian faith and life for themselves. Christ and culture *in paradox* holds that Christians are called to live in two worlds. Martin Luther explained it as the duality of the worlds of Christ and Caesar, to which the Christian owes allegiance at different times and in different ways. Advocates seek to live by the gospel in a society they view as unredeemable. Niebuhr attributes the Christ as *transformer* of culture viewpoint to Augustine and Calvin. Advocates maintain that Christ can and will convert both man and society to biblical practice. The position is consistent with the social gospel movement in America begun by Walter Rausenbusch during

[43] Quoted in Stafford, "Mere Mission," 39–41.

[44] Quoted in Stafford, "N.T. Wright: Making scholarship a tool for the church," 42–46.

[45] Niebuhr, *Christ and Culture*.

the turn of the nineteenth century.[46] However, numerous contemporary Christian organizations who believe that Christians should be transformers of culture would resist the social gospel label.

Regardless of their theology of Christ and culture, Christians have initiated many social reforms, from abolition of slavery and child labor to humane treatment of leprosy and the Dalits (untouchables) of India, to establishment of hospitals, orphanages, and soup kitchens. More recently the Christian "Just War" tradition has been applied to nuclear weapons, a theology of creation care has been developed, right-to-life legislation has been passed, and calls for limitations on genome manipulation and human cloning have been sounded. Technology is used to help spread the gospel, and technology can be used for much of the healing in the physical, aesthetic, and sociological realms. All of these actions qualify as "redemption of society" or "transformation of the social order."

Purposes and Limitations of Technology

Redemption and restoration is the "interim" between Christ's first and second advents; between the disclosure of the kingdom and its fulfillment.[47] Full realization of God's kingdom awaits the consummation, but the process is underway.[48] Thus we are full of hope, but we also have responsibility. According to Moltmann "the other side of reconciliation [is] mankind filled with hopeful expectation but at the same time responsibility and decision for the world of history is required of him." "Salvation aims at reconciliation with God (2 Cor 5:18ff.), at forgiveness of sins, and abolition of godlessness," he writes. "But salvation—σωτηρια—must also be understood as *shalōm*—שָׁלוֹם—in the Old Testament sense. This does not mean merely salvation of the soul, individual rescue from the evil world, comfort for the troubled conscience, but also the realization of the eschatological *hope of justice*, the humanizing of man, the socializing of humanity, peace for all creation." [49]

The responsibility that Moltmann refers to includes technology, not only because technology can help relieve suffering, but because Western

---

[46] Ferguson et al., "Social Gospel," 646–47.

[47] Niebuhr, "The Nature and Destiny of Man," 326. The war between David and Saul seems to illustrate the situation (2 Sam 3:1). Samuel had anointed David King of Israel, but he did not sit upon the throne until the House of Saul had been defeated, thirty years later.

[48] Eph 1:10; cf. Brunner, *loc. cit.*, 451; Niebuhr "The Nature and Destiny of Man," 325.

[49] Moltmann, *loc. cit.*, 328–29.

culture *is* technological. But we must extract the authentically biblical applications from the list of possible purposes that I have discussed in this chapter and preceding ones. The broad list includes:

1. exercising the abilities that God gave us
2. helping to fulfill the mandates—including culture and mission
3. relieving toil and suffering that ensued from the fall
4. recovering powers that Adam lost
5. achieving powers that Adam never had
6. establishing the kingdom of God on Earth

Collectively, the six purposes portend a high calling not only for Christians who develop technology, but also for all of us who use it. Thus credit for positive impacts and responsibility for negative ones belong to both developer and user. But each purpose must also be evaluated in light of other scriptures. I have argued that technology cannot be morally neutral because it is developed by humans with an objective in mind and a worldview at work. Moreover, technology is used by humans for the design intent or misused for other purposes, and emergent properties are usually realized only after the causative technology is widely disseminated in the economy.

The first three purposes seem readily supportable on biblical grounds. When biblically managed, technology can be a "force multiplier" to help mankind carry out the mandates, spread the gospel, and exercise his dominion and stewardship duties. Except for mission, these duties existed before the fall. Technology can be (and has been) employed to relieve suffering and reduce toil and drudgery that came to be associated with human endeavor subsequent to the fall. But we must be careful that our zeal for the ends does not seduce us into undiscerning acceptance of any or all means.

Purpose 4 is in the gray area, because we know Adam's powers only in a general sense. Purposes 5 and 6 are fraught with risks of presumption and arrogance, because it is tempting to embrace technology as a means to regain lost paradise—and surpass it. The fully realized kingdom will be better than the Garden of Eden; but that knowledge also opened the door to the idea that modern technology can enable us to bypass the limits imposed on first humans. Biotechnology comes to mind immediately, as do artificial intelligence, transhumanism, and eugenics. God intervened when mankind determined to use civil engineering to design and construct a tower that reached to heaven. Perhaps this is symbolic language, perhaps not; but the offense of *presumption* is the same one that caused the downfall of Satan and the eviction of Adam and Eve from the Garden. Genetic engineering and biotechnology are not biblically sanctioned, but neither are they condemned unless they are pursued with the objective of attaining god-like powers.

In carrying out their duties, Adam and Eve were to recognize limits and care for the Garden. They were (and we are) to subdue and rule in a way that brings out the beauty and excellence that God designed into the creation. The psalmist clarifies the point by explaining that products of culture should bring praise to the Creator.[50] All the God-given limits or constraints that mankind encountered in Genesis were made much more specific in the Mosaic Law. Idol worship and covetousness stand out as particular problems most likely to be exacerbated by technology, and the concept of justice becomes much more complex. For many Christians, "Thou shall not kill" indicts abortion, cloning, euthanasia, and modern warfare. But the underlying principles did not change with the giving of the Law or with the inauguration of the kingdom. Our present understanding of the biblical purposes of technology and its limitations can be summarized in the following general terms:

- Adam (first man) was given responsibilities (to develop taxonomy of creatures, to work and keep the Garden). This is culture and creation care mandates.

- He (and first woman) had enormous freedom—including fellowship with the Creator—but limits were imposed ("You shall not eat of the tree . . ."). These directives provide a foundation for responsible technology and imply limits to human endeavor.

- The effects of the fall will not be fully rescinded until the consummation. Hence technology as a means to regain lost paradise is destined to end in disappointment.

- The spiritual and psychological separations may not be accessible to technological repair, even though great progress has been made in the fields of neuroscience and psychopharmacology. On the other hand, technology can affect the human psyche and spirit in both positive and negative ways.

[50] Ps 104, 108.

Additional Biblical Guidance

At this stage our nascent "theology of technology" is still too theoretical to be of much practical use. It must be supplemented with additional biblical principles including justice, love, and compassion. A complete theology of technology must also honor the covenants, help us love God and neighbor, and care for God's creation. But neither technology nor nature can be viewed as sacred. We must maintain a distinction between creation and Creator; only the transcendent God is to be worshipped. According to Psalm 8 and the *Westminster Larger Catechism,* "the chief purpose of mankind to worship God and enjoy Him forever." This transcendent calling trivializes the thesis of evolutionary psychology, which claims that the ultimate purpose of biological life is to propagate its genes. Several of the aforementioned additional principles require further consideration before they can be applied to technology. The following sections on creation care, wisdom, Jesus' hierarchy of values, and the grand objectives summarize the important work that has been done in this regard.

Creation Care

According to scripture Jesus was the creator, the agent of the Trinity during the creation process.[51] He also is the sustainer,[52] such that without his moment-by-moment upholding the cosmos as we know it would cease to exist. The mandates given before the fall from grace provide the first reasons for technology. The cultural mandate was first.[53] Humans were to create order from the natural tendency to disorder and make nature productive for its dependents—but in a way that is responsive to the creator.[54] "Subdue" (Heb. *kabash*) in Gen 1:28 is used in conjunction with "replenish" or "fill." "Dominion" (Heb. *radah*) means *rule over*—but it is to be a Godly rule, as illustrated in Psalm 72:7–8, where *radah* also characterizes the reign of a righteous king.[55] According to Psalms 104, 108, and 148 the purpose of development is the glory and service of the Lord. That would include all the tools and techniques mankind develops to carry out the culture mandate.

---

[51] Col 1:16; Heb 1: 2.

[52] Col 1:17; Heb 1:3.

[53] Gen 1:28–30, 2:15.

[54] Monsma, *loc. cit.,* 37ff; Wauzzinski, *loc. cit.,* 35, 137.

[55] cf. Ps 72:8.

Creation care is the second mandate given before the fall. "Work" or "till" (Heb. *abad*) in Gen 2:15 contains the meaning of *serve*, and is followed by "keep" or "take care of" (Heb. *shamar*), which incorporates our responsibility to study and watch over. Repeatedly in the Old Testament the same word refers to serving God. *Shamar* is used in the Aaronic blessing "the Lord bless you and *keep* you."[56] Cain used *shamar* when he asked: "Am I my brother's *keeper*?"[57] God replied (in essence): "You are his brother."[58] In Psalm 23 *shamar* is used to describe the shepherd's care, and in Psalm 121 "The Lord will *keep* you from all harm."

Biblical technology will be protective of all living things because God values biodiversity; he established the "Noahic Covenant" with mankind "and every living thing."[59] Heb 1:3 attributes sustainability to Jesus: "upholding (sustaining) all things by the word of His power" (NIV). Heb 1:2 reads " . . . by His Son, whom he appointed heir of all things and through whom He made the Universe" (NIV). Eugene Peterson translates the passage "By his Son, God created the world in the beginning, and it will all belong to the Son at the end."[60] Notice the continuity: Jesus as creator, sustainer, and final owner. As I said earlier, biblical history is the gradual unfolding of God's plan. But the fact that Jesus is the sustainer does not absolve his followers from responsibility any more than his death and resurrection absolves us from evangelization. Why would God give his Son an inheritance that was hopelessly polluted and about to be destroyed? At the end of history "all nature will be redeemed."[61] The Son will inherit a *new* heaven and a *new* earth, but does that mean a new creation ex-nihilo? Possibly so; but equally likely it means a *renewed* cosmos, purified from the contaminating consequences of the fall from grace.

In the twenty first century, as we have seen, land, water, and atmosphere are under stress from human activity; and some of the stresses are global in extent and perhaps incipiently catastrophic. The stresses on the land have damaged its productive capacity in some areas and destroyed it in others. God's desire that biodiversity be maintained is codified in the Noahic covenant. In the book of Job, we read of God's delight in creatures that have no apparent usefulness to humans—thereby discrediting a

[56] Num 6:24.
[57] Gen 4:9.
[58] Woodley, *Living in Color*. 26–27.
[59] Gen 9: 8–17.
[60] Peterson, *The Message*.
[61] Rom 7:21; Col 1:20.

purely utilitarian worldview. Human activity that results in extinction of species is not only a biological concern for the ecosystems that support human life, it is in opposition to God's intent. So our theology of technology must elevate maintenance of biodiversity to obedience to God.

Evangelicals struggle to value environmental care against the urgency of evangelism.[62] Allegedly biblical environmental ethics that have been championed range from a property-rights platform called "wise use," to its opposite "Earthkeeping," or creation care, the term adopted here.[63] On the renewed Earth when healing is completed, mountains and hills will sing, trees will clap hands, the earth will be glad, the seas will roar, and fields will be joyful in praise of the Creator. Therefore creation care, environmental protection, and sustainable use are consistent with Jesus' work of sustaining, and repair of past environmental damage with his work of redemption. When we meditate on the fact that God called the creation "good," maintains ownership, and loves His *entire creation*, we derive additional motivation.[64]

Wisdom

Biblical wisdom is woven throughout Scripture, but especially in Psalms, Proverbs, and Ecclesiastes. "The fear of the Lord is the beginning of wisdom," Solomon wrote; "and knowledge of the Holy One is understanding."[65] In studying the wisdom literature, James Crenshaw extracted seven characteristics of biblical wisdom: time and place, moderation and restraint, fear of God, a capacity to reason, and no separation of religion and ethics. Properly applied, wisdom leads to "skepticism," by which Crenshaw meant doubt and questioning about the disparity between the actual state of affairs and a vision of what should be.[66] The application of wisdom principles to the issues of technology leads to *wise practice of technology*, characterized by recognition of limits, moderation and restraint,

---

[62] Ball, "The Use of Ecology in the Evangelical Protestant Response to the Ecological Crisis," 32–39. Evangelicals are also conflicted about biblical economics. But claims for biblical political economy range from free market capitalism to socialism; cf. Sine, *The Mustard Seed Conspiracy*; Sider, *Living More Simply*; Sider, *Rich Christians in an Age of Hunger*. Also "Green Products by Design"; Lane, *The Market Experience*; Reijnders, "The Factor X Debate," 13–22.

[63] Berry, "Creation and the Environment," 21–43; Van Dyke et al., *Redeeming Creation*.

[64] The Greek word *cosmos* that is translated *world* in John 3:16 refers to all of nature at least, and more likely to the entire universe.

[65] Prov 9:10.

[66] Crenshaw, *Old Testament Wisdom*. Cited in Stahl, *God and the Chip*, 121.

and by faith that skeptical reason and debate are a superior way to the good life—whereas the doctrines of technological experts or religious belief in the universal efficacy of technology are not.[67] Wise practice leads to a different way of practicing technology, one that requires changes in culture *and* organizations *and* techniques.[68]

The central principles of the new technological paradigm—Ursula Franklin's term is *redemptive technology*—are reciprocity and holism.[69] Reciprocity is fundamental to dialogue and is therefore the essence of democracy, as well as justice, fairness, and equity. Holism is the key to recognizing limits, building community, including marginalized people, and protecting nature.[70] Discerning progress toward redemptive technology requires judgment and evaluation; in other words, technology assessment. In order to accomplish this in a biblical way, values, ethics, and politics have to become an integral part of our thinking. Although he devotes an entire chapter to the subject, William Stahl comes to a disappointing conclusion. "I cannot even offer a definitive technique for assessing technology," he says. "What I do is offer an invitation to talk."[71] I believe that the methodologies of industrial ecology can provide the missing ingredient.

Jesus' Hierarchy of Values

Technology must be judged with respect to its instrumental value in realizing the good and fulfilling the moral obligations that Jesus taught.[72] To begin with, he taught that the whole of creation is valuable, and that people are more valuable than other created things.[73] Jesus valued human life, because he raised people from the dead and dreaded his own death. He valued health, for most of his recorded miracles involved healing. He considered food and clothing to be good, for he taught that even though they are not the highest good, God knows that we need them.[74] That he considered shelter to be good is clear, otherwise the parable of the wise and foolish builders would have been pointless.[75] Jesus valued family, for as a boy

---

67 Stahl, *loc. cit.*, 122.

68 Stahl, *loc. cit*, 128. Also see Conway, *Choices at the Heart of Technology*, 62–63.

69 Franklin, *The Real World of Technology.*

70 Franklin, *loc. cit.*, 144.

71 Stahl, *God and the Chip*, 165.

72 Funk, "Technology and Christian Values."

73 Gen 2:15; Matt 6:26, 28, 29.

74 Matt 6:31–32.

75 Matt 7:24–27.

he was obedient to his parents,[76] as a man dying on the cross he entrusted his mother's care to his disciple John,[77] and in his ministry he used fatherly love for children as a metaphor for God's love for us.[78] Friendship and community were valuable to him, for he had a deep friendship with Mary, Martha, and their brother Lazarus,[79] and throughout most of his Earthly ministry he surrounded himself with a small community of friends, his disciples. He valued knowledge and understanding, for he prominently displayed them in his first recorded public appearance.[80] Though no hedonist, he did consider happiness a good, for he described it as a reward of the good and faithful servants in the parable of the talents.[81]

But Jesus taught that the highest good is God and His kingdom.[82] From this hierarchy of values follows our moral obligations to do what is right and love the good. We are to be good stewards of the creation and we are to love our neighbors as ourselves. Most importantly, we are to love God with all our hearts and seek His kingdom. According to Jesus the highest good is God and the highest good that we can realize is to participate in the kingdom of God.

The Grand Objectives

The four "grand objectives" that philosophically underpin industrial ecology putatively pertain to "life on earth, its maintenance, and its enjoyment"[83]; but their goal is environmental sustainability. The objectives to be maintained and enjoyed include the existence of the human species, the capacity for sustainable development, the diversity of living things, and the aesthetic richness of the planet. Because they are naturalistic as written, it is not possible to reason from the four grand objectives to a biblical worldview. The reverse process, however, is illuminating. The first objective is clearly anthropocentric, but also consistent with Imago Dei[84]

---

[76] Luke 2:51

[77] John 19:26–27.

[78] Luke 11:11–13.

[79] John 11:5.

[80] Luke 2:46–47.

[81] Matt 25:14–23.

[82] Mark 10:17–18. Here Jesus is drawing on the Old Testament tradition of God as the greatest good.

[83] Graedel, *Streamlined Life-Cycle Assessment*, 5. See p. 283.

[84] Gen 1:26–27.

and the command to be fruitful and multiply.[85] Because the command to multiply was given to all the creatures, in principle the second and third objectives are also consistent with Scripture. However, a biblical derivation would insist that the purpose of the human species is more than propagation; it is to worship God and honor Him.[86]

Scripture provides considerable support for maintaining Earth's capacity for sustainable development,[87] which in turn invokes the biblical concept of limits. Limits to human endeavor began with the commandment about presumption[88] and proceeded to limits for technology.[89] There are many admonitions against unlimited acquisition, from greed and covetousness to unjust gain[90] and materialism.[91] Voluntary self-restraint is emphasized instead, illustrated in the Old Testament by rules regarding tithing, gleaning, and the Sabbath. Jeremiah asks "does it make you a king to have more and more cedar?" i.e. a bigger and fancier house.[92] In addition to Jesus' many warnings about material things, Paul equates greed with idolatry.[93]

The biblical portrayal of God cherishing the diversity of His creation supports the diversity objective.[94] A biocentric ethic is readily apparent,[95] but a biblical version would elevate maintenance of biodiversity to the level of obedience to God. The aesthetic objective can be derived from the many biblical passages about the beauty of the creation and passages that describe nature's joy at its eschatological restoration.[96] The message is negatively reinforced by passages expressing God's anger toward and punishment of those who defile the land.[97] The grand objectives were postulated ad-hoc in order to provide a philosophical or moral foundation for industrial ecology. Because they are derivable from scripture, however,

---

[85] Gen 1:22, 24, 28.

[86] Psalm 8.

[87] Ps 104:27–30; Jer 2:7; Ezek 34:17–18; Hos 4:1–3; Rom 8:22; Heb 1:3; Rev 11:15.

[88] Gen 2:16–17.

[89] Genesis 11.

[90] Exod. 20:17; Prov 30:15–16; Jer 22:13–17; Hab 2:9–11; Mark 7:22; Col 3:5.

[91] Matt 6:24, 19:23–24; Mark 10:21–22; Luke 12:15; Acts 2:45.

[92] Jer 22:15.

[93] Col 3:5.

[94] Gen 1:22, 6:19–20, 7:7–10; Job 12:10; Hos 2:18.

[95] Spaling and Wood, "Greed, Need, or Creed," 230–40.

[96] Neh 9:6; Job 37:14–24; Ps 8, 19:1–6, 66:4, 96:11–12; Isa 55:12; Rom 1:20.

[97] e.g. Jer 2:7; Rev 11:18.

some correspondence between the principles of industrial ecology and biblical themes should be expected. The parallels are evident from the entries in Table 10.1.

Table 10.1. Corresponding themes in scripture and industrial ecology

Biblical Theme	IE Principles
Voluntary self restraint tithing gleaning Sabbath/Jubilee simplicity	*Constraints on society* sustainable living sustainable design environmental justice environmental protection
Dissipation wasted lives dominion mandate to bring order from chaos	*Dissipative use* irrecoverable loss nonrenewable resources
Living more simply equipoise society the theology of enough	*Dematerialization* materials productivity per-capita GDP vs. quality of life
Irreducible complexity intelligent design	*Complex systems* emergent properties
Theism the purposeful hand of God in history toward consummation	*Evolution of complex systems* Guided by engineers, business-persons, and politicians toward sustainability

Synthesis: A Theology of Technology

God's plan for human activity is *heteronomy*—the direct opposite of autonomy. It means basing our lives on His precepts.[98] Philosophically speaking, this requires revealed principles; a *structural* framework.[99] All the foregoing biblical principles and mandates pertaining to technology can be collected and distilled into a "chronology" that categorizes them according to (1) those given before the fall when nature and human spirits were undamaged; (2) directions given after the fall that channel human interaction with other humans and nature; and (3) principles that lead to substantial healing in the present age of redemption and reconciliation.

[98] Wauzzinski, *loc. cit.*, 31, 160.
[99] Ibid.

Before the Fall: Develop Culture and Care for Creation

Technology is a legitimate response to the mandates. It is a cultural activity by which—with the aid of tools and procedures—untamed nature can be transformed into a social environment. Natural resources and technology are to be used for human benefit.[100] In fact, God assigned to the land the "duty" to produce vegetation.[101] But in reaping the benefits we must not damage Earth's ability to regenerate. With respect to a biblical ethic for agricultural land use, steward-like care of farmland means that humans may enjoy the fruit of the land, but we may not diminish its fruitfulness.[102] This ethic seems suitable for the seas as well.

Technology helps us realize the possibilities (unfortunately, for both benefit and harm) latent in creation. Because we are to simultaneously develop and respect God's creation, however, we should develop but must not destroy Earth's life support systems. This might mean clearing land for agriculture, building cities and water systems, and doing forestry. Technology should complement, not dominate, life; no "mere" technical solutions are permitted.[103] Social, spiritual, and aesthetic needs must be addressed in addition to physical ones. Technological solutions must be culturally sensitive and appropriate, respecting and preserving existing cultural patterns that are not unbiblical.[104] And we are to subdue and rule in such a way that nature is served as well in the sense of bringing out the excellence that God has placed in His creation. The latter principle has been fleshed out in the Christian literature of Earthkeeping and creation care. Sustainability can be substituted as an operative term in secular discussions.

After the Fall

Were engineers not needed until the fall? If my understanding of the cultural mandate is correct, Adam and Eve would have practiced engineering in a rudimentary sense as they pursued their tending, keeping, and dominion duties. After the fall humans continued to develop animal husbandry, musical instruments, and tools of bronze and iron; but these developments were now accompanied by jealousy, pride, murder, and greedy am-

---

[100] cf. Isa 45.

[101] Gen 1:11–12. One might extend that assignment to the production of fossil fuels; but the land also provides minerals for industrial civilization.

[102] Spaling and Wood, *loc. cit.*, 117.

[103] Wauzzinski, *loc. cit.*, 137, 156, 160, 164.

[104] Foster, *Freedom of Simplicity*, 168; Monsma, *loc. cit.*, 71; Wauzzinski, *loc. cit.*, 173.

bition.[105] As a result, engineering became essential to relieve the newfound toil and drudgery, to create shelters and surety, and to design prosthetics and weapons.

After the fall God reaffirmed the culture mandate to Noah;[106] and David, Isaiah, and Paul acknowledged its continuance.[107] Additional instruction became necessary, however, and these were provided in the *Shema*, the Ten Commandments, and the Law of Moses. The *Shema*, which Jesus called the Great Commandment, is "Hear, O Israel: the Lord our God is one. You shall love the Lord thy God with all your heart, and with all your soul, and with all your strength," and the additional "love your neighbor as yourself."[108] We are to love God first and our neighbors in consequence. The first Commandment warns us to have no other gods before Yahweh.[109] The second expands the theme: we must make, or have, no idols. God created humans "in His image," and the Ten Commandments explain that we are to *be* His images—we are to image Him by our behavior. All this means we must reflect love for God and neighbor, and to expand (not constrict) opportunities for men and women to be the joyful, loving creatures God intended. Technologies that we develop and the use we make of them must reflect these directives and in so doing bring praise to the Creator.[110]

Substantial Healing

A final reason for engaging in technology is to participate in God's work of redemption and reconciliation. The Bible teaches that the earth presently "groans" under human-caused impacts, but substantial healing of the effects of the fall can be realized in the present age before the consummation. If Israel had been faithful to the Law and the prophets a living testimony to God's character would have emerged, a redeemed community that served as God's agents. But Israel wasn't up to the task, and God enacted His ultimate plan in Jesus Christ. Jesus explained and demonstrated that redemption and reconciliation are kingdom ministries. This teaching provides positive vision for the engineering profession and many other human endeavors if they are practiced with the objective of participating

[105] See Gen 4 and Monsma, *loc. cit.*, 45–46.

[106] Gen 9:1–7.

[107] Ps 8; Isa 45:18; Col 1:15–20.

[108] Lev 19:18; Deut 6:4; Mark 12:29–31.

[109] Exod 20:2.

[110] Gen 1:31; Pss 104, 108.

in God's work of redemption. In other words, technology can be redemptive—with careful consideration.

Human activities that repair past damage and promote four-fold sustainability in the future can be redemptive. Many specific scriptures address environmental sustainability; or to put it another way, they impose constraints on our use of Earth's sinks as waste repositories and on human perturbation of natural global systems. Waste production and resource extraction are measures of the economy's departure from sustainability, and they also involve justice—intergenerational and social justice in particular. Resource usage must be sustainable because we do not know how many future generations must live until the consummation, and waste deposition into air, water, or land often disproportionately affects the poor. Sustainability should be one of the objectives of technology assessment, the outcomes of which should guide a collective self-limitation that will permit civilization to operate within the constraints set forth in Scripture.

At first look some technologies seem inherently redemptive. Many medical devices and procedures must qualify, as would technologies that expand the reach of missionaries, facilitate education, assist biblical archeology and cosmology, and enable on-line theological research. Industrial ecology practices can be redemptive because they provide a method for assessing the environmental sustainability technologies before they are deployed—and for comparing alternative solutions to existing problems. But because all technologies and practices have unintended consequences and technological successes can lead to presumption, the technological endeavor must be pursued with deliberation and humility. Biblical technology must be concerned for aesthetic, social, and spiritual impacts in addition to environmental ones. More specifics for redemptive technology will be provided in the next chapter.

A simple example will help clarify the kinds of issues that Christians must wrestle. How is the value of a fruit tree to be compared with a thousand-year-old redwood? The fruit tree may be valued only for its production, whereas the redwood tree has aesthetic value in the wild but is economically productive only when reduced to lumber. Should the redwood become a fence or deck, or should it be valued for the praise that it can bring to its Creator? Schaeffer and Monsma argue for the latter,[111] and because we live close enough to the redwoods to enjoy them on an afternoon outing, Nancy and I regularly experience those feelings of praise. And we are helping our grandchildren do likewise. The motivation for de-

---

[111] Schaeffer, *loc. cit.,* 76–77; Monsma, *loc. cit.,* 69.

veloping "engineered materials" such as structural beams and planks made from wood chips and recycled plastic may have been economic, but the technology is biblical. The engineered materials are every bit as durable and workable as new wood, but they are made from industrial residues and hybrid trees that grow much faster than redwood. Unfortunately, the engineered materials are also slower to biodegrade when eventually they are disposed as waste.

The collected principles from Scripture that are set out in the foregoing can be distilled into eight principles for biblical technological activity. Biblical technology should:

1. bring praise to the Creator;

2. stimulate humanity's thirst for God's kingdom of activity, dynamism, vibrancy, peace, harmony, and joy;

3. serve and promote justice;

4. serve God, fellow humans, and nature;

5. enhance life without dominating it;

6. respect (cherish), preserve, care for, and utilize nature while meeting human needs;

7. be culturally appropriate and protect cultural traditions that are not unbiblical; and

8. be trustworthy (reliable and repairable) and transparent (full disclosure of impacts).

Chapter 11

What Then Should We Be Doing?

THE TITLE of this chapter is taken from Acts 2:37. The Apostle Peter had just finished explaining to the crowd that Jesus whom they had crucified was their promised messiah. "When the people heard this," Luke writes, "they were cut to the heart and said to Peter and the other apostles 'Brothers, what shall we do?'" Peter answered "Repent and be baptized." He warned them, and he pleaded with them "Save yourselves from this corrupt generation."[1] Many scriptures make clear that Peter was not instructing the people to physically separate themselves from the culture. Instead, they were to live in society without being caught up in the pervading culture.[2] They were to serve as preservatives and provide guidance.[3] As we have seen, technology has been part of the problem, but it also can be part of the solution.

Secular and anthropocentric purposes for technology were described in chapter 1, and biblical purposes in chapter 10. Only two of the six secular purposes—protection from nature and relief of toil and suffering—are obviously consistent with the biblical ones. Attaining peace and security by technical means may be supportable from Scripture, but not unambiguously, as attested by the widely differing views on the subject within the Church. In the worldview survey that I conducted (chapter 8), I asked respondents if they could "opt out" of technology whenever they wished, and to identify a place in their lives that was unaffected by it. Most acknowledged that they couldn't choose to live apart from technology. But a significant number of evangelicals reported that their spiritual lives were exempt. These same folk view technology—if they reflect upon it at all—as morally and spiritually neutral. Such responses imply that spirituality is a private matter, disconnected from the material realm. This idea

---

[1] Acts 2:38–40.

[2] John 17:15.

[3] Matt 5:13–16; 1 Pet 2:12.

is dualistic and inconsistent with the Scriptural framework for technology developed in the preceding chapter.

Technology has always been presumed to be in service to humans in one way or another. Since the Enlightenment, however, technology has become synonymous with progress, and today represents the manifestation of the operative Western worldview, as set forth in Table 11.1. Certainly technology is not limited to relieving the effects of the fall from grace. Some is used for evil purposes, most has unintended consequences, and pervasive technology leads to materialism and weariness of spirit. I hope that by now the reader understands the *quotidian nature* of technology and its pervasiveness in our culture and in our lives.[4]

Table 11.1. Operative worldview of Western culture

- Progress should be continuous
  - progress is inevitable and irreversible
- Growth is progress
  - *magnitude* of growth is the measure of progress
  - *directing* growth is outside the domain of government
  - in fact, the direction is unpredictable
- The "invisible hand" of the market will provide direction
- Science and technology are the keys
  - for solving societal problems and
  - for creating economic growth and raising standards of living

In contemporary Western culture nearly every action that we take, every decision that we make, involves technology. If we aren't directly using technology at any given moment, almost certainly the material we are using—or consuming—was fashioned and supplied to us by technological means. But pervasiveness generates dependency. Dietrich Bonhoffer wrote: "Technology is the power with which the Earth grips man and subdues him. We do not rule; we are ruled. We do not rule because we do not know the world as God's creation and because we do not receive our dominion as God-given but grasp it for ourselves."[5] Technology that

---

[4] Borgmann, *Power Failure.*

[5] Bonhoeffer, *Creation and Fall,* 40; also Bonhoffer, *Temptation.*

is both designed and used under biblical guidelines will be sensitive to the four-fold (environmental, aesthetic, social, and spiritual) impacts upon humans and the rest of creation. Spiritual sustainability includes commitment, perseverance, waiting, longsuffering, forbearance, grace, freedom, and renewal.

Steering Progress

Technological and economic optimists believe that economic growth always points toward higher standards of living. Most of us do see technology more as an ally than a threat. Technological pessimists, on the other hand, believe that we are headed toward catastrophe. The catastrophe could be social, in the sense of a technology-enabled war, a terrorist attack, or moral collapse; or it could be environmental—a result of pollution or resource exhaustion. Richard Swenson has argued that lethal things are proliferating along with beneficial ones, and one or more of these inevitably must reach its threshold of lethality.[6] While I am not as pessimistic as he, I do believe the present course of Western industrial civilization is not sustainable in *any* of the four dimensions, and I feel a sense of urgency about redirecting our course before we move too far down the present path. The path is unsustainable in the environmental and aesthetic dimensions because irreversible changes are occurring in the planet's life support systems; and it is unsustainable in the spiritual and social dimensions because of the impacts of the scientific-technological worldview that underpins contemporary culture. The marriage between the Christian faith and the present paradigm implicates the Church in the problems and greatly impedes its corporate witness to the culture.

Even if progress can be directed, won't the effort amount to planning the economy, which most Americans believe is a process doomed to fail? "If we do what we've always done, we'll get what we've always gotten," the aphorism says. And one definition of insanity is continuing to do the same thing over and over again with the hope of getting different results. In the words of sociologist Daniel Sarweitz "The fact that our current state of scientific and technological sophistication, and current levels of material well-being, derive from a certain view about human relation to nature . . . does not imply that such views will serve humanity well for the future."[7] But all levels of government *do* try to stimulate and focus economic growth, in the belief that growth is progress. Steering is implicit, manifest

[6] Swenson, *Hurtling Toward Oblivion.*

[7] Sarewitz, *Frontiers of Illusion,* 105.

at the very least by the choices regarding where public funds will be spent. Options range from technologies for law enforcement to deciding which research fields to sponsor. In the U.S., public investment in technology development and acquisition has long been heavily weighted toward military applications.[8] From the Manhattan Project through the end of the Cold War, physics dominated the national research agenda. Since then the pendulum has swung toward the medical and biological sciences. But because growth entails qualitative direction in addition to magnitude, these investments de facto put the government in the business of steering progress. Therefore an essential element of our mission is to show how economic growth is inevitably directional and unavoidably value-laden.

Unsustainable trends continue unabated in the U.S. (and the world), including overuse of aquifers, urbanization of agricultural land, destruction of wilderness and habitat, increasing dependence upon petroleum, increasing reliance on asocial or antisocial technologies, and widening economic stratification. The suggestion that consumption needs to be constrained by sustainability often invokes denial (limits are illusory) or hostility (accusations of anti-technology Luddism or utopian pastoralism). Both reactions derive from fears that the economy and "the American way of life" would be threatened by the proposed changes. Following the 9/11/2001 terrorist attacks, Vice President Cheney said he hoped Americans would "stick their thumb in the eye of the terrorists and . . . not let what's happened here in any way throw off their normal level of economic activity."[9] He mocked conservation by calling it "a sign of personal virtue, but . . . not a sufficient basis for a sound, comprehensive energy policy."[10] House Minority Leader at the time, Dick Gephardt, proclaimed that Americans were: "not giving up on America, they're not giving up on our markets," and President Bush asked Americans for their "continued participation and confidence in the American economy."[11] The foregoing counsel is derivable from the Enlightenment worldview. It stands in marked contrast to Jesus' teaching about materialism, self-denial, and suffering servant-hood.

According to theologian Howard Snyder, the Church's first task is to *be* the redeemed community. He wrote "The genuine demonstration of Christian community is the first step toward accomplishing God's cosmic plan. This is miracle, and miracle attracts. God's plan calls for the Church

[8] Sarewitz, *loc. cit.*, 5.

[9] Reich, "The American Prospect Online."

[10] Vice President Dick Cheney, from a speech in Toronto, ON; April 30, 2002.

[11] Reich, *loc. cit.*

to be a microcosm of that cosmic reconciliation which He is bringing. Thus to the extent that the Church grows and expands throughout the world and demonstrates true Christian community, to that extent the kingdom of God has come on Earth!"[12] Voluntary self-restraint from the excessive consumption that technology makes so seductive would not only reduce the environmental, social, aesthetic and spiritual impacts, such action would also make the Church a role model for society.[13]

The Church's second task, Snyder says, is to do the works of God and carry on Jesus' mission, and in so doing the Church will transmit kingdom values to the broader culture.[14] "The kingdom of God works like yeast. It leavens cultures and social systems, replacing the false with the true."[15] Operating as a prototype kingdom community, the Church would bring about substantial healing of the effects of the fall. Toward this objective, God's people are to demonstrate a biblical way of life and to work to redirect culture toward the same end. It would also move contemporary Western practice of the Christian faith considerably closer to Jesus' teaching. In the process, the arrow of progress would swing toward biblical norms.

Implementation

In its ongoing application to contemporary culture, the culture mandate means subsuming technological culture into a framework of God's laws. It means transformation—redirecting society toward biblical norms, and it must begin with discernment of the scientific-technological worldview. It is a directional change, not a renunciation of science and technology.[16] The process that I propose for going about this mission parallels the sequence Thomas Graedel developed for deriving actions from the grand objectives for environmental sustainability, as shown in Figure 11.1.[17]

Grand Objectives   Crucial Concerns   Targeted Activities   Directed Actions

Figure 11.1. Linking actions to objectives

[12] Snyder, *The Community of the King*, 69.

[13] I don't think that sustainability requires hardship, suffering, deprivation, or rejection of technology.

[14] Snyder, *loc. cit.,* 71.

[15] Snyder, *loc. cit.,* 135.

[16] Schuurman, *Faith and Hope in Technology*, 180, 182, 186.

[17] Graedel, *Streamlined Life-Cycle Assessment*, 6–13.

Graedel began with four "Grand (Ω) Objectives for life on Earth, its' maintenance, and its' enjoyment." The grand objectives can be derived from Scripture. However, *four-fold sustainability* contains a broader and more biblical purpose—equivalent to setting forth a set of "biblical grand objectives." Beginning with the Ω objectives, Graedel identifies major societal problems that directly bear on them. He labels these problems *crucial concerns*. Global warming is a crucial concern for environmental sustainability, as is resource exhaustion, ozone shield destruction, and loss of biodiversity. Albeit for somewhat different reasons, these concerns are as valid for the biblical grand objectives as for they are for industrial ecology.

The next step in Graedel's method is to identify a set of human activities that directly impact the crucial concerns. These activities become targets for change—hence they are *targeted activities*. Activities that impact global warming include those that release greenhouse gases—especially fossil fuel combustion and certain agricultural practices such as rice growing and ruminants (cattle, sheep, and goats), and also deforestation, urbanization, and covering land surface with pavement. The parallel process derived from the biblical grand objectives would include additional tasks—such as identifying technologies that damage families and cultures, intrude on solitude and silence, deface aesthetic beauty solely for the benefit of a few wealthy persons, and so forth.

When the targeted activities are identified, a set of *directed actions* is developed to reduce the impact(s) of the targeted activity. Fossil energy use is a targeted activity because of its contribution to global warming. The associated directed actions will reduce fossil energy use—such as funding (and using) commuter rail, building bicycle paths, and developing and installing renewable energy systems. Associated policies would promote "smart growth" or "new urbanism" and encourage local producers as a means to reduce long-distance shipping.[18]

I believe the foregoing methodology can lead to a biblical technology practice which in turn would redirect Western civilization toward four-fold sustainability. Clearly, the number of issues grows rapidly as we move through the sequence; detailed development could fill a separate book for each of the four sustainability domains that comprise the biblical grand objectives. Fortunately, scholarship has already produced much that will be of value in this endeavor, and a biblical foundation was laid in chapter 10. Several other Christian writers have worked on developing biblical

---

[18] Grunwald, "Warming to the Inconvenient Facts," 23.

guidelines for technology[19]; and these can be supplemented by sound—biblically admissible—guidelines from secular works.[20] In Table 11.2 I have condensed the results into a list entitled "directed actions for biblical technology." The list approximates the ones presented by Monsma[21] and Schuurman.[22] Although couched in terms of products and devices, the guidelines apply equally well to development of services or technique.

Table 11.2. Directed actions for biblical technology

1. *Cultural appropriateness.* Technologies should be appropriate for the cultures that will use them. Technology should provide tools to alleviate human burdens but without damaging traditions that are wholesome and good in a given culture. Technologies appropriate for Western cultures are often unsuitable in developing countries.

2. *Openness and communication.* Social and communication values should be upheld, as illustrated by the following attributes: Product information should be accurate and open. Value judgments made during the design process should not be secret; alternate but rejected concepts should be made available (together with the reasons for their rejection), and information should be made available regarding known and possible side effects, hazards (including hazards from possible misuse), energy consumption and toxics contained in the product and used during materials extraction and processing, manufacture, packaging and shipping, and disposition.

3. *Economics and stewardship.* Profit must not be at the expense of stewardship of nonrenewable resources (human, material, and energy). Supporting principles include design for durability, repairability, and recyclability. Environmental impacts must be minimized; species and open spaces protected. Brownfields should be redeveloped before greenfields.

---

[19] Schumacher, *Small is Beautiful*; Schuurman, *Technology and the Future*; Schuurman, *Perspectives on Technology and Culture*; Monsma, *Responsible Technology*, 68–74, 170–77; Conway, *Choices at the Heart of Technology*,. 83–85, 114.

[20] Franklin, *The Real World of Technology*, 127*ff*; "Green Products by Design"; Graedel and Allenby, *Industrial Ecology*, 173–89, 310; Papanek, *The Green Imperative*; Papanek, *Design for the Real World*.

[21] Monsma, *loc. cit.*

[22] Schuurman, *loc. cit.*, 195–200.

4. *Aesthetics.* The technology should facilitate whole relationships between humans and the rest of creation. The creation should be respected as God's very good work. The design and the application must value the beauty and harmony of the creation, and promote harmony between cultures and between societies. There should be beauty of form and of ergonomic function. The technology should do what it purports to do, and do it well. Operation, including the user interface, should be intuitive.

5. *Justice.* Societies, humans, cultures, and the creation must be treated justly. The technology and its application should help justice prevail—including social, economic, legal, spatial, and temporal dimensions. All persons should be accorded rights as God's image-bearers, and all should have equal access to the benefits of technology. The poor should not disproportionately bear negative impacts. The technology and its application should not violate family stability, extinguish plant and animal species, or use information for misanthropic purposes. Examples of technologies of special concern include those that eliminate jobs, facilitate misuse of information, damage wild and scenic areas, or invite repressive use by one group over another.

6. *Morality.* The technology should promote love and caring. This goes beyond justice; in both creating and using technology we are to act as servants. The technology and its application should safeguard the well-being of neighbors near and far and the natural creation. It should care for the well-being of production worker and user and not require dehumanizing or exhausting work.

7. *Faith.* This requirement implies trust and belief. The user, serviceperson, salesman, and recycler should be able to trust the product as safe and dependable. The manufacturer and the retailer must stand behind the product or service. But our ultimate faith must be in God, not technology, to save us. The design process should proceed with humility and the product should not portray hubris.

Would not any company adopting these guidelines quickly go bankrupt? Would not any industrial nation that adopted them lose its productivity edge to overseas competitors? In the present state of our economy, in many instances the answer would be affirmative. But I have argued for redirection of our culture to a state where these practices could be profitable. Imagine looking back on our era from a hundred years hence, with the knowledge that the brief period of consumer society lasting roughly from 1950 to 2050 had created grave and irreversible environmental and social ills that could have been substantially avoided or eased. What would one think of an educator who had failed to teach his or her students how to avert the disaster? What would one think of a practicing engineer who had not resisted the excesses, who even had collaborated actively in them? No one can know for sure whether such a future is coming, but the arrow of technological progress presently points in that direction. To some extent the arrow has always pointed in an unsustainable direction, inasmuch as technology has been an endeavor of fallen mankind. But since the Industrial Revolution the scientific-technological worldview has exacerbated the problem. The vision of redemptive technology (which would include sustainability as a measure) represents a radical departure from the present paradigm.

Hippocratic Engineering

As the number of concerns, activities, and directed actions for redirecting progress multiply, prioritizing among them becomes important. Graedel assumes expert testimony to be the best source of such guidance. For environmental concerns he appealed to the World Commission on Environment and Development and the EPA Science Advisory board. The extracted wisdom prioritizes environmental concerns according to "critical," "highly important," and "less important."[23] A technical expert might propose that all necessary guidance can be obtained from risk analysis, root cause or fault tree assessment, failure modes and effects analysis, or other rational methodologies.[24] And once the presumed cause is identified, they would propose a scientific-technological solution such as Surety Science and Engineering to prevent violence in schools (chapter 2). Such tools are attractive to scientists and engineers because most tend to be convergent thinkers. And they have a powerful argument—have not rational-scientific methods such as these delivered the amazing technological progress that we have enjoyed since the beginning of the Enlightenment?

[23] Graedel, *loc. cit.*, 6–9.

[24] Kepner and Tregoe, *The New Rational Manager.*

Some social scientists are concerned, however, about the degree to which industrial ecology is based upon the risk paradigm—i.e. because of its total reliance upon the judgment of highly trained experts for impact assessments. The concern is that the outcomes will favor technological and industrial interests over the welfare of the populace.[25] The social scientists argue that the decision processes that control development and deployment of technology should be democratic rather than expert, because only when marginalized and powerless peoples—or their advocates—participate in the decision-making process will their rights be protected.[26] "The poor and the marginal have little influence," sociologist William Stahl observed, and by noting that "nature has no vote" (except through its advocates), he extended the scope of the discussion to include the rights of non-human creation.[27] According to technology policy analyst social scientist Daniel Sarewitz, who worked on science policy issues for the U.S. Congress, "If the public is not directly involved in deciding which trade-offs to make, then the influence of experts, acting within their own subjective frame of reference, can only grow more significant over time, while citizens are increasingly cut off from the forces that shape their lives."[28] The "subjective frame of reference" that Sarewitz alludes to is, of course, the scientific-technological worldview. This may come as a surprise to technologists, because most consider their practice wholly rational—which they also believe to be a virtue. The notion that the technological method can advance to an all-encompassing worldview is a difficult pill to swallow.

But we have seen that Western cultures are inclined to seek technical remedies for problems whose "root causes" are actually social or spiritual.[29] Philosophers attribute this tendency to technological determinism or to technicism. Most of my readers will agree that no purely rational analyses can provide insights into spiritual impacts and spiritual causes, and that technical solutions may preclude searches for deeper causes. But admitting democratic processes into technological decision-making is as difficult for

---

[25] Howard, "Integrating Intelligent Trial and Error into Industrial Ecology."

[26] Howard, "Toward Intelligent, Democratic Steering of Chemical Technologies"; Morone and. Woodhouse, *The Demise of Nuclear Energy*; Sarewitz, *loc. cit.*; Thornton, *Pandora's Poison*; Wauzzinski, *Discerning Promethius*.

[27] Stahl, William A., *God and the Chip*, 160.

[28] Sarewitz *loc. cit.*, 182.

[29] Chapters 2–3. Also cf. Winner, *The Whale and the Reactor*; Sarewitz, *loc. cit.*, 164; Howard, "Toward participatory ecological design of technological systems"; Howard, "Environmental 'nasty surprise' as a window on precautionary thinking," 19–22; Howard et al., "Body burdens of industrial chemicals in the general population," 163–200.

technologists as it is for medical doctors and lawyers. This is primarily because these professions require years of training and the technical details are often beyond the comprehension of the lay person, a fact that does make highly trained professionals vulnerable to elitism.

An analogous critique of decision making applies to contemporary medicine, where the portents for the poor and powerless are much more apparent, and perhaps more ominous as well. The subject of Hippocratic medicine pertains to ethical practice in the field of medicine. It is widely believed that the *Hippocratic Oath* was written by Hippocrates, the father of Western medicine, in the 4th Century B.C., or by one of his students.[30] The Oath presumed that the heart of medical practice was philanthropic moral commitment; a covenant between the physician, his god, and his patient. These were controversial values when the Hippocratic Oath first demanded them, and we are frequently reminded of their controversial character. This is because advancing technologies for making, shaping, maintaining, and taking human life are confronting medical personnel with ethical dilemmas far beyond those that their predecessors had to face. The adjunct problem of just (equitable) allocation of ever more costly high-tech medical technologies only compounds the problem.

Tragically, the response from within Western medicine has been to retreat from the Hippocratic consensus of a purely philanthropic endeavor, and to shift to a "post-Hippocratic" practice in which "technique is divorced from values, and clinical skill imparted without regard to moral commitment."[31] The shift began with the 1948 *Declaration of Geneva*, which sought to re-state hippocratism in the wake of Nazi medical atrocities.[32] Unfortunately, the Declaration wound up marking the beginnings of post-Hippocratic decline. The sanctity of life was de-rated to "utmost respect for life" thereby shifting from vertical to merely horizontal ethics.[33] A new, secular, and malleable medical philosophy emerged, one that denies any transcendent, theistic grounds for its ethics and thereby turns covenant into mere code. The door was formally opened to something quite new: two fundamentally divergent understandings of the practice of medicine. As a philanthropic service Hippocratic medicine offered healing or, if that were not possible, palliation to the sick. In contrast, post-Hippocratic medicine serves the interests of the powerful, whether in their

---

[30] "Hippocratic Oath."

[31] Cameron, *The New Medicine*, 151.

[32] "Hippocratic Oath," *loc. cit.*

[33] Cameron, *loc. cit.*, 156.

own healing, or in their destruction, or in the healing or destruction of the powerless.

Zygotes, embryos, severely impaired persons, and comatose patients are powerless—they cannot speak for themselves. In the absence of the Hippocratic Oath, what set of values guides the physician—or medical researcher—in his course determining what is best for the patient? If he or she does not see all human life as created in the image of God, the physician must instead make judgments about quality of life or about a life worth living.[34] According to bioethicist Nigel M. de S. Cameron, post-Hippocratic medicine underlies the recent pressure for "lay" involvement in ethical committees and a growing tendency to seek judicial review of clinical judgments. "Rather than address the substantive ethical issues which are focused by technical developments and general ethical flux," he writes, "physicians and ethicists alike respond by concentrating on the way in which decisions are made . . . With the ebbing of the Western ethical consensus it is easier to agree on the procedures which will allow individuals to make their own choices."[35] He believes that the trend should be understood as a defensive response to the inevitable uncertainty produced by the absence of ethical consensus at the heart of contemporary medical practice.

Like medicine, engineering is a profession. Its original purpose was—and still is advertised to be—purely philanthropic. The differences from medicine are the absence of an oath or a covenant equivalent to the Hippocratic Oath, and the possibility of practicing in industry without the requirement of professional licensing. However, engineering does require satisfactory completion of an accredited formal course of education, a period of apprenticeship (as "engineer-in-training" or "junior engineer" or both), and professional licensing if the engineer is to be involved in projects that affect "public safety." Each engineering school documents the set of values that supposedly guide the education of its undergraduates, and professional engineering societies publish a "code of ethics" for their membership. In essence the practice of engineering proceeds under a covenant between the engineer, his professional colleagues, and his clients. Here "clients" should be understood to be not only the users of the technology, but anyone who encounters the product during its life cycle.

As is the case in medicine, ethical dilemmas for engineers and technologists are not new. Engineers have always been asked to apply their

---

[34] Cameron, *loc. cit.,* 157.

[35] Cameron, *loc. cit.,* 146.

knowledge and skills in less-than-philanthropic and even sociopathic pursuits. For legitimate defense of the state, the ethics may at first appear straightforward, but problems often become evident on deeper examination. Consider WMD. Some have argued—using just war principles—that WMD can never be moral. But if an engineer settles this matter in his own mind and conscience and (for example) decides to work in nuclear weapons development (as I did), should he/she work on accuracy, reliability, and effectiveness that allow reduced yield, or would it be better to work on use control (denial of access to unauthorized personnel), fire and accident safety, or arms control and dismantlement? WMD provide an obvious illustration of an ethically charged technology. But it should be evident from the examples given in this book that in addition to the outcome intended by design, all technology has unintended and unanticipated consequences. In the case of nuclear weapons, one of the unintended consequences was an arms race of fifty years duration and a "balance of terror" between the two ideological blocs that came to be known as "West" and "East." I have also argued that that the technology development process is inherently infused with value judgments by developer and sponsor. And I have argued that the technological enterprise is the most significant force in our culture, and that it is underpinned by a worldview that is de-facto religious.

Medicine may be moving away from its Hippocratic consensus, but engineering would do well to move *toward* it. I am proposing that the practice of engineering be "hippocratized" by approaching it as a covenant. The covenant will have a vertical dimension—between the technologist and his god—and a horizontal dimension between the technologist, his peers, and his clients. The engineer, or technologist, will vow to apply his knowledge and expertise for philanthropic and sustainable ends. The secular practitioner will have to adopt the covenant on purely utilitarian or pragmatic grounds, but, for the Christian engineer, the covenant will value human life as created imago Dei, and nature as the creator's possession. As the Hippocratic physician devoted his life and art to the care of his patients, so should the new engineer devote his life and art to the wellbeing of his clients. As the Hippocratic physician is (or was) subject to the philanthropic and professional demands of medicine, so the "Hippocratic engineer" should accept a distinct ethical framework as the basis for professional practice. The economic benefit of the sponsor should be secondary to the philanthropic benefit to the users and to society.

This knitting together of technical skill and moral commitment amounts to a covenant between engineer and client(s). The covenant would limit the engineer's freedom of action; he or she would be bound by the principles of philanthropy, and the Christian engineer would also be bound by the biblical principles set forth earlier. I have argued that industrial ecology offers a promising procedure for deriving targeted activities from biblical objectives. But once the covenant is accepted the client would be freed from subjective judgments made by the engineer as was the case for Hippocratic medicine.

The parallel between medicine and engineering at the spiritual level draws even closer when we consider the shared objective of healing. The physician (under the covenantal Hippocratic Oath) is committed to healing the human being in body and mind. The philanthropic moral purpose of engineering is to mitigate the effects of the fall from grace, by relieving burdensome toil and providing food, shelter, and material needs. More pragmatically, engineering achievements can provide *substantial healing* of the creation from the damage that resulted from the fall. In this sense engineering can be a Godly pursuit.

How Can a Minority Change the World?

Hippocratic medicine was not representative of the medical practice of ancient Greece, but rather the tradition of only a small minority within the wider medical community. And so it remained for some time. Yet the Hippocratic Oath was a manifesto for reform, and reform was solely needed in the medicine of the day.[36] The infusion of Judeo-Christian ethics ensured the final triumph of hippocratism in the Greco-Roman world and its establishment as the medical tradition of the West. The equivalences in the practice of engineering are straightforward. The engineering profession is the primary agency of change in technological culture, and engineers are the agents. They possess specialized knowledge that is beyond the comprehension of the average layperson—hence the practice is cloaked in an aura of mysticism—and they produce products or outcomes that are so profound as to be sometimes labeled "magic."[37] The industrial organizations that employ the majority of engineers and choose the assignments they work on provide the engineering equivalent of the powerful that control the allocation of medical technology for themselves and for the less powerful.

My call for "Hippocratic engineering" is certain to upset several groups whose interests are vested in maintaining the status quo. Certainly

[36] Edelstein, *The Hippocratic Oath*. Cited in Cameron, *loc. cit.*, 155.
[37] Stahl, *loc. cit.*

free-market advocates and economic determinists are among them, because they will argue that any attempt to steer the course of technology development will kill the enterprise goose that lays the golden eggs of technological progress. As I mentioned in chapter 8, engineering apologist Samuel Florman has argued that professionals' primary duty is to meet the expectations of their clients and employers. "Professional restraints should be derived from laws and governmental regulations," he wrote, "not personal conscience."[38] Unfortunately, teaching the customer about sustainability and an equipoise society is not part of the Total Quality Management process, and in Florman's view actually could be construed as a violation of the implied contract between engineer and employer.[39] But unless the employer directs, this leaves us without basis to approach many of the four-fold sustainability issues described in this book.

Jesus' teaching of "extra mile lifestyle" in the Sermon on the Mount and the Parable of the Good Samaritan asks much more of Christian technical professionals. He challenges them to voluntarily assume risk of monetary or physical loss in the pursuit of ethical ends. At first this may sound a little like "Erin Brockovich" (except for the sensationalism in the movie), and it could also include "whistle blowing" or even "tree sitting." However, those illustrations are negative in the sense that they have as their goal to stop something that is perceived to be damaging. In contrast, the application to business ethics is positive in that it seeks not opposition and blockage, but redirection. For example, while working for his/her employer on the project that has emerged from the design definition process, a Christian engineer might search on his/her own time for sustainable alternatives.[40] If the employer remains unresponsive, the engineer may have to make a decision about remaining on the payroll. This is but one example of a larger set of choices that a Christian must make in order to work out his/her biblical relationship to creation.

Moral relativists or postmodernists will insist that all values are merely personal preferences and that individual autonomy is the only universal value. Environmental regulations and liability laws are of some help, but these are far from delivering a sustainable society. The Precautionary Principle in the pharmaceutical industry has the objective of providing

---

[38] Florman, *The Civilized Engineer*, 32.

[39] The term "equipoise society" was coined by Bishop John Taylor of Winchester (Taylor, *Enough is Enough*). Taylor's aphorism calls for equity plus balance.

[40] Victor Papanek first suggested that "the designer should perform all the requested work but do a voluntary study of an alternative solution as well" (Papanek, *loc. cit.,* 74).

consumer protection, but the principle is often attacked for its role in slowing the introduction of new drugs.

Consideration of the history of the Hippocratic tradition, however, provides evidence that big things can start small. And surely the impact of twelve uneducated working men in Palestine two millennia ago provide proof that—empowered by the Holy Spirit—a few committed activists can change the world. If this seems a tall order for today, it can be no taller than in pre-Hippocratic Greece or Palestine of 30 AD. Biblical guidelines for Hippocratic engineering—collected from all the foregoing discussion—might be briefly summarized as follows:

1. Get wisdom: make use of the good potential of technology without falling prey to technological optimism or technicism.

2. Develop technologies that support or further the culture mandate, creation care and redemption and reconciliation.

3. Include in the design process consideration of the possible social, cultural, aesthetic, spiritual and environmental impacts of new technologies, processes, and products.

4. Assess the potential impacts of new technologies *while they are being developed.*

5. Include affected groups in the impact assessment process: developers, users, and collaterally affected persons.

6. Deploy green chemistry: if possible avoid synthesis of new compounds not seen in nature, especially chlorinated hydrocarbons.

7. For potentially high-impact technologies, utilize Intelligent Trial and Error and the Precautionary Principle design approaches.

8. Include the costs of impacts in the price of the products.

Guided Evolution

Ultimately, the prevailing cultural value system displayed in Table 11.1 will have to be re-ordered before industrial civilization can be redirected to sustainable norms. The changes don't have to be accomplished overnight, but based on the most recent forecasts for global warming and petroleum exhaustion, I think that we have less than a century—more likely a half century—to accomplish the change. It took more than a century to build our present non-sustainable technological civilization; now we must re-build our way toward a sustainable one. An undertaking of this magnitude will take national leadership and commitment. Eventually the world's nations will need to "get on board," but the U.S. is in the best position to take a leading role. If public and private sectors agree on the necessity of redirecting cultural evolution toward sustainability, and if new or revised policy instruments represent shared sacrifice, then market forces—adjust-ed for true costs of operations and directed toward sustainability—can in-fluence the economy in that direction. That is why the concept of guided evolution is attractive. Society can begin moving toward sustainability in a deliberate way, by using the price system and evaluating the results of modest steps as they are tried. The process will be "guided" in the sense that appropriate public and private drivers are deliberately instituted, and the response "evolutionary" because the economy will be allowed to re-spond to these revised drivers, and the policy instruments will be subject to continuing evaluation and revision. As a consequence, development of "appropriate" technology will be stimulated by the economy, in contrast to the present situation where the economy rides on the shoulders of technol-ogy, powerless to consider or influence its direction.

As the principle enablers (dare I say "priests"?) of technological cul-ture, engineers have an important role in redirecting that culture. But they will have only modest impact without cooperation of other key sectors of society: sociologists, economists, business executives, and consumers. The Bible assigns the lead role to God's people, the Church. Secular environ-mentalists have no motivation other than pragmatism to live sustainably, and over the long term pragmatism will fail to keep people motivated.[41] That is why, even though he postulated the grand objectives ad-hoc, Graedel appealed to religious worldviews for support.[42] For the Church to function as prototype kingdom communities does not mean separation from culture, but rather living as a sub-culture that demonstrates *substan-tial healing* of the four-fold alienation.[43]

Sustainable living as part of the work of redemption is not a brand new thought. The Lausanne Covenant of 1974 outlined the actions deemed necessary for effective worldwide evangelism in the late twentieth

---

[41] White, "The Historical Roots of Our Ecologic Crisis," 1203–7; Sagan, "To Avert a Common Danger, 10–14; Gordon, "Invoking the Spirit."

[42] Graedel, *loc. cit.,* 5.

[43] Schaeffer, *Pollution and the Death of Man.* Healing of the alienation of nature from itself might include protection from "acts of God" like tidal waves, hurricanes, and earthquakes; but getting the lion to lie down with the lamb will have to await Christ's return.

century. One suggestion was that affluent Christians begin to live simpler lifestyles, not as an end in itself but in order to permit generous contributions to relief and evangelism.[44] Richard Foster explained that inner and outer simplicity are the keys to real freedom;[45] and Ursula Franklin argued for "redemptive technologies."[46] Albert Borgmann urged consumers to simplify their lives and reconnect with people and nature in order to wrest control from the technological culture.[47] But foundational to these efforts is for the Church to understand the scientific-technological worldview and its consequences, and for us to teach discernment to our children. In addition, we will have to commit to participating in the democratic decision processes that will redirect technological culture.

Whatever actions a Christian might choose, passive compliance within an inequitable or non-sustainable system is not an option. One who "sees the sword coming and fails to warn the people" fails in his or her duty as a watchman.[48] Nor can it suffice for technical professionals merely to work quietly to increase the efficiency with which industry and its products operate (although this is a worthy objective). Instead, a serious review of the current state of our culture, the direction that it is headed, and the driving role of technology must lead to fundamental reconsideration of technical professionals' work, and all of our lifestyles. Participation with the Creator and ruler of the cosmos in substantial healing of the effects of the fall will be an exhilarating pursuit, consistent with the ministry of reconciliation.

[44] Sider, *Living More Simply*, 13.

[45] Foster, *Freedom of Simplicity*.

[46] Franklin, *loc. cit.*

[47] Borgmann, *loc. cit.*

[48] Isa 21:11; Jer 16:1; Ezek 6:17–19, 33:2–10.

Bibliography

Accreditation Board for Engineering and Technology. "Criteria for Accrediting Programs in Engineering in the United States, 2001."

Adler, Robert. "Entering a Dark Age of Innovation." *New Scientist.com news service*, http://www.newscientist.com/articlens?id=dn7616, 07/02/06. Last visited 06/14/06.

Alcorn, Randy. *Heaven.* Carol Stream, IL: Tyndale House, 2004.

Alden, Lori. "Reducing Demand for Lumber." Santa Rosa, CA: *The Press-Democrat* (10/01/2002).

Allenby, Braden R. *Industrial Ecology: Policy Framework and Implementation.* Upper Saddle River, NJ: Prentice Hall, 1999.

Amato, Ivan. *Stuff: The Materials the World is Made of.* New York, NY: Basic Books, 1997.

Ambrose, Steven E. *Nothing Like it in the World.* New York, NY: Touchstone/ Simon & Schuster, 2000.

"America's Oceans in Crisis." Pew Oceans Commission (June 2003). http://www.pewoceans.org/oceans/index.asp. Last visited 1/20/04.

Anderson, Craig A., and Karen E. Dill. "Video Games and Aggressive Thoughts, Feelings, and Behavior in the Laboratory and in Life." *Journal of Personality and Social Psychology* 78 (April 2000) 772–90.

Anderson, David R. "Black Market Spreads in Sales of Illicit Access Cards for Satellite TV." Portland, OR: *The Oregonian* (02//29/2000) B1, B6.

Anderson, W. French. "Gene Therapy." *Scientific American* (September, 1995) 124–28.

Apel, Andrew. "Are Risk Assessment and the Precautionary Principle Equivalent?" *International Society of Regulatory Toxicology and Pharmacology Workshop on the Precautionary Principle* (Arlington, VA, June 20–21, 2002). http://www.cei.org/utils/printer.cfm?AID=3162. Last visited 09/09/2003.

Applebaum, Anne. "Mission to Nowhere," *Washington Post National Weekly Edition* (January 12–18, 2004) 27.

Auster, Bruce. "Striking Back at Terrorism," *ASEE Prism* (February, 2000) 16–21.

Ausubel, J. "Regularities in Technological Development: An Environmental View." In *Technology and Environment.* Washington, DC: National Academy Press, 1989.

Baal-Schem, J., and D. Shinar. "The telepresence era: global village or media slums?" *IEEE Technology and Society Magazine* (Spring 1998).

Baker, Allen and Steven Zahniser. "Ethanol reshapes corn market." *Wheat Life* 49 No. 8 (2006) 51–54.

Baker, Bob. "Electronic Device Converts Windows into Speakers" (October 20, 2003). http://www.whispering-windows.com/news/electronic_device_converts.cfm. Last visited 03/24/2004.

Ball, Jeffrey. "'Peak-oil' theorist sees global supply dwindling, process soaring." Wall Street Journal/ Santa Rosa, CA: *The Press Democrat* (09/21/2004) E1–E2.

Ball, Jim. "The Use of Ecology in the Evangelical Protestant Response to the Ecological Crisis." *Perspectives on Science and Christian Faith* 50 No. 1 (1998) 32–39.

Barlow, David. "Crash Site Secrets." In *Innovation Episode 5*. PBS Television, http://www. pbs.org/wnet/innovation/about_episode5.html. Last visited 07/11/2006.

Barlow, Edward. "Creating the Future." Society of Manufacturing Engineers Annual Meeting and Leadership Forum (Seattle, WA, May 29–June 3, 2001).

Baumgartner, M.P. *The Moral Order of a Suburb*. New York, NY: Oxford University Press, 1991.

Beck, John. "Monster Jam: Jacked-up, gas guzzling monster trucks in Wine Country: You bet." Santa Rosa, CA: *The Press Democrat* (04/15/2004) D1, D8.

Bee, Richard. "Highway Numbers." *Mechanical Engineering* (September, 2000) 8.

Belcher, Angela. "Viruses Put to Work to Make High-Tech Materials." *Nanoscience— Where Physics, Chemistry and Biology collide*. Canberra, AUS.: Australian Academy of Science (2 May 2003). http://www.science.org.au/sats2003/belcher.htm. Last visited 3/09/2004.

Bell, Daniel. *The Coming of Post-Industrial Society: A Venture in Social Forecasting*, New York, NY: Basic Books, 1973.

Benefield, Kerry. "Not so fast." Santa Rosa, CA: *The Press Democrat* (09/03/2006) A1, A15.

Bernardini, O., and R. Galli. "Dematerialization: long-term trends in the intensity of use of materials and energy." *Futures* (May, 1993) 431–48.

Berry, John M. "Doing More With Fewer Workers." *Washington Post National Weekly Edition* (December 8–14, 2003) 19.

Berry, R.J. "Creation and the Environment." *Science and Christian Belief 7* (1995) 21–43.

"Beyond Sprawl: New Patterns of Growth to fit the New California." San Francisco: Bank of America Environmental Policies and Programs Office, 1996.

Bhattacharjee, Yudhijt. "In Wake of Disaster, Scientists Seek Out Clues to Prevention." *Science* 307 (January 7, 2005) 22–23.

Bingenheimer. Jeffrey B., et al. "Firearm Violence, Exposure, and Serious Violent Behavior," *Science* 308 (May 27, 2005) 1323–26.

Birkerts, Sven. *The Gutenberg Elegies*, New York, NY: Ballantine Books, 1994.

Blanchard, Benjamin S., and Wolter J. Fabrycky. *Systems Engineering and Analysis*. 3d ed. Upper Saddle River, NJ: Prentice Hall, 1998.

Blanchflower, David, and Andrew Oswald. "Well-being over time in Britain and the USA." *Journal of Public Economics* 88 Issues 7–8 (2004) 1359–86.

Bonhoeffer, Dietrich. *Creation and Fall: A Theological Interpretation of Genesis 1–3*. (1937). New York, NY: Macmillan, 1959.

———. *Temptation*. (1953). New York, NY: Macmillan, 1959.

Boorstin, Daniel J. "Technology and Democracy." In *The Dolphin Reader*, edited by Douglas Hunt., 152–66. Boston, MA: Houghton Mifflin, 1986.

Borgmann, Albert. *Power Failure: Christianity in the Culture of Technology*. Grand Rapids, MI: Brazos Press, 2003.

Bouma-Prediger, Steven. "Creation Care and Character: The Nature and Necessity of the Ecological Virtues." *Perspectives on Science and Christian Faith* 50 No. 1 (1998) 6–21.

Boylan, Michael. *Environmental Ethics*. Upper Saddle River, NJ: Prentice Hall, 2001.

Bradsher, Keith. *High and Mighty; SUVs: The World's Most Dangerous Vehicles and How they Got that Way*. New York, NY: PublicAffairs, 2002.

Brindle, David. "GPs Report Rise in Stress." *The Guardian* (May 30, 1994) 3.

Broad, Robert, and John Cavanagh. "The Corporate Accountability Movement: Lessons and Opportunities." A Study for the World Wildlife Fund's (WWF) Project on International Financial Flows and the Environment (1998) 12, 30.

Brooks, David. "Our Sprawling, Supersize Utopia." *New York Times Magazine* (April 4, 2004), 38.

Brooks, Rodney. "The Other Exponentials." *Technology Review* (November, 2004) 33. www.technologyreview.com. Last visited 11/07/2004.

Brophy, Beth, "Kindergartners in the Prozac nation," *US News & World Report* (November 13, 1995).http://www.keepmedia.com/pubsUSNewsWorldReport/1995/11/13/231993. Last visited 10/17/2004.

Brown, Steve. "Homes growing as families shrink." Dallas Morning News/ Santa Rosa, CA: *The Press Democrat* (01/13/2006) E5.

"Brownfields Glossary of Terms." *Brownfields Home Page*. Environmental Protection Agency Office of Solid Waste and Emergency Response. http://www.epa.gov/swerosps/bf/ glossary.htm. Last visited September, 1998.

"Brownfields Major Milestones and Accomplishments." *Brownfields Home Page*. Environmental Protection Agency Office of Solid Waste and Emergency Response. http://www.epa.gov/swerosps/bf/glossary.htm. Last visited Jan. 20, 2004.

Buehand, R. A. "Dead End." Review of *Dead End: The Automobile in Mass Transportation*, by G.L. Houseman. *Society* 13 (1975) 89–90.

———. Review of "The Death of the Automobile: The Fatal Effect of the Golden Era, 1955–1970, by J. Jerome. *Society* 13 (1975) 89–90.

Brunner, Emil. *Man in Revolt: A Christian Anthropology*. Cambridge, England & Philadelphia, PA: The Westminster Press, 1939.

Burkdoll, Amy. "Eavesdropping on cops doomed by technology." Associated Press/ Vancouver, WA: *The Columbian* (11/27/1998).

Burke, Edmund. "Selected Letters." In *The Portable Edmund Burke*. New York, NY: Penguin, 1999.

Burns, Ken, and Stephen Ives. "The West: Fight no More Forever." In *American Stories*. Washington, D.C.: PBS, 1996.

Burroughs, Chris. "Sandia team investigates use of Labs' technology to ensure 'farm-to-fork' safety of the nation's food supply." Albuquerque, NM: *Sandia Lab News* (December 14, 2001) 9.

Cabanatuan, Michael S. "Only 15% participate in Spare the Air day." *San Francisco Chronicle* (September 10, 2004) B1, B5.

Caldiera, Ken, and Michael E. Wickett. "Oceanography: Anthropogenic carbon and ocean pH." *Nature* 425 (September 25, 2003) 365–69.

Cameron, Nigel M. de S., *The New Medicine: Life and Death After Hippocrates*. New ed. Chicago, IL: Bioethics Press, 2001.

Campbell, Colin J. "Oil and Gas Liquids 2004 Scenario, Updated 05/15/04." Uppsala Hydrocarbon Depletion Study Group. http://www.peakoil.net/uhdsg/Default.htm. Last visited 11/03/2004.

Carpenter, Novella. "Hit and Run." Sonoma County, CA: *The Bohemian* 25.18 (2003).

Carter, Steven L. *Civility*. New York, NY: HarperCollins Perennial, 1999.

Cevero, Robert. "Why Go Anywhere?" *Scientific American* (September, 1995) 118–20.

Chan, Vincent W.S. "All-Optical Networks." *Scientific American* (September, 1995) 72–76.

Chandler, Daniel. "Technological or Media Determinism." http://www.aber.ac.uk/media/ Documents/tecdet.html. Last visited 09/25/2003.

Chang, Kenneth, and Andrew Pollack. "Sniffing Out Pathogens." New York Times/ Portland, OR: *The Oregonian* (11/01/2001) A14.

Chang, Kenneth. "Scientists find less sunshine reaching Earth." New York Times/ Santa Rosa, CA: *The Press-Democrat* (05/13/2004) A6.

Chatzky, Jean. *You Don't Have to Be Rich: Comfort, Happiness, and Financial Security On Your Own Terms.* Woodland, TX: Portfolio, 2003.

"Chicago: City of the Century." In *American Experience.* PBS Television. http://www.pbs. org/wgbh/amex/chicago/filmmore/pt.html. Last visited 11/20/03.

Chu, Paul C.W. "High-Temperature Superconductors." *Scientific American* (September, 1995) 162–65.

Clayton, Philip. *God and Contemporary Science.* Grand Rapids, MI: Eerdmans, 1997.

Clouse, Robert G., ed. *Wealth and Poverty: Four Christian Views.* Downers Grove, IL: InterVarsity Press, 1984.

Coates, P. *Nature.* Berkeley, CA: University of California Press, 1998.

Coghlan, Andy. "'Too little' oil for global warming." *New Scientist* 180 Issue 2415 (2003) 18.

"Cognition and Behavior." *Science Magazine special issue* (October 15, 2004).

Colson, Charles. "The Moral Home Front." *Christianity Today* (October 2004) 152.

Commoner, Barry. *The Poverty of Power.* New York, NY: Alfred A. Knopf, 1976.

Constable, George, and Bob Somerville, *A Century of Innovation: The Engineering that Transformed Our Lives.* Washington, D.C.: National Academies /Joseph Henry Press, 2003.

"Converging Technologies for Improving Human Performance: Nanotechnology, Biotechnology, Information Technology and Cognitive Science." National Science Foundation, 2001. http://wtec.org/ConvergingTechnologies. Last visited 03/31/2004.

Conway, Ruth. *Choices at the Heart of Technology: A Christian Perspective.* Harrisburg, PA: Trinity Press International, 1999.

Cook, Gary, ed. "2002 Research Review." NREL/JA-810-31967. US Department of Energy National Renewable Energy Laboratory, July 2002.

Cornehls, James. "The Automobile Society." *Traffic Quarterly* 90 (1977) 52–53.

Coursey, David, "How Recycling Your PC Just Got Easier." http://msn.zdnet.com/zdfeeds/ msncobrand/reviews/0,13828,2913478,00.html. Last visited 5/01/2003.

Crenshaw, James L. *Old Testament Wisdom: An Introduction.* Atlanta, GA: John Knox Press, 1981.

"Criteria for Accrediting Programs in Engineering in the United States." Accreditation Board for Engineering and Technology, 2001.

Cropley, Ed. "More Than 15,000 Species Facing Extinction." *Reuters News Service.* http://news.yahoo.com/news?tmpl=story&cid=570&u=/nm/20041117/sc_nm/ environment_species_dc&printer=1. Last visited 11/17/04.

Crouch, Andy. "Eating the Supper of the Lamb in a Cool Whip Society: Albert Borgmann's post-technological feast." *Books & Culture* (Jan/Feb 2004) 26–27.

Daggatt, Russell. "Satellites for a Developing World." *Scientific American* (September, 1995) 94.

DeGaspari, John. "Retooling CAFÉ." *Mechanical Engineering* 126 No. 4 (2004) 24–27.

———. "Layered Security." *Mechanical Engineering* (May, 2005) 35.

DeLong, J. Bradford. "Productivity Growth in the 2000s, Draft 1.2." http://econ161. berkeley.edu/Econ_Articles/macro_annual/delong_macro_annual_05.pdf. Last visited 04/25/2004.

DeNora, T. *Music in Everyday Life.* Cambridge, UK: University Press, 2000.

Dieter, George E. *Engineering Design: A Materials and Processing Approach.* 2d ed. New York, NY: McGraw-Hill, 1993.

Douglas, J.D., ed. *The New Bible Dictionary.* Grand Rapids, MI: Eerdmans, 1979.

Doxiadis, Constantinos. "The Coming World City: Ecumenopolis." In *Cities of Destiny,* ed. Arnold Toynbee, 12–28. New York, NY: McGraw-Hill, 1967.

Durbin, Dee-Ann. "15,000 saved by air bags." Associated Press/ Santa Rosa, CA: *The Press Democrat* (07/11/2004) A5.

———. "Car Sales Fall in November." Associated Press/Santa Rosa, CA: *The Press Democrat* (12/02/2005) E2.

Durning, Alan Thein. "The Car and the City." Seattle, WA: *Northwest Environmental Watch,* 1966.

Dyson, Freeman J. "21st-Century Spacecraft." *Scientific American* (September, 1995) 114–116A.

Eastham, Tony. "High-Speed Rail: Another Golden Age?" *Scientific American* (September, 1995) 100–101.

"Easy on the Starch, I, Robot." *Engineering Education News—Connections* (May, 2005).

Edelson, Martin. "EED Member Survey results." *ASME Environmental Engineering News* (Spring 2003) 3.

Edelstein, Ludwig. *The Hippocratic Oath: Text, Translation, and Interpretation.* Baltimore, MD: The Johns Hopkins Press, 1943.

Ehrenman, Gayle. "New Retinas for Old." *Mechanical Engineering* 125 No. 10 (2003) 42–46.

Ehrlich, Paul, and Stephen Schneider. "A $15,000 Counteroffer." *San Francisco Chronicle* (05/18/1995).

Eilperin, Juliet, "U.S. to expand tsunami alarm net." Washington Post/Santa Rosa, CA: *The Press Democrat* (01/15/2005) A10.

"Electronics Waste: A New Opportunity for Waste Prevention, Reuse, and Recycling." US Environmental Protection Agency Report EPA530-F-01-006 (July, 2001). http://www.epa.gov.epr. Last visited 1/20/2004.

Elias, Paul. "Bioengineered Bugs Alarm Some Scientists." Associated Press/ Santa Rosa, CA: *The Press Democrat* (01/26/04) D3.

Ellis, Ed. "Excess capacity a thing of the past." *Trains* (October, 1998) 16–17.

Ellul, Jacques. *The Technological Society.* New York, NY: Vintage Press, 1964.

Engelberger, Joseph F. "Robotics in the 21st Century." *Scientific American* (September, 1995) 166.

Epps, Garrett. "The prying eye of government." Portland, OR: *The Oregonian* (09/26/1999).

Estabrook, Barry. "A Paycheck Weekly, Insults Daily." *New York Times* (02/15/2004) 5, 11.

Evangelistica, Benny. "The Machine that Changed the World." *San Francisco Chronicle* (01/24/2004) A1–A2.

"Even in Texas, the cars are smaller." Washington Post/ Spokane, WA: *The Spokesman Review* (09/09/2005) A10, A13.

Ewing, Reid, et al. "Relationship Between Urban Sprawl and Obesity, Physical Activity, and Morbidity." *American Journal of Health Promotion* 18 No. 1 (2003) 47–57. http://www.rwjf.org/publications/publicationsPdfs/AJHP18Ewing47–57.pdf.

Falcioni, John G. "Terrorism on Alert." *Mechanical Engineering* (May, 2003) 4.

Featherstone, Rene. "B–2 in Odessa: A big nudge in canola biodiesel demand locally makes for 'the best prospects for our agriculture in a long time.'" *Wheat Life* 49 No. 9 (2006) 4–16.

———. "The frame around WAWG." *Wheat Life*. 47 No. 9 (2004) 31.

Ferguson et al., "Social Gospel." In *New Dictionary of Theology*, edited by Sinclair Ferguson et al., 646–47. Downers Grove, IL: InterVarsity Press, 1998.

Fischer, Dick. "Young-Earth Creationism: A Literal Mistake." *Perspectives on Science and Christian Faith* 55 No. 4 (2003) 222–31.

Flatow, Ira. "Micro Biochemical Processors." *Talk of the Nation-Science Friday*. National Public Radio (January 9, 2004.)

Florman, Samuel. *The Civilized Engineer*. New York, NY: St. Martins Griffins, 1987.

———. *The Existential Pleasures of Engineering*. New York, NY: St. Martins Griffins, 1994.

Foster, Richard J. *Freedom of Simplicity*. San Francisco, CA: Harper and Row, 1981.

———. *Celebration of Discipline*. San Francisco, CA: Harper San Francisco, 1998.

Frank, Robert H. *Luxury Fever: Why Money Fails to Satisfy in an Era of Excess*. New York, NY: The Free Press, 1999.

Franklin, Ursula. *The Real World of Technology*. Toronto, ON: Anansi Press, 1992.

Friedel, Robert. "Scarcity and Promise: Materials and American Domestic Culture during World War II." In *World War II and the American Dream: How Wartime Building Changed a Nation*, edited by Donald Albrecht. Cambridge, MA: MIT Press, 1995.

Fukyama, Frances. "Are We at the End of History?" *Fortune* 121 No. 2 (1990) 75–78.

Funk, Kenneth. "Technology and Christian 'Values." http://web.engr.oregonstate.edu/~funkk/Technology/index.html. Last visited 07/14/06.

Fysh, Graham. "Expert Predicts Housing Problems for Seattle." Portland, OR: *The Oregonian* (01/10/1997).

"Gadget puts TV haters in control." Santa Rosa, CA: *The Press Democrat* (10/20/2004) A2

Gaither, Norman. *Production and Operations Management*. 7th *Ed*. Belmont, CA: ITP Duxbury, 1996.

Gallagher, Noel. "Computer, TV Recycling Ordered." Santa Rosa, CA: *The Press Democrat* (01/20/2004) E1–E2.

Gamel, Jay. "St. Joseph Health System: Queen of the Valley Hospital." *Northbay Biz* 29 No. 2 (2004) 28–33.

Garreau, Joel. "Evolution of Our Species." *Washington Post National Weekly Edition* (June 20–26, 2005) 6–7.

"Gasoline Cost Externalities: Security and Protection Services—An Update to CTA's "Real Price of Gasoline." International Center for Technology Assessment http://www.icta.org/doc/RPG20%security%20update.pdf. Last visited 07/16/2006.

Gawel, Richard. "Groups Aim to Make Molehill out of Mountain of Electronic Trash." *Electronic Design* (Feb. 19, 2001) 34. http://www.elecdesign.com/Articles/Index.cfm?ArticleID=4185. Last visited 02/03/2004.

Getlin, Josh. "Our Violent Nature." Portland, OR: *The Oregonian* (04/25/1999).

Gilligan, C. *In a Different Voice: Psychological Theory and Women's Development*. Cambridge, MA: Harvard University Press, 1993.

Gillis, Justin. "And Now, Designer Insects." *Washington Post National Weekly Edition* (January 26—February 1, 2004) 31.

Ginsberg, Steven. "How About a Road Just for Trucks?" *Washington Post National Weekly Edition* (April 5–11, 2004) 31.

Glassner, Berry. *The Culture of Fear: Why Americans are Afraid of the Wrong Things*. New York, NY: Basic Books, 2000.

Gleick, James B. *Faster: The Acceleration of Just About Everything*. New York, NY: Vintage Books, 2000.

"Global Biodiversity Outlook 2002." UN Environmental Programme Convention on Biodiversity, 2002. http://www.biodiv.org/doc/publications/gbo/gbo-summ-en.pdf. Last visited 01/26/2004.

"Global Warming, Ozone, and Acid Rain." *Ecocentre Home Page*. http://www.ecocentre.org.uk/resources/global_warming.htm. Last visited 1/27/04.

Goddard, Stephen B. *Getting There: The Epic Struggle between Road and Rail in the American Century*. New York, NY: Basic Books, 1994.

Goetsch, David L & Stanley B. Davis. *Quality Management*. 3d. ed. Upper Saddle River, NJ: Prentice Hall, 2000.

Goodman , Ellen. "Warning: Your car is making you fat." Boston Globe/ Santa Rosa, CA: *The Press Democrat* (02/06/2004) B5.

———. "Have your toothbrush call my laptop." Boston Globe/ Santa Rosa, Ca: *The Press Democrat* (05/28/2006) G1, G6.

Goodman, Peter, "Where Old Computers Go: China." *Washington Post National Weekly Edition* (March 3–9, 2003).

Gordon, Gary. "Invoking the Spirit: Religion and Spirituality in the Quest for a Sustainable World." *Worldwatch Institute Paper No. 164*, 2002. http://www.worldwatch.org/pubs/paper/164/. Last visited 07/07/04.

Gordon, Sarah H. *Passage to Union: How the Railroads Transformed American Life*. Chicago, IL: Ivan R. Dee, 1996.

Goudzwaard, Bob. *Idols of Our Time*. Downers Grove, IL: InterVarsity Press, 1984.

Graedel, T.E., and Allenby, B.R. *Industrial Ecology*. Englewood Cliffs, NJ: Prentice Hall, 1995.

Graedel, Thomas E. *Streamlined Life-Cycle Assessment*. Upper Saddle River, NJ: Prentice Hall, 1998.

Granelli, James S. "Study: Headsets don't reduce accident rate for drivers on cell phones." Los Angeles Times/Santa Rosa, CA: *The Press Democrat* (07/12/2005) A1, A13.

Grant, George. *Technology and Empire: Perspectives on North America*. Toronto, ON: House of Anansi, 1991.

———. *Lament for a Nation*. Toronto, ON: McLellan and Stewart, 1965.

"Green Light for Guzzlers." *Washington Post National Weekly Edition* (Sept. 5–11, 2005) 24.

"Green Products by Design: Choices for a Cleaner Environment." U.S. Congress Office of Technology Assessment. Washington, DC: U.S. Government Printing Office, September, 1992.

Green, Mary W. "The Appropriate and Effective Use of Security Technologies in US Schools," *National Institute of Justice Research Report #178265*, September 1999.

Grossman, Elizabeth, "A Digital Dumping Ground: Discarded computer parts heap hazards at sites in Nigeria and elsewhere in Africa." *Washington Post National Weekly Edition* (December 19–25, 2005) 35.

Grossman, Lev. "Forward Thinking." *Time* 164 Issue 15 (2004) 136.

Grunwald, Michael. "Warming to the Inconvenient Facts." *Washington Post National Weekly Edition* (July 31—August 6, 2006) 23.

Guilder, George. *Life after Television: The Coming Transformation of Media and American Life*. New York, NY: WW Norton and Co., 1992.

Hagerbaumer, Chris. "Make the most of it." Portland, OR: *The Oregonian* (09/06/1997).

Hakim, Danny. "SUV sales plunge as gas prices take off." New York Times/ Santa Rosa, CA: *The Press Democrat* (10/02/2005) E1, E6.

Hales, Dianne. "The New Family Car: A Special Report." *Parade* (January 5, 2003) 8–10.

———. "What your Car Says About You." *Parade* (May 15, 2005) 8.

Hall, Kevin. "Future of U.S. oil flows through Canada." Knight Ridder/ Santa Rosa, CA: *The Press Democrat* (10/09/2005) A1, A17.

Hallinan, Kevin, et al. "Balancing Technical and Social Issues: A New First-Year Design Course." *IEEE Technology and Society Magazine* 21 No. 3 (2001) 4–14.

Har, Janie. "Survey: 1 in 8 teen-agers tote weapons." Portland, OR: *The Oregonian* (12/08/1999).

Harden, Blaine. "The Greening of Evangelicals: The Christian Right Turns, Sometimes Warily, to Environmentalism." www.washingtonpost.com/ac2/wp-dyn/A1491-2005-Feb5? Last visited 2/26/2005.

Hardin, Garrett. "The Tragedy of the Commons." *Science* 162 (1968) 1243–48.

Harris, Ron, "Floor-scrubbing robot sticks to its turf." Associated Press/ *San Francisco Chronicle* (12/26/05) F3.

Harrop, Froma. "Young and deadly: Is the Isolation of life outside cities driving some children to violence?" Portland, OR: *The Oregonian* (05/30/1998).

Hartley, Dorothy. *Lost Country Life*. New York, NY: Panthenon, 1979.

Hartley, Troy W. "Environmental Justice: An Environmental Civil Rights Value Acceptable to All World Views." *Environmental Ethics* 17 (1995) 277–89.

Hawken, Paul. "Natural Capitalism." *Mother Jones* (March/April 1997) 44ff.

Haws, David R. "Ethics Instruction in Engineering: a (Mini) Meta Analysis." *ASEE Journal of Engineering Education* (April 2001) 223–29.

Hayles, N. Katherine. *How We Became Posthuman: Virtual Bodies in Cybernetics, Literature, and Informatics*. Chicago, IL: University of Chicago Press, 1999.

Hayward, Steven. "Broken Cities: Liberalism's Urban Legacy." *Policy Review* 88 (1998). http://www.policyreview.com/heritage/p_review/mar98/cities/html. Last visited 11/1998.

———. "Land-Use Planners Don't Understand Urban Complexities." San Ramon, CA: *Valley Times* (06/15/1996) 3B.

Hefner, Philip. *Technology and Human Becoming*. Minneapolis, MN: Fortress Press, 2003.

Heinberg, Richard. *The Party's Over: Oil, War, and the Fate of Industrial Society*. Gabriola Island, BC: New Society Publishing, 2003.

Hendershot, Heather. *Shaking the World for Jesus: Media and the Evangelical Conservative*. Chicago, IL: University of Chicago Press, 2004.

Hendren, John. "Detection system gets the dirt on employees who fail to wash hands." Associated Press/Portland, OR: *The Oregonian* (05/25/1997).

Henry, Carl F.H. *A Plea for Evangelical Demonstration*. Grand Rapids, MI: Baker, 1971.

Herkert, Joseph R. "Sustainable Development, Engineering and Multinational Corporations: Ethical and Public Policy Implications." *Science and Engineering Ethics* 4 No. 3 (1998) 333–46.

Hildrith, Susan. "No reason to fear privacy invasion from library books." *San Francisco Chronicle* (05/06/2004) B9.

"Higher speed limits, deaths tied." Portland, OR: *The Oregonian* (01/15/1998) A10.

Hinds, James R., and Edmund Fitzgerald. *Bulwark and Bastion*. Revised ed. Union City, TN: Pioneer Press, 1966.

"Hippocratic Oath." In *Wikipedia*. http://en.wikipedia.org/wiki/Hippocratic_Oath. Last visited 11/01/2006.

Hittinger, Russell. "Christopher Dawson's Insights: Can a Culture Survive the Loss of its Religious Roots?" In *Christianity and Western Civilization*. Ft. Collins, CO: Ignatius Press, 1995.

————. "Christopher Dawson on Technology and the Demise of Liberalism, Christianity and Western Civilization." *Proceedings of the Wethersfield Institute* 7 (1995) 73–95.

Ho, David. "Jammers Quash Cell Calls in Public." Cox News Service/Santa Rosa, CA: *The Press Democrat* (02/16/2004) D1, D8.

Hoagland, William. "Solar Energy." *Scientific American* (September, 1995) 170–73.

Hoffman, David. "Radioactivity Threatens a Mighty River." In *World After the Cold War* (August 17, 1998) A1. http://www.washingtonpost.com/wp-srv/inatl/longterm/coldwar/siberiaa.htm. Last visited 10/14/2006.

Holdren, John. P. "*Energy Agenda for the 1990s*." In *The Energy-Environment Connection*, 378–91.Washington, DC: Island Press, 1992.

Hollander, Jack. "Introduction by the Editor." In *The Energy-Environment Connection,* Jack Hollander, ed., xv–xxvi. Washington, DC: Island Press, 1992.

Hook, C. Christopher. "The Techno Sapiens are Coming." *Christianity Today* (January, 2004) 37–40.

Hooper, F. Bodfield. *Reciprocity, Overproduction v. Overconsumption*. London: Elliott Stock, 1879. Available on microfiche from Chadwyk-Healey Ltd., Cambridge (1987).

Hopkins, David. "Weapons and Oregon teens: what is the risk?" Oregon Health Division 1999. www.oshd.org/cdpe/chs/statinfo.htm. Last visited 02/2000.

Hopper, David. *Technology, Theology, and the Idea of Progress*. Louisville, KY: Westminster/John Knox Press, 1991.

Horbert, Bob. "Violent toys take a sad toll on Youth." *New York Times* (12/01/2002).

Howard, Jeff. "Eight tenets of precaution: Commentary on the Wingspread statement [on the precautionary principle]." *The Networker* 3 No. 1 (1998). http://www.sehn.org/Volume_3-1_5.html.

————. "Environmental 'nasty surprise' as a window on precautionary thinking." *IEEE Technology and Society Magazine* 21 No. 4 (Winter, 2002/2003) 19–22.

————. "Integrating Intelligent Trial and Error into Industrial Ecology." Leiden, Netherlands: Annual Meeting of the International Society for Industrial Ecology, November 12–14, 2001.

————. "Toward participatory ecological design of technological systems." *Design Issues* 20 No. 3; special issue on Science and Technology Studies and Design (Summer, 2004).

————. "Toward Intelligent, Democratic Steering of Chemical Technologies: Evaluating Industrial Chlorine Chemistry as Environmental trial and Error." Ph.D. diss., Renesselaer Polytechnic University, 2004.

————, et al. "Body burdens of industrial chemicals in the general population." In *Life Support: The Environment and Human Health*, ed. Michael McCally, 163–200. Cambridge, MA: MIT Press, 2002.

Howe, Maggy. "Must Haves: Ten features new home buyers demand." Santa Rosa, CA: *The Press Democrat* (04/23/2005) 34–39.

Hughes, J.D. *Pan's Travail: Environmental Problems of the Ancient Greeks and Romans*. Baltimore, MD: The Johns Hopkins University Press, 1994.

"Hunting Buried Danger." *Mechanical Engineering* (June, 2004) 19.

Hutchinson, Harry. "Calculating Risks: Can the science that judges the safety of nuclear plants secure the infrastructure of a nation?" *Mechanical Engineering* (January, 2005) 40–41.

———. "Easy on the Gas." *Mechanical Engineering* (July 2006) 24–33.

———. "Technology vs. Terrorism." *Mechanical Engineering* (January, 2002) 48–52.

Hyman, Barry. *Fundamentals of Engineering Design.* Upper Saddle River, NJ: Prentice Hall, 1998.

"Is that a Verichip Under Your Skin?" *Time* 16 Issue 17 (2004), 67.

Jackson, David. "Feds Put Billions into Terrorist Fight." Dallas Morning News/ Vancouver, WA: *The Columbian* (04/19/1999).

Jackson, Maggie. "Is the boss watching? Surveillance becoming common." Associated Press/Vancouver, WA: *The Columbian* (05/26/1997).

Jackson, Wes. "Letter from the Land Institute." Salina, KS (November, 2003).

Jacobs, Jane. *The Death and Life of Great American Cities.* New York, NY: Vintage Books, 1992.

Jeeves, Malcolm A. *The Scientific Enterprise and Christian Faith.* Downers Grove, IL: InterVarsity Press, 1971.

Jewett, Dave. "V-chip? What V-chip?" Vancouver, WA: *The Columbian* (02/04/2000).

Johnson, James Turner. "Just War, As It Was and Is." *First Things* 149 (2005) 14–24.

Johnston, Bob. "Riders are an afterthought in the battle to save or dismantle Amtrak." *Trains* (April, 1998) 61–65.

Johnston, Don. "Commuters may trade cars for trains." Lawrence Livermore National Laboratory: *Newsline* (0/17/1995) 1, 4.

Joy, Bill. "Why the Future Doesn't Need Us." *Wired Magazine* 8.04 (2000). http://www.wired.com/wired/archive/8.04/joy_pr.html. Last visited 02/19/2003.

Kahn, Herman, et al. *The Next 200 Years: A Scenario for America and the World.* New York, NY: Morrow, 1976.

Keay, Davidson. "Saving the Universe by Restricting Research." *San Francisco Chronicle* (04/14/2003) A6.

Kenyon, William, "New design thinking can minimize electronic waste" *Surface Mount Cleaning* (October, 2001) 22–24.

Kepner, C.H., and B.B. Tregoe. *The New Rational manager.* Princeton, NJ: Princeton University Press, 1981.

Kidder, Tracie. "Because we can." *Parade Magazine* (April 3, 2005) 4–6.

Kirby, Richard Shelton, et. al. *Engineering in History.* Mineola, NY: Dover Publications, 1990.

Kirk, Andrew. *Good News of the Kingdom Coming.* Downers Grove, IL: InterVarsity Press, 1983.

Kishlansky, Mark, and Henry G. Weisser. "Early Stages of Industrialization." In *Microsoft® Encarta® Encyclopedia 2000.* ©1993–1999 Microsoft Corporation. All rights reserved.

Klauer, S. G., et al. "The Impact of Driver Inattention on Near-Crash/Crash Risk: An Analysis Using the 100-Car Naturalistic Driving Study Data." Study Performed by Virginia Tech Transportation Institute, Blacksburg, VA. DOT HS 810 594. Washington, D.C.: National Highway Traffic Safety Administration, April 2006.

Knox, Noelle. "Sales to schools a major market for security firms." Associated Press/ Portland, OR: *The Oregonian* (04/29/1999).

Kohlberg, Lawrence, *Essays in Moral Development* New York, NY: Harper and Row, 1981.

Kosko, Bart. *Heaven in a Chip: Fuzzy Visions of Society and Science in the Digital Age.* New York, NY: Three Rivers Press, 1999.

Kotkin Joel. "Beyond White Flight." *Washington Post National Weekly Edition* (March 18–24, 1996) 26–27.

———. "Reinventing Suburbia." Santa Rosa, CA: *The Press Democrat* (02/13/2005) G1, G8.

Kozlowski, Carl. "*High-Tech Surveillance.*" Chicago Tribune/ Vancouver, WA: *The Columbian* (12/30/1999).

Krane, Jim. "It's Gadget Time in Las Vegas." Associated Press/Santa Rosa, CA: *The Press Democrat* (01/06/2003) D10.

Kuhn, Thomas S. *The Structure of Scientific Revolutions.* 2d. ed. Chicago, IL: University of Chicago Press, 1970.

Kuhns, William. *Environmental Man.* New York, NY: Harper & Row, 1969.

Kurzweil, Ray. "Promise and Peril of the 21st Century." *CIO Magazine* (Fall/Winter, 2001). http://www.cio.com/archive/092203/kurzweil.html. Last visited 03/23/2005.

———. "Technology in the 21st Century: an Imminent Intimate Merger." http://www.kurzweilai.net/meme/frame.html?main=/articles/art0465.html. Last visited 06/16/06.

Kusnetz, Ilyse. "Cyborgs No Longer Science Fiction." Orlando Sentinal/ Santa Rosa, CA: *The Press Democrat* (10/12/2003) D1.

Ladika, Susan. "South Asian Tsunami: DNA Helps Identify Missing in the Tsunami Zone." *Science* 307 (January 28, 2005) 504.

Landry, Peter. *Thomas Robert Malthus.* http://www.blupete.com/Literature/Biographies/Philosophy/Malthus.htm. Last visited 04/06/2004.

Lane, Robert E. *The Decline of Happiness in Market Democracies.* New Haven, CT: Yale University Press, 2000.

———. *The Market Experience.* London, UK: Cambridge University Press, 1991.

Langer, Robert, and Joseph P. Vacanti. "Artificial Organs." *Scientific American* (September 1995) 130–133.

Lankard, Tom, and John Lehrer. "Axles to Grind." *Washington Journey* (November/ December, 1999) 34–38.

Lanza, Joseph. *Elevator Music: A surreal History of Muzak, Easy Listening and other Moodsong.* East Lansing, MI: University of Michigan Press, 2003.

Larzelere, Robert E. "Values and Social Science: Modernism, Post-Modernism, and Faith," Annual meeting of the American Scientific Affiliation (Manhattan, KS, July 22, 2001).

Lassila, Kathrin Day. "The New Suburbanites: How America's plants and animals are threatened by sprawl." *Amicus Journal* (Summer, 1999) 16–21.

Laszlo, Ervin. *The World System: Models, Norms, Variations.* New York, NY: George Braziller Inc., 1973.

Laurel, Brenda, "Virtual Reality." *Scientific American* (September, 1995) 90.

Lave, Lester B., et al. "Recycling Decisions and Green Design." *Issues in Science and Technology* 28 No. 1 (1994) 18A–24A.

Layton, David. "Make the Future Work, Appropriate Technology: A Teachers' Guide." In *Values in Design and Technology,* edited by Catherine Budgett-Meatkin. Harlow: Longman Group UK for Intermediate Technology, 1992.

Lebacqz, Victor, and Robert Pearce. "Future Air Traffic, 100 Years of Flight." *Special supplement to Mechanical Engineering* (2003) 35.

Lee, Charles. "Environmental Justice, Urban Revitalization and Brownfields: the Search for Authentic Signs of Hope." National Environmental Justice Advisory Council/ Waste and Facility Siting Subcommittee: *Brownfields Home Page.* http://www.epa. gov/swerops/bf/html.doc. Last visited 11/1998.

Lenat, Douglas. "Artificial Intelligence." *Scientific American* (September, 1995) 80–82.

Levy, Steven. "A High-Tech Home Front." *Newsweek* (October 8, 2001). http://www. msnbc.com/news/635417.asp. Last visited 12/11/2001.

Lewis, C.S. *The Abolition of Man.* HarperSanFrancisco, 1974.

Lewis, T., & .J.K. Wang, "Geothermal evidence for deforestation induced warming: Implications for the climatic impact of land development." *Geophysical Research Letters* 25 No.4 (1998) 535.

Lieberman, John K. "Constitution of the United States." In *Microsoft® Encarta® Encyclopedia 2000,* ©1993–1999. All Rights Reserved.

Lindblom, Charles E., and Edward J. Woodhouse. *The Policy-Making Process.* 3d. ed. Englewood Cliffs, NJ: Prentice Hall, 1993.

List, Peter C. *Environmental Ethics and Forestry.* Philadelphia, PA: Temple University Press, 2000.

Loeb, Vernon. "You Still Feel Like You Have a Hand." *Washington Post National Weekly Edition* (October 27—November 2, 2003) 35.

Lohr, Steve. "A Time Out for Technophilia." *New York Times* (11/18/2001).

Long. Doug J. "Robert Oppenheimer." http://www.doug-long.com/oppie/htm. Last visited 07/22/2006.

Lord, Lewis, and Sarah Burke. "America before Columbus." *US News and World Report* (July 8, 1991) 22–37.

Louderback, Jim. "2004: Welcome to the Wonderful World of Wireless." *USA Weekend* (Dec. 12–14, 2003) 6.

———. "Cars go High-tech." http://story.news.yahoo.com/news?tmpl=story&u=/ ttzd/20040205/tc_techtues_zd/118388&cid=1739&ncid=1729. Last visited 02/10/2004.

Lucky, Robert W. "What Technology Alone Cannot Do." *Scientific American* (September, 1995) 204–5.

Lynch, James. *A Cry Unheard: New Insights into the Medical Consequences of Loneliness.* Baltimore, MD: Bancroft Press, 2000.

Lyon, David. *Surveillance After September 11.* Cambridge, UK: Polity Press, 2003.

———. *Surveillance Society: Monitoring Everyday Life.* Philadelphia, PA: Open University Press/McGraw-Hill, 2001.

Maas, Winy, et al. *Fairmax: Excursions on Density.* Rotterdam, The Netherlands: 010 Publishers, 1998.

Maes, Pattie. "Intelligent Software." *Scientific American* (September, 1995) 84–86.

Makew, C. and R. Simmon, "Earth at Night." National Aeronautics and Space Administration, NOAA/GSFC. http://antwrp.gsfc.nasa.gov/apod/image/0011/ earthlights_dmsp_big.jpg. Last visited 9/29/2006.

Mann, Catherine L. "Globalization of IT Services and White Collar Jobs: The Next Wave of Productivity Growth." Institute for International Economics: *International Economics Policy Brief No. PB03–11* (2003) 6.

Manserus, Laura. "Turbulent Manners Unsettle Fliers." *New York Times* (02/15/2004) 5, 11.

Markhoff, John. "Some Voices in Silicon Valley Speak Out for Slowing Down." New York Times/ *San Francisco Chronicle* (04/14/ 2003).

Marshall, Paul. *Their Blood Cries Out.* Waco, TX: World Publishing, 1997.

Martin, Mike W., & Roland Schinzinger. *Ethics in Engineering.* 3d. ed. New York, NY: McGraw Hill, 1996.

Mascie-Taylor, C.G. Nicholas, and Enamul Karim. "The burden of chronic diseases." *Science* 302 (12 December, 2003) 1921–22.

Mathews, Jessica. "Once a Blessing, automobiles turn into a curse." *Washington Post National Weekly Edition* (October, 1966).

McEvoy, S.P., et al. "Role of mobile phones in motor vehicle crashes resulting in hospital attendance: a case-crossover study." *British Medical Journal Online First.* doi:10.1136/bmj.38537.397512.55 (July 12, 2005).

Mead, Walter Russell. "Apocalypse Now-or Soon." *Washington Post National Weekly Edition* (February 10–16, 2003) 22–23.

Meagher, Bill, and Peter Seidman. "Slow and go costs jobs." Santa Rosa, CA: *NorthBay Biz* (April, 2004) 88–95.

"Measure to tax diapers introduced." Santa Rosa, CA: *The Press Democrat* (02/14/2003).

Miller, Ruth Douglas. "Gasoline Consumption and Stewardship: A Survey of Christian Choices for Automobile Transportation." Joint Meeting of the American Scientific Affiliation, Canadian Scientific & Christian Affiliation, and Christians in Science (Trinity Western University, July 23–26, 2004).

Minkin, Barry H. "More Shocking Future." *Hemispheres* (November, 1995) 47–52.

————. *Future in Sight.* New York, NY: MacMillan, 1995.

"Missile Defense: actions are needed now to enhance testing and accountability." General Accounting Office: *GAO Highlights.* http://www.gao.gov/highlights/do4409/high.pdf. Last visited 04/24/2004.

Mitcham, Carl. *Thinking Through Technology: The Path between Engineering and Philosophy.* Chicago, IL: University of Chicago Press, 1994.

"Model forecasts four choices in Central Valley." *California Farmer* (April, 2005) 30.

"Modern Marvels: Landmines." *The History Channel Video AAE–433799* (November, 2003).

Moffett, Bruce. "Whales." National Geographic Television and Film, 2004.

Moltmann, Jergen. *Theology of Hope.* New York, NY: Harper & Row, 1965.

Monsma, Steven V. *Responsible Technology.* Grand Rapids, MI: Eerdmans, 1986.

Moore, Matt. "Tech to the rescue." Associated Press/ Santa Rosa, CA: *The Press Democrat* (12/30/2004) E1, E6.

Moran, John M. "A Face in the Crowd." The Hartford Courant/Vancouver, WA: *The Columbian* (10/19/2001) D1.

Moreland, J.P. *Christianity and the Nature of Science.* Grand Rapids, MI: Baker, 1989.

Morone, Joseph G.. & Edward J. Woodhouse. *The Demise of Nuclear Energy? Lessons for Democratic Control of Technology.* New Haven, NJ: Yale University Press, 1989.

————. *Averting Catastrophe: Strategies for Regulating Risky Technologies.* Berkeley CA: University of California Press, 1986.

Morrell, Virginia. "Tomb of Key Maya Ruler Found." *Science* 252 (May 24, 1991) 1067.

Mouw, Richard J. *When the Kings Come Marching In.* Grand Rapids, MI: Eerdmans 1983.

Mumford, Lewis. *The Pentagon of Power.* London: Secker and Warburg, 1971.

Munro, Donald. "The Executive Director's Corner." *Newsletter of the American Scientific Affiliation and Canadian Scientific and Christian Affiliation* (Jan/Feb, 2004) 2.

Murphy, Bill. "Author Tom Reed's 'insider's' account of Cold War fascinates Sandia Audiences." *Sandia Lab News* (April 16, 2004) 7.

Myers, D.G. and E. Diener. "The Pursuit of Happiness." *Scientific American* 274 (May, 1996) 70–72.

Myers, Ransom, and Boris Worm. "Rapid worldwide depletion of predatory fish communities." *Nature* 423 (2003) 280–83.

Nanotechnology: Shaping the World Atom by Atom. National Science and Technology Council Committee on Technology, Interagency Working Group on Nanoscience, Engineering, and Technology (September, 1999). http://wtec.org/loyola/nano/IWGN.Public.Brochure/IWGN.Nanotechnology.Brochure.pdf. Last visited 03/31/04.

National Nanotechnology Initiative. National Science and Technology Council Committee on Technology, Subcommittee on Nanoscale Science, Engineering and Technology (July, 2000). http://wtec.org/loyola/nano/IWGN.Implementation.Plan/nni.implementation.plan.pdf. Last visited 03/31/04.

Naugle, David K. *Worldview: The History of a Concept.* Grand Rapids, MI: Eerdmans, 2002.

Newberry, Paul. "NASCAR Drives Religion in the Fast Lane." Associated Press/ Santa Rosa, CA: *The Press Democrat* (02/10/2004) C1–C2.

Niebuhr, H. Richard. *Christ and Culture.* New York, NY: Harper & Brothers, 1951.

Niebuhr, Reinhold, "The Nature and Destiny of Man." Vol. II (1943). In *Readings in Christian Thought,* edited by Hugh T. Kerr. Nashville, TN: Abingdon Press, 1966.

Noble, David F. *The Religion of Technology: The Divinity of Man and the Spirit of Invention.* New York, NY: Penguin Books, 1999.

Noguchi, Yuki. "Teens: Gold mine for cell-phone industry." Washington Post/ Santa Rosa, CA: *The Press Democrat* (05/11/2004) D8.

Norman, Donald A. "Designing the Future." *Scientific American* (September, 1995) 194–98.

Nusser, Janet. *Leslie Allen White.* http://www.mnsu.edu/emuseum/information/biography/uvwxyz/white_leslie.html. Last visited 09/15/05.

O'Keefe, Mark. "Parent's dilemma: to snoop on kids or not." Portland, OR: *The Oregonian* (05/01/1999).

Oakes, Robert. "Amtrak hopes to keep up with budget streamline." San Ramon, CA: *Valley Times* (09/12/1995) 10A.

"Obese fliers weigh down planes." *Associated Press* (11/02/2004). http://www.msnbc.msn.com/id/6409403. Last visited 01/17/05.

Offner, Avner. *The Challenge of Affluence: Self-Control and Well-Being in the United States and Britain since 1950.* Oxford, GB: Oxford University Press, 2006.

Oppenheimer, J. Robert. In "Brainy Quote." http://www.brainyquote.com/quotes/authors/j/j_robert_oppenheimer.html. Last visited 10/20/2006.

Orr, David. "The Ecology of Giving and Consuming." In *Consuming Desires: Consumption, Culture, and the Pursuit of Happiness,* edited by Roger Rosenblatt, 137–54, Washington, DC: Island Press, 1999.

"Our Common Future." World Commission on Environment and Development. New York, NY: Oxford University Press, 1987.

Ozberkhan, Hasan. "The Triumph of Technology—'can' implies 'ought.'" In *Man-Made Futures: Readings in Society, Technology, and Design,* edited by David Nigel et al. London: Hutchinson, 1974.

Papanek, Victor. *Design for Human Scale.* New York, NY: Van Nostrand Reinhold, 1983.

———. *Design for the Real World.* 2d ed. New York, NY: Van Nostrand Reinhold, 1984.

————. *Design for the Real World: Human Ecology and Social Change.* Chicago, IL: Academy Chicago Publishers, 1999.

————. *The Green Imperative: Natural Design for the Real World.* London, UK: Thames and Hudson, 1995.

Parker, Laura, and Martin Kasindorf. "Schools taking security to heart." *USA Today* (May 21–23, 1999) 1.

Patcek, T.W. "Thermodynamics of the Corn-Ethanol Biofuel Cycle." In *Critical Reviews in Plant Sciences* 23 No. 6 (2004) 519–67. http://petroleum.berkeley.edu/papers/patzek/thermodynmaics%20of%20cornethanol.htm. Last visited July 18, 2005.

Patterson, David A. "Microprocessors in 2020." *Scientific American* (September, 1995) 62–67.

Paula, Greg. "Crime Fighting Sensors." *Mechanical Engineering* (January, 1998) 66–68.

Payne, Melanie. "Drug testing gives birth to cheating industry." Knight-Rider/Tribune Information Service/Portland, OR: *The Oregonian* (01/20/1999).

Pearse, Meic. *Why the Rest Hates the West.* Downers Grove, IL: InterVarsity Press, 2004.

Perrow, Charles. *Normal Accidents: Living With High-Risk Technologies.* New York: Basic Books, 1984.

Peterson, Eugene. *The Message.* Colorado Springs, CO: Navpress, 2002.

Phillips, Don. "The new millennium: rail requiem or rebirth?" *Trains* (January, 2000) 12–13.

Plucknett, Donald L., and Donald Winkelmann. "Technology for Sustainable Agriculture." *Scientific American* (September, 1995) 182–86.

"Pollution." In *Microsoft® Encarta® Encyclopedia 2000.* © 1993–1999 Microsoft Corporation.

Poniewozik, James. "Why we're So Obsessed with 'Next.'" *Time* 162 Issue 10 (2003) 171.

Postef, S.L., et al. "Human Appropriation of Renewable Fresh Water." *Science 271* (1996) 785–88.

Postman, Neil. *Amusing Ourselves to Death: Public Discourse in the Age of Show Business.* New York, NY: Penguin Books, 1986.

————. *Technopoly: The Surrender of Culture to Technology.* New York, NY: Vintage Books, 1993.

Pressler, Margaret Webb. "New products flooding market, but few care." Washington Post/Santa Rosa, CA: *The Press Democrat* (05/06/2004) E6.

————. "Building a Better Burger." *Washington Post National Weekly Edition* (Jan 25—Feb 1, 2004) 10–11.

"Proceedings of a Conference to Determine Whether or Not There is a Public Health Question in the Manufacture, Distribution, or Use of Tetraethyl Lead in Gasoline." *Public Health Bulletin #158.* Washington, DC: US Public Health Service, GPO (1925).

Pucket, Jim, et al. "The Digital Divide: Exporting Reuse and Abuse to Africa." *Basel Action Network Report* (October, 2005).

————. "Exporting Harm: The High-tech Trashing of Asia." Basel Action Network/Silicon Valley Toxics Coalition (February 25, 2004).

Purcell, Carroll. *White Heat.* London: BBC, 1994.

Putnam, Robert D. *Bowling Alone: Civic Disengagement in America.* New York, NY: Simon and Schuster, 2000.

Raghu, S., et al., "Adding Biofuels to the Invasive Species Fire," *Science* 313 No. 5794 (2006) 1742.

Redefining Progress Institute. http://redefiningprogress.org/projects/gpi. Last visited 05/30/2004.

Reed, Thomas. *At the Abyss: An Insider's History of the Cold War.* Novato, CA: Presidio Press, 2004.

Rees, Sir Martin. *Our Final Hour.* New York, NY: Basic Books, 2003.

Regal, Philip J. "Metaphysics in Genetic Engineering: Cryptic Philosophy and Ideology in the 'Science' of Risk Assessment." In *Coping with Deliberate Release: The Limits of Risk Assessment, edited by* Ad Van Dommelen, 25. Amsterdam: Free University of Amsterdam, 1996.

Reich, Robert W. "The American Prospect Online." (09/23/2001). http://www.prospect. org/webfeatures/2001/09/reich-r-09-23.html. Last visited 06/24/2004.

Reijnders, L. "The Factor X Debate: Setting Targets for Eco-efficiency." *Journal of Industrial Ecology* 2 No. 1 (1998) 13–22.

Reitkirk, Wim. *The Future Great Planet Earth.* Landour Mussourie UP India: Nivedit Good Books Distributors Pvt. Ltd., 1989.

Renberg, Ingemar, et al. "Pre-Industrial Atmospheric Lead Contamination Detected in Swedish Lake Sediment." *Nature* 368 (1994) 323–26.

Rennie, John. "A Conversation with James D. Watson." *Scientific American* (April, 2003). www.sciam.com/issue.cfm?issueddate=Apr-03. Last visited 12/09/03.

———. "Custom Manufacturing." *Scientific American* (September, 1995) 160–161.

———. "The Uncertainties of Technological Revolution." *Scientific American* (September, 1995) 57–58.

Rhodes, Richard. *Why They Kill: The Discoveries of a Maverick Criminologist.* New York, NY: Alfred A. Knopf/ Random House, 1999.

Rickles, R.N. "Suburbia Isn't What It Used to Be." *New York Times* (01/06/1974) 27.

"RoadPeace." (January 5, 2003). http://www.roadpeace.org/articles/WorldFirstDeath. html. Last visited 04/13/2004.

"Road Safety: A Public Health Issue." World Health Organization, March 29, 2004. http:// www.who.int/features/2004/road_safety/en/. Last visited 04/13/2004.

Robinson, John P. "The Time Squeeze." *American Demographics* 12 (1990) 30–33.

"Robo-cat is out of the bag." http://news.bbc.co.uk/1/hi/sci/tech/1602677.stm (10/16/01). Last visited 06/26/2006.

Rodin, Scott, et al. "A theology of Technology: Raising the Theological Questions." http:/ www.palmerseminary.edu/theology of technology.htm. Last visited 04/15/2006.

Roeburn, Paul, "A childhood epidemic," *USA Today* (September 16, 2004). http://www. keepmedia.com/pubs/USATODAY/2004/09/16/580189. Last visited 10/17/2004.

Rogers, Craig A. "Intelligent Materials." *Scientific American* (September, 1995) 154–57.

Rorty, Richard. "Science as Solidarity." In *The Rhetoric of the Human Sciences,* edited by S. Nelson et al., 38–52. Madison, WI: U. of Wisconsin Press, 1987.

Rose, Bleys W. "Stashing the Goods." Santa Rosa, CA: *The Press Democrat* (8/1/2005) D2, D8.

Rosen, Jay. "Car or Truck: Politics of the SUV." Review of *High and Mighty: SUVs: The World.s Most Dangetrous Vehicles and How They Got That* Way, by Keith Bradsher. New York Times News Service/Santa Rosa, CA: *The Press Democrat* (12/01/2002).

Rosenblith, Lara Jill. "Fact Sheet - Electronics Waste (e-waste)." http://environment.about. com/cs/ewaste/a/ewaste.htm. Last visited 1/20/2004.

Rosensweig, Barbara H. "The Middle Ages." In *Microsoft® Encarta® Encyclopedia 2000,* © 1993–1999 Microsoft Corporation. All rights reserved.

Rule, James B. *Private Lives and Public Surveillance.* London: Allan Lane, 1973.

Russakoff, Dale. "Chasing After That Pie in the Sky." *Washington Journal* (10/1989).

Russell, Roberta, and Robert Taylor. *Operations Management.* Upper Saddle River, NJ: Prentice Hall, 1997.

Sagan, Carl. "To Avert a Common Danger: Joint Appeal by Science and Religion for the Environment." *Parade Magazine* (1 March, 1992) 10–14.

Sambursky, S. *The Physical World of the Greek.* Routledge and Kegan Paul, 1963.

Samples, Kenneth Richard. "Just another Animal?" *Connections* 8 No. 1 (2006). http://www.reasons.org/resources/connections/200604_connections_q2/index.shtml#just_another_animal. Last visited 06/15/06.

Samuelson, Robert J. "Affluence and Its Discontents." *Washington Post National Weekly Edition* (May 15–21, 2006) 26.

Sanchez, Jose L. Jr. "Council Approves parking System." Santa Rosa, CA: *The Press Democrat* (01/04//2005) B1–B2.

Sandin, Per, et al. "5 Charges against the Precautionary Principle." *Journal of Risk Research* 5 No. 4 (2002) 287–99.

Sarewitz, Daniel. *Frontiers of Illusion: Science, Technology, and the Politics of Progress.* Philadelphia, PA: Temple University Press, 1996.

Schaeffer, Francis A. *Pollution and the Death of Man: The Christian View of Ecology.* Wheaton, IL: Tyndale House Publishers, 1970.

———. *The God Who is There.* Downers Grove, IL: InterVarsity Press, 1968.

Schoch, Deborah. "Fading Glory: Light Pollution Robs Night Skies of Starry Splendor." Los Angeles Times/ *The Santa Fe New Mexican* (10/20/2003) D1–D2.

Schor, Juliet B. *The Overspent American: Upscaling, Downshifting, and the New Consumer.* New York, NY: Basic Books, 1998.

———. *The Overworked American: The Unexpected Decline of Leisure.* New York, NY: Basic Books, 1992.

Schumacher, Ernst F. *Small is Beautiful: Economics as if People Mattered.* New York, NY: Harper and Row, 1973.

Schuurman, Egbert. *Faith and Hope in Technology.* Toronto, ON: Clements Publishing, 2003.

———. *Perspectives on Technology and Culture.* Sioux Center, IA: Dordt College Press, 1995.

———. *Technology and the Future: A philosophical Challenge.* Toronto, ON: Wedge Publishing, 1980.

Schwartz, Barry. *The Paradox of Choice: Why More is Less.* New York, NY: HarperCollins Echo, 2004.

Schwartz, John. "Does Your Seat Mate Have a 'Mute' Button?" *New York Times* (02/15/2004) 5, 10.

Sciano, Joseph. "Honk if You Think I'm Rude." *New York Times* (02/15/2004) 5, 11.

Science and Health Network Home Page. http://www.sehn.org/precaution.html. Last visited 03/11/2004.

Sclove, Richard. *Democracy and Technology.* New York: Guilford Press, 1995.

Seu, Andre. "Risky Business: Livelihood insurance and other charms for the safe and secure life." *World* (July 23, 2005) 35.

Shallis, Michael. *The Silicon Idol: The Micro Revolution and its Social Implications.* Oxford, U.K.: Oxford University Press, 1984.

Sider, Ronald J. *Living More Simply: Biblical Principles and Practical Models.* Downers Grove, IL: InterVarsity Press, 1980.

———. *Cry Justice.* Downers Grove, IL: InterVarsity Press, 1980;

————. *Rich Christians in an Age of Hunger.* Downers Grove, IL: InterVarsity Press, 1984.

Siegfried, Michael L. "The Inner City in the 21st Century: Huxley's Brave New World Revisited?" *Journal of Interdisciplinary Studies* VIII (1996) 19–30.

Simon Julian L., ed. *The State of Humanity.* Oxford, UK: Blackwell, 1995.

————. "Earth's Doomsayers are Wrong." *San Francisco Chronicle* (05/12/1995).

————. "Finite doesn't fit here," Knight-Ridder Tribune Information Services/ Portland, OR: *The Oregonian* (02/11/1997).

————. *The Ultimate Resource.* Princeton, NJ: Princeton University Press, 1981.

Sine, Tom. *The Mustard Seed Conspiracy.* Waco, TX: Word Inc., 1981.

Singer, Neal. "Desktop Computers to Counsel Users on Decisions." *Sandia Lab News* (January 23, 2004) 6.

Singletary, Michelle. "Materialism At Heart of American Dream Kills Contentment." Washington Post/Santa Rosa, CA: *The Press Democrat* (08/06/2003) E2.

————. "Study Finds More Money Doesn't Make People Much Happier." Washington Post/ Santa Rosa, CA: *The Press Democrat* (12/09/2003) E2.

Sleeth, Peter. "Watching your step: ubiquitous cameras that tape your commute, your shopping and your stroll down the street raise moral questions that rarely are discussed." Portland, OR: *The Oregonian* (02/28/1999) G1–G2.

SmallTimes. http://www.smalltimes.com. Last visited 03/14/2004.

Smith, Emily. "New "X" in DFX: Sabotage." *Mechanical Engineering* (September, 2002). http://www.memagazine.org/backissues/sept02/features/sabotage/sabotage.html. Last visited 12/16/2002.

Smith, Ted. "Health Concerns and Electronics Products." Silicon Valley Toxics Coalition Computer Take-back campaign (April, 2004). http://www.svtc.org/cleancc/greenprocurement/CleanMed_presentation_4_04.ppt. Last visited 11/16/2004.

Snoke, David. "Why Were Dangerous Animals Created?" *Perspectives on Science and Christian Faith* 56 No. 2 (2004) 117–25.

Snyder, Howard A. *The Community of the King.* Downers Grove, IL: InterVarsity Press, 1978.

Snyder, Susan. "High-tech student ID card sounds alarm if class is cut." Knight Ridder/ Vancouver, WA: *The Columbian* (03/06/2000) A5.

"Societal Implications of Nanoscience and Nanotechnology." National Science Foundation, September 1999. http://wtec.org/loyola/nano/NSET.Societal.Implications/. Last visited 03/31/2004.

Sorenson, A. Ann, et al. *Farming at the Edge.* DeKalb, IL: American Farmland Trust Center for Agriculture in the Environment/ Northern Illinois University, 1997.

Sowell, Thomas. *A Conflict of Visions.* New York, NY: William Morrow and Company, 1987.

Spaling, Harry, and Annette Dekker. "Cultural Sustainable Development: Concepts and Principles." *Perspectives on Science and Christian Faith* 48 No. 4 (1996) 230–40.

————, and John Wood. "Greed, Need, or Creed: Farmland Ethics in the Rural-Urban Fringe." *Land Use Policy* 5 No. 2 (1998).

Stafford, Tim. "N.T. Wright: Making scholarship a tool for the church." *Christianity Today* (February 8, 1999) 42–46.

————. "Mere Mission: N. T. Wright talks about how to present the gospel in a postmodern world." *Christianity Today* (January, 2007) 39–41.

————. *Surprised by Jesus.* Downers Grove, IL: IVPBooks, 2006.

Stahl, William A. *God and the Chip: Religion and the Culture of Technology.* Waterloo, ON: Wilfrid Laurier University Press, 1999.

Statistical Abstracts. US Bureau of the Census, 2000.

St. John, Warren. "The World at Ear's Length." *New York Times* (02/15/2004) 9.1–9.2.

Stokes, Robert. "Environmentalists Work Harder, Smarter at Communications than Natural Resource Users." *Wheat Life* (November, 2003) 10–11.

Sturdevant, Cameron. "When a transmitter becomes a blabbermouth." *San Francisco Chronicle* (05/06/2004) B9.

Summers, Donna C. *Quality.* Englewood Cliffs, NJ: Prentice-Hall, 1997.

"Surety White Paper." In *Surety Science and Engineering Workshop* (September 23, 1998). Washington, D.C.: National Academy of Sciences. http://www.sandia.gov/Surety/SurWP.htm. Last visited April 2002.

Swearengen, J. C. "Arms Control and God's Purpose in History." *Perspectives on Science and Christian Faith* 44 No. 1 (1992) 25–35.

———. "Brownfields and Greenfields: an Ethical Perspective on Land Use." *Environmental Ethics* 21 No.3 (1999) 277–92.

———. "Property Rights versus Stewardship." *IEEE Technology and Society Magazine* (Summer 1999) 12–24.

———, and Alan P. Swearengen. "Comparative Analysis of the Nuclear Weapons Debate: Campus and Developer Perspectives." *Perspectives on Science and Christian Faith* 42 No. 2 (1990) 75–85.

———, and Edward J. Woodhouse. "Overconsumption as an Ethics Challenge for Engineering Education." *International Journal of Mechanical Engineering Education* 31 No.1 (2003) 15–31.

———, and E. J. Woodhouse. "Cultural Risks of Technological Innovation: the Case of School Violence." *IEEE Technology and Society Magazine* 20 No.1 (2001) 15–28.

———, and E. J. Woodhouse. "Overconsumption, Engineering Design, and Christian Ethics." *Perspectives on Science and Christian Faith* 54 No. 2 (2002) 1–12.

Swenson, Richard A. *Hurtling Toward Oblivion.* Colorado Springs, CO: NavPress, 1999.

———. *Margin.* Colorado Springs, CO: NavPress, 1992.

Tackett, Timothy N. "The Enlightenment." In *Microsoft® Encarta® Encyclopedia 2000* ©1993–1999 Microsoft Corporation. All rights reserved.

"Taming the Beast." *The Economist* (June 22–28, 1996) 1–18.

Taylor, John. *Enough is Enough.* London, UK: Westminster, 1975.

Technology & Society Newsletter. American Society of Mechanical Engineers (1993).

"Technology focus: Think It, Move It." *Mechanical Engineering* (June, 2005) 22.

Tenner, Edward. "Beware Our Diminishing Curiosity." *Washington Post National Weekly Edition* (September 1–7, 2003) 28.

———. *Why Things Bite Back: Technology and the Revenge of Unintended Consequences.* New York, NY: Vintage Books, 1997.

"The Land Institute." http://www.landinstitute.org/vnews/display.v. Last visited 03/18/2004.

"The Real Price of Gasoline." International Center for Technology Assessment (11/16/1998). http://www.icta.org/template/index.cfm.

"The Tragedy of the Commons?" *Science* 302 (12 December, 2003) 1861–1928. 1993.

Thomas, Chris D. et al. "Extinction Risk from Climate Change." *Nature* 427 (2004) 145–48. http://www.nature.com/nature/links/040108/040108-1.html. Last visited 01/09/2004.

Thomas, Keith. *Man and the Natural World.* New York, NY: Pantheon, 1983.

Thornton, Joe. *Pandora's Poison: Chlorine, Health, and a New Environmental Strategy.* Boston, MA: MIT Press, 2000.

Tickner, Joel, et al. "The Precautionary Principle in Action: a Handbook." *Science and health Network* (1998). http://www.sehn.org/rtfdocs/handbook-rtf.rtf. Last visited 03/11/2004.

"To Establish Truth, Insure Domestic Tranquility." Washington D.C: Milton S. Eisenhower Foundation, 1999.

Toffler, Alvin. *Previews and Premises: An Interview with Alvin Toffler.* Boston, MA: South End Press, 1983.

————. *Future Shock.* New York, NY: Bantam, 1970.

————. *Previews and Premises.* London: Pan Books 1983.

Touryan, Kenell. "ASA in the 21st Century: Expanding Our Vision for Serving God, the Church, and Society through Science and Technology." *Perspectives on Science and Christian Faith* 56 No. 2 (2004) 82–88.

Toynbee, Arnold. "Cities in History." In *Cities of Destiny,* edited by Arnold Toynbee, 12–28. New York, NY: McGraw-Hill, 1967.

"Traffic Fatalities vs. Crashes." Nebraska Office of Highway Safety. http://www.dmv.state.ne.us/highwaysafety/pdf/tr2fatals.pdf. Last visited 10/30/2006.

Transportation Energy Data Book: Edition 25. US Department of Energy, 2006.

Trefy, J.H, et al. "A Decline in Lead Transport by the Mississippi River." *Science* 230 (1985) 439–41.

"Truckers Mostly In the Right." *Mechanical Engineering* (December, 1999) 16.

Truesdale, Albert. "Last Things First: The Impact of Eschatology on Ecology." *Perspectives on Science and Christian Faith* 46 No. 2 (June, 1994) 116–22.

Turkle, Sherry. *The Second Self: Computers and the Human Spirit.* Cambridge, MA: MIT Press, 2005.

Tyson, Rae. "DOT Releases Preliminary Estimates of 2003 Highway Fatalities." http://www.nhtsa.dot.gov/nhtsa/announce/press/pressdisplay.cfm. Last visited 05/04/2004.

Ullman, David G. *The Mechanical Design Process.* 2d ed. New York, NY: McGraw-Hill, 1997.

"US Department of Homeland Security Home Page." http://www.dhs.gov/dhspublic/theme_home1.jsp. Last visited 02/09/2004.

Van Dyke, Fred, et al. *Redeeming Creation: The Biblical Basis for Environmental Stewardship.* Downers Grove, IL: InterVarsity Press, 1966.

Van Slambrouck, Paul. "From the land of high tech comes a human connection." *The Christian Science Monitor* (04/15/1999).

VanderLeest, Steven. In *Connection.* American Society for Engineering Education (November, 2003).

Vargas, Jose Antonio. "A Substitute for War." *Washington Post National Weekly Edition* (February 20–26, 2006) 20–21.

Vice President Dick Cheney. From a speech in Toronto, ON, April 30, 2002. http://www.princeton.edu/~iyohai/Classical_Political_Statements.html. Last visited 06/26/2004.

Vogtner, Jennifer. "Recycling Your PC." *Going Places* (May/June, 2000) 8.

Wackernagel, Mathis, et al. "Tracking the Ecological Overshoot of the Economy." *Proceedings of the National Academy of Science (USA)* 99 Issue 14 (July 9, 2002) 9266–71.

Waks, Leonard J. "Value Judgment and Social Action in Technological Studies." *International Journal of Technology and Design Education* 4 No. 1 (1994) 35–47.

Wallis, Jim. *God's Politics: How the Right Gets It Wrong and the Left Doesn't Get It.* San Francisco, CA: Harper Collins, 2005.

Wauzzinski, Robert A. *Discerning Promethius: The Cry for Wisdom in our Technological Society.* Madison, NJ: Fairleigh Dickinson University Press, 2001.

———. "Technological Pessimism." *Perspectives on Science and Christian Faith* 46 No. 2 (June, 1994) 98–114.

Wayne, Leslie. "Developing smart weapons." Portland, OR: *The Oregonian* (06/17/1999).

Weeks, Linton. "no muss, no fuss with robo-pets." Washington Post/Santa Rosa, CA: *The Press Democrat* (06/07/2005) D1, D2.

Weiss, Rick. "Fish Out of Water." *Washington Post National Weekly Edition* (June 28, 2003) 35.

———. "Missing Links: Electronic Archivists Attempt to Keep Records of Fast-Vanishing Internet Documents." *Washington Post National Weekly Edition* (December 1–7, 2003) 34.

———. "Monkey Brains Run Robot." Washington Post/ Santa Rosa, CA: *The Press Democrat* (10/1320/2003).

———. "The Last Buffalo Hunt." *Washington Post National Weekly Edition* (June 9–15, 2003) 35.

———. "The Fears and Hopes Offered by Nanotech," Washington Post/Santa Rosa, CA: *The Press Democrat* (02/24/2004) D1.

Wenz, Peter S. *Environmental Ethics Today.* New York, NY: Oxford University Press, 2001.

White, Jerry. "*Landmine Survivors' Network*" (2003). http://www.landminesurvivors.org/. Last visited 10/12/2006.

White, John. *The Golden Cow.* Downers Grove, IL: InterVarsity Press, 1979.

White, Lynn Jr. "The Historical Roots of Our Ecologic Crisis." *Science* 155 (March, 1967) 1203–7.

———. "Cultural Climates and Technological Advance in the Middle Ages." *Viator* 2 (1971) 172–73.

Whiteley, Nigel. *Design for Society.* London, UK: Reaktion Books, 1993.

Whitesides, George M. "Self-Assembling Materials." *Scientific American* (September, 1995) 146–49.

Wigley, T.M.L. "Could Reducing Fossil Fuel Emissions Cause Global Warming?" *Nature* 349 (1991) 503–5.

Wilson, David Gordon. "Pedals vs. Fuel Cells" (Letter). *Mechanical Engineering* (April, 2004).

Winfree, Eric. "The DNA and Natural Algorithms Group: Research Perspective." http://www.dna.caltech.edu/DNAresearch_perspective.html. Last visited 03/19/2004.

Winner, Langdon. *Autonomous Technology: Technics-Out of-Control as a Theme in Political Thought.* Cambridge, MA: MIT Press, 1977.

———. *The Whale and the Reactor: A Search for Limits in an Age of High Technology.* Chicago, IL: University of Chicago Press, 1986.

Winters, Rebecca. "What's Always Next?" *Time* 162 Issue 10 (September 8, 2003) 62.

Woodhouse, Edward, and Daniel Sarewitz. "Small is Powerful." In *Living With the Genie: Essays on Technology and the Quest for Human Mastery,* edited by Alan Lightman et al., 63–83. Washington, D.C.: Island Press, 2003.

———, and Dean Nieusma. "Democratic Expertise: Integrating Knowledge, Power, and Participation." In *Policy Studies Review Annual* Vol. 12: *Knowledge, Power, and*

Participation in Environmental Policy Analysis, edited by Matthijs Hisschemoller et al., 73–96. New Brunswick, NJ: Transaction Publishers, 2001.

Woodley, Randy. *Living in Color: Embracing God's Passion for Ethnic Diversity.* Downers Grove, IL: InterVarsity Press 2001.

Woodward, Steve. "Modern World Faces Specter of 'Netwar.'" Portland, OR: *The Oregonian,* (09/17/2001) B1.

"World Petroleum Assessment 2000 Description and Results." U.S. Geological Survey World Energy Assessment Team. U.S. Geological Survey Digital Data Series—DDS-60, 2000.

Wright, N.T. *Jesus and the Victory of God.* Minneapolis, MN: Fortress Press, 1996.

Yaffee, Martin D., ed. *Judaism and Environmental Ethics.* Lanham, MD: Lexington Books, 2001.

Yates, Brock. "California Dreaming: Our Nightmarish Future." *The Washington Post Magazine* (January 8, 1989) 31–32.

Zetche, Dieter. "The Automobile: Clean and Customized." *Scientific American* (September, 1995) 102–6.

Zysman, George. "Wireless Networks." *Scientific American* (September, 1995) 68–71.

Index